INTERNATIONAL MARINE ENVIRONMENTAL LAW AND POLICY

Several disturbing issues pose a threat to the marine environment and its wellbeing, among them marine environmental pollution and degradation of marine biodiversity. Most troubling is that these issues are overwhelmingly caused by human activities which are sometimes transboundary, and their consequences will become more severe and complicated if not properly curbed. Thus, these activities require comprehensive policies, laws, and principles to manage them effectively. Linked to these solutions is the need for responsibilities, cooperation and commitments at local, national, regional and international levels.

Contemporary Marine Environmental Law and Policy presents a thorough appraisal of the main issues, actors and institutions engaged in the legal aspects of marine environmental conservation. With contributions from an international range of authors, the book provides a concise account of the legal and policy framework underlying international marine environmental issues, and of the fundamental concepts and strategies that are important to the protection of the marine environment. Some of the topics explored include: the prevention of marine pollution caused by land based activities, ships, and offshore hydrocarbon and mineral resources exploration; the conservation and management of marine living resources; the marine environment in the polar regions; and the settlement of marine environmental disputes.

This book provides a solid foundation for anyone studying International Environmental Law and the Law of the Sea. It will also appeal to anyone seeking to gain a deeper understanding of this hugely important subject.

Daud Hassan is the Director of International Centre for Ocean Governance (ICOG), Western Sydney University, Australia.

Md Saiful Karim is the Director International at the School of Law, Queensland University of Technology, Australia.

INTERNATIONAL MARINE ENVIRONMENTAL LAW AND POLICY

INTERNATIONAL MARINE ENVIRONMENTAL LAW AND POLICY

Edited by Daud Hassan and Md Saiful Karim

LONDON AND NEW YORK

First published 2019
by Routledge
2 Park Square, Milton Park, Abingdon, Oxon OX14 4RN

and by Routledge
711 Third Avenue, New York, NY 10017

Routledge is an imprint of the Taylor & Francis Group, an informa business

© 2019 selection and editorial matter, Daud Hassan and Md Saiful Karim; individual chapters, the contributors

The right of Daud Hassan and Md Saiful Karim to be identified as the author of the editorial material, and of the authors for their individual chapters, has been asserted in accordance with sections 77 and 78 of the Copyright, Designs and Patents Act 1988.

All rights reserved. No part of this book may be reprinted or reproduced or utilised in any form or by any electronic, mechanical, or other means, now known or hereafter invented, including photocopying and recording, or in any information storage or retrieval system, without permission in writing from the publishers.

Trademark notice: Product or corporate names may be trademarks or registered trademarks, and are used only for identification and explanation without intent to infringe.

British Library Cataloguing-in-Publication Data
A catalogue record for this book is available from the British Library

Library of Congress Cataloging-in-Publication Data
Names: Hassan, Daud, editor. | Karim, Saiful, editor.
Title: International marine environmental law and policy / edited by Daud Hassan & MD Saiful Karim.
Description: Abingdon, Oxon [UK] ; New York, NY : Routledge, 2018. | Includes bibliographical references and index.
Identifiers: LCCN 2018014698 | ISBN 9781138651111 (hardback) | ISBN 9781138651135 (pbk.)
Subjects: LCSH: Marine pollution—Law and legislation. | Marine resources conservation—Law and legislation. | Marine parks and reserves—Law and legislation. | Environmental law, International.
Classification: LCC K3590.4 .I69 2018 | DDC 344.04/6—dc23
LC record available at https://lccn.loc.gov/2018014698

ISBN: 978-1-138-65111-1 (hbk)
ISBN: 978-1-138-65113-5 (pbk)
ISBN: 978-1-315-62492-1 (ebk)

Typeset in Bembo
by Apex CoVantage, LLC

Printed and bound by CPI Group (UK) Ltd, Croydon, CR0 4YY

CONTENTS

Notes on the contributors viii
Acknowledgements xii

PART I
Introduction and general framework for the international marine environmental law 1

1 Contemporary issues in the protection and conservation of the marine environment: an overview 3
  Sandya Nishanthi Gunasekara and Md Saiful Karim

2 Ocean governance and marine environmental conservation: concepts, principles and institutions 16
  Abul Hasanat and Md Saiful Karim

PART II
Prevention of marine pollution 43

3 Prevention, reduction and control of marine pollution from land-based sources and activities 45
  Daud Hassan and Stan Palassis

4 Prevention, reduction and control of marine pollution from ships 60
  Md Mahatab Uddin and Md Saiful Karim

5 Control and prevention of marine pollution from offshore
   hydrocarbon and mineral resources exploration and
   production activities   69
   Hossein Esmaeili

6 Climate change, ocean acidification and the marine
   environment: challenges for the international legal regime   87
   Tavis Potts

7 Marine spatial planning and the new frontiers of marine
   governance   101
   Niko Soininen and Daud Hassan

PART III
Conservation and management of marine living resources 121

8 Conservation of marine living resources and
   fisheries management   123
   Daud Hassan and Emdadul Haque

9 Marine protected areas: contemporary challenges and
   developments   153
   Erika Techera

10 Recognition of Indigenous rights in governance of marine
   protected areas: applying international law and Australian
   experiences   173
   Donna Craig

PART IV
Polar regions 191

11 Protection of the Antarctic marine environment:
   dimensions, relationships and fields   193
   Tuomas Kuokkanen

12 Protection of the Arctic marine environment   206
   Timo Koivurova and Nengye Liu

PART V
Settlement of disputes and conclusions 223

13 Contemporary marine environmental disputes 225
    Daud Hassan and Beatriz Garcia

14 Future of international marine environmental law and
    policy: concluding remarks 252
    Daud Hassan and Asraful Alam

Index 257

CONTRIBUTORS

Daud Hassan is the Director of the International Ocean Governance Centre and Associate Professor at the School of Law, University of Western Sydney. Dr Hassan has published widely in international comparative marine environmental law, the study of the problems, prospects and issues of marine pollution and its effect on the marine environment. His current research interest includes sustainable ocean governance with reference to marine spatial planning. Dr Hassan held visiting positions in international and comparative marine environmental law in various Universities in Asia and Europe.

Md Saiful Karim is the Director International at the School of Law, Queensland University of Technology (QUT), Australia. Dr Karim is the author of *Prevention of Pollution of the Marine Environment from Vessels: The Potential and Limits of the International Maritime Organisation* (Springer, 2015); *Maritime Terrorism and the Role of Judicial Institutions in the International Legal Order* (Brill-Nijhoff, 2017) and *Shipbreaking in Developing Countries: A Requiem for Environmental Justice from the Perspective of Bangladesh* (Routledge, 2018). Dr Karim is a lead author of the IPCC Special Report on the Ocean and Cryosphere in a Changing Climate and the Global and Asia Pacific Assessment Reports of the IPBES. Dr Karim is a member of the World Commission on Environmental Law and the World Commission on Protected Areas.

Contributors

Asraful Alam is a Lecturer of the Department of Maritime Law and Policy, Bangabandhu Sheikh Mujibur Rahman Maritime University, Bangladesh. Currently, Mr Alam is pursuing his PhD under School of Law, Western Sydney University. His research interest is ocean governance and marine environmental law.

Contributors ix

Donna Craig is a Professor of School of Law, University of Western Sydney University. Professor Craig is the Deputy Director of the International Centre for Ocean Governance (ICOG). Donna served as Foundation Board Member of the IUCN Academy of Environmental Law, Regional Vice-Chair for Oceania of the IUCN Commission of Environmental Law, Regional Governor of the International Council on Environmental Law, Board Member of the Northern Territory Environmental Protection Authority and Member of Advisory Board of Greenland-based International Training Centre of Indigenous Peoples. Professor Craig is a specialist in international, comparative and national environmental law and policy at Western Sydney University.

Hossein Esmaeili is an Associate Professor of Law at Flinders University. He previously taught at the School of Law, University of New England, and Faculty of Law, University of New South Wales and School of Law, University of Western Sydney. Dr Esmaeili's teaching areas include Real Property Law, Trusts, Immigration and Refugee Law, Comparative Law and Public International Law. He is the author of The Legal Regime of Offshore Oil Rigs in International Law (2001, Ashgate, Aldershot) and has published scholarly articles in leading law journals in Australia, Europe and the United States.

Beatriz Garcia is a lecturer at the School of Law, University of Western Sydney. Dr Garcia worked in the Climate Change and Sustainable Development branch of the United Nations Conference on Trade and Development (UNCTAD) in Geneva, Switzerland, managing climate and biodiversity projects. She was a research fellow at the Australian Centre for Climate and Environmental Law at Sydney Law School. She held positions as an advisor at government agencies in Brazil and several other organisations, such as the German Technical Cooperation, the Earth Council Geneva and various United Nations' agencies. She is the author of the book *The Amazon from an International Law Perspective* published by Cambridge University Press in 2011, as well as journal articles, chapters in books and several technical reports.

Sandya Nishanthi Gunasekara is a Senior Lecturer at the University of Kelaniya, Sri Lanka, teaching undergraduate and postgraduate courses in the areas of international studies. She is currently a PhD candidate at the Faculty of Law, Queensland University of Technology (QUT), Australia. Her PhD research provides a comprehensive explanation of the ocean governance through ecosystem-based management in the Bay of Bengal region.

Emdadul Haque is a Joint District Judge in Bangladesh. He completed his PhD from the School of Law, University of Western Sydney, on the Delimitation of Maritime Boundaries in the Bay of Bengal Sub-region in South Asia. He has special interests in the law of the sea with reference to South Asian Seas region.

Abul Hasanat is a Joint District Judge at Bangladesh Judicial Service and a PhD candidate at the Faculty of Law, Queensland University of Technology (QUT), Australia. He also worked as a Deputy Director at the Judicial Administration Training Institute, Dhaka. He was a Visiting Researcher at the Institute of Human Rights, Åbo Akademi University, Finland.

Timo Koivurova is a Research Professor and the Director of Arctic Centre, University of Lapland, Finland. Professor Koivurova worked as the Director of the Northern Institute of Environmental and Minority Law at the Arctic Centre. His research work addresses the interplay between different levels of environmental law, law of the sea in the Arctic waters and the integrated maritime policy in the EU. Professor Koivurova has been involved as an expert in several international processes globally and in the Arctic region and has published on the aforementioned topics extensively.

Tuomas Kuokkanen (Doctor of Laws, University of Helsinki) is Docent of International Environmental Law, University of Eastern Finland, and Docent of International Law, University of Helsinki. Previously, he has worked as a Ministerial Adviser with the Ministry of the Environment of Finland and as a part-time Professor of International Law at the University of Eastern Finland. Mr Kuokkanen is currently working as the Justice of the Supreme Administrative Court of Finland. His research interest is in International Environmental Law and Public International Law. He was a co-leader for the University of Eastern Finland – UN Environment Course on Multilateral Environmental Agreements.

Nengye Liu holds a PhD from Ghent University, Belgium. Currently he is a Senior Lecturer at Adelaide Law School, University of Adelaide. He worked at King & Wood Mallessons (Shenzhen, China), Singapore International Arbitration Centre, Future Ocean Cluster of Excellence (Kiel, Germany) and University of Dundee (United Kingdom). Dr Liu's research centres on enhancing a global governance regime for better protection of the oceans, with focus on the Polar Regions. He has published extensively in the fields of the law of the sea and international environmental law.

Stan Palassis is a Senior Lecturer at the Faculty of Law, University of Technology Sydney. He holds a Doctor of Juridical Studies (SJD) from the University of Sydney. Dr Palassis served as the Director of Post Graduate Program at the Faculty of Law, University of Technology Sydney. He has special interest in International and Comparative Environmental law with a particular focus on marine environmental governance. Dr Palassis has widely published in his areas of interest.

Tavis Potts (PhD) is a Senior Lecturer in Environmental Geography and Director of the MSc in Environmental Partnership Management at the University of Aberdeen, Scotland. Dr Potts has an interest in the social and political dimensions of marine spatial planning, coastal management and sustainable resource management. He has a focus on the political economy of ecosystem services and MPAs; non-state sustainable fisheries and seafood governance; and critical perspectives on the development of the blue economy.

Niko Soininen holds a Doctoral Degree from the University of Eastern Finland. Mr Soininen is a lecturer in Environmental Law and Jurisprudence, University of Eastern Finland. Expanding on his scholarly work to marine environmental law, Soininen has written about MSP from a rule of law perspective and has studied the implementation of MSP in northern Europe. Outside academia, Dr Soininen has also worked briefly as an adviser to HELCOM in transboundary MSP-related matters. Mr Soininen holds visiting positions in different universities.

Erika Techera is a Professor in the Law School and Oceans Institute at the University of Western Australia. Professor Techera is an international and comparative environmental lawyer with a strong focus on marine environmental governance, the conservation and management of marine species, Indo-Pacific island States and cultural heritage related to the ocean. Her work also explores inter-disciplinarity and the intersection of law with humanities and social sciences including ethics, philosophy, history, archaeology and anthropology, as well as science, technology and engineering.

Md Mahatab Uddin holds a PhD from Aarhus University, Denmark. He is an Assistant Professor at East West University, Dhaka, Bangladesh, where he teaches Public International Law, International Environmental Law and Laws of International Organisations. Dr Uddin's arenas of research interest mostly concern transboundary environmental issues such as climate change, ocean governance, Arctic governance and sustainable development. Dr Uddin is an Advocate of the Supreme Court of Bangladesh.

ACKNOWLEDGEMENTS

This book is the result of a collaborative effort of a group of international marine environmental law scholars. The book provides a concise and critical account of the international legal and policy framework for some major aspects of contemporary marine environmental issues. It assembles a team of leading and emerging scholars to analyse the different aspects of international marine environmental law and policy. It focuses on the strategic importance of the protection of the marine environment and also assesses the contemporary marine environmental management regimes from practical and operational perspectives. With the promise of better and more comprehensive understanding of marine environmental law and policy, it is no wonder that there has been considerable academic knowledge and this book sheds light on that.

A book such as this includes a considerable amount of effort and support. First and foremost, we would like to thank all the chapter authors for their valuable contribution to the book. We would like to thank all our colleagues at Western Sydney University (WSU) and Queensland University of Technology (QUT). We would particularly like to thank our colleagues at the International Centre for Ocean Governance (ICOG), WSU, for facilitating many valuable comments and informative discussions in marine environmental law and policy.

Hector Gutierrez-Bocaz and Asraful Alam deserve appreciation for proofreading and putting all the chapters together. We are grateful to the publishers for accepting our book proposal for publication and their continuing efforts in finalising the publication of the book.

Finally, we would like to express our sincerest gratitude to our families for their encouragement, tolerance, support and understanding. We dedicate this book to them.

Daud Hassan and Md Saiful Karim
Sydney and Brisbane
March 2018

PART I

Introduction and general framework for the international marine environmental law

1
CONTEMPORARY ISSUES IN THE PROTECTION AND CONSERVATION OF THE MARINE ENVIRONMENT

An overview

Sandya Nishanthi Gunasekara and Md Saiful Karim

Introduction

The protection and conservation of the ocean warrant increased attention from the global community. Several disturbing issues pose a threat to the marine environment and its well-being (Von Heland, Clifton & Olsson, 2014, pp. 4470–4496), among them are marine environmental pollution and the degradation of marine biodiversity – two well-known challenges that must be overcome. Combined, they are striking challenges to the marine environment. Moreover, most troubling is that they are caused by an overwhelming level of human activities (von Heland, Clifton & Olsson, 2014), which are sometimes transboundary, and whose consequences will become more severe and complicated if not properly curbed. Thus, it is common knowledge that these activities require comprehensive policies, laws and principles to manage them effectively. Linked to these solutions is the need for responsibilities, cooperation and commitments at local, national, regional and international levels. Altogether, the actions required for the protection of the ocean from human activities in responsible ways has become a necessity rather than an option. However, despite the challenges becoming more acute, and the use of the ocean less sustainable and more harmful, a durable solution to reverse these impacts is unlikely.

Considering these issues, this chapter lays the foundation for subsequent chapters by describing why and how ocean-related issues should be addressed responsibly, immediately and systematically, and how and why ocean pollution and threats to marine biodiversity are challenges to overcome. The exploration in this chapter guides the discussion in the subsequent chapters, which critically examine the current legal and institutional frameworks governing different issues of marine environmental protection and conservation.

Responsible ocean governance

Ocean governance is a complex and highly technical sub-discipline of international law (Kotze, 2008, pp. 11–30). The contemporary notion of ocean governance supports stronger initiatives towards the responsible use of the ocean (Pyć, 2016, pp. 159–162), and it has now been established as a collective process of decision-making, underpinned by the necessity to strengthen the ecosystem structure and sustain its functions (Rochette et al., 2015). Consequently, there has been a development of ocean policies (Bateman, 2000, pp. 5–11) through legal and institutional mechanisms and through local, national, regional and international levels of implementation (Bailet, 2002; Houghton & Rochette, 2014, pp. 81–84). As a result, the contemporary notion of ocean governance supports stronger initiatives towards the responsible use of the ocean.

According to the United Nations Convention on the Law of the Sea (UNCLOS), protection of the marine environment is an obligation of State parties. For example, such responsible efforts are highlighted in the 1992 Rio Declaration, Chapter 17 of Agenda 21, the 2002 Johannesburg Declaration, a number of International Maritime Organization (IMO) legal instruments, regional seas conventions and other marine environment–related international legal instruments.

The structure of the ocean governance framework is heavily influenced by the key objective of sustainable development (Cicin-Sain, 1993, pp. 11–43; Ittekkot, 2015, pp. 46–49; Mitchell & Hinds, 1999, pp. 235–244; Visbeck et al., 2013). The framework covers both maritime areas under the jurisdiction of the coastal States and in areas beyond national jurisdictions (ABNJ) (Bhatia et al., 2017). Similarly, collective engagement in ABNJ – high seawater columns and the deep seabed area, which cover almost 60% of the global ocean – should be designated a high level of importance in international marine conservation and environmental-based management (Drankier et al., 2012, pp. 375–433; Jørem & Tvedt, 2014, pp. 321–343; Narula, 2016, pp. 65–78).

Avoiding harm to the ocean through marine pollution and protecting marine biodiversity from a plethora of dangers calls for more attention and responsibilities. The following discussion attempts to reassess these impacts on the ocean.

Unsustainable use of marine living resources

Studies focusing on the sustainability of marine resources have made the illegal, unreported and unregulated (IUU) fishing (Agnew & Barnes, 2004, pp. 169–200; Baird, 2006; Karim, 2011, pp. 101–127; Miller, 2010, pp. 75–100; Schmidt, 2005, pp. 479–507), and overfishing or over-exploitation of fish (Perissi et al., 2017, pp. 285–292; Rosenberg, 2003, pp. 102–106), a constitutive part of their analyses. These activities are detrimental to marine biodiversity, which is a composition of 'the living resources that compose it and the ecological processes that sustain it' (Coll et al., 2008). Both IUU fishing and the over-exploitation of fish constitute 'unsustainable fishing', thus contradicting the spirit of UNLOCS, and can be treated as an unacceptable pattern of fishing (Food and Agriculture Organisation of the United Nations, 2009). These activities are also 'leading to long-term losses in the biological and economic productivity, biological diversity, or impacting ecosystem structure in a way that impairs functioning of the exploited system across several generations' (Food and Agriculture Organisation of the United Nations, 2009). Unsustainable fishing poses a severe threat to the world's future food security, denies the use of sustainable fishing practices and undermines existing environmental regulations and national, regional and international agreements, resulting in significant losses for national economies (Agnew et al., 2009; Sodik, 2008, pp. 129–164).

IUU fishing may represent '26 million tonnes of fish a year, or more than 15 percent of the world's total annual capture fisheries output' (FAO, 2016). Illegal fishing[1] is carried out by national or foreign vessels violating national legal provisions, regional fisheries management measures or international obligations (Food and Agriculture Organization of the United Nations, 2001). It has been outlined that, each year, between USD11 and USD23.5 billion is lost to illegal fishing (de Coning & Witbooi, 2015, pp. 208–215). Unreported fishing has adverse effects on economies when fish harvests are not recorded systematically or are misreported. The damage inflicted by IUU fishing activities is of major concern because, apart from the economic damage, 'such practices can threaten local biodiversity and food security in many countries' (Food and Agriculture Organisation of the United Nations, 2016). Altogether, IUU fishing denotes unsustainable fisheries' practices, endangering marine biodiversity in the ocean.

A consequence of unsustainable fishing practices is over-exploitation of fish, which directly affects the marine biodiversity, causing depletion and excessive mortalities of targeted fish populations as well as non-targeted fish populations (Coll et al., 2008), and which in practice remains a serious challenge to the conservation of marine living resources (Ahmad, 2011; Tanaka, 2011, pp. 291–330). According to the FAO Code of Conduct, overfishing of marine resources, resulting in habitat loss, is an irresponsible activity. Because of the unsustainable use of marine resources, more than 90% of global fish stocks have been exploited or overfished, either to the limits of sustainability (Federal Ministry for Economic Cooperation and Development, 2016) or to an extent that is higher than the carrying capacity of the marine system (Perissi et al., 2017, pp. 285–292). Another report indicated that almost a quarter of all the fish caught never reach the market and that 27 million tonnes of fish caught are thrown back dead into the ocean (Giuliani et al., 2004).

Such destructive fishing practices are harmful for marine biodiversity, especially when conducted using bottom trawling (Chuenpagdee et al., 2003, pp. 517–524), a method that inflicts damage to the seafloor (Giuliani et al., 2004). Watling and Norse (1998, pp. 1180–1197) revealed that bottom trawling gear scrapes approximately 14.8 million square kilometres of ocean bed annually. These unregulated practices lead to a significantly negative aftermath for marine biodiversity (Morgan & Chuenpagdee, 2003), including the capturing of non-targeted marine animals (Stiles et al., 2010), and eventually leading to habitat destruction. Non-targeted fish, or 'by-catch', which are caught and released later show a very low rate of survival (Morgan & Chuenpagdee, 2003); moreover, the majority of these unwanted fish are juvenile (Harrington, Myers & Rosenberg, 2005, pp. 350–361). Fish comprising by-catch are also vulnerable to damage caused by bottom trawlers (Morgan et al., 2005). The pressure exerted by fishing vessels on marine biodiversity in ABNJ is significant, and more profound given the slow reproductive rates and considerably low growth rates (Morgan et al., 2005).

Seabed habitat disturbances due to bottom trawling are well documented. Trawling endangers the lives of seabed habitats of coral reefs, rocks, seagrasses and seamounts, which protect fish and other species from predators, and provide them with food and refuge (Auster et al., 1996, pp. 185–202; Hourigan, 2009, pp. 333–340; Roberts et al., 2005). Thus, these seabed habitats are extremely vulnerable to destructive fishing activities (Fosså, Mortensen & Furevik, 2002, pp. 1–12; Hall et al., 2002, pp. 507–511).

The growing extent worldwide of unsustainable fishing exerts a considerable pressure for change in international legal and normative frameworks. Such international legal and normative initiatives for combatting unsustainable fishing activities in the aftermath of the UNCLOS have been epitomised in the introduction of a series of binding and non-binding global fisheries instruments. Simultaneously, there is a parallel development of regional and national scale actions and efforts to combat irresponsible fishing. Nevertheless, an examination of these frameworks is critical regarding the extent to which marine biodiversity is addressed as a challenge and counter measures provided.

Impacts of climate change

Climate change presents overwhelming challenges to the ocean ecosystems (Howden et al., 2003). There is strong evidence that climate change leads to unprecedented shifts in marine environment conditions. These shifts, which often result from human activities, contribute significantly to global warming, ocean acidification, coral bleaching, changes in species distribution and other biological changes to the sea (Bijma et al., 2013, pp. 495–505; Pörtner et al., 2014, pp. 411–484). Moreover, international legal and institutional frameworks implemented to overcome these challenges are inadequate (Galland, Harrould-Kolieb & Herr, 2012, pp. 764–771). Despite a reference to the ocean in the Paris Agreement, a significant gulf exists between scientific and government understanding (Gallo, Victor & Levin, 2017, pp. 833–838; Magnan et al., 2016, pp. 770–780), which will create bottlenecks in existing governance regimes (Brandt & Kronbak, 2010, pp. 11–19; Galaz et al., 2012, pp. 21–32).

Ocean acidification places the marine environment and its biodiversity in danger (Doney et al., 2009, pp. 169–192; Gattuso & Hansson, 2011). The ocean's healthy absorption of carbon dioxide plays a key role in ensuring a fair chemical balance; however, this balance is vulnerable to change when the ocean is no longer able to fully absorb carbon dioxide (Harrould-Kolieb, Huelsenbeck & Selz, 2010). Thus, the changing acidity of the ocean instigates changes in the balance of ocean chemistry upon which marine living resources depend. Corals, shellfish and plants take the brunt of these changes in that these marine animals become less fit for survival. In their struggle to survive, although some animals tolerate these changes well ('winners'), others are adversely and negatively affected (Brown & Thatje, 2015, pp. 173–180). However, corals are severely and easily affected, leaving scientists predicting that they may be seriously damaged or completely lost in the future. To the extent that ocean acidification continues, and climate change consequences such as global warming persist, the calcification of corals will continue to decline (Mongin et al., 2016). As an example, the calcification of the reefs of the Great Barrier Reef has seriously declined (De'ath, Lough & Fabricius, 2009, pp. 116–119).

Of the evidence proving that the impact of carbon dioxide emissions and climate change is real and unavoidable, the bleaching of corals is the most visible sign of destruction. While the vulnerability of corals has been increasing in magnitude and volume over the last decade, it was not a phenomenon of investigation or one known to researchers prior to 1979 (Hoegh-Guldberg, Berkelmans & Oliver, 1997). Such a vulnerable scenario is relevant to the sensitivity of coral; for instance, an increase of only $1.0°C$ in the tropics for a few weeks is enough to produce mass bleaching (Goreau & Hayes, 1994). Australia's icon, the Great Barrier Reef, characterised as a one of the country's main tourist destinations, has been experiencing unusually warm temperatures recently. Consequently, in 2002 – one of Australia's warmest years of the 21st century – coral reefs near Great Keppel Island on the Great Barrier Reef were considerably threatened by high temperatures and unusual summers (Great Barrier Reef Marine Park Authority, 2007; Marshall & Schuttenberg, 2006). In 1998 alone, 50% of corals in the Great Barrier Reef were affected by bleaching (Swann & Campbell, 2016). Brierley and Kingsford (2009) predicted that 'waters of the Great Barrier Reef are expected to warm by between 1 and 3 °C over the next 100 years, so the risk of high temperature press events that could be fatal to corals is increasing' (p. 610).

Since temperature controls the distribution of ocean species (Sunday, Bates & Dulvy, 2012, pp. 686–690) and global patterns of marine biodiversity are strongly driven by ocean temperature (Proelss & Krivickaite, 2009, pp. 437–445), the rising temperature acts as the main catalyst of marine biodiversity deterioration. Given that the survival of marine species is often linked to temperature and that the species distribution is ensured by the 'geographic range boundaries' set by temperature (Sunday, Bates & Dulvy, 2012, pp. 686–690), shifts in ocean temperature affect biodiversity.

Land-based marine pollution

Even though land-based marine pollution is a relatively new area of ocean-related law, in the last decades it has been established as the most frequent and most harmful cause of marine pollution (Schumacher, Hoagland & Gaines, 1996, pp. 99–121). Thus, it is a threat to the ocean sustainability that affects marine ecosystems and coastal areas, which are sites of high biological productivity (Tanaka, 2016). According to the United Nations Environment's *Regional Seas Programme*, land-based marine pollution 'account[s] for as much as 80 percent of all marine pollution' (United Nations Environment Programme, 2014).

While the causes of damage inflicted on the marine environment vary, it should be considered that industrial, municipal and agricultural sources are jointly responsible for the catastrophic results (Hassan, 2003, pp. 61–94). The damage is transboundary in nature, so that the severe consequences are distributed over large parts of the ocean. Given this scenario, States ought to ensure that in accordance with the United Nations Charter and the principles of international law:

> the sovereign right to exploit their own resources pursuant to their own environmental and developmental policies, and the responsibility to ensure that activities within their jurisdiction or control do not cause damage to the environment of other States or of areas beyond the limits of national jurisdiction.
>
> *(1992 Rio Declaration on Environment and Development, Principle 21)*

In a broad context, owing to the consequences of land-based marine pollution and its transcending nature, there are calls for more specific control of the causes of the pollution such as sewage, garbage, fertilisers, pesticides and industrial pollution. Despite a general obligation established under UNCLOS, the development of regulations for land-based pollution at the global level is challenging and slow. However, several regional legal instruments exist that deal with the issue.

Pollution from ships

The threats of pollution to human health in coastal areas and surroundings, and to marine life provide the States with additional incentives to prevent marine pollution from vessels (Endresen et al., 2003, pp. 10–17; Maragkogianni & Papaefthimiou, 2015). Since the signing of the International Convention for the Prevention of Pollution of the Sea by Oil, commonly known as the OILPOL Convention, a number of international conventions have come into being. Examples include the International Convention for the Prevention of Pollution from Ships (MARPOL, 1973, amended in 1978, replacing the OILPOL Convention) and the International Convention for the Safety of Life at Sea (adopted in 1974 under the auspices of the IMO). The MARPOL Convention represents a plausible step to assign responsibilities towards protecting the ocean from oil, chemicals, harmful matter transported in any form of packages, sewage and garbage and emissions of harmful gases (Karim, 2009, pp. 51–82; Karim, 2010, pp. 303–337; Karim, 2015; Renken, 2010).

The growth of the international shipping industry, and the increase in number of commercial ships and ship traffic density has been drastic. Concomitant with this, pollutant emissions with a high sulphur content from ships, and discharge of vessels' sewage, garbage and ballast have also seen a dramatic and continuous increase (Nelson, 1995). Communities living close to coastal areas are exposed to emissions from ships and thus are easily affected by premature death, cancer, heart and respiratory diseases (Han, 2010, pp. 7–29). Emissions from ships, mainly nitrogen, sulphur, carbon dioxide and hydrocarbons, cause interrelated environmental impacts, for example 'emission of greenhouse gases changes the radiative balance of the atmosphere. Sulphur and nitrogen compounds emitted from ships oxidising in the atmosphere to form sulphate and nitrate, and thus contribute to acidification' (Endresen et al., 2003, p. 3).

Pollution of the ocean environment produced by vessels' sewage, also known as black water, contains various harmful substances that cause the death of marine life and present a threat to human health if discharged irresponsibly (Koboević, Komadina & Kurtela, 2011, pp. 377–387). For example, sewage and garbage dumped in the sea have caused disturbances to marine corals and their ecological balance (Aston, 2006).

Different types of environmental distress occur because of oil spills. The release of substantial quantities of oils into marine water from large oil spills, for example, the Niger Delta oil spills, Exxon Valdez in 1989 and Prestige in 2002, have contaminated large areas and endangered marine lives (Brussaard et al., 2016). Planktonic organisms (such as algae, bacteria, protozoa, plants and drifting or floating animals) are directly affected by oil spills (Jernelöv, 2010, pp. 353–366). Moreover, seabirds that come into direct contact with oil are affected by 'plumage fouling'; as a result, their flying and swimming abilities are reduced. It is estimated that around 250,000 seabirds died as a result of the Exxon Valdez oil spill incident (Piatt & Ford, 1996, pp. 712–719). Further, marine mammals and reptiles are highly affected. For example, killer whale populations decreased in the aftermath of the Exxon Valdez oil spill (Matkin et al., 2008, pp. 269–281). Highly sensitive organism corals are also damaged by floating oil.

Since 1987, more than 700 marine pollution cases have been reported (Aston, 2006). Nevertheless, to date, oil spill incidents – from minor to major – have been on a downward trend (Renken, 2010). Despite this positive trend, minor oil spills continue to take place. However, ignorance of small-scale oil spills may lead to misleading conclusions, for example, that they are not harmful. Despite such presumptions, Redondo and Platonov (2009) argued that smaller and undetected oil spills from ships in the oceans between 1996 and 2004 contributed to the long-term damage of the marine environment.

Offshore hydrocarbon exploration and mining

The International Energy Agency predicts that the growth of global oil demands could be increased by more than 35% from 2010 to 2035, which is an increase of 6,900 million tonnes of oil in 2010 to 9,400 by 2035 (Wilson Center, 2013). According to the British Petroleum *Statistical Review of World Energy*, the global consumption of gas is also growing by 1.5% (63 billion cubic metres) – quite a bit weaker than its 10-year average of 2.3% (British Petroleum, 2017).

Given the rising demand, there is concern that offshore oil and gas explorations are also now dramatically rising, particularly when considering that these activities have been linked to damage to marine lives such as corals (Loya & Rinkevich, 1980, pp. 167–180). Hydrocarbon exploration and exploitation activities are gradually shifting towards 'previously inaccessible deep waters and other frontier regions', creating several challenges, including *inter alia* 'threats to ecosystems and marine species from oil spills, negative impacts on native biodiversity from invasive species colonising drilling infrastructure, and increased political conflicts that can delay conservation actions' (Kark et al., 2015, p. 1573). The Deepwater Horizon blowout in 2010 illustrates the potential devastating impact of offshore hydrocarbon exploration and exploitation (Joye, 2015, pp. 592–593) by having severely affected marine lives and contributed to deaths of protected species such as sea turtles and dolphins (Wallace et al., 2017, pp. 1–7).

The problem is now expanding to the Polar Regions. There is potential for considerable harm to the marine living resources in the Arctic Ocean from drill cutting, especially from the noise it generates (Koivurova, Hossain & Arctic Transform, 2008). Moreover, transportation of oil through ocean routes carries the risk of oil spills (Koivurova, Hossain & Arctic Transform, 2008). Further, the increasing possibility of deep sea mineral exploration and exploitation may create further pressures on the marine environment and biodiversity (Durden et al., 2017, pp. 193–201; Gollner et al., 2017, pp. 76–101).

Conclusion

This chapter identifies some existing and emerging challenges in the conservation of the marine environment, particularly concerning the prevention of marine pollution and the protection of marine biodiversity. The chapter emphasises the critical importance of discussion of international regulatory frameworks for overcoming these issues. The subsequent chapters of the book concisely present the international regulatory frameworks covering the issues identified in this chapter.

Note

1 'Illegal fishing refers to activities: 3.1.1 conducted by national or foreign vessels in waters under the jurisdiction of a State, without the permission of that State, or in contravention of its laws and regulations; 3.1.2 conducted by vessels flying the flag of States that are parties to a relevant regional fisheries management organisation but operate in contravention of the conservation and management measures adopted by that organisation and by which the States are bound, or relevant provisions of the applicable international law; or 3.1.3 in violation of national laws or international obligations, including those undertaken by cooperating States to a relevant regional fisheries management organization'. International Plan of Action to Prevent, Deter and Eliminate Illegal, Unreported and Unregulated Fishing (IPOA-IUU), 2001, www.fao.org/3/contents/faadeaa5-d06e-5df3-9cea-14a536d66cf5/y1224e00.htm.

References

Agnew, D.J., & Barnes, C. (2004). Economic aspects and drivers of IUU fishing: Building a framework, in K. Gray, F. Legg & E. Andrews-Chouicha (eds), *Fish Piracy: Combating Illegal, Unreported and Unregulated Fishing*, OECD Publishing, Paris, pp. 169–200.

Agnew, D.J., Pearce, J., Pramod, G., Peatman, T., Watson, R., Beddington, J.R., & Pitcher, T.J. (2009). Estimating the worldwide extent of illegal fishing. *PLoS ONE*, e44570, viewed 20 November 2017, https://doi.org/10.1371/journal.pone.0004570.

Ahmad, M.Z. (2011). International legal and normative framework for responsible fisheries, with reference to Malaysia's offshore EEZ fisheries management, PhD thesis, University of Wollongong, Wollongong, Australia.

Aston, J. (2006). The state of the Great Barrier Reef on-line, in A. Chin (ed.), *Shipping and Oil Spills*, Great Barrier Reef Marine Park Authority, Townsville, QLD.

Auster, P.J., Malatesta, R.J., Langton, R.W., Watting, L., Valentine, P.C., Donaldson, C.L.S., Langton, E.W., Shepard, A.N., & Babb, W.G. (1996). The impacts of mobile fishing gear on seafloor habitats in the Gulf of Maine (Northwest Atlantic): Implications for conservation of fish populations. *Reviews in Fisheries Science*, vol. 4, no. 2, pp. 185–202.

Bailet, F. (2002). Ocean governance: Towards an oceanic circle. *DOALOS/ UNITAR Briefing on Developments in Ocean Affairs and the LOS: 20 Years After the Conclusion of UNCLOS* International Ocean Institute, viewed 17 December 2017, www.un.org/depts/los/convention_agreements/convention_20years/presentation_ocean_governance_frbailet.pdf.

Baird, R.J. (2006). *Aspects of Illegal, Unreported, and Unregulated Fishing in the Southern Ocean*, Springer, Dordrecht, The Netherlands.

Bateman, S. (2000). Australia's oceans policy and the maritime community [The Annual Boulton Lecture 1999]. *Journal of the Australian Naval Institute*, vol. 26, no. 1, pp. 5–11.

Bhatia, R., Boteler, B., Kraemer, R.A., Herédia, M., Krüger, I., Martinez, G., Mathur, A., Pendleton, L., e Cunha, T.P., & Rochette, J. (2017). Sustainable ocean economy, innovation and growth: A G20 initiative for the 7th largest economy in the world. *Policy Area: 2030 Agenda for Sustainable Development*, viewed 22 October 2017, www.g20-insights.org/policy_briefs/sustainable-ocean-economy-innovation-growth-g20-initiative-7th-largest-economy-world/.

Bijma, J., Pörtner, H.-O., Yesson, C., & Rogers, A.D. (2013). Climate change and the oceans: What does the future hold? *Marine Pollution Bulletin*, vol. 74, no. 2, pp. 495–505.

Brandt, U.S., & Kronbak, L.G. (2010). On the stability of fishery agreements under exogenous change: An example of agreements under climate change. *Fisheries Research*, vol. 101, no. 1, pp. 11–19.

Brierley, A.S., & Kingsford, M.J. (2009). Impacts of climate change on marine organisms and ecosystems. *Current Biology*, vol. 19, no. 14, pp. 602–614.

British Petroleum (2017). *BP Statistical Review of World Energy-2017* 66 edn, British Petroleum, London.

Brown, A., & Thatje, S. (2015). The effects of changing climate on faunal depth distributions determine winners and losers. *Global Change Biology*, vol. 21, no. 1, pp. 173–180.

Brussaard, C.P., Peperzak, L., Beggah, S., Wick, L.Y., Wuerz, B., Weber, J., Arey, J.S., Van Der Burg, B., Jonas, A., & Huisman, J. (2016). Immediate ecotoxicological effects of short-lived oil spills on marine biota. *Nature Communications*, vol. 7, doi: 10.1038/ncomms11206.

Chuenpagdee, R., Morgan, L.E., Maxwell, S.M., Norse, E.A., & Pauly, D. (2003). Shifting gears: Assessing collateral impacts of fishing methods in US waters. *Frontiers in Ecology and the Environment*, vol. 1, no. 10, pp. 517–524.

Cicin-Sain, B. (1993). Sustainable development and integrated coastal management'. *Ocean and Coastal Management*, vol. 21, no. 1–3, pp. 11–43.

Coll, M., Libralato, S., Tudela, S., Palomera, I., & Pranovi, F. (2008). Ecosystem overfishing in the ocean. *PLoS ONE*, vol. 3, no. 12, viewed 15 November 2017, https://doi.org/10.1371/journal.pone.0003881.

De'ath, G., Lough, J.M., & Fabricius, K.E. (2009). Declining coral calcification on the Great Barrier Reef. *Science*, vol. 323, no. 5910, pp. 116–119.

de Coning, E., & Witbooi, E. (2015). Towards a new 'fisheries crime' paradigm: South Africa as an illustrative example. *Marine Policy*, vol. 60, pp. 208–215.

Doney, S.C., Fabry, V.J., Feely, R.A., & Kleypas, J.A. (2009). Ocean acidification: The other CO_2 problem. *Annual Review of Marine Science*, vol. 1, no. 1, pp. 169–192.

Drankier, P., Oude Elferink, A.G., Visser, B., & Takács, T. (2012). Marine genetic resources in areas beyond national jurisdiction: Access and benefit-sharing. *The International Journal of Marine and Coastal Law*, vol. 27, no. 2, pp. 375–433.

Durden, J.M., Murphy, K., Jaeckel, A., Van Dover, C.L., Christiansen, S., Gjerde, K., Ortega, A., & Jones, D.O.B. (2017). A procedural framework for robust environmental management of deep-sea mining projects using a conceptual model. *Marine Policy*, vol. 84, pp. 193–201.

Endresen, Ø., Sørgård, E., Sundet, J.K., Dalsøren, S.B., Isaksen, I.S., Berglen, T.F., & Gravir, G. (2003). Emission from international sea transportation and environmental impact. *Journal of Geophysical Research: Atmospheres*, vol. 108, no. D17, doi: 10.1029/2002JD002898.

Federal Ministry for Economic Cooperation and Development. (2016). Marine conservation and sustainable fisheries: Ten point plan of action. Federal Ministry for Economic Cooperation and Development, Bonn, Germany, viewed 18 October 2017, www.bmz.de/en/publications/topics/environment/Materialie262_marine_conservation.pdf.

Food and Agriculture Organization of the United Nations. (2001). *International Plan of Action to Prevent, Deter and Eliminate Illegal, Unreported and Unregulated Fishing*. Food and Agriculture Organization of the United Nations, Rome.

Food and Agriculture Organisation of the United Nations. (2009). FAO/UNEP expert meeting on impacts of destructive fishing practices, unsustainable fishing, and illegal, unreported and unregulated (iuu) fishing on marine biodiversity and habitats. *FAO Fisheries and Aquaculture Report No. 932*.

Food and Agriculture Organisation of the United Nations. (2016). *The State of World Fisheries and Aquaculture 2016. Contributing to Food Security and Nutrition for All*. Food and Agriculture Organisation of the United Nations, Rome.

Fosså, J.H., Mortensen, P.B., & Furevik, D.M. (2002). The deep-water coral Lophelia pertusa in Norwegian waters: Distribution and fishery impacts. *Hydrobiologia*, vol. 471, no. 1, pp. 1–12.

Galaz, V., Crona, B., Österblom, H., Olsson, P., & Folke, C. (2012). Polycentric systems and interacting planetary boundaries – Emerging governance of climate change – ocean acidification – marine biodiversity. *Ecological Economics*, vol. 81, pp. 21–32.

Galland, G., Harrould-Kolieb, E., & Herr, D. (2012). The ocean and climate change policy. *Climate Policy*, vol. 12, no. 6, pp. 764–771.

Gallo, N.D., Victor, D.G., & Levin, L.A. (2017). Ocean commitments under the Paris Agreement. *Nature Climate Change*, vol. 7, no. 11, pp. 833–838.

Gattuso, J.-P., & Hansson, L. (2011). *Ocean Acidification*, Oxford University Press, Oxford.

Giuliani, G., De Bono, A., Kluser, S., Peduzzi, P., & United Nations Environment Programme (2004). Overfishing, a major threat to the global marine ecology, viewed 22 November 2017, http://archive-ouverte.unige.ch/unige:23129.

Gollner, S., Kaiser, S., Menzel, L., Jones, D., O.B, Brown, A., Mestre, N.C., Van Oevelen, D., Menot, L., Colaço, A., & Canals, M. (2017). Resilience of benthic deep-sea fauna to mining activities. *Marine Environmental Research*, vol. 129, pp. 76–101.

Goreau, T.J., & Hayes, R. L. (1994). Coral bleaching and ocean "hot spots". Ambio-Journal of Human Environment Research and Management, 23(3), pp. 176–180. Great Barrier Reef Marine Park Authority. (2007). Great Barrier Reef coral bleaching surveys 2006. no. 87, Great Barrier Reef Marine Park Authority, Townsville, QLD.

Hall – Spencer, J., Allain, V., & Fosså, J.H. (2002). Trawling damage to Northeast Atlantic ancient coral reefs. *Proceedings of the Royal Society of London. Series B: Biological Sciences*, vol. 269, no. 1490, pp. 507–511.

Han, C. (2010). Strategies to reduce air pollution in shipping industry. *The Asian Journal of Shipping and Logistics*, vol. 26, no. 1, pp. 7–29.

Harrington, J.M., Myers, R.A., & Rosenberg, A.A. (2005). Wasted fishery resources: Discarded by catch in the USA. *Fish and Fisheries*, vol. 6, no. 4, pp. 350–361.

Harrould-Kolieb, E., Huelsenbeck, M., & Selz, V. (2010). Ocean acidification: The untold stories. *Oceana*, vol. 3.

Hassan, D. (2003). Land-based sources of marine pollution-a global framework for control. *Australian International Law Journal*, vol. 61, pp. 61–94.

Hoegh-Guldberg, O., Berkelmans, R., & Oliver, J. (1997). Coral bleaching: Implications for the Great Barrier Reef Marine Park. *The Great Barrier Reef Science, Use and Management Conference*, 25–29 November, 1996, Great Barrier Reef Marine Park Authority, Townsville, Australia, Townsville, Australia, pp. 210–224.

Houghton, K., & Rochette, J. (2014). Introduction: Advancing governance of areas beyond national jurisdiction. *Marine Policy*, vol. 49, pp. 81–84.

Hourigan, T.F. (2009). Managing fishery impacts on deep-water coral ecosystems of the USA: Emerging best practices. *Marine Ecology Progress Series*, vol. 397, pp. 333–340.

Howden, M., Hughes, L., Dunlop, M., Zethoven, I., Hilbert, D., & Chilcott, C. (2003). *Climate Change Impacts on Biodiversity in Australia*, Commonwealth of Australia, Canberra.

Ittekkot, V. (2015). Oceans, seas and sustainable development: Preparedness of developing countries. *Environmental Development*, vol. 13, pp. 46–49.

Jernelöv, A. (2010). The threats from oil spills: Now, then, and in the future. *AMBIO: A Journal of the Human Environment*, vol. 39, no. 6, pp. 353–366.

Jørem, A., & Tvedt, M.W. (2014). Bioprospecting in the high seas: Existing rights and obligations in view of a new legal regime for marine areas beyond national jurisdiction. *The International Journal of Marine and Coastal Law*, vol. 29, no. 2, pp. 321–343.

Joye, B.S. (2015). Deepwater horizon, 5 years on. *Science*, vol. 349, no. 6248, pp. 592–593.

Karim, M.S. (2009). Implementation of the MARPOL convention in Bangladesh. *Macquarie Journal of International and Comparative Environmental Law*, vol. 6, no. 1, pp. 51–82.

Karim, M.S. (2010). Implementation of the MARPOL convention in developing countries. *Nordic Journal of International Law*, vol. 79, pp. 303–337.

Karim, M.S. (2011). Conflicts over protection of marine living resources: The Volga Case. *Goettingen Journal of International Law*, vol. 3, no. 1, pp. 101–127.

Karim, M.S. (2015). *Prevention of Pollution of the Marine Environment from Vessels: The Potential and Limits of the International Maritime Organisation*, Springer, Heidelberg, Germany.

Kark, S., Brokovich, E., Mazor, T., & Levin, N. (2015). Emerging conservation challenges and prospects in an era of offshore hydrocarbon exploration and exploitation. *Conservation Biology*, vol. 29, no. 6, pp. 1573–1585.

Koboević, Ž., Komadina, P., & Kurtela, Ž. (2011). Protection of the seas from pollution by vessel's sewage with reference to legal regulations. *Promet-Traffic and Transportation*, vol. 23, no. 5, pp. 377–387.

Koivurova, T., Hossain, K., & Arctic Transform. (2008). *Offshore Hydrocarbon: Current Policy Context in the Marine Arctic*, Arctic Centre, Rovaniemi, Finland.

Kotze, L. (2008). Fragmentation of international environmental law: An oceans governance case study, in E. Couzens & T. Honkonen (eds), *International Environmental Law-Making and Diplomacy Review 2008*, University of Joensuu, Joensuu, Finland, pp. 11–30.

Loya, Y., & Rinkevich, B. (1980). Effects of oil pollution on coral reef communities. *Marine Ecology Progress Series*, vol. 3, pp. 167–180.

Magnan, A.K., Colombier, M., Billé, R., Joos, F., Hoegh-Guldberg, O., Pörtner, H.-O., Waisman, H., Spencer, T., & Gattuso, J.-P. (2016). Implications of the Paris agreement for the ocean. *Nature Climate Change*, vol. 6, no. 8, pp. 732–735.

Maragkogianni, A., & Papaefthimiou, S. (2015). Evaluating the social cost of cruise ships air emissions in major ports of Greece. *Transportation Research Part D: Transport and Environment*, vol. 36, pp. 10–17.

Marshall, P.A., & Schuttenberg, H. (2006). *A Reef Manager's Guide to Coral Bleaching*, Great Barrier Reef Marine Park Authority, Townsville, QLD.

Matkin, C., Saulitis, E., Ellis, G., Olesiuk, P., & Rice, S. (2008). Ongoing population-level impacts on killer whales Orcinus orca following the 'Exxon Valdez' oil spill in Prince William Sound, Alaska. *Marine Ecology Progress Series*, vol. 356, pp. 269–281.

Miller, G.M. (2010). Occupying the high ground: Technology and the war on IUU fishing, in D. Vidas (ed.), *Law, Technology and Science for Oceans in Globalization*, Martinus Nijhoff Publishers, Leiden/Boston, pp. 75–100.

Mitchell, C.L., & Hinds, L.O. (1999). Small island developing states and sustainable development of ocean resources. *Natural Resources Forum*, vol. 23, no. 3, pp. 235–244.

Mongin, M., Baird, M.E., Tilbrook, B., Matear, R.J., Lenton, A., Herzfeld, M., Wild-Allen, K., Skerratt, J., Margvelashvili, N., Robson, B.J., Duarte, C.M., Gustafsson, M.S.M., Ralph, P.J., & Steven, A.D.L. (2016). The exposure of the Great Barrier Reef to ocean acidification'. *Nature Communications*, vol. 7.

Morgan, L.E., & Chuenpagdee, R. (2003). *Shifting Gears: Addressing the Collateral Impacts of Fishing Methods in U.S. Waters*, Island Press, Washington, DC.

Morgan, L.E., Norse, E.A., Rogers, A.D., Haedrich, R.L., & Maxwell, S.M. (2005). Why the world needs a time-out on high-seas bottom trawling. *The Deep Sea Conservation Coalition*, viewed 22 November 2017, https://mcbi.marine-conservation.org/publications/pub_pdfs/TimeOut_english.pdf.

Narula, K. (2016). Ocean governance: Strengthening the legal framework for conservation of marine biological diversity beyond areas of national jurisdiction. *Maritime Affairs: Journal of the National Maritime Foundation of India*, vol. 12, no. 1, pp. 65–78.

Nelson, P (1995). Pollution from ships: A global perspective, in Gunningham, N, Norberry, J and McKillop, S (eds), AIC Conference Proceedings: Environmental Crime, 26, Australian Institute of Criminology, Canberra, pp. 175–188.

Perissi, I., Bardi, U., El Asmar, T., & Lavacchi, A. (2017). Dynamic patterns of overexploitation in fisheries. *Ecological Modelling*, vol. 359, pp. 285–292.

Piatt, J.F., & Ford, R.G. (1996). How many seabirds were killed by the Exxon Valdez oil spill. *American Fisheries Society Symposium*, vol. 18, no. 1993, pp. 712–719.

Pörtner, H.-O., Karl, D.M., Boyd, P.W., Cheung, W., Lluch-Cota, S.E., Nojiri, Y., Schmidt, D.N., Zavialov, P.O., Alheit, J., & Aristegui, J. (2014). Ocean systems, in C.B. Field, V.R. Barros, D.J. Dokken, K.J. Mach, M.D. Mastrandrea, T.E. Bilir, M. Chatterjee, K.L. Ebi, Y.O. Estrada, B. Genova, B. Girma, E.S. Kissel, A.N. Levy, S. MacCracken, P.R. Mastrandrea & L. White (eds), *Climate Change 2014: Impacts, Adaptation, and Vulnerability. Part A: Global and Sectoral Aspects. Contribution of Working Group II to the Fifth Assessment Report of the Intergovernmental Panel on Climate Change*, Cambridge University Press, Cambridge, pp. 411–484.

Proelss, A., & Krivickaite, M. (2009). Marine biodiversity and climate change. *Carbon & Climate Law Review*, vol. 3, no. 4, pp. 437–445.

Pyć, D. (2016). Global ocean governance. *TransNav: International Journal on Marine Navigation and Safety of Sea Transportation*, vol. 10, no. 1, pp. 159–162.

Redondo, J.M., & Platonov, A.K. (2009). Self-similar distribution of oil spills in European coastal waters. *Environmental Research Letters*, vol. 4, no. 1, doi: 10.1088/1748-9326/4/1/014008, p. 014008.

Renken, H. (2010). Global trends in ship-sourced marine pollution, paper presented to the *Oil in the Sea Conference, 17–19 November*, Hamburg, Germany.
Rio Declaration on Environment and Development. (1992). Agenda 21. New York: United Nations.
Roberts, S., Aguilar, R., Warrenchuk, J., Hudson, C., & Hirshfield, M. (2005). Deep sea life: On the edge of the abyss: Protecting the World's Oceans. New York: USA. Retrieved from http://oceana.org/reports/deep-sea-life-edge-abyss
Rochette, J., Wright, G., Chabason, L., Unger, S., Ardron, J., & Houghton, K. (2015). Advancing governance of marine areas beyond national jurisdiction. *Brief for Global Sustainable Development Report 2015*, viewed 27 October 2017, https://sustainabledevelopment.un.org/content/documents/5774Brief%20ABNJ%20GSDR_rev.pdf.
Rosenberg, A.A. (2003). Managing to the margins: The overexploitation of fisheries. *Frontiers in Ecology and the Environment*, vol. 1, no. 2, pp. 102–106.
Schmidt, C.-C. (2005). Economic drivers of illegal, unreported and unregulated (IUU) fishing. *The International Journal of Marine and Coastal Law*, vol. 20, no. 3, pp. 479–507.
Schumacher, M., Hoagland, P., & Gaines, A. (1996). Land based marine pollution in the Caribbean: Incentives and prospects for an effective regional protocol. *Marine Policy*, vol. 20, no. 2, pp. 99–121.
Sodik, D.M. (2008). Non-legally binding international fisheries instruments and measures to combat illegal, unreported and unregulated fishing. *Australian International Law Journal*, vol. 15 no. 1, pp. 129–164.
Stiles, M.L., Stockbridge, J., Lande, M., & Hirshfield, M.F. (2010). *Impacts of Bottom Trawling*, Oceana, Washington, DC.
Sunday, J.M., Bates, A.E., & Dulvy, N.K. (2012). Thermal tolerance and the global redistribution of animals. *Nature Climate Change*, vol. 2, no. 9, pp. 686–690.
Swann, T., & Campbell, R. (2016). *Great Barrier Bleached: Coral Bleaching, the Great Barrier Reef and Potential Impacts on Tourism*, The Australia Institute, Canberra.
Tanaka, Y. (2011). The changing approaches to conservation of marine living resources in international law. *Heidelberg Journal of International Law*, vol. 71, pp. 291–330.
Tanaka, Y. (2016). *A Dual Approach to Ocean Governance: The Cases of Zonal and Integrated Management in International Law of the Sea*, Routledge, New York.
United Nations Environment Programme. (2014). *Land Based Pollution*, viewed 18 November 2017, http://web.unep.org/regionalseas/about/what-we-do/land-based-pollution.
Visbeck, M., Kronfeld-Goharani, U., Neumann, B., Rickels, W., Schmidt, J., & van Doorn, E. (2013). Establishing a sustainable development goal for oceans and coasts to face the challenges of our future ocean. *Kiel Working Paper, No. 1847*, Kiel Institute for the World Economy (IfW), Kiel, Germany.
von Heland, F., Clifton, J., & Olsson, P. (2014). Improving stewardship of marine resources: Linking strategy to opportunity. *Sustainability*, vol. 6, no. 7, pp. 4470–4496.
Wallace, B.P., Brosnan, T., McLamb, D., Rowles, T., Ruder, E., Schroeder, B., Schwacke, L., Stacy, B., Sullivan, L., & Takeshita, R. (2017). Effects of the Deepwater Horizon oil spill on protected marine species. *Endangered Species Research*, vol. 33, pp. 1–7.
Watling, L., & Norse, E.A. (1998). Disturbance of the seabed by mobile fishing gear: A comparison to forest clearcutting. *Conservation Biology*, vol. 12, no. 6, pp. 1180–1197.
Wilson Center. (2013). *Opportunities and Challenges for Arctic Oil and Gas Development*, Wilson Center, Washington, DC, viewed 2 November 2017, www.wilsoncenter.org/sites/default/files/Artic%20Report_F2.pdf.

2
OCEAN GOVERNANCE AND MARINE ENVIRONMENTAL CONSERVATION

Concepts, principles and institutions

Abul Hasanat and Md Saiful Karim

Introduction

The oceans comprise approximately three-quarters of the Earth's surface (United Nations, 2015). Oceans play a crucial role in maintaining the Earth's ecosystem as well as the socio-economic welfare of human beings (United Nations Economic and Social Council, 2016). Oceans 'nurture life and shape the planet's weather and climate' (Sands & Peel, 2012, p. 342). However, oceans are now under serious threat due to excessive fishing, violent fishing practices, ocean acidification, habitat loss, coastal pollution, rise of alien species and climate change (Sands & Peel, 2012, p. 342; Rochette et al., 2015, p. 9). These practices must be mitigated and kept under careful control under a united, strategic and legally binding strategy. A variety of theories, principles, legal instruments and institutions have emerged and are working toward creating a more effective regulatory framework for protecting and preserving the marine environment and living resources. Most of these theories and principles have derived from existing international environmental jurisprudence, and relevant regulatory instruments are being adopted for the sustainable governance of different components of oceans and seas, both on an international and regional level. Although regional mechanisms are generally considered more effective than international mechanisms, some problems are also apparent in domestic implementation of regional environmental legal imperatives. Certain global organisations have long been working toward governance of the marine environment and biodiversity from different perspectives, and certain regional organisations, particularly the bodies operating under various treaties are actively working toward protecting the marine environment in their respective jurisdictions under the mandate and supervision of international institutions such as the International Maritime Organization (IMO) and the United Nations Environment Programme (UNEP), and instruments such as the United Nations Convention on the Law of the Sea, 1982 (UNCLOS).

Global ocean governance and protection of the marine environment: conceptual framework

Marine environmental problems are in many ways transnational and mostly 'complex, multiple, and often overlapping or synergistic' (Spalding et al., 2013, p. 213). Such problems generally attract States' mutual cooperation and commitment, and global initiatives and governing mechanisms (World Commission on Environment and Development, 1987, p. 43). As a concerted response to managing such problems, a series of international and regional instruments – both binding and persuasive – have emerged for the purpose of preserving and protecting the marine environment as a whole. More than 60 years ago, the International Convention for the Prevention of Pollution of the Sea by Oil, 1954 (OILPOL Convention, 1954) was adopted with the aim of protecting the sea from pollution by oil discharged from ships. Thereafter, the Convention on the Prevention of Marine Pollution by Dumping of Wastes and Other Matter, 1972 (London Convention, 1972)[1] was adopted for controlling and prohibiting the dumping of different hazardous materials, and the International Convention for the Prevention of Pollution from Ships, 1973 (MARPOL 73/78)[2] was adopted for preventing marine pollution by ships from accidental or operational discharge of hazardous substances.

In 1982, UNCLOS was adopted a with a desire for

> a legal order for the seas and oceans which will facilitate international communication, and will promote the peaceful uses of the seas and oceans, the equitable and efficient utilization of their resources, the conservation of their living resources, and the study, protection and preservation of the marine environment.[3]

Despite having some normative deficiencies, this instrument has provided a 'clear jurisdictional framework' (Churchill, 2015, p. 30) according to which State parties can take domestic policies and actions for the protection of their respective marine environments. In fact, UNCLOS, its annexes, and the implementing Agreement to its Part XI have developed a consolidated and holistic regime for maintaining a balance between the marine interests of different categories of States – coastal, land-locked and geographically disadvantaged (Miles, 1999, p. 1). Usually treated as the 'constitution for the oceans', UNCLOS has laid down the legal and philosophical foundations for an entire domain of laws of the sea and prevails over all prior marine environmental legal instruments (Churchill, 2015, p. 4). In addition, there are a significant number of laws that require enforcement in accordance with the spirit of UNCLOS (Churchill, 2015, p. 4). UNCLOS works as a unifying and flexible legal framework, and hence provides a comprehensive legal avenue for new norms and principles of marine governance to be incorporated within the relevant legal instruments (Spalding et al., 2013, p. 216).

In addition, the Convention on Biological Diversity, 1992 (CBD, 1992), and the United Nations Fish Stock Agreement, 1995, created a legal regime for the conservation and protection of marine living resources (Chang, 2010, p. 591). In addition, the International Convention for the Regulation of Whaling, 1946 has long contributed to the global protection of whales.

Besides the major treaties on ocean governance presented previously, many international instruments – such as the Convention on the International Trade in Endangered Species of Wild Flora and Fauna, 1973 (CITES, 1973), the Convention Concerning the Protection of the World Cultural and Natural Heritage, 1972 (World Heritage Convention, 1972), the Ramsar Convention on Wetlands of International Importance especially as Waterfowl Habitat, 1971, and a number of IMO conventions and protocols – are also playing important roles in the protection of the marine environment and biodiversity. In addition to these global legal tools for the protection of marine environment, UNCLOS has also mandated that States develop regional legal instruments, standards, procedures and practices that are consonant with UNCLOS.[4] Several regional seas conventions and regional fisheries agreements have been adopted according to this UNCLOS mandate.

In dealing with the most pressing problems of human beings, the United Nations Sustainable Development Goals (SDGs) 2030 stress the sustainable use of different resources, and many of the directives are directly or indirectly related to the protection of the environment as a whole. For example, Goal 14 specifically recognises the importance of oceans, seas and marine resources, and calls for their 'careful management'.[5] This goal delineates various 'facts and figures' and provides 14 targets related to the use of marine and coastal resources.[6] In fulfilling the aim of the sustainable use of targeted resources, including the marine environment, the SDGs necessitate a joint effort from all sectors and actors on every level.[7] In fact, most of the binding and non-binding international instruments ultimately reflect the principles of international cooperation and collaboration between States in the governance of local, regional and international marine environments and resources (Chang, 2010, p. 592). An analysis suggests that the legal and political governance of the oceanic environment may be grounded in certain broad concepts such as the 'rule of law, participatory, transparency, consensus-based decision-making, accountability, equity and inclusiveness, responsiveness and coherence' (Chang, 2010, p. 592). Chang (2010, pp. 592, 605) argues that to ensure good marine governance, particularly at the domestic level, people need to be informed of the new law, and it ought to be applied even-handedly and enforced strictly.

Ocean governance and principles of international environmental law

Oceans, seas and coastal areas have transnational and international implications in terms of their preservation and protection. International laws should not be treated merely as a body of rules and principles but embody some well-designed mechanisms and procedures for promoting international relations between and among global communities at large (Crawford, 2012, p. xviii). This governing system in relation to international marine environmental law has been developed through the incorporation of certain long-standing principles of environmental law in different international legal instruments. For example, UNCLOS has largely embodied general environmental rules and principles for the protection of the ocean and seas in general. Such principles are most often elaborated through the adoption of international policy documents such as the Declaration of the United Nations Conference on the Human Environment, 1972 (Stockholm Declaration, 1972) and certain framework created by international organisations through the development of their resolutions or declarations embracing innovative principles (e.g., UNEP Draft Principles) and by international non-government organisations through the adoption of certain instruments embodying new environmental rules and principles (e.g., the Helsinki Rules on the Use of Waters of International Rivers, 1996) (Paradell Trius, 2000, p. 97). However, some of these principles remain objects of 'considerable uncertainty and disagreement' (Paradell Trius, 2000, p. 94).

Despite this uncertainty and disagreement, the development of such principles is accepted by the international community for three main reasons. First, global social, economic and environmental issues cannot be solved by any specific, binding rules due to their diverse circumstances, and, in such conditions, environmental principles may function for the world's communities as 'general norms' to be followed when designing domestic or regional legal rules and regulations (Paradell Trius, 2000, p. 93). Second, when making international decisions during a period of urgency and utmost necessity, they can provide 'standards or objectives which are expected to be taken into account as international cannons of environmental conduct' (Paradell Trius, 2000, p. 94). Third, due to the principles' 'indeterminacy and abstraction', they can lay down a minimum obligation for States to take appropriate measures according to scientific advancements (Paradell Trius, 2000, pp. 93–94). In line with such arguments, Sands (1995, p. 66) states that 'in the absence of clear, substantive obligations such principles can play an important secondary role in the emerging international law of sustainable development'. In consideration of international environmental instruments and other jurisprudence, Sands and Peel (2012, p. 187) identify the following seven such principles: the State's sovereignty over its natural resources and its duty not to cause transboundary environmental harm; precautionary measures; preventive measures; cooperation; polluter-pays principle; common but differentiated responsibilities and sustainable development. Apart from these well recognised principles, other emerging principles and approaches have been recognised by scholars and institutions.[8]

State sovereign rights over natural resources

The principle of State sovereignty over its natural resources is an 'extension of the sovereignty principle' (Sands & Peel, 2012, p. 191), which conditionally permits States to conduct any activities in their respective territories, including those that have a potentially detrimental environmental effect (Sands & Peel, 2012, p. 191). The Stockholm Declaration, 1972 incorporates this extended principle in the first part of its Principle 21, which affirms the following: 'States have, in accordance with the

Charter of the United Nations and the principles of international law, the sovereign right to exploit their own resources pursuant to their own environmental policies'.

The Stockholm Declaration, 1972, had manifest influence on the creation, design and content of UNCLOS. The principle of sovereignty over natural resources was specifically included in Article 193 of UNCLOS, which affirms the following: 'States have the sovereign right to exploit their natural resources pursuant to their environmental policies and in accordance with their duty to protect and preserve the marine environment'. While exercising this right, State parties must also consider their general obligations of protecting and preserving the marine environment as enshrined in UNCLOS Article 192. This obligation seems to be a condition precedent to the exploitation of such resources because this obligatory provision comes before that of the right expressed in UNCLOS Article 193. In addition, this right expressed in UNCLOS Article 193 cannot be exercised arbitrarily, as the United Nations General Assembly Resolution 1803 (XXVII) stipulates that the 'rights of peoples and nations to permanent sovereignty over their natural wealth and resources must be exercised in the interest of their national development of the well-being of the people of the State concerned'.[9]

This principle of State sovereignty also appears in several previous United Nations resolutions adopted after 1952 (Sands & Peel, 2012, p. 191) and in Principle 2 of the Rio Declaration on Environment and Development, 1992 (Rio Declaration, 1992).[10] These United Nations resolutions aim to create a fair balance between States' sovereignty over their natural resources and the 'legal certainty in the stability of investments' (Sands & Peel, 2012, p. 191) made by foreign companies (mainly) in developing States. The principle has been treated by international judicial bodies as a reflection of customary international norms.[11] This principle has also been reflected in a series of international instruments.[12]

Duty not to cause transboundary harm

A State has no right to perform or allow activities within its territory that can injure the interests of other States – this rule is commonly termed the 'no-harm principle'. This principle developed from the principle of the good neighbourliness (Sands & Peel, 2012, p. 197). This principle is frequently used and explained in discourses of environmental protection and environmental justice. The Stockholm Declaration, 1972, incorporated this principle in the second part of its Principle 21, which stipulates that States have the 'responsibility to ensure that activities within their jurisdiction or control do not cause damage to the environment of other States or of areas beyond the limits of national jurisdiction'. The jurisdiction of a State refers also to its domestic territory, which includes marine areas. The no-harm principle is also included in the second part of Principle 2 of the Rio Declaration, 1992.[13] The no-harm principle may appear to impose restrictions indirectly on a State's sovereign right to use its domestic natural resources; however, the violation of this principle is qualified or conditional. That is, whether a State has infringed this principle is assessed on questions and facts relating to the description, intensity and consequence of the damage, and the category and extent of liability of the State for that damage (Sands & Peel, 2012, p. 196). The no-harm principle was first formally identified in the *Trail Smelter* case,[14] where it was stated:

> Under the principles of international law as well as of the law of the United States, no State has the right to use or permit the use of its territory in such a manner as to cause injury by fumes in or to the territory of another or the properties or persons therein, when the case is of serious consequence and the injury is established by clear and convincing evidence.

The application of this principle is not confined only to the situation of transboundary pollution, but extends to 'the protection of the high seas or the global atmosphere' (Tanaka, 2015, p. 37). No-harm principle has been incorporated in Article 194(2) of UNCLOS, which stipulates the following:

> States shall take all measures necessary to ensure that activities under their jurisdiction or control are so conducted as not to cause damage by pollution to other States and their environment, and that pollution arising from incidents or activities under their jurisdiction or control does not spread beyond the areas where they exercise sovereign rights in accordance with this Convention.

To prevent (among others factors) transboundary harm affecting the other States, responsible States must manage all sources of pollution and take all possible measures to minimise different categories of pollution.[15] UNCLOS Article 194(4) stipulates that even in 'taking measures to prevent, reduce or control pollution of the marine environment, States shall refrain from unjustifiable interference with activities carried out by other States in the exercise of their rights and in pursuance of their duties in conformity with this Convention'.[16] In other words, the process of controlling one transboundary harm should not give rise to another.

In addition, the no-harm principle was reflected by many earlier agreements, including the International Plant Protection Convention, 1959[17] and the Nuclear Test Ban Treaty, 1963[18] and the World Heritage Convention, 1972.[19] The United Nations and other international organisations have consciously incorporated the no-harm principle into their resolutions and legal instruments, and it has been treated by United Nations General Assembly Resolution 2996 (XXVII)[20] as one of the few fundamental cannons in environmental governance between the States (Sands & Peel, 2012, p. 198). In the *Corfu Channel* case, the International Court of Justice (ICJ) stated that the sovereignty principle also imposes a duty on States that they must not use their territories in such a way that can affect the rights of the other States.[21] Similarly, an upstream State cannot divert the water of an international river, ignoring the right of the downstream State.[22]

Intergenerational and intragenerational equity

The principle of intergenerational equity refers to maintaining a fair balance between the interests of the present and future generations. The principle of *intra-generational* equity refers to the just distribution of the global wealth and resources between the current generations of different populations (e.g., those of developed and developing countries). Brown Weiss (1990, p. 198) states the following in relation to intergenerational equity:

> What is new is that now we have the power to change our global environment irreversibly, with profoundly damaging effects on the robustness and integrity of the planet and the heritage that we pass on to future generations.

Brown Weiss creates an idea of partnership between the past, present and future generations and emphasises that the present generation of human beings, which has moral sense, is a temporal trustee of the Earth for future generations, which are entitled to 'an equal access to and sharing of resources and environmental quality' (Jansen, 2002, pp. 12–13). Intra-generational equity developed from the principle of intergenerational equity (Des Jardins, 1997, pp. 27–28). Intra-generational equity involves two principal dimensions: human beings' relationship with other human beings, and human beings' relationship with the entire natural system, of which human beings are also an element (Brown Weiss, 1990, p. 199). The main problems related to the principles of intergenerational equity and intra-generational equity emerged from the continuous 'depletion of resources, global warming, ozone depletion and elimination of biodiversity' (Jansen, 2002, p. 3).

Intra-generational equity appears to be difficult to achieve because it involves the redistribution of world resources and must affect global, political, economic and social-reality factors (Jansen, 2002, p. 33). However, this principle is reflected in some international instruments. For example, the Preamble to UNCLOS states the aim to achieve the 'realization of a just and equitable international economic order which takes into account the interests and needs of humankind as a whole and, in particular, the special interests and needs of developing countries, whether coastal or land-locked'. This Preamble also notes that the components of the sea including seabed, ocean floor, subsoil thereof and their resources shall be 'the common heritage of mankind, the exploration and exploitation of which shall be carried out for the benefit of mankind as a whole, irrespective of the geographical location of States'.[23] The Preamble further states that even developing countries must receive preference in the allocation of required funds, technical assistance and specialised services 'for the purposes of prevention, reduction and control of pollution of the marine environment or minimization of its effects'.[24] Similarly, the Preamble to the CBD, 1992, states that 'special provision is required to meet the needs of developing countries, including the provision of new and additional financial resources and appropriate access to relevant technologies'[25] and that it is necessary to consider 'the special conditions of the least developed countries and Small Island States'.[26]

This approach is also somewhat reflected in the principle of common but differentiated responsibilities. However, the principle of intergenerational equity first attracted attention in the *Pacific Fur Seal* arbitration of 1893.[27] Thereafter, this principle has been included in many international and regional conventions and agreements, including those that directly and indirectly manage the preservation and protection of marine environment and resources. The first part of the Preamble to CITES, 1973, asserts that 'wild fauna and flora [. . .] must be protected for this and the generations to come'.[28] This means that water resources must be protected in an efficient manner 'so that the needs of the present generation are met without compromising the ability of future generations to meet their own needs'.[29] The Preamble to the CBD, 1992, also affirms that State parties hold the determination to 'conserve and sustainably use biological diversity for the benefit of present and future generations'.[30] The Preamble to UNCLOS affirms that the State parties shall ensure an equitable use of their resources and the 'realization of a just and equitable international economic order which takes into account the interests and needs of mankind as a whole'.[31] The Stockholm Declaration, 1972 also asserts that each human being 'bears a solemn responsibility to protect and improve the environment for present and future generations'.[32] With the aim of protecting the marine environment, several regional environmental agreements also embody the principle of intergenerational equity. For example, the Preamble to the Kuwait Regional Convention for Co-operation on the Protection of the Marine Environment from Pollution, 1978, holds that State parties will think of mutual cooperation and coordination 'with the aim of protecting the marine environment of the region for the benefit of all concerned, including future generations'.[33] The same principle, using the same linguistic pattern, is used in the Jeddah Convention, 1982, which aims to protect the 'marine environment of the Red Sea and Gulf of Aden'.[34] Article 1(1) of the Jeddah Convention, 1982, specifically notes that the present generation will exploit the living and non-living marine and coastal resources while considering 'the needs and aspirations of future generations'.[35] The States in the Caribbean region also agreed to save their marine environment 'for the benefit and enjoyment of present and future generations'.[36] This principle has also been incorporated in other international instruments for protecting other components of the environment and nature (Sands & Peel, 2012, pp. 209–210).

Precaution

There is controversy as to whether 'precaution' in relation to conservation principles should be termed a 'precautionary principle' or a 'precautionary approach' (Vanderzwaag, 2002, p. 166). The term 'precautionary approach' usually implies 'a softer, non-binding nature', whereas the term 'precautionary principle' seems to bear some legal binding-ness (Freestone, 1999). However, some researchers believe these terms have a similar meaning, and the Rio Declaration, 1992, uses both the terms 'precautionary principle' and 'precautionary approach' (Vanderzwaag, 2002, p. 167). Any activity, including coastal development within marine areas, may entail serious environmental damage and, given this, the precautionary principle or approach has been included in most of the international instruments related to marine environment (Freestone & Hey, 1996; Hohmann, 1994).

It is not surprising that UNCLOS did not incorporate the precautionary principle or approach for ocean and marine governance since this principle (or approach) was recognised in international law after the adoption of UNCLOS on 10 December 1982 (Rayfuse, 2012, p. 774). During evolution of the precautionary principle (or approach), it worked well for the governance of the marine resources and the environment, and achieved recognition in a number of international legal tools (Rayfuse, 2012, p. 774). For example, the Rio Declaration, 1992, concretely asserts the following:

> In order to protect the environment, the precautionary approach shall be widely applied by States according to their capabilities. Where there are threats of serious or irreversible damage, lack of full scientific certainty shall not be used as a reason for postponing cost-effective measures to prevent environmental degradation.[37]

The same principle and its conceptual elements were included in the London Protocol, 1996, which stipulates the following:

> Contracting Parties shall apply a precautionary approach to environmental protection from dumping of wastes or other matter whereby appropriate preventative measures are taken when there is reason to believe that wastes or other matter introduced into the marine environment are likely to cause harm even when there is no conclusive evidence to prove a causal relation between inputs and their effects.[38]

This principle is also found in the provision of the Fish Stock Agreement, 1995, that State parties, including the coastal States, will protect their fish stock through the assessment of the 'impacts of fishing, other human activities and environmental factors on target stocks and species belonging to the same ecosystem'.[39] The Fish Stock Agreement, 1995, also imposes a strong legal duty on State parties to 'apply the precautionary approach widely to conservation, management and exploitation of straddling fish stocks and highly migratory fish stocks' (Tanaka, 2015, p. 41).

For State parties to protect their marine environment and resources, some regional treaties incorporate stricter obligations in relation to the provision of precautionary measures. For example, the Convention for the Protection of the Marine Environment of the North-East Atlantic, 1992 (OSPAR Convention, 1992)[40] embraces the 'precautionary principle' and prescribes the following:

> [The States will take] more stringent measures with respect to the prevention and elimination of pollution of the marine environment or with respect to the protection of the marine environment against the adverse effects of

human activities than are provided for in international conventions or agreements with a global scope.[41]

The precautionary principle is incorporated as a fundamental principle in the Helsinki Convention, 1992, which affirms the following fundamental obligation of States:

> [To] take preventive measures when there is reason to assume that substances or energy introduced, directly or indirectly, into the marine environment may create hazards to human health, harm living resources and marine ecosystems, damage amenities or interfere with other legitimate uses of the sea even when there is no conclusive evidence of a causal relationship between inputs and their alleged effects.[42]

Similarly, the precautionary principle was reflected in the Food and Agricultural Organization (FAO) Code of Conduct for Responsible Fisheries, 1995, which urges that State parties utilise the precautionary approach in total governance of the 'living aquatic resources' and 'aquatic environment'.[43]

Prevention

Generally, the principle of prevention obliges the State to take adequate measures so that its acts or omissions do not cause any damage to the environment. This principle binds a State not only to prevent transboundary damage to other States but to protect its own environment (Singh, 1986, pp. xi–xii). The principle has been treated as a 'principle of general international law' or as a 'customary rule', which is derived from due diligence in State practices (Sands & Peel, 2012, p. 200). This due diligence refers to the following:

> an obligation which entails not only the adoption of appropriate rules and measures but also a certain level of vigilance in their enforcement and the exercise of administrative control applicable to public and private operators, such as the monitoring of activities undertaken by such operators.[44]

Principle of prevention also requires the States to adopt careful measures at the initial stage of activity before any damage affects the environment.[45] That is, States must undertake preventive measures with 'due diligence' that is appropriate according to the attending circumstances.[46] This principle of prevention has similarities to the concepts underlying the principles of no harm and precaution.[47] The principle of prevention is reflected in many international and regional agreements made for the protection of environmental elements, including the oceans, seas and marine living resources.

UNCLOS incorporates the principle of prevention to be followed by the States while taking measures against the 'pollution of the marine environment from any source'.[48] The OSPAR Convention, 1992, also includes this principle, stipulating that State parties must take required measures to 'prevent and eliminate pollution and shall take the necessary measures to protect the maritime area against the adverse effects of human activities [and] prevent an increase in pollution of the sea outside the maritime area or in other parts of the environment'.[49] In an older convention, the Convention Relative to the Preservation of Fauna and Flora in Their Natural State, 1933, mutual cooperation was made compulsory in relation to preventing the extinction of fauna and flora in the territories of the Contracting Parties.[50] The principle of prevention is also included in the Convention for the Conservation of Antarctic Marine Living Resources, 1982 (CAMLR Convention, 1982), for preventing the decrease of harvested populations of different living organisms and 'recognising the importance of safeguarding the environment and protecting the integrity of the ecosystem of the seas surrounding Antarctica'.[51] Preamble to the MARPOL 73/78 discloses that the States have agreed to adopt mutual steps for preventing the 'pollution of the sea by oil discharged from ships'. The General Fisheries Council for the Mediterranean was endowed with the function of preventing occupational diseases of fishermen with the aim of 'development and proper utilization of the resources of the Mediterranean and contiguous waters'.[52] To protect the marine environment as a whole in the Black Sea, the provisions of preventive measures have been incorporated in several places in the Protocol to the Black Sea Convention, 2009.[53]

In some other instruments, there are similar provisions for preventive measures to be taken against the 'pollution of the seas from the dumping of radioactive waste',[54] the 'pollution of water resources generally',[55] the 'pollution of the marine environment by the discharge of harmful substances or effluents containing such substances',[56] the pollution of seas by land-based substances and energy,[57] the loss of fish stocks[58] and the hazards created by shipwrecks to the marine environment.[59] With a substantive analysis of the implementing environmental legislations in different countries, it is clear that the preventive principle influenced the State parties greatly in protecting the important components of the environment, including the oceans, seas and marine living resources (Sands & Peel, 2012, pp. 201–201).

Cooperation

No single State acting alone can ensure the adequate protection and preservation of the Earth's environmental elements, including the oceans, seas and marine resources. Such protection and preservation require international cooperation. Thus, the Stockholm Declaration, 1972, states the following:

> International matters concerning the protection and improvement of the environment should be handled in a cooperative spirit by all countries, big and small, on an equal footing. Cooperation through multilateral or bilateral arrangements or other appropriate means is essential to effectively control, prevent, reduce and eliminate adverse environmental effects resulting from

activities conducted in all spheres, in such a way that due account is taken of the sovereignty and interests of all States.[60]

Similarly, the Rio Declaration, 1992, specifically asserts the following:

> States and people shall cooperate in good faith and in a spirit of partnership in the fulfilment of the principles embodied in this Declaration and in the further development of international law in the field of sustainable development.[61]

The UNCLOS also holds that the State parties desire to solve all legal matters relating to the sea 'in a spirit of mutual understanding and cooperation'.[62] This principle of cooperation was also upheld by the International Tribunal for the Law of the Sea (ITLOS) in the *MOX Plant* case, where it was stated that the 'duty to cooperate is a fundamental principle in the prevention of pollution of the marine environment under Part XII of the Convention and general international law'.[63] ITLOS unanimously prescribed provisional measures for Ireland and the United Kingdom that they must cooperate through consultation to ensure the following:

> (a) exchange further information with regard to possible consequences for the Irish Sea arising out of the commissioning of the MOX plant; (b) monitor risks or the effects of the operation of the MOX plant for the Irish Sea; (c) devise, as appropriate, measures to prevent pollution of the marine environment which might result from the operation of the MOX plant.[64]

ITLOS applies the principle of cooperation in the *Land Reclamation* case, in which it directed the parties (i.e., Malaysia and Singapore) to cooperate with each other so as to agree on a point that a panel of experts would assess the effects of the disputed land reclamation and suggest required measures for avoiding any adverse effects from such reclamation and to exchange necessary information.[65]

Several provisions are included in UNCLOS that emphasise the principle of cooperation in protecting the marine environment and resources. For example, UNCLOS imposes a duty on the Member States to cooperate with other States to conserve the 'living resources of the high seas'.[66] In addition, UNCLOS Article 118 holds that 'States shall cooperate with each other in the conservation and management of living resources in the areas of the high seas'. It also holds that States must cooperate with each other internationally and regionally 'in formulating and elaborating international rules, standards and recommended practices and procedures consistent with [. . .] [UNCLOS] for the protection and preservation of the marine environment'.[67] In case of imminent danger or any pollution, UNCLOS states that 'competent international organizations shall cooperate [. . .] in eliminating the effects of pollution and preventing or minimising the damage [and] shall jointly develop and promote contingency plans for responding to pollution incidents in the marine environment'.[68] States are bound also to follow the principle of cooperation in promoting studies, undertaking and conducting research (and the exchange of information and data) and, in view of such data and information, they must collaboratively determine 'appropriate scientific criteria for the formulation and elaboration of rules, standards and recommended practices and procedures for the prevention, reduction and control of pollution of the marine environment'.[69] In addition, the substantive role of the international legal instruments, the relevant international and regional bodies and the international judicial institutions is crucial in advancing cooperation between the Contracting States for the purpose of governing the oceanic environment and living resources (Tanaka, 2015, pp. 53–54).

Polluter-pays principle

The polluter-pays principle implies that the cost of any pollution will be paid by the polluter. However, its meaning and application attract different interpretations in different situations, including in the determination of the actual nature of environmental liability. Some countries interpret that the principle is enforceable in governing domestic affairs but not international issues (Sands & Peel, 2012, pp. 228–229). Although this principle has not yet obtained as much international legal recognition as have the principles of prevention and precaution (Sands & Peel, 2012, p. 229), it is reflected in several international and regional instruments. For example, Principle 7 of the Rio Declaration, 1992, has indirectly incorporated this principle from a global perspective in the clause that stipulates that the 'developed countries acknowledge the responsibility that they bear in the international pursuit of sustainable development in view of the pressures their societies place on the global environment and of the technologies and financial resources they command'. This principle is initially found in the Paris Convention, 1960,[70] and the Vienna Convention, 1963,[71] in relation to compensation for different nuclear damages.

To safeguard the marine environment, including flora and fauna, the OSPAR Convention, 1992, has embraced the polluter-pays principle, asserting that the 'costs of pollution prevention, control and reduction measures are to be borne by the polluter'.[72] The International Convention on Oil Pollution Preparedness, Response and Co-operation, 1990, has also absorbed the polluter-pays principle with the aim of preserving the 'human environment in general and the marine environment in particular'.[73]

The polluter-pays principle has also been recognised in some regional instruments aiming to protect the marine environment. For example, the Antigua Convention, 2002, holds that the Member States must apply the polluter-pays principle to make the polluters responsible for paying the 'full costs of measures to prevent, control, reduce and remedy such pollution' from the sense of obligation to 'protect the environment and contribute to the sustainable management, protection and conservation of the marine environment of the region'.[74] Similarly, for protecting and preserving the environment of Baltic Sea area, the State parties in the Helsinki Convention, 1992, unconditionally agreed to apply the polluter-pays principle.[75]

Common but differentiated responsibilities

The principle of common but differentiated responsibilities is principally based on the global recognition of the concept of equity and the consideration of the different and reasonable treatment of developing countries 'in the development, application and interpretation of rules of international environmental law' (Sands & Peel, 2012, p. 233). Principle 7 of the Rio Declaration, 1992, states the following:

> States shall co-operate in a spirit of global partnership to conserve, protect and restore the health and integrity of the Earth's ecosystem. In view of the different contributions to global environmental degradation, States have common but differentiated responsibilities. The developed countries acknowledge the responsibility that they bear in the international pursuit of sustainable development in view of the pressures their societies place on the global environment and of the technologies and financial resources they command.

That is, to protect the climate system, State parties must take action 'on the basis of equity and in accordance with their common but differentiated responsibilities and respective capabilities'.[76] The principle of common but differentiated responsibilities mainly consists of two concepts: that all nations have a common duty to protect the environment in general but that the degree of such duty may vary in accordance with their respective ability and the historical liability for the global climate situation.

The Preamble to the UNFCCC also includes the principle of common but differentiated responsibilities. According to the Basel Convention, to protect human health and the environment in general from different hazardous wastes, the State parties agreed to consider the 'limited capabilities of the developing countries'.[77] The Preamble to the CBD, 1992, embodies the principle that while the 'conservation of biological diversity is a common concern of humankind', special needs are acknowledged for developing countries and special conditions are felt for the least developed countries and the small island States.

UNCLOS reflects this principle based on fairness and equity (Deleuil, 2012, p. 1) in its Preamble and in other provisions. One of the vital goals of the State parties is to ensure the 'equitable and efficient utilisation of their [marine] resources' through the establishment of a common 'legal order for the seas and oceans'.[78] Such 'goals will contribute to the realization of a just and equitable international economic order which takes into account the interests and needs of humankind as a whole and, in particular, the special interests and needs of developing countries, whether coastal or land-locked'.[79]

In relation to governance of marine environment and resources, this principle of common but differentiated responsibilities is clear in the UNCLOS, which holds that the State parties must adopt individual and joint measures for the common purpose of preventing, reducing and controlling marine environment pollution 'in accordance with their capabilities'.[80] In addition, UNCLOS Article 207(4) stipulates the following:

> States [...] shall endeavor to establish global and regional rules, standards and recommended practices and procedures to prevent, reduce and control pollution of the marine environment from land-based sources, taking into account characteristic regional features, the economic capacity of developing States and their need for economic development.[81]

Therefore, the constituent elements of the principle of common but differentiated responsibilities is incorporated in UNCLOS. The objectives of the London Protocol, 1996 also embody the principle of common but differentiated responsibilities:

> Contracting Parties shall individually and collectively protect and preserve the marine environment from all sources of pollution and take effective measures, according to their scientific, technical and economic capabilities, to prevent, reduce and where practicable eliminate pollution caused by dumping or incineration at sea of wastes or other matter.[82]

Sustainable development

While the term 'sustainable development' was first used in the Brundtland Report, the principle of sustainable development is first found in the Preamble to the Agreement on the European Economic Area, 1992 (Sands & Peel, 2012, p. 206). The Brundtland Report defines sustainable development as the 'development that meets the needs of the present without compromising the ability of the future generations to meet their own needs' (World Commission on Environment and Development, 1987, p. 43). The principle of sustainable development generally holds that development activities be conducted considering environmental concerns while recognising that ecological protection must not absolutely override the priorities of development plans, programmes and projects. The principle holds that a balance should be maintained between the environment and development. In environmental studies, this principle is synonymously used with concepts such as 'sustainable use' and 'sustainability'. The principle of sustainable development comprises four elements: intergenerational equity, sustainable use, equitable use or intragenerational equity and integration (Sands & Peel, 2012, p. 207). However, some scholars include a broad array of principles within the concept of sustainable development.[83] Although the functioning of the concept of sustainable development largely depends on the national policies of a country, the ICJ has held that States duly consider this concept as a new norm and standard in economic decision-making so that the environment is also protected.[84]

Despite UNCLOS not specifically referring to the principle of sustainable development, all the elements of this principle are reflected in the text and philosophy of UNCLOS. For example, UNCLOS affirms that in dealing with the seas and oceans, the State parties desire to establish a legal order that 'will promote the peaceful uses of the seas and oceans, the equitable and efficient utilization of their resources, the conservation of their living resources, and the [. . .] protection and preservation of the marine environment'.[85] Here, the clause the 'equitable and efficient utilization of their resources' also suggests the principle of intergenerational equity, and 'peaceful uses of the seas and oceans' and the 'conservation of their living resources' suggest the principle of sustainable use, while 'protection and preservation of the marine environment' suggests the concept of integration. UNCLOS also includes intragenerational equity by describing that the State parties intend to realise an 'international economic order which takes into account the interests and needs of mankind as a whole and, in particular, the special interests and needs of developing countries, whether coastal or land-locked'.[86]

The principle of sustainable development is also included in several other international instruments that aim to protect different elements of seas and oceans. For example, the principle of sustainable development is found in the Preamble to and in Articles 2, 5(b) and 5(h) of the United Nations Fish Stocks Agreement, 1995.[87] The State Parties to the Agreement intend to 'ensure the long-term conservation and sustainable use of straddling fish stocks and highly migratory fish stocks through effective implementation of the relevant provisions of the [UNCLOS]'.[88] In addition, the principle of sustainable development is incorporated in Article 1 of the CBD, 1992, which states that one of its objectives is to ensure the 'sustainable use of its components'. Agenda 21 also embodies the principle of sustainable development in relation to the protection of oceans, seas, coastal areas and marine living resources.[89] Code of Conduct for Responsible Fisheries, 1995, states that the 'long-term sustainable use of fisheries resources is the overriding objective of conservation and management' for the Contracting Parties.[90] The Rome Declaration on the Implementation of the Code of Conduct for Responsible Fisheries, 1999, also agrees that parties will work together to 'seek the optimum and sustainable use of the world's fishery resources'.[91] The principle of sustainable development is also reflected in the Reykjavik Declaration on Responsible Fisheries in the Marine Eco-system, 2001, which emphasises 'an effort to reinforce responsible and sustainable fisheries in the marine ecosystem'.[92]

Role of international and regional institutions

The oceanic environment has different national, regional and international dimensions, and requires joint, cooperative approaches for its protection and conservation. The United Nations General Assembly has developed many global measures to attempt to smooth the governance of 'marine biodiversity and ecosystems' (Sands & Peel, 2012, p. 437). Since 1997, the United Nations General Assembly has adopted at least one resolution annually for the purpose of protecting marine spaces and ecosystems. Moreover, the IMO and the FAO have significantly contributed on a global level to the protection and preservation of the marine environment and marine living resources in general. UNCLOS has focused on the importance of the legal and policy cooperation of States on the global and regional levels in governing the ocean and seas. UNCLOS Article 197 holds the following:

> States shall cooperate on a global basis and, as appropriate, on a regional basis, directly or through competent international organizations, in formulating and elaborating international rules, standards and recommended practices and procedures consistent with this Convention, for the protection and preservation of the marine environment, taking into account characteristic regional features.[93]

Prior to the adoption of UNCLOS, several legal tools and institutions also existed to apply global and regional ocean governance.

IMO

UNCLOS has stipulated a major role for the international organisations, particularly the IMO, in managing activities occurring in oceans and seas, including the task of creating rules and regulations for the Member States (Oxman, 1995, p. 467). The IMO is one of the specialised agencies of the United Nations. It was established in 1948 and initially it did not incorporate in its constitution any objectives such as the prevention of marine pollution. However, the IMO Constitution was amended by incorporating the clause 'Control of marine pollution from ships' as one of its purposes in Article 1(a). In 1975, the IMO also established the Legal Committee and the Marine Environment Pollution Committee (MEPC), which work to ensure the overall legal protection and safety of the marine environment and ecosystems from vessel-source pollution. The IMO has delivered outstanding service in the legal protection and preservation of the oceanic environment (De La Fayette, 2001, p. 158).

The IMO has the global duty of adopting necessary legal and policy measures to ensure the safety and security of shipping and to prevent marine pollution by ships.[94] It works as the 'global standard-setting authority for the safety, security and environmental performance of international shipping'.[95] That is, the IMO acts as a global platform by which the Contracting Parties negotiate, develop and implement the rules and regulations of international legal tools that address the prevention of pollution and risk in the oceans (Roberts, 2006, p. 53). However, the IMO does not regulate international shipping, but rather functions as a forum 'for both [the] harmonisation of existing standards and for creating new ones' (Roberts, 2006, p. 56).

In addition, the IMO has also developed essential technical rules to supplement the norms and standards accepted by the Contracting Parties and these rules play an important role in the protection and preservation of marine spaces from ship-driven pollution (Dzidzornu & Tsamenyi, 1991, p. 75). Moreover, the concerned conventions can mandate the IMO to review, amend and approve necessary amendments and regulatory proposals, and the IMO is also able to adopt relevant soft-law instruments such as guidelines and standards for protecting the marine environment (Roberts, 2006, p. 54). Oxman (1995, p. 468) identifies three roles of the IMO: 1) the forum role, which is fulfilled by promoting global cooperation, information sharing and consultation on international policy matters; 2) the standard-setting role, which is fulfilled by the creation and development of required legal instruments and procedures; 3) the approval role, which is fulfilled by the process of reviewing the existing legal standards and approving new proposals from the Member States.

MARPOL 73/78 is the principal international legal tool against marine pollution from vessels caused by operational and accidental factors (Karim, 2009, p. 57). The IMO has achieved significant success in reducing marine pollution by ships through the implementation of MARPOL 73/78, particularly through the modification of the equipment standard of oil tankers (Mitchell, 1994). The IMO developed conventions such as the Intervention Convention, 1969,[96] the International Convention for the Safety of Life at Sea, 1974 (SOLAS Convention, 1974),[97] and the OPRC Convention, 1990,[98] which play important roles in protecting the marine environment from pollution from ships (McGrath & Julian, 2000, p. 195). The IMO has also provided the essential coordinating or secretarial services in the consultation and conclusion of a series of subsequent global conventions, particularly those aimed at creating compensatory liability for any marine pollution by oil from ships,[99] 'control and management of ships' ballast water and sediments',[100] 'safe and environmentally sound recycling of ships'[101] and 'control of harmful anti-fouling systems on ships'.[102]

Regional organisations

To create a legal regime for the oceans and seas, UNCLOS emphasises global and regional cooperation in ensuring the protection and preservation of the marine environment.[103] Given that it is a highly complex issue, marine governance needs speedy and specific regional attention and activities to ensure its effectiveness. Before the adoption of UNCLOS, ocean governance was accomplished under regional arrangements such as UNEP's Regional Seas Programme (RSP) (Sands & Peel, 2012, p. 352). UNEP is now considered a vital organisation for implementing the measures adopted under UNCLOS (Techera, 2013, p. 78). UNEP's RSP was created in 1974 as a governing system to protect the marine environment on the regional level. In 2017, it addressed the marine protection of 18 regions of the world, making it one of the largest global initiatives.[104] Among these RSPs, 14 regional programmes are now active under their respective regional treaties and the remaining four have not yet adopted their conventions (Techera, 2013, p. 78). These regional seas programmes can broadly be classified into three types: the partner or independent programmes,[105] UNEP-administered programmes[106] and non-UNEP-administered programmes.[107] Most of the RSPs conduct their work through different action plans, each of which determine the essential strategies and contents of the programme in consideration of the 'region's particular environmental challenges as well as its socio-economic and political situation'.[108]

The RSP mainly deals with the following six areas of marine protection: 'coastal area management, eco-system and biodiversity, land-based activities, marine litter, sea based pollution and small islands' (Oral, 2015, p. 343). UNEP has helped the RSP to fulfil its responsibilities to achieve to the priorities set by the UNEP Governing Council and the United Nations Environment Assembly, and toenable it to achieve certain global targets and goals such as the SDGs.[109]

To achieve the legal protection and preservation of the marine environment and ecosystem, UNEP has developed multilateral environmental agreements (MEAs) that incorporate the universal principles of environmental law and procedures relating to their implementation at regional and national levels, but these MEAs face significant challenges in national implementation (Oral, 2015, p. 339). In addition, these legal mechanisms now must consider critical issues, such as climate change, and new concepts, such as precautionary measures, that are difficult to harmonise with the existing legal mechanisms (Oral, 2015, p. 343). Most of the regional agreements or conventions follow identical legal structures and contents, including in their 'basic substantive and procedural obligations, institutional arrangements and mechanisms for the adoption of protocols and annexes' (Sands & Peel, 2012, p. 358). Therefore, most of these regional agreements need to be amended or to adopt additional instruments to adequately address new situations arising in the field of ocean governance.

Some international environmental issues can be solved adequately at the regional level, thus requiring no direct global action (Alhéritière, 1982). States or regional entities are now demonstrating their ability to ensure the protection and conservation of the marine living resources through regional mechanisms (Rochette et al., 2015, p. 10). Moreover, the mandate for regional cooperation in UNCLOS,[110] and the principle of regionalism have promoted the States to develop specific regional organisations that aim to protect and preserve marine and coastal environments. UNCLOS encourages such regional initiatives:

> States whose nationals exploit identical living resources, or different living resources in the same area, shall enter into negotiations with a view to taking the measures necessary for the conservation of the living resources concerned [and] cooperate to establish sub-regional or regional fisheries organizations to this end.[111]

Moreover, the Fish Stock Agreement, 1995, states that if there is no regional or sub-regional organisation or arrangement for the protection and management of fish stock in marine and coastal areas, then the concerned States can 'establish such an organisation or enter into other appropriate arrangements to ensure conservation and management of such stock and shall participate in the work of the organisation or arrangement'.[112] As a result, some regional bodies for fisheries management are actively engaged in the supervision and monitoring of fishing in marine spaces, most often in response to the influence of the Fish Stock Agreement, 1995, and the FAO Code of Conduct for Responsible Fisheries, 1995 (Harrison, 2015, pp. 63–64).

Generally, all the RSPs have a Regional Coordinating Unit (RCU) that coordinates, communicates and cooperates to implement different policies for marine environment protection. On behalf of RSP, the RCU also liaises with different organisations, including United Nations bodies, government agencies, non-government organisations and intergovernmental organisations (Techera, 2013, p. 78). Some programmes have a Regional Activity Centre (RAC) that publishes data in papers and reports to assist the States in designing appropriate policies, arranges conferences and workshops to promote regional cooperation and supplies 'legal and technical assistance for the implementation of conventions, protocols and action plans' (Rochette et al., 2015, p. 10). The principal role of the regional mechanisms is to engage with programmes related to research, monitoring and assessment and management (Grip, 2017, p. 414).

Under the authority of relevant legal instruments,[113] some regional organisations, including commissions, were created to protect and preserve the marine and natural environment in the territorial jurisdiction of the European Union (Grip, 2017, p. 419). These regional organisations conduct their collective ventures through mutual cooperation and coordination under the regulatory framework of the IMO to save their marine environments from various types of pollution by ships and related activities (Grip, 2017, p. 419). For example, the Nordic Council of Ministers (NCM) accomplishes one of its major tasks, marine environment protection, with the help of the Nordic Marine Group (Grip, 2017, p. 419). In addition, the Helsinki Commission under the Helsinki Convention has adopted an action plan with a set of targets designed to save the environment and resources of the Baltic Sea (Backer et al., 2010). Similarly, the Regional Organization for the Protection of Marine the Environment (ROPME) is working to design action plans for preventing pollution in the marine environments of the territories of the Member States (Porkareh et al., 2013). Every region has organisations, groups or forums that manage the protection and preservation of different components of the environment, including the marine environment.[114]

Conclusion

The world's ocean has ecological, social and economic importance, and must therefore be protected and preserved under a comprehensive regulatory system. To fulfil this purpose, a growing number of environmental legal norms, instruments and organisations have emerged at all levels. Indeed, the principles of international environmental law are generally reflected in all the global and regional agreements and instruments designed to govern the marine environment. Among the legal instruments, UNCLOS provides the broadest framework for the governance, management, regulation and protection of the marine environment and resources. The guiding environmental principles related to sovereign rights over natural resources, responsibility for transboundary harm, intergenerational and intragenerational equity, precaution, prevention, cooperation, polluter-pays principle, common but differentiated responsibilities and sustainable development play a catalytic role in protecting and conserving the marine environment and its living resources. The Member States have deliberately incorporated these principles in their international and regional agreements, and some of these principles have attained the status of customary international law. In addition, these principles constitute important legal norms and standards in designing the domestic legislations of Member States and international and regional marine environmental agreements. Most of the principles are directly or indirectly interrelated and, sometimes, overlap with one another.

Generally, the agreements by the States embody the provisions of regulatory mechanisms through creating new institutions or referring to established organisations such as the IMO or UNEP. The IMO has been actively working in marine environment protection, particularly in relation to pollution by ships. However, before the adoption in 1982 of UNCLOS, UNEP initiated the regional seas programmes to endeavour to preserve and protect oceans and seas through regional cooperation, and the programmes it promoted are quite successful in their mission despite certain difficulties in national implementation. Since 1982, UNCLOS has also stated the importance of a regional regulatory approach to be adopted along with global governing mechanisms to protect and preserve the oceans, seas and marine living resources. The environmental principles, instruments and institutions are continuously evolving and adopting new dimensions in following new global circumstances and scientific and moral understanding such as climate change, globalisation and technological developments that have a great effect on the marine environment, the biggest ecosystem on Earth.

Notes

1 Convention on the Prevention of Marine Pollution by Dumping of Wastes and Other Matter, London, 29 December 1972, in force 30 August 1975.
2 International Convention for the Prevention of Pollution from Ships, 1973, as modified by the Protocol of 1978 relating thereto (MARPOL 73/78), London 1973 and 1978.
3 United Nations Convention on the Law of the Sea (hereinafter UNCLOS), 1982, Montego Bay, 10 December 1982, in force 10 November 1994, 21 *International Legal Materials* (1982) 1261 Preamble para 4.
4 United Nations Convention on the Law of the Sea (UNCLOS), 1982, Montego Bay, 10 December 1982, in force 10 November 1994, 21 *International Legal Materials* (1982) 1261, Article 197.
5 Goal 14 states that the 'world's oceans – their temperature, chemistry, currents and life – drive global systems that make the Earth habitable for humankind. Our rainwater, drinking water, weather, climate, coastlines, much of our food, and even the oxygen in the air we breathe, are all ultimately provided and regulated by the sea. Throughout history, oceans and seas have been vital conduits for trade and transportation. Careful management of this essential global resource is a key feature of a sustainable future'.
6 See "Goal 14: Conserve and sustainably use the oceans, seas and marine resources", viewed 21 June 2017, www.un.org/sustainabledevelopment/oceans/.

7 See "Multi-sectoral partnerships and voluntary commitments", viewed 21 June 2017, https://sustainabledevelopment.un.org/sdinaction.
8 Paradell-Trius identifies some new principles such as the "principles of non-discrimination, equitable use and concerted management of natural shared resources, intergenerational equity, and integration of environmental considerations into economic and development project" (Tanaka, 2015, p. 32). The International Union for Conservation of Nature has developed ten principles for governing the sea area: "conditional freedom of activity on the high seas, protection and preservation of the marine environment, international cooperation, science-based approach to management, public availability of information, transparent and open decision making processes and precautionary approach" (Tanaka, 2015, p. 32).
9 GA Res. 17/1803, UN GAOR, 17th sess, 1194th plen mtg, Agenda Item 39, *UN Doc A/RES/17/1803* (14 December 1962).
10 Principle 2 of the Rio Declaration, 1992 affirms the following: "States have, in accordance with the Charter of the United Nations and the principles of international law, the sovereign right to exploit their own resources pursuant to their own environmental and developmental policies".
11 *Texaco Overseas Petroleum Co. and California Asiatic Oil Co. v Libya*, 53 ILR 389 (1977), para 87.
12 For example, Convention on the Prevention of Marine Pollution by Dumping of Wastes and Other Matter, 1972, Article 9(6); Ramsar Convention on Wetlands of International Importance especially as Waterfowl Habitat, 1971, Article 2(3); International Tropical Timber Agreement, 2006, Article 1; Basel Convention on the Control of Transboundary Movements of Hazardous Wastes and their Disposal, 1989, Preamble; United Nations Framework Convention on Climate Change, 1992, Preamble; CBD, 1992, Preamble; Nagoya Protocol to the CBD, Article 6.
13 Principle 2 of the Rio Declaration, 1992 says, "States have [. . .] the responsibility to ensure that activities within their jurisdiction or control do not cause damage to the environment of other States or of areas beyond the limits of national jurisdiction".
14 *United States v Canada* [1941] 3 RIAA 1905, 1907.
15 UNCLOS, Article 194(3): 'These measures shall include, *inter alia*, those designed to minimise to the fullest possible extent: (a) the release of toxic, harmful or noxious substances, especially those which are persistent, from land-based sources, from or through the atmosphere or by dumping; (b) pollution from vessels, in particular measures for preventing accidents and dealing with emergencies, ensuring the safety of operations at sea, preventing intentional and unintentional discharges, and regulating the design, construction, equipment, operation and manning of vessels; (c) pollution from installations and devices used in exploration or exploitation of the natural resources of the seabed and subsoil, in particular measures for preventing accidents and dealing with emergencies, ensuring the safety of operations at sea, and regulating the design, construction, equipment, operation and manning of such installations or devices; (d) pollution from other installations and devices operating in the marine environment, in particular measures for preventing accidents and dealing with emergencies, ensuring the safety of operations at sea, and regulating the design, construction, equipment, operation and manning of such installations or devices'.
16 UNCLOS, Article 194(4).
17 See Preamble.
18 See Article I (1) (b).
19 See Article 6(3).
20 GA Res. 27/2996, UN GAOR, sess 27, Supp No 30, U.N. Doc. A/2996 (15 December 1972).
21 *UK v Albania* [1949] ICJ Rep 4, 22.
22 *Spain v France* [1957] 12 RIAA 281, 285.
23 UNCLOS Preamble para 8.

24 UNCLOS, Article 203.
25 Convention on Biological Diversity (CBD), Rio de Janeiro, 5 June 1992, in force 29 December 1993, 31 International Legal Materials (1992) 822, <www.biodiv.org>, Preamble para 17.
26 Convention on Biological Diversity (CBD), Rio de Janeiro, 5 June 1992, in force 29 December 1993, 31 International Legal Materials (1992) 822, <www.biodiv.org>, Preamble para 18.
27 See Pacific Fur Seal Arbitration, Proceedings of the Tribunal of Arbitration, convened at Paris, under the treaty between the United States and Great Britain, concluded in Washington, 29 February 1892, for the determination of questions between the two governments concerning the jurisdictional rights of the United States in the waters of Bering Sea, viewed 6 December 2017, https://archive.org/stream/fursealarbitrati02bering/fursealarbitrati02bering_djvu.txt.
28 Convention on International Trade in Endangered Species of Wild Fauna and Flora, (CITES), Washington, DC, 3 March 1973 in force 1 July 1975, Preamble para 2.
29 Convention on the Protection and Use of Trans-boundary Watercourses and International Lakes, Helsinki, 17 March 1992, in force in 6 October 1996, Article 2(5)(c).
30 Convention on Biological Diversity (CBD), Rio de Janeiro, 5 June 1992, in force 29 December 1993, 31 International Legal Materials (1992) 822, <www.biodiv.org>, Preamble para 24.
31 UNCLOS Preamble para 6; also see Preamble para 4.
32 Stockholm Declaration on Human Environment, Stockholm, 5–16 June 1972, Principle I.
33 Kuwait Regional Convention for Co-operation on the Protection of the Marine Environment from Pollution, Kuwait City, 24 April 1978, in force 30 June 1979, Preamble para 9.
34 Regional Convention for the Conservation of the Red Sea and of the Gulf of Aden Environment, Jeddah, 14 February 1982, in force 20 August 1985, Preamble para 3.
35 Regional Convention for the Conservation of the Red Sea and of the Gulf of Aden Environment, Jeddah, 14 February 1982, in force 20 August 1985.
36 Convention for the Protection and Development of the Marine Environment of the Wider Caribbean Region, Cartagena, 24 March 1983, in force 11 October 1986, Preamble para 3.
37 Rio Declaration, 1992, Principle 15.
38 1996 Protocol to the Convention on the Prevention of Marine Pollution by Dumping of Wastes and Other Matter, 1972, Article 3(1).
39 Fish Stock Agreement, 1995, Article 5(d).
40 Convention for the Protection of the Marine Environment of the North-East Atlantic, 1992.
41 Convention for the Protection of the Marine Environment of the North-East Atlantic, 1992, Preamble.
42 Convention on the Protection of the Marine Environment of the Baltic Sea Area, 1992, Article 3(2).
43 FAO Code of Conduct for Responsible Fisheries, 1995, para 7.5.1; reference to a precautionary approach is also used in paras 7.5.2 and 6.5.
44 *Pulp Mills on the River Uruguay (Argentina v Uruguay)* (order on the Request for the Indication of Provisional Measures) [2006] ICJ Rep 135, para 197.
45 *Gabčíkovo-Nagymaros Project (Hungary v Slovakia)* (1997) ICJ Reports 7, 78 para 140; see also Sands and Peel (2012, p. 201).
46 See the Responsibilities and Obligations of States Sponsoring Persons and Entities with Respect to Activities in the Area (Advisory Opinion) (Seabed Dispute Chamber of ITLOS Case No. 17), para 117.
47 Goba (2004) considers that the principle of prevention has some inherent conformity to the principle of no harm.

48 UNCLOS, Article 194(1).
49 UNCLOS, Article 2.
50 Convention Relative to the Preservation of Fauna and Flora in Their Natural State, London, 8 November 1933, in force 14 January 1936, Article 12(2).
51 Convention for the Conservation of Antarctic Marine Living Resources, Canberra, 1 August 1980, in force 7 April 1982, Article 2(3)(a).
52 Agreement for the Establishment of a General Fisheries Council for the Mediterranean, Rome, 24 September 1949, in force 20 February 1952, Premable.
53 See Articles 1, 4, 6, 14 and 15.
54 Article 25.
55 Lake Victoria Basin Protocol, 2003, Article 4; also see, Sands and Peel (2012, p. 202).
56 MARPOL 73/78, Article 1(1).
57 Convention for the Prevention of Marine Pollution from Land-based Sources, Article 1.
58 Fish Stocks Agreement, 1995, Article 5(h).
59 Wrecks Convention, 2007, Article 1(7).
60 Stockholm Declaration, 1972, Principle 24.
61 Rio Declaration, 1992, Principle 27.
62 UNCLOS, Preamble para 2.
63 *MOX Plant Case (Ireland v United Kingdom) (Provisional Measures)*, ITLOS Case No. 10 (2002), para 82.
64 *MOX Plant Case (Ireland v United Kingdom) (Provisional Measures)*, ITLOS Case No. 10 (2002), para 89.
65 *Malaysia v Singapore* (2003), ITLOS Case No. 12, para 92.
66 UNCLOS, Article 117.
67 UNCLOS, Article 197.
68 UNCLOS, Articles 198 and 199.
69 UNCLOS, Articles 200 and 201.
70 Convention on Third Party Liability in the Field of Nuclear Energy, 1960.
71 Vienna Convention on Civil Liability for Nuclear Damage, 1963.
72 Article 2(2)(b).
73 International Convention on Oil Pollution Preparedness, Response and Co-operation, London, 30 November 1990, in force 13 May 1995, Preamble para 2.
74 Convention for Cooperation in the Protection and Sustainable Development of the Marine and Coastal Environment of the Northeast Pacific, Antigua, 18 February 2002, (not yet in force), Article 5(6)(c).
75 Convention on the Protection of the Marine Environment of the Baltic Sea Area, 1992, Article 3(4).
76 United Nations Framework Convention on Climate Change, 1992, Article 3(1).
77 Basel Convention on the Control of Transboundary Movements of Hazardous Wastes and their Disposal, 1989, Preamble.
78 UNCLOS, Preamble para 5.
79 UNCLOS, Preamble para 6.
80 UNCLOS, Article 194(1).
81 UNCLOS, Article 207(4).
82 1996 Protocol to the Convention on the Prevention of Marine Pollution by Dumping of Wastes and Other Matter, 1972, Article 2.
83 These principles are the principle of integration between the environment and development, precautionary principle, principle for common concern of humanity, principle of State sovereignty with State responsibility, principle of common but differentiated responsibility, principle of global partnership and cooperation, polluter-pays principle and principle of participatory and informed decision-making (see Dupuy, 1997, pp. 888–891; Tanaka, 2015).
84 See *Gabčíkovo – Nagymaros Project (Hungary v Slovakia)* [1997] ICJ Reports, 78, para 140.
85 UNCLOS, Preamble, para 4.

86 UNCLOS, Preamble, para 5.
87 Original name of this instrument is 'The United Nations Agreement for the Implementation of the Provisions of the United Nations Convention on the Law of the Sea of 10 December 1982 relating to the Conservation and Management of Straddling Fish Stocks and Highly Migratory Fish Stocks' adopted on 4 August 1995 and entered into force on 11 December 2001.
88 United Nations Fish Stocks Agreement, 1995, Article 2.
89 See Chapter 17 of Agenda 21.
90 Article 7.2.1.
91 Rome Declaration on the Implementation of the Code of Conduct for Responsible Fisheries, 1999, para 12(n).
92 Reykjavik Declaration on Responsible Fisheries in the Marine Eco-system, 2001, Preamble para 21.
93 UNCLOS, Article 197.
94 See 'Introduction to IMO', viewed 9 July 2017, www.imo.org/en/About/Pages/Default.aspx.
95 See 'Introduction to IMO', viewed 9 July 2017, www.imo.org/en/About/Pages/Default.aspx.
96 International Convention Relating to Intervention on the High Seas in Cases of Oil Pollution Casualties, 1969.
97 International Convention for the Safety of Life at Sea, 1974.
98 International Convention on Oil Pollution Preparedness, Response and Co-operation, 1990.
99 International Convention on Civil Liability for Oil Pollution Damage, 1992.
100 *International Convention* for the *Control and Management of Ships' Ballast Water and Sediments*, 2004.
101 International Convention for the Safe and Environmentally Sound Recycling of Ships, 2009.
102 International Convention on the Control of Harmful Anti-fouling Systems on Ships, 2001.
103 See UNCLOS, Article 197; see also Articles 198–201.
104 RSP, viewed 11 July 2017, www.unep.org/regionalseas/who-we-are/regional-seas-programmes.
105 These are active in the Antarctic, Arctic, Baltic, Caspian and North-East Atlantic seas.
106 These are active in the Caribbean, East Asian, Eastern African, Mediterranean, Northwest Pacific and Western African seas.
107 These are active in the Black Sea region, Northeast Pacific, Red Sea and Gulf of Aden, South Asian Seas, Southeast Pacific, Pacific and the ROPME Sea Area.
108 RSP, viewed 11 July 2017, www.unep.org/regionalseas/who-we-are/regional-seas-programmes.
109 RSP, viewed 11 July 2017, www.unep.org/regionalseas/who-we-are/regional-seas-programmes.
110 See Article 197; see also Articles 198–201.
111 Article 118.
112 Article 8(5).
113 These are the Helsinki Convention on the Protection of the Marine Environment of the Baltic Sea Area, 1992; the Convention for the Protection of the Marine Environment of the North-East Atlantic, 1992; the Convention for the Protection of the Mediterranean Sea Against Pollution, 1995, and the Protocols to the Convention on the Protection of the Black Sea Against Pollution, 2009.
114 For example, institutions such as the Secretariat of the Pacific Community, the Forum Fisheries Agency and the Secretariat of the Pacific Regional Environment Programme aim to protect and preserve of the environment of the Pacific Island region.

References

Alhéritière, D. (1982). Marine pollution control regulation: Regional approaches. *Marine Policy*, vol. 6, no. 3, pp. 162–174.
Backer, H., Leppänen, J.-M., Brusendorff, A.C., Forsius, K., Stankiewicz, M., Mehtonen, J., Pyhälä, M., Laamanena, M., Paulomäkia, H., Vlasova, N., & Haaranenc, T. (2010). HELCOM Baltic Sea action plan – A regional programme of measures for the marine environment based on the ecosystem approach. *Marine Pollution Bulletin*, vol. 60, no. 5, pp. 642–649.
Brown Weiss, E. (1990). What obligation does our generation owe to the next? An approach to global environmental responsibility: Our rights and obligations to future generations for the environment. *American Journal of International Law*, vol. 84, no. 1, pp. 198–207.
Chang, Y.C. (2010). International legal obligations in relation to good ocean governance. *Chinese Journal of International Law*, vol. 9, no. 3, pp. 589–605.
Churchill, R. (2015). The LOSC regime for the protection of the marine environment – Fit for the twenty-first century, in R. Rayfuse (ed.), *Research Handbook on International Marine Environmental Law*, Edward Elgar, Cheltenham, pp. 3–30.
Crawford, J. (2012). *Brownlie's Principles of Public International Law*, 8th edn, Oxford University Press, Oxford.
De La Fayette, L. (2001). The marine environment protection committee: The conjunction of the law of the sea and international environmental law. *The International Journal of Marine and Coastal Law*, vol. 16, no. 2, pp. 155–238.
Deleuil, T. (2012). The common but differentiated responsibilities principle: Changes in continuity after the Durban conference of the parties. *Review of European, Comparative & International Environmental Law*, vol. 21, no. 3, pp. 271–281.
Des Jardins, J.R. (1997). *Environmental Ethics: An Introduction to Environmental Philosophy*, Wadsworth Publishing Company, Belmont, CA.
Dupuy, Voir Aussi P.M. (1997). Où en est le droit international de l'environnement à la fin du siècle? *Revue General du Droit International Public*, vol. 101, no. 4, pp. 873–903.
Dzidzornu, D.M., & Tsamenyi, B.M. (1991). Enhancing international control of vessel source oil pollution under the law of the sea convention, 1982: A reassessment. *University of Tasmania Law Review*, vol. 10, pp. 269–291.
Freestone, D. (1999). Implementing precaution cautiously: The precautionary approach in the straddling and highly migratory fish stocks agreement, in E. Hey (ed.), *Developments in International Fisheries Law*, Kluwer Law International, The Hague, pp. 287–325.
Freestone, D., & Hey, E. (1996). Origins and development of the precautionary principle, in D. Freestone & E. Hey (eds), *The Precautionary Principle and International Law: The Challenge of Implementation*, Kluwer Law International, The Hague, pp. 3–18.
Grip, K. (2017). International marine environmental governance: A review. *Ambio*, vol. 46, no. 4, pp. 413–427.
Harrison, J. (2015). Actors and Institutions for the Protection of the Marine Environment, in R. Rayfuse (ed.), *Research Handbook on International Marine Environmental Law*, Edward Elgar, Cheltenham, pp. 57–78.
Hohmann, H. (1994). *Precautionary Legal Duties and Principles of Modern International Environmental Law*, Graham & Trotman/Martinus Nijhoff, London.
Jansen, T.C. (2002). Intergenerational and intra-generational equity and transboundary movements of radioactive wastes, Master's Thesis, McGill University, Montreal.
Karim, M.S. (2009). Implementation of the MARPOL convention in Bangladesh. *Macquarie Journal of International and Comparative Law*, vol. 5, pp. 51–82.
McGrath, P.M., & Julian, M. (2000). Protection of the marine environment from shipping operations: Australian and international responses, in D. Rothwell & S. Bateman (eds),

Navigational Rights and Freedoms and the New Law of the Sea, Martinus Nijhoff Publishers, The Hague & Boston, pp. 198–199.

Miles, E.L. (1999). The concept of ocean governance: Evolution toward the 21st century and the principle of sustainable ocean use. *Coastal Management*, vol. 27, no. 1, pp. 1–30.

Mitchell, R.B. (1994). *International Oil Pollution at Sea*, MIT Press, Cambridge, MA.

Oral, N. (2015). Forty years of the UNEP regional seas programme: From past to future, in R. Rayfuse (ed.), *Research Handbook on International Marine Environmental Law*, Edward Elgar, Cheltenham, pp. 339–362.

Oxman, B.H. (1995). Environmental protection in archipelagic waters and international straits-the role of the international maritime organization. *International Journal of Marine and Coastal Law*, vol. 10, no. 4, pp. 467–481.

Paradell Trius, L. (2000). Principles of international environmental law: An overview. *Review of European Community & International Environmental Law*, vol. 9, no. 2, pp. 93–99.

Porkareh, M.H., Monavari, S.M., Molaei, Y., & Fard, M.A. (2013). Comparison of regional organization for the protection of the marine environment (ROPME) and the convention of Caspian sea protection. *Annals of Biological Research*, vol. 4, no. 7, pp. 27–34.

Rayfuse, R. (2012). Precaution and the protection of marine biodiversity in areas beyond national jurisdiction. *The International Journal of Marine and Coastal Law*, vol. 27, no. 4, pp. 773–781.

Roberts, J. (2006). *Marine Environment Protection and Biodiversity Conservation: The Application and Future Development of the IMO's Particularly Sensitive Sea Area Concept*, Springer, Berlin.

Rochette, J., Billé, R., Molenaar, E.J., Drankier, P., & Chabason, L. (2015). Regional oceans governance mechanisms: A review. *Marine Policy*, vol. 60, pp. 9–19.

Sands, P. (1995). International law in the field of sustainable development, in W. Lang (ed.), *Sustainable Development and International Law*, Graham Trotman, London.

Sands, P., & Peel, J. (2012). *Principles of International Environmental Law*, 3rd edn, Cambridge University Press, Cambridge.

Singh, J.N. (1986). Foreword, in R.D. Munro & J.G. Lammers (eds), *Environmental Protection and Sustainable Development: Legal Principles and Recommendations*, Graham & Trotman/Martinus Nijhoff, London.

Spalding, M.D., Meliane, I., Milam, A., Fitzgerald, C., & Hale, L.Z. (2013). Protecting marine spaces: Global targets and changing approaches. *Ocean Yearbook Online*, vol. 27, no. 1, pp. 213–248.

Tanaka, Y. (2015). Principles of international marine environmental law, in R. Rayfuse (ed.), *Research Handbook on International Marine Environmental Law*, Edward Elgar, Cheltenham, pp. 31–56.

Techera, E. (2013). *Marine Environmental Governance: From International Law to Local Practice*, Routledge, Oxford.

United Nations. (2015). *Sustainable Development Goals*, viewed 19 June 2017, www.un.org/sustainabledevelopment/oceans/.

United Nations Economic and Social Council. (2016). *Progress Towards the Sustainable Development Goals*, Report of the UN Secretary-General, UNESC, New York, https://unstats.un.org/sdgs/files/report/2016/secretary-general-sdg-report-2016—EN.pdf.

Vanderzwaag, D. (2002). The precautionary principle and marine environmental protection: Slippery shores, rough seas, and rising normative tides. *Ocean Development & International Law*, vol. 33, no. 2, pp. 165–188.

World Commission on Environment and Development. (1987). *Our Common Future*, Oxford University Press, Oxford.

PART II
Prevention of marine pollution

3
PREVENTION, REDUCTION AND CONTROL OF MARINE POLLUTION FROM LAND-BASED SOURCES AND ACTIVITIES

Daud Hassan and Stan Palassis

Introduction

The world's oceans provide a range of benefits essential for long-term human well-being and prosperity. The oceans are an important medium for climate stability, they guarantee food security and they provide a range of indispensable services that include transportation and recreation. Various human activities have, however, put the oceans and marine ecosystems at risk of irreversible damage. These activities include overfishing, increased pollution, ocean acidification from absorbed carbon emissions, climatic change, unsustainable coastal zone development and impacts from resource extraction. As one of the most significant threats to marine life, pollution dramatically affects the health of the oceans (Stevenson and Oxman, 1994). The prevention, reduction and control of marine pollution is therefore critical for the long-term protection of marine ecosystems and key to improving the health of the oceans (Gouilloud, 1981).

There are a variety of sources of pollution of the marine environment, including ship-sourced, sea dumping, sea-bed activities and land-based sources of marine pollution (LBSMP). Of these various sources of marine pollution, LBSMP are by far the greatest threat to the marine environment. According to a 1990 global assessment by the United Nations Joint Group of Experts on the Scientific Aspects of Marine Pollution (GESAMP) on the state of marine environment, LBSMP constitutes approximately 77% of the total marine pollution.[1] Consistent with statistics compiled by the GESAMP in 1993, major sources of marine pollution consisted of 44% from land-based discharge, 33% from atmospheric inputs from land, 12% from marine transport, 10% from dumping and 1% from oil exploration and production (Gold, 1997). Aside from being the greatest of the sources of marine pollution, LBSMP enter the marine environment through various pathways and have diverse environmental effects (Hassan, 2006). Furthermore, the severe environmental consequences of LBSMP can be demonstrated in the areas of public health, food resources, marine species integrity and health and survival.

Although LBSMP is a major problem affecting the world's marine and coastal zone environments, at present there is no global treaty which exclusively deals with LBSMP control. Furthermore, despite a range of legal and policy developments undertaken internationally in the prevention and control of LBSMP, questions remain as to how far the present legal frameworks have gone for the effective protection of the marine environment from LBSMP.[2]

The emphasis of the chapter is on analysing the global framework for the prevention, reduction and control of LBSMP. The chapter commences by examining the initial legal control of LBSMP through customary international law. The chapter then examines treaty regimes in the law of the sea and sea dumping. The chapter then moves on to examining the problems, challenges and prospects of reducing and controlling LBSMP for the protection of the marine environment by analysing key sustainability instruments. The chapter then examines and analyses international soft law instruments specific to LBSMP. The chapter then moves to examine regional initiatives in the control of LBSMP. Finally, the chapter critically evaluates the congruencies and discrepancies between international environmental management principles and the international legal framework in controlling LBSMP. The reasons for the inadequacies of the current regimes are also explored in the chapter.

Initial international customary law development

Initially the control of LBSMP occurred through the application of certain broad and general principles of customary international law. As an unwritten source of international law, customary international law comprises two interrelated elements: a consistent and general international practice amongst States and an acceptance by States of this practice as being driven by a sense of legal obligation. Customary international law can be reflected in practice and claim including physical acts and omissions, such as General Assembly resolutions, national laws and national judgements (Akehurst, 1976). Non-State activities, such as decisions of the International Court of Justice (ICJ) and of other international courts and tribunals as well as the writing of publicists, are also relevant as they can lead to a declaration of the existence of a customary rule. These decisions and writings are thus useful legal documents that demonstrate the emergence of new rules of customary international law (Hickey, 1978).

It was not until the second half of 20th century that LBSMP was identified as an important issue of international, regional and national concern. As awareness about the impact of LBSMP increased during this period, control mechanisms of LBSMP began to emerge as a response to an issue of increasing popular environmental concern. This led to the development of certain, well-recognised and interrelated principles of customary international law, which formed the initial basis for the control of LBSMP. These principles formed the origins from which the customary international law of marine pollution derived, and, in particular, the rules relating to cross-jurisdictional marine pollution. In this context, the principle of good neighbourliness and the principle of reasonableness of use are most notable.

The principle of good neighbourliness advocates that no State may conduct, promote or sustain in its territory activities which may cause anything other than the inconsiderable and usual damage in the territory of a neighbouring State (Hakapää, 1981). In its broader sense, the principle refers to State relations in general. For example, in the preamble to the 1945 United Nations Charter 'the peoples of the United Nations' have expressed their determination to 'live together in peace with one another as good neighbours' (UN Charter, 1945). Whereas the principle of reasonableness of use denotes a positive obligation on States in terms of utilisation of the high seas for the sake of the interest of others,[3] in the *Fisheries Jurisdiction* case (UK v Iceland, 1973), the ICJ considered this provision and required the contesting parties to duly take into account the interests of other States in the conservation and equitable exploitation of high seas fisheries resources. However, as these principles only addressed cross-jurisdictional impacts, and not domestic impacts, they left issues surrounding national marine pollution control to the will of sovereign States. This shortcoming of customary international law resulted in the call for the creation of conventional and instrument-driven international law on the issue of LBSMP (Goering, 1980). This in turn paved the way for new beginnings in the international control of LBSMP to emerge from the 1970s onwards.

The 1972 United Nations Conference on the Human Environment (UNCHE), also known as the Stockholm Conference, is often regarded as the beginning of a new journey of hope reflecting the commencement point in the genesis of international environmental law. The Conference addressed all aspects of the human environment through the adoption of the Declaration of the United Nations Conference on the Human Environment (Stockholm Declaration)[4] as well as a corresponding Action Plan.[5] Furthermore, the Conference also reflected a strong sense of dedication by States in establishing the basic rules of international marine environmental law (Birnie and Boyle, 1995). For the first time, the urgent necessity for control of LBSMP was explicitly recognised by international law. Principle 7 of the Stockholm Declaration specifically obligates States to prevent marine pollution. Since then many hard law[6] and soft law[7] instruments at global as well as regional levels have been concluded relevant to LBSMP control. Instruments adopted include: the 1972 *Convention on the Prevention of Marine Pollution by Dumping of Wastes and other Matters*; the 1982 *United Nations Convention on the Law of the Sea*; the 1985 *Montreal Guidelines for the Protection of the Marine Environment from Land Based Sources*; the *Rio Declaration on Environment and Development* of the 1992 *United Nations Conference on Environment and Development; Agenda 21* of the 1992 *United Nations Conference on Environment and Development*; the 1985 *Montreal Guidelines for the Protection of the Marine Environment from Land Based Sources of Marine Pollution*; and the 1995 *Global Programme of Action for the Protection of the Marine Environment from Land Based Sources* (GPA).

The role of treaty instruments

United Nations Convention on the Law of the Sea

In 1982 States adopted the United Nations Convention on the Law of the Sea (LOSC)[8]. The LOSC is an outstanding example of a treaty that carefully balances the competing interests of maritime and coastal States. The treaty is comprehensive in its scope covering every human usage of the oceans and seas. Part XII of the treaty is devoted to the protection and preservation of the marine environment and provides a comprehensive framework of marine environmental protection. Part XII is a fundamental legal instrument of marine environmental protection and conservation. It creates a regime that addresses all forms of marine pollution, along with the specific duties of States with respect to these sources of pollution (Charney, 1994). It is important to note that the treaty also establishes a framework for the conservation of and development of marine living resources.

Article 192 commences with a general recognition that all States have the duty to protect the marine environment. Article 194 expands on this duty by providing that:

1 States shall take, individually or jointly as appropriate, all measures consistent with this Convention that are necessary to prevent, reduce and control pollution of the marine environment from any source, using for this purpose the best practicable means at their disposal and in accordance with their capabilities, and they shall endeavour to harmonise their policies in this connection.
2 States shall take all measures necessary to ensure that activities under their jurisdiction or control are so conducted as not to cause damage by pollution to other States and their environment, and that pollution arising from incidents or activities under their jurisdiction or control does not spread beyond the areas where they exercise sovereign rights in accordance with this Convention.

The LOSC recognises the obligation in combating all forms of marine pollution, including LBSMP. In this regard Article 194 continues on to provide that:

3 The measures taken pursuant to this Part shall deal with all sources of pollution of the marine environment. These measures shall include, *inter alia*, those designed to minimise to the fullest possible extent:

   (a) The release of toxic, harmful or noxious substances, especially those which are persistent, from land-based sources, from or through the atmosphere or by dumping;

The LOSC is the most important treaty law to deal with LBSMP. It is the only global treaty with specific provisions on LBSMP. Article 207 of the LOSC provides:

1 States shall adopt laws and regulations to prevent, reduce and control pollution of the marine environment from land-based sources, including rivers, estuaries, pipelines and outfall structures, taking into account internationally agreed rules, standards and recommended practices and procedures.
2 States shall take other measures as may be necessary to prevent, reduce and control such pollution.

3   States shall endeavour to harmonise their policies in this connection at the appropriate regional level.
4   States acting especially through the competent international organisations or diplomatic conference shall endeavour to establish global and regional rules, standards and recommended practices and procedures to prevent, reduce and control pollution of the marine environment from land-based sources, taking into account characteristic regional features, the economic capacity of developing States and their need for economic development. Such rules, standards and recommended practices and procedures shall be re-examined from time to time as necessary.
5   Laws, regulations, measures, rules, standards and recommended practices and procedures referred to in paragraphs 1, 2 and 4 shall include those designed to minimise to the fullest extent possible, the release of toxic, harmful or noxious substances, especially those which are persistent, into the marine environment.

Article 207 the LOSC thus obligates States to: take into account internationally agreed rules, standards and recommended practices and procedures; endeavour to harmonise their policies at the appropriate regional level; and, act through the competent international organisations or diplomatic conferences to establish rules to control LBSMP.[9] Thus the LOSC does not specifically create detailed rules but rather is a framework in nature by emphasising cooperation on a global and regional basis and thus directing States to create more specific rules in the regulation of marine pollution.

Finally, it is also important to note that the LOSC emphasises cooperation with respect to the protection of enclosed and semi-enclosed seas.[10] In this regard the LOSC does not provide a comprehensive management system with the application of sustainable management principles.

London Dumping Convention

In 1972 States adopted the Convention for the Prevention of Marine Pollution by Dumping of Wastes and Other Matter (London Convention).[11] The Convention is relevant to the control of LBSMP as most marine dumping is of land-generated industrial waste or land-dredged silt.[12] The Convention prohibits substances listed in Annex I from being dumped at sea, substances that can be dumped subject to special permit are listed in Annex II and all other substances require a prior general permit.[13] In 1996 a Protocol to the London Convention was adopted which enhanced environmental protection of the regime through the requirement of a precautionary approach.[14] The 1996 Protocol both widens the ambit of 'dumping' so that it includes the deliberate disposal of wastes into the sea and extends it to the storage of wastes or other matter on the seabed and sub-soils and the abandonment at sea of platforms or other man-made structures.[15]

The sustainability instruments

Sustainable development

Protection and preservation of the marine environment in an integrated and sustainable manner has been enunciated in various global and regional forums, including the United Nations. Sustainable development has been defined as 'development that meets the needs of the present without compromising the ability of future generations to meet their own needs' (Brundtland, 1987, p. 8). Sustainable protection relates to an improved control of wastes and the development of contingency plans for dealing with accidents harmful to the marine environment.

The United Nations Conference on Environment and Development (UNCED), also known as the Earth Summit, was convened in 1992 at Rio de Janeiro. The Earth Summit was convened exactly 20 years after the historic Stockholm Conference of 1972 and provided the international community with the opportunity to establish new environmental priorities. At the Earth Summit, important treaties were adopted on climate change,[16] biological diversity[17] and the process was commenced for a treaty on desertification that would subsequently be adopted in 1994.[18] In addition, a number of soft law instruments were adopted, in particular the Rio Declaration on Environment and Development (Rio Declaration),[19] Agenda 21[20] and a Statement of Forestry Principles.[21] Of all the treaties and soft law instruments adopted at the Earth Summit the Rio Declaration and Agenda 21 are of most relevance to the prevention, reduction and control of LBSMP.

Rio Declaration

The Rio Declaration is important in its identifying the key principles necessary for States to implement in their attainment of sustainable development. The Rio principles of sustainable development are to be utilised by States through their implementing strategies and programmes for environmental protection and resource conservation. Despite being non-legally binding, the principles of the Rio Declaration are important principles of international environmental policy and management.[22] Furthermore, certain of the Rio principles are candidates for customary international law status (Palassis, 2011). Some of the Rio Declaration's most pertinent sustainability principles relevant to the protection of the marine environment from the effects of pollution include the following:

- Environmental impact assessment (EIA) is an important management tool that ensures sound environmental development activities and an evaluation of environmental effects of proposed developments.[23]
- The precautionary principle ensures that a substance or activity posing a threat to the environment is prevented from adversely affecting the environment, even if there is no scientific proof linking that particular substance or activity to environmental damage (Cameron and Abouchar, 1991).

- As a tool of minimising international competitive distortions arising from LBSMP, the polluter-pays principle advocates that the costs of environmental pollution should be internalised. In the international context, it is an attempt to shift the burden of pollution prevention and clean-up costs to States or other groups or bodies involved in polluting activities, rather than permitting that burden to continue to be imposed on international society as a whole.
- As a management tool, the cleaner production principle offers an effective solution for tackling LBSMP problems by providing the opportunity to conserve and clean up coastal waters and by ensuring environmentally sustainable use of resources by firms and industries in marine and coastal areas (efficient resource utilisation). It also provides an effective solution for protecting the marine and coastal environment from the negative impacts of human activities (reducing waste disposal charges).

Agenda 21

Chapter 17 of Agenda 21 titled 'Protection of the Oceans, all Kinds of Seas, Including Enclosed and Semi-enclosed and Coastal Areas, and the Protection, Rational Use and Development of their Living Resources' is devoted to the protection and preservation of the marine environment. Chapter 17 makes many useful recommendations to prevent, reduce and control LBSMP. These include the following: the application of preventive, precautionary and anticipatory approaches to avoid degradation of the marine environment; prior assessment of activities which have significant impacts upon the marine environment; the integrated protection of the marine environment; the development of economic incentives to apply clean technologies and the application of the polluter-pays principle.

Chapter 17 also prescribes the specific actions that are needed to prevent, reduce and control LBSMP. In this context, the document prescribes that States should take action at the national levels to control LBSMP and take into account Montreal Guidelines in this respect;[24] consider updating, strengthening and extending the Montreal Guidelines, as appropriate; assess the effectiveness of existing regional agreements and action plans, where appropriate; develop policy guidance for relevant global funding mechanisms;[25] convene, as soon as practicable, an intergovernmental meeting on the protection of the marine environment from LBS;[26] give priority to sewage discharge and establish regulatory and monitoring programmes to control effluents' discharges;[27] eliminate the discharge of organohalogen compounds,[28] reduce use of synthetic organic compounds, control inputs of nitrogen and phosphorus into the seawater, promote the use of less harmful pesticides and fertilisers and undertake new initiatives at national, sub-regional and regional levels for controlling the input of non-point source pollutants;[29] control and prevent coastal erosion and siltation due to anthropogenic factors related to, *inter alia*, land use and construction techniques and practices.[30]

Instruments specifically dealing with LBSMP

Montreal Guidelines

Following on from the Stockholm Conference international attention turned to focus on more prescriptive standards for LBSMP control.[31] As an initiative of the Governing Council of the United Nations Environment Programme (UNEP), the *Montreal Guidelines for the Protection of the Marine Environment from Land Based Sources of Pollution* (Montreal Guidelines)[32] were adopted in 1985 with a view to assist States in the process of developing appropriate bilateral, regional and multilateral agreements and, in particular, national legislation for the protection of the marine environment from LBSMP. The Montreal Guidelines have defined LBSMP as

> Land-based sources means: Municipal, industrial or agricultural sources, both fixed and mobile, on land, discharges from which reach the marine environment, in particular:
>
> From the coast, including from outfalls discharging directly into the marine environment and through run-off; and through rivers, canals or other water-courses, including underground water courses; and via the atmosphere.
> Sources of marine pollution from activities conducted on offshore fixed or mobile facilities within the limits of national jurisdiction save to the extent that these sources are governed by appropriate international agreement.[33]

The Guidelines provide a checklist of provisions which governments may select, adopt or elaborate, as appropriate, to meet the needs of specific regions to control LBSMP (Guidelines, 1985). As the first global instrument directed exclusively at LBSMP, the Montreal Guidelines set out responsibilities to protect and preserve the marine environment; prevent transboundary pollution; adopt measures against marine pollution from land-based sources; cooperate on a global, regional and bilateral basis; prevent transfer or transformation of pollution from land-based sources; establish marine sanctuaries and reserves;, engage in scientific and technological cooperation and assist developing countries for the purpose of improving their capacities to prevent, reduce and control LBSMP.[34] It is important to note that these guidelines are virtually identical to provisions contained in Articles 192 to 1982 LOSC.

Global Programme of Action to Prevent, Reduce and Control LBSMP

In direct response to the recommendations made in Chapter 17 of Agenda 21 the Conference on the Protection of the Marine Environment from LBSMP was held in Washington in 1995 (Washington Conference). The Washington Conference was convened and coordinated by UNEP, in close cooperation with intergovernmental and non-governmental organisations (NGOs). The Conference was attended by over 100 States, 17 global and regional international organisations and 27 NGOs.[35] The aim of the Washington Conference was to develop a Global Programme of Action (GPA) to Prevent, Reduce and Control LBSMP, which was unanimously adopted by the participants of the Conference. The GPA provides valuable insights as to what is needed to deal more effectively with the LBSMP problem and how States might be persuaded, encouraged or assisted.[36]

The GPA provides certain criteria to ensure successful implementations of its programme, such as these: establishing and strengthening regional and global networks, encouraging and facilitating interregional cooperation and establishing and supporting the necessary Secretariat services for regional cooperative arrangements (Basiron, 1996). Furthermore, the GPA has initiated and proposed a coherent strategy and methodology to develop programmes of action at national, regional and international levels and has established the programmatic links between various GPA activities and integrated legal, economic and technological policies.[37]

The regional regulation of LBSMP

The importance of regionalism

The effects of LBSMP are most intensely felt at regional levels (Schumacher, Hoagland and Gaines, 1996). They are particularly critical in coastal waters.[38] In general, the coastal zone includes coastal waters and all areas to the landward side of the coastal waters (Kay and Alder, 1998). However, the coastal zone can be more closely defined as:

> The land and waters extending inland for one kilometre from the high-water mark on the foreshore and extending seaward to the 30 metre depth contour line and also including the waters, beds, and banks of all rivers, estuaries, inlets, creeks, bays, or lakes subject to the ebb and flow of the tide.
>
> *(Beer, 1996)*

Furthermore, the effects of LBSMP are highly specific for different regions. Due to 'their special hydrographical and ecological characteristics, as well as the predominant patterns of industrial and economic development' (Kuwabara, 1984, p. 20) the nature and scope of land-based pollutants differ from region to region. This is particularly true in shallow, enclosed or semi-enclosed seas, as they are especially sensitive and receive substantial contamination from the land and coasts.[39] In this context, the Gulf of Mexico, the Gulf of Thailand, the Baltic Sea and the South China Sea are all pertinent examples.

Due in large to the reasons stated previously, the regional approach has proven to be enormously attractive and, to a certain extent, successful for LBSMP since the late 1960s. The 1969 Bonn Convention on the Prevention of Pollution of the North Sea, 1969,[40] was the first regional legal regime for marine pollution control. This was followed by the Paris Convention on the Prevention of Marine Pollution from Land-based Sources, 1974,[41] and the Convention on the Protection of the Marine Environment of the Baltic Sea Area, 1974.[42] These regimes can all be considered as the pioneer legal instruments for regional marine pollution control.

The regional seas programme

Following on from these regional initiatives, the UNEP regional seas program (RSP) was formulated in 1974. Since its inception the RSP has been playing a key role in the control of LBSMP. The RSP is the cornerstone of the oceans management programme in various regional seas of the world's oceans and at present it includes 16 regions.[43] In 1985 the name of UNEP's RSP was changed to the Ocean and Coastal Areas Program (OCA) and its headquarters, the Program Activity Centre (PAC), was moved from Geneva to Nairobi (Caldwell, 1990). Nevertheless, the programme is still commonly called the RSP as it was originally known.

The RSP is a global programme implemented through regional components wherein each RSP includes a Regional Action Plan (RAP). The RSP aimed at enabling countries of a given region to meet and formulate common commitments under a RAP adopted by them. These Action Plans are formulated according to the practical needs of the region, as perceived by the governments of the States concerned. They serve to coordinate the efforts of national institutions, identify their capabilities and needs (Neuman, 1985) and provide generic support to control LBSMP. The adoption of the Action Plan for the East Asian Seas region and other regional initiatives and activities in the region are examples in this respect.

Most regions of the RSP have established regional trust funds for the major financial support of marine environmental programmes. However, utilising such trust funds, regions are succeeding in implementing their marine environmental programmes where regional convention and specific protocol on LBSMP control are concluded, such as such as Mediterranean Sea region, but not succeeding where such legal framework is yet to be adopted.

UNEP coordination office

As mentioned previously, the GPA is presently being implemented under the auspices of the UNEP's RSP. Realising the nature of LBSMP and the need to promote the implementation of the GPA at regional levels, a UNEP coordinating office for the GPA was established in November 1997 in The Hague and which become fully operational in 1999. The GPA coordination office has put in place various mechanisms as part of a process of implementing the GPA. Central to this process have been a series of regional technical workshops that it has conducted for the programme of 'regional implementation'.[44] The main objectives of these workshops were to finalise regional overviews of land-based activities, agree on the development of regional components of the Clearing-House mechanism and develop regional programmes of action to address impacts of land-based activities in the marine environment.[45]

Problems and future challenges

The institutional components to control LBSMP at the global and regional levels are currently very weak. There are some successful examples of progress in the regional seas areas where the region consists of developed States, such as that of the North-East Atlantic. Furthermore, success can also be seen in the regional seas areas where there are both developed and developing States, such as in the Mediterranean and Baltic Sea regions. However, conditions are still rudimentary where the particular regional seas area consists of developing States, such as that of South Asia and certain areas of Africa.

The attainment of goals of sustainable development continues to allude. The 2002 World Summit on Sustainable Development (WSSD) held in Johannesburg, South Africa, put emphasis on the implementation of GPA. The WSSD urged for coordinated international action for LBSMP control. It calls on legislators and governments to commit to the implementation of the GPA effectively. In order to achieve a relative success of the United Nations 2030 Agenda for Sustainable Development, particularly Sustainable Development Goal 14 that requires States 'to conserve and sustainably use the oceans, seas and marine resources' a better functional and more sustainable and comprehensive management regime is required.

The current governance framework needs to be strengthened by incorporating and effectively implementing ecologically sustainable management principles and concepts including Ecosystem Based Management (EBM) and Integrated Coastal Zone Management (ICZM). The Organization for Economic Cooperation and Development (OECD) Environment Directorate has defined ICZM as

> [M]anagement of the coastal zone as a whole in relation to local, regional, national and international environmental goals. It imposes a particular focus on the interaction between the various activities that occur in the coastal zone and between coastal zone activities and activities in other regions.[46]

This integration in coastal management may embrace a number of dimensions including intergovernmental, geographical (land-water interface), intersectoral and interdisciplinary.

Neither the LOSC nor any other global instrument contains a legally binding obligation to pursue either ICZM or EBM. However, some non-binding commitments have been agreed to pursue these though various global bodies and soft law instruments. These include the following: United Nations General Assembly Resolutions, UNEP, the Conference of the Parties (COP) to the CBD, Agenda 21, Rio+20 and International Union for Conservation of Nature and Natural Resources (IUCN). In many instances, these commitments are complemented by specific guidance on implementation

Adequate integration in resource management to maximise the success of its planning and management measures is required (Hassan, 2013). A better understanding about the oceans by awareness building and strengthening research are significant to keep our oceans healthy, resilient and productive. Strengthening national and regional leadership and cooperation on sustainable oceans governance issues are similarly important.

Furthermore, concrete and positive cooperation on LBSMP control can only be achieved when political commitment is present and is supported financially.[47] Further attention is needed to establish an adequate and strengthened regime that would reinforce the commitment and support to control LBSMP effectively.

All of these considerations point to the need for a comprehensive, legally binding framework entailing detailed and appropriate support systems, including dynamic legal, administrative and financial inputs to support and facilitate private sector participation and to promote compliance.

Notes

1 United Nations Joint Group of Experts on the Scientific Aspects of Marine Pollution (GESAMP), The State of the Marine Environment, *GESAMP Report and Studies* No 39, 1990, UNEP, Nairobi). See also Kimball L, 'The United Nations Convention on the Law of the Sea and Marine Environmental Protection', (1995) 7 *Georgetown International Environmental Law Review* 745.
2 Effectiveness refers, first, to the mechanisms set forth in the treaty to ensure its implementation and compliance and whether, and to what extent, these measures ensure the achievement of the treaty objectives, and, second, it refers to whether the obligations are written in such concrete terms that they actually can be put into effect domestically. See Nordic Council of Ministers, *The Effectiveness of Multimedia Environmental Agreements-A Report from a Nordic Project*, Tema Nord 1996:513, pp. 5–6.
3 Article 2, Convention on the High Seas, (1958) 450 UNTS 11.
4 U.N. Doc. A/Conf.48/14/Rev. 1(1973); 11 ILM 1416 (1972)
5 UN Documents, A/CONF.48/14/Rev.1.
6 Hard law refers to treaty law. Soft laws are non-legally binding declarations and guidelines, which may serve as 'quasi legal guide post'. See Brubaker, D. (1993).
7 Soft law instruments are a relatively recent phenomenon in respect of the growing body of international agreements between States. They offer strategies, impose obligations in an imprecise and flexible way and are shaped by normative guidelines rather than constrained by precise rules. See: Abbott, K.W., & Snidal, D. (2000).
8 *United Nations Convention on the Law of the Sea* adopted by the Third United Nations Conference on the Law of the Sea (UNCLOS III). Montego Bay, 10 December 1982. 21 ILM 1261, 1833 UNTS 3 and 1835 UNTS 261 (Final Act) (in force 16 November 1994).
9 1833 UNTS 3; 21 ILM 1261 (1982).
10 Articles 122–23, LOSC.
11 The *Convention for the Prevention of Marine Pollution by Dumping of Wastes and Other Matters* (11 ILM [1972] 1291).
12 UNEP, Marine Pollution from Land Based Sources, UNEP Industry and Environment, June 1992, p. 3.
13 London Convention, Article IV.
14 The *1996 Protocol to the 1972 Convention on the Prevention of Marine Pollution by Dumping of Wastes and Other Matters* (36 ILM 1997).
15 1996 Protocol, Article 1 (4.1).

Marine pollution from land-based sources   57

16 U.N. Framework Convention on Climate Change 31 ILM (1992), 851. Entered into force 21 March 1994.
17 International Convention on Biological Diversity 31 ILM (1992), 818. Entered into force 21 December 1993.
18 International Convention Combatting the Effects of Desertification in Those Countries Experiencing Serious Drought and/or Desertification, Particularly in Africa, U.N. Doc. A/AC.241.27 (12 September 1994).
19 Rio Declaration on Environment and Development, UN Doc. A/CONF.151/26/Rev.1, Report of the UNCED, vol. 1 (New York).
20 Agenda 21, U.N. Conference on Environment and Development, U.N. Doc. A/CONF. 151.26 (1992).
21 Non-Legally Binding Authoritative Statement of Principles for a Global Consensus on the Management, Conservation and Sustainable Development of All Types of Forests, U.N. Doc. A/CONF.151.26 Vol. III.
22 UN Doc. A/CONF.151/26 (vol. I); 31 ILM 874 (1992).
23 EIA, *UNEP Regional Seas Reports and Studies No.* 130, UNEP, 1990, at p. 1.
24 Chapter 17.24.
25 Chapter 17.25.
26 Chapter 17.26. Agenda 21 requested the governing council of the UNEP to make more concrete measures, and to implement its recommendations and directives related to LBSMP.
27 Chapter 17.27.
28 Organohalogen compounds contain at least one halogen (fluorine, chlorine, bromine) or iodine bonded to carbon.
29 Chapter 17.28.
30 Chapter 17.29.
31 Hassan D, supra note 5 at p. 89.
32 The 1985 Montreal Guidelines for the Protection of the Marine Environment from Land Based Sources of Marine Pollution (UNEP, 'Protection of the Marine Environment against Pollution from Land-based Sources' 14(2–3) Environmental Policy and Law 1985 at 77, UNEP/WG 120/3 Part IV.
33 Ibid.
34 Ibid.
35 UNEP Report, Rio Follow up Marine Environment 26 Environmental Policy and Law, (1996) at p. 11.
36 Hassan D, *supra* note 5 at p. 96.
37 Hassan D, *supra* note 5 at p. 98.
38 Gouilloud MR, *supra* note 3 at p. 197.
39 On this problem refer to UK Department of Environment, Quality status of the North Sea (1987); Kuwabara, S, *The Legal Regime of the Protection of the Mediterranean against Land-based Sources* (Tycooly International Publishing Ltd. 1984) Chapter 1; Clark (ed), *Marine Pollution* (Oxford 1986), Chapter 10; Sibthorp (ed), *The North Sea: Challenge and Opportunity* (London 1975), 22 ff; Helsinki Commission, First Periodic Assessment of the state of the Marine Environment of the Baltic Sea Area (Helsinki 1985).
40 09.06.1969, i.f. 09.08.1969 (704 UNTS), as revised in 1983.
41 13 ILM 1974 at 352.
42 13 ILM 1974 at 546.
43 The regions in UNEP's RSP are as follows: Black Sea, Caribbean, East-Asian Seas, Eastern Africa, Kuwait region, Mediterranean, North-West Pacific, Red Sea and Gulf of Aden, South-Asian Seas, South-East Pacific, South Pacific, South-West Atlantic, West and Central Africa, Arctic, Baltic and North-East Atlantic.
44 UNEP, *Institutional Arrangements for Implementation of the Global Program of Action for the Protection of the Marine Environment from Land-based Activities*, (UNEP/GC.19/INF.4, 8 November 1996) at p. 19.

45 UNEP, Leaflet from UNEP/GPA Coordination Office of the Global Program of Action for the Protection of the Marine Environment from Land-based Activities, 1999 at p. 6.
46 Organization for Economic Cooperation and Development (OECD) Environment Directorate Committee (1991), *Report on Coastal Zone Management: Integrated Policies and Draft Recommendation of the Council on Integrated Coastal Zone Management*, Paris.
47 Hassan, Daud (2006). Protecting the Marine Environment from the Land-Based Sources of Pollution, Ashgate Publishing, UK, p. 206.

References

Abbott, K., & Snidal, D. (2000). Hard and soft law in international governance. *International Organization*, vol. 54, no. 3, pp. 421–456.

Akehurst, M. (1976). Custom as a source of international law. *British Yearbook of International Law*, vol. 47, no. 1, pp. 1–53.

Basiron, N. (1996). The global program of action for the protection of the marine environment from land-based activities. *Malaysian Institute of Maritime Affairs Bulletin*, vol. 3, pp. 62–68.

Beer, T. (1996). *Environmental Oceanography*, Vol. 11, CRC Press, Boca Raton, Finland.

Birnie, P., & Boyle, A. (1995). *Basic Documents on International Law and the Environment*, Oxford University Press, Oxford.

Brubaker, D. (1993). *Marine Pollution and International Law: Principles and Practice*, Belhaven Press, London, pp. 64–66.

Brundtland, G. (1987). *Report of the World Commission on Environment and Development: "our common future"*, United Nations, Oxford University Press, UK.

Caldwell, L. (1990). *International Environmental Policy: Emergence and Dimensions*, Rev. Ed. 2, Duke University Press, North Carolina, USA.

Cameron, J., & Abouchar, J. (1991). The precautionary principle: A fundamental principle of law and policy for the protection of the global environment. *Boston College International and Comparative Law Review*, vol. 14, no. 2.

Charney, J. (1994). The marine environment and the 1982 United Nations convention on the law of the sea. *The International Lawyer*, pp. 879–901.

Goering, K. (1980). Mediterranean protocol on land-based sources: Regional response to a pressing transnational problem. *Cornell International Law Journal*, vol. 13, pp. 331–332.

Gold, E. (1997). *Gard Handbook on Marine Pollution*, Gard, Arendal, Norway.

Gouilloud, M. (1981). Prevention and control of marine pollution, in D.M. Johnston (ed.), *The Environmental Law of the Sea*, Erich Schmidt Verlag, Berlin 1981, p. 193.

Guidelines, M. (1985). Protection of the marine environment against pollution from land-based sources. *Environmental Policy and Law*, vol. 14, nos. 2–3, pp. 77–83.

Hakapää, K. (1981). *Marine Pollution in International Law: Material Obligations and Jurisdiction with Special Reference to the Third United Nations Conference on the Law of the Sea*, Vol. 28, Suomalainen Tiedeakatemia, Distribution, Akateeminen Kirjakauppa.

Hassan, D. (2006). *Protecting the Marine Environment from Land-Based Sources of Pollution: Towards Effective International Cooperation*, Ashgate Publishing, Ltd., Aldershot.

Hassan, D. (2013). The Great Barrier Reef-maritime spatial planning. *Environmental Policy and Law*, vol. 43, nos. 4/5.

Hickey Jr, J. (1978). Custom and land-based pollution of the high seas. *San Diego Law Review*, vol. 15, pp. 409–414.

Kay, R., & Alder, J. (1998). *Coastal Planning and Management*, CRC Press, London.

Kuwabara, S. (1984). *The Legal Regime of the Protection of the Mediterranean Against Pollution from Land-Based Sources*, Tycooly International Publishing Limited, Dublin.

Neuman, L. (1985). The United Nations regional seas program. *Marine Technology Society Journal*, vol. 19, no. 1, pp. 46–52.

Palassis, S. (2011). Beyond the global summits: Reflecting on the environmental principles of sustainable developments. *Colorado Journal of International Environmental Law and Policy*, vol. 22, p. 41.

Schumacher, M., Hoagland, P., & Gaines, A. (1996). Land-based marine pollution in the Caribbean Incentives and prospects for an effective regional protocol. *Marine Policy*, vol. 20, no. 2, pp. 99–121.

Stevenson, J., & Oxman, B. (1994). The future of the United Nations convention on the law of the sea. *American Journal of International Law*, vol. 88, no. 3, pp. 488–499.

UN Charter. (1945). *Charter of the United Nations*, Signed at the United Nations Conference on International Organisation, San Francisco, California, June 1945 (Washington, DC, U.S. Government Printing Office, 1945).

v Iceland, U.K. (1973). Fisheries jurisdiction case. *International Court of Justice Reports*, vol. 3.

4

PREVENTION, REDUCTION AND CONTROL OF MARINE POLLUTION FROM SHIPS

Md Mahatab Uddin and Md Saiful Karim

Introduction

Various sources of marine pollution from ships have prompted the development of many international conventions under the auspices of the International Maritime Organization (IMO). Of these, the International Convention for the Prevention of Pollution from Ships (hereinafter MARPOL 73/78/MARPOL Convention) is the most important. It covers the issues of prevention of vessel-source pollution by oil, noxious liquid substances in bulk, harmful substances carried in packaged form, sewage and garbage and also of air pollution from ships. This chapter presents a brief overview of the IMO conventions on vessel-source marine pollution preparedness, response, cooperation and intervention as well as marine pollution liability and compensation. In addition to conventional vessel-source pollution, international shipping has many unintended effects on the marine environment. One such effect is that harmful aquatic organisms carried by ballast water and harmful aquatic organisms, which accumulate on marine vessels through biofouling, are transferred to another marine environment. This chapter also presents a brief overview of legal instruments covering these issues. Further, it examines the issue of marine environmental pollution by the ship recycling industry. A major contemporary issue is reducing emissions of greenhouse gases (GHGs) owing to international shipping. This issue has created a serious North–South divide, leading to debate between developed and developing countries. This chapter covers this issue briefly.

Development of international legal framework

The international regime for the protection of the marine environment includes the legal and jurisdictional framework for prevention, reduction and control of marine pollution from ships. This international regime has arguably been based on two mutually dependent bodies of laws. The first can be denoted as the international framework or jurisdictional instruments establishing general rules and principles, while the second can be denoted as the international regulatory regime that adopts technical rules and standards aimed at ensuring compliance with the general rules and principles adopted under this framework (Karim, 2015, pp. 29–37; Ringbom, 2015, p. 105).

International environmental conventions, such as the Convention on Biological Diversity, 1992, the Ramsar Convention on Wetlands of International Importance especially as Waterfowl Habitat, 1971, and the Convention Concerning the Protection of the World Cultural and Natural Heritage, 1972, are relevant for protection of the marine environment and marine biodiversity. However, the United Nations Convention on the Law of the Sea, 1982 (UNCLOS), as the umbrella convention for global ocean affairs, provides the jurisdictional framework for the prevention of marine pollution from ships. UNCLOS establishes the flag, coastal port States' prescriptive and enforcement jurisdiction for prevention of such pollution.

As aforementioned, the international regulatory regime for technical rules and standards for the prevention of pollution from ships is mainly developed under the auspices of the IMO, of which the most important convention is the MARPOL Convention. In fact, at the time of concluding UNCLOS in 1982, a set of technical rules and standards regarding the prohibition of vessel-source marine pollution were already established under the MARPOL Convention. In addition, one reason that UNCLOS avoided introducing new technical rules and standards concerning the prohibition of vessel-source marine pollution is the technical nature of the issue that requires examination by an expert forum possessing technical expertise. Therefore, UNCLOS has general rules and principles for prevention, control and reduction of vessel-source marine environmental pollution and urges States to adopt necessary 'international rules and standards' acting through a 'competent international organisation' (Karim, 2015, pp. 31–36). Article 211(1) of UNCLOS stipulates:

> States, *acting through the competent international organization* or general diplomatic conference, shall establish international rules and standards to prevent, reduce and control pollution of the marine environment from vessels and promote the adoption, in the same manner, wherever appropriate, of routing systems designed to minimize the threat of accidents which might cause pollution of the marine environment, including the coastline, and pollution damage to the related interests of coastal States. Such rules and standards shall, in the same manner, be re-examined from time to time as necessary (emphasis added).

Although UNCLOS does not directly refer to the IMO as the 'competent international organisation' for the purpose of Article 211(1), the IMO is widely recognised as such (Karim, 2015, pp. 31–36; Wolfrum, 1999, p. 234). Table 4.1 lists some important international legal and other instruments the IMO has adopted for prevention, preparedness, response and cooperation as regards marine pollution from ships.

TABLE 4.1 Major IMO Instruments for Prevention, Preparedness, Response and Cooperation for Marine Pollution from Ships

Convention and other instruments	Issues covered
International Convention for the Prevention of Pollution from Ships, 1973 (MARPOL 73/78)	Oil pollution Noxious liquid substances carried in bulk Harmful substances carried in packaged form Sewage Garbage Air pollution Energy efficiency and GHG emissions Special areas
International Convention on Oil Pollution Preparedness, Response and Co-operation, 1990 (OPRC)	Pollution preparedness and response, intervention and cooperation
Protocol on Preparedness, Response and Co-operation to Pollution Incidents by Hazardous and Noxious Substances, 2000 (OPRC-HNS Protocol)	
International Convention Relating to Intervention on the High Seas in Cases of Oil Pollution Casualties, 1969 (Intervention)	
International Convention for the Control and Management of Ships' Ballast Water and Sediments, 2004 (BWM)	Ships' ballast water and sediments
Guidelines for the Control and Management of Ships' Biofouling to Minimize the Transfer of invasive aquatic species, 2011 (Biofouling Guidelines)	Biofouling and harmful anti-fouling
International Convention on the Control of Harmful Anti-fouling Systems on Ships, 2001(AFS)	
International Convention for the Safe and Environmentally Sound Recycling of Ships, 2009 (Hong Kong Convention)	Recycling of ships
Resolution A.982(24) on Revised Guidelines for the Identification and Designation of Particularly Sensitive Sea Areas (PSSAs), 2006	Particularly sensitive sea areas
International Convention on Civil Liability for Oil Pollution Damage, 1992 (CLC, 1992) Replacing the 1969 CLC	Liability and compensation for marine pollution
International Convention on the Establishment of an International Fund for Compensation for Oil Pollution Damage, 1992 (FUND, 1992), Replacing the 1971 Fund Convention	
International Convention on Liability and Compensation for Damage in Connection with the Carriage of Hazardous and Noxious Substances by Sea, 2010	
International Convention on Civil Liability for Bunker Oil Pollution Damage, 2001	

Oil, chemical, dangerous goods, sewage and garbage pollution from ships

Different technical issues regarding vessel-source pollution, such as pollution by oil, chemical, sewage and garbage discharged from ships, are extensively covered in the MARPOL Convention. Annex I of this Convention has regulations for the prevention of pollution by oil, Annex II has regulations for the control of pollution by noxious liquid substances (chemicals) carried in bulk, Annex III has regulations for the prevention of pollution by harmful substances (dangerous goods) carried by sea in packaged form, Annex IV has regulations for the prevention of pollution by sewage from ships and Annex V has regulations for the prevention of pollution by garbage from ships. The MARPOL Convention generally prohibits discharge of oil, chemical, sewage and garbage from ships unless specific preconditions are met, including those on discharge rate, discharge speed and distance from the nearest coast.

Annex I of the MARPOL Convention introduced some new technical measures and also reintroduced some technical measures on the basis of established practices. Such measures include those related to establishing oil discharge criteria and managing discharge of dirty bilge water into the sea, segregated ballast tanks and crude oil washing system (Karim, 2015, pp. 44–48). However, the most significant change Annex I introduced was phasing out single-hull oil tankers by 2010 by mandating the use of only double-hulled tankers (Karim, 2015, p. 46).

Discharges of noxious liquid substances (NLS), whether by accident or intentionally, can cause major harm to the marine environment. Annex II of the MARPOL Convention establishes criteria for management of NLS carried in bulk and lists several substances for which discharge of residues is only permitted in designated reception facilities (Karim, 2015, pp. 49–40).

Annex III specifies general requirements related to harmful substances carried in packaged form.[1] It also lists general requirements for port State control on operational requirements for preventing pollution by harmful substances.[2] Disposal of harmful substances from ships into the ocean is strictly prohibited, unless it is essential to secure the safety of the ship or save life at sea.[3]

Annex IV generally prohibits discharge of sewage from ships into the sea and establishes specific requirements for allowable discharge.[4]

Annex V of the MARPOL Convention considers the control of marine pollution caused by garbage, including plastic from ships. It generally prohibits disposal of plastic into the sea, other than for ensuring the security of the ship, saving life at sea and accidental loss of garbage under certain circumstances.[5]

Apart from the general provisions about pollutant discharge, the MARPOL Convention also introduced a system for certification, survey and provision for reception facilities. The IMO also developed legal instruments for pollution preparedness, response and intervention. The International Convention on Oil Pollution Preparedness, Response and Co-operation, 1990 (OPRC); the Protocol on Preparedness, Response and Co-operation to Pollution Incidents by Hazardous and Noxious Substances, 2000 (OPRC-HNS Protocol) and the International Convention

Relating to Intervention on the High Seas in Cases of Oil Pollution Casualties, 1969 (Intervention), are relevant in this regard.

The IMO also developed a legal regime for liability and compensation for marine pollution. The most important legal instruments in this regime are the International Convention on Civil Liability for Oil Pollution Damage, 1992 (CLC, 1992, Replacing the 1969 CLC); the International Convention on the Establishment of an International Fund for Compensation for Oil Pollution Damage, 1992 (FUND, 1992, Replacing the 1971 Fund Convention); the International Convention on Liability and Compensation for Damage in Connection with the Carriage of Hazardous and Noxious Substances by Sea, 2010, and the International Convention on Civil Liability for Bunker Oil Pollution Damage, 2001.

The MARPOL Convention Annexes also contain provisions for designating special pollution and emissions control areas. Following these provisions, many special areas have been established under the Convention. The IMO also established a system for designating Particularly Sensitive Sea Areas (PSSAs). The IMO (2006, p. 3) defines PSSA as 'an area that needs special protection through action by IMO because of its significance for recognised ecological, socio-economic, or scientific attributes where such attributes may be vulnerable to damage by international shipping activities'. Having an area declared a PSSA by the IMO allows the coastal State to introduce especial protective measures, including ship routing, ship reporting and Vessel Traffic Services. The IMO has designated several areas as PSSAs, starting from the Great Barrier Reef PSSA in 1990.

Air pollution, energy efficiency and GHG emissions

A new Annex of the MARPOL Convention, namely, Annex VI, was adopted in 1997 for the prevention of air pollution from ships. It regulates emissions of nitrogen oxides (NOx) and sulphur oxides (SOx) and imposes a prohibition on deliberate emissions of ozone-depleting substances (IMO, 2017b; Lin & Lin, 2006). It also contains provisions for regulating shipboard incineration and emissions of volatile organic compounds from tankers. It was amended to progressively introduce more stringent emissions standards for NOx and SOx as well as for introducing emissions control areas (IMO, 2017b).

In 2011, the IMO adopted mandatory energy efficiency measures for international shipping (Karim, 2011; Karim, 2015, p. 108; Karim & Alam, 2011). A new chapter was added to Annex VI of MARPOL (IMO, 2011a). This chapter introduced a compulsory Energy Efficiency Design Index (EEDI) for new ships. The EEDI has binding obligations of GHG emissions reduction and establishes a minimum energy efficiency level per capita mile. This minimum level would vary by ship type and size (IMO, 2011a). The amendment also introduced the Ship Energy Efficiency Management Plan for all ships to improve energy efficiency of ships through adopting some operational measures. However, it only requires a plan and does not establish a specific standard for the plan or emissions reduction target for ships (IMO, 2011a). Therefore, the IMO is currently considering further technical and operational measures to enhance the energy efficiency of international shipping and to reduce GHGs emissions from ships (IMO, 2017a).

Ballast water and biofouling

In addition to the marine pollution mentioned in the previous sections of this chapter, two important sources of vessel-source pollution are dangerous aquatic organisms carried by ballast water and aquatic invasive species introduced by biofouling. (Davidson & Simkanin, 2012; Karim, 2015, p. 67).

In 2004, the IMO adopted the International Convention for the Control and Management of Ship's Ballast Water and Sediments (hereinafter BWM Convention) (Gollasch et al., 2007).[6] It requires all ships to implement a Ballast Water and Sediments Management Plan and a ballast water management process.[7] The Convention came into force in September 2017, that is, 12 years after the IMO adopted it. It requires each ship to have on board and implement a ship-specific Ballast Water Management Plan containing some minimum requirements it lists.[8] It also introduces a Ballast Water Record Book for recording every action concerning ballast water (Karim, 2015, p. 73).

Transfer of invasive aquatic species through biofouling is a major threat to the marine environment. The 'Guidelines for the Control and Management of Ships' Biofouling to Minimize the Transfer of Invasive Aquatic Species' was adopted by the IMO in 2011. It defines biofouling as 'the accumulation of aquatic organisms such as micro-organisms, plants and animals on surfaces and structures immersed in or exposed to the aquatic environment' and 'invasive aquatic species' as 'a species which may pose threats to human, animal and plant life, economic and cultural activities and the aquatic environment' (IMO, 2011b, p. 4). The guidelines were adopted to harmonise the global approach towards biofouling management. Although the guideline is only recommendatory and not mandatory (Karim, 2015, p. 79), it embodies a 'decisive step towards reducing the transfer of invasive aquatic species by ships' (IMO, 2017c).

Ships use anti-fouling paints to stop the accumulation of marine creatures on the hull because such accumulation slows down the ships. However, some substances used in these paints, including organotin tributyltin, are harmful to marine life (IMO, 2018). Therefore, the International Convention on the Control of Harmful Anti-fouling Systems on Ships (AFS Convention) prohibits and controls application, re-application, installation and use of harmful anti-fouling systems.[9]

Disposal of obsolete ships

Disposal of obsolete or end-of-life ships, also known as shipbreaking, leads to marine and coastal pollution as well as poses a serious threat to workers' safety in some developing countries (Karim, 2009a; Karim, 2010b; Karim, 2018, pp. 4–8). The Basel Convention on the Control of Transboundary Movements of Hazardous Wastes and their Disposal (Basel Convention) partly deals with the issue of transboundary movement and environmentally sound disposal of obsolete ships.

Enforcement of the provisions of this Convention to the transboundary movement of end-of-life vessels were technically and practically difficult (Karim, 2010b; Karim, 2018). Hence, ship recycling activities are now also regulated by the Hong Kong International Convention for the Safe and Environmentally Sound Recycling of Ships, 2009 (hereinafter Hong Kong Convention), adopted by the IMO.[10] The Hong Kong Convention is applicable to both 'ships entitled to fly the flag of a Party', and 'Ship Recycling Facilities operating under the jurisdiction of a Party'.[11] Therefore, the Convention obliges both flag States and ship recycling States to adopt measures so that the concerned ships and recycling facilities of both groups of States comply with the provisions of Convention.

As a general obligation to all parties, the Hong Kong Convention obliges parties 'to prevent, reduce, minimise and, to the extent practicable, eliminate accidents, injuries and other adverse effects on human health and the environment caused by Ship Recycling'.[12] However, to prevent various 'adverse effects on human health and the environment caused by Ship Recycling', the Convention requires the State parties to 'enhance ship safety, protection of human health and the environment throughout a ship's operating life'.[13]

In connection with 'green shipbuilding', the Convention obliges parties to 'prohibit and/or restrict the installation or use of Hazardous Materials listed in Appendix 1' of the Convention.[14] The Convention also introduced an inventory system for hazardous materials.[15]

Regarding ship recycling procedure, the Convention specifically requires that ships be recycled at authorised recycling facilities only[16] and that ship owners provide the concerned recycling facility with 'all available information relating to the ship for the development of the Ship Recycling Plan'.[17] Moreover, prior to entering a recycling facility, ship owners are required to take essential steps for minimising 'the amount of cargo residues, remaining fuel oil, and wastes remaining on board'.[18]

The Hong Kong Convention has received a few ratifications and is yet to come into force. It is a highly controversial legal instrument. Its future effectiveness is doubtful owing to some limitations:

> including ambiguity in ensuring standards of shipbreaking facilitates, lack of provision for pre-cleaning of ships, lack of provision for downstream management of hazardous materials, lack of effective provision for Safe-for-Hot-Work and Safe-for-Entry Certificates, and disregarding of international environmental law principles, human rights and global environmental justice.
>
> *(Karim, 2018, p. 83)*

Conclusion

Over the years, the IMO has developed numerous legal instruments introducing technical and operational measures for combating marine pollution from ships. Many of these instruments are arguably successful. However, their implementation in developing countries is generally lacking. The commitments within these instruments to provide technical and financial assistance to these countries have not been implemented or honoured (Karim, 2009b; Karim, 2010a). Moreover, there is a lack of political will in the developing world for implementation and enforcement of these instruments (Karim, 2009b; Karim, 2010a; Karim, 2015). Further, the flag State enforcement is weakened because of widespread use of flags of convenience.

Notes

1. International Convention for the Prevention of Pollution from Ships, opened for signature 2 November 1973, 1340 UNTS 184 as modified by the Protocol of 1978 to the 1973 Convention, opened for signature 17 February 1978, 1341 UNTS 3 (entered into force 2 October 1983), (hereinafter MARPOL 73/78/ MARPOL Convention), Annex III, regs. 2, 3, 6, 5, 4.
2. MARPOL Convention, Annex III, reg. 8.
3. MARPOL Convention, Annex III, reg. 7.
4. MARPOL Convention, Annex IV, reg. 2.
5. MARPOL Convention, Annex V, regs. 3, 4, 5, 6 and 7.
6. International Convention for the Control and Management of Ship's Ballast Water and Sediments, IMO Doc. BWM/CONF/36 (16 February 2004) (entered into force 8 September 2017 (hereinafter BWM Convention).
7. BWM Convention, reg. B-1 and reg. B-3.
8. BWM Convention, Annex, reg. B-1.
9. International Convention on the Control of Harmful Anti-fouling Systems on Ships 2001, IMO Doc. AFS/CONF/26 (5 October 2001) (entered into force 17 September 2008) (hereinafter AFS Convention), art 4(1).
10. Hong Kong International Convention for the Safe and Environmentally Sound Recycling of Ships, opened for signature 1 September 2009, IMO Doc. SR/CONF/45 (19 May 2009) (not yet in force) (hereinafter Hong Kong Convention).
11. Hong Kong Convention, Art. 3(1).
12. Hong Kong Convention, Art. 1(1).
13. Ibid.
14. Hong Kong Convention, Annex, reg. 4.1.
15. Hong Kong Convention, Annex, reg. 5.1.
16. Hong Kong Convention, Annex, reg. 8.1.
17. Hong Kong Convention, Annex, reg. 8.4.
18. Hong Kong Convention, Annex, reg. 8.2.

References

Davidson, I.C., & Simkanin, C. (2012). The biology of ballast water 25 years later. *Biological Invasions*, vol. 14, no. 1, pp. 9–13.

Gollasch, S., Matej David, M., Voigt, M., Dragsund, E., Hewitt, C., & Fukuyo, Y. (2007). Critical review of the IMO international convention on the management of ships' ballast water and sediments. *Harmful Algae*, vol. 6, no. 4, pp. 585–600.

International Maritime Organization (IMO). (2006). Resolution A.982 (24), Adopted on 1 December 2005, Revised Guidelines for the Identification and Designation of Particularly Sensitive Sea Areas. IMO Doc. A 24/Res.982 (6 February 2006).

International Maritime Organization (IMO). (2011a). *Report of the Marine Environment Protection Committee on Its Sixty-Second Session*, Annex 19, IMO Doc. MEPC 62/24/Add.1 (26 July 2011).

International Maritime Organization (IMO). (2011b). *Guidelines for the Control and Management of Ships' Biofouling to Minimize the Transfer of Invasive Aquatic Species*, Annex 26, IMO Doc. MEPC 62/24/Add.1.

International Maritime Organization (IMO). (2017a). *Report of the Marine Environment Protection Committee on Its Seventy-First Session*, IMO Doc. MEPC 71/17 (24 July 2017).

International Maritime Organization (IMO). (2017b). *Prevention of Air Pollution from Ships*, viewed 8 January 2018, www.imo.org/en/OurWork/environment/pollutionprevention/airpollution/pages/air-pollution.aspx.

International Maritime Organization (IMO). (2017c). *Biofouling*, viewed 5 January 2018, www.imo.org/en/OurWork/Environment/Biofouling/Pages/default.aspx.

International Maritime Organization (IMO). (2018). *Anti-Fouling Systems*, viewed 8 January 2018, www.imo.org/en/OurWork/Environment/Anti-foulingSystems/Pages/Default.aspx.

Karim, M.S. (2009a). Violation of Labour Rights in the Ship-Breaking Yards of Bangladesh: Legal Norms and Reality. *International Journal of Comparative Labour Law and Industrial Relations*, vol. 25, no. 4, pp. 379–394.

Karim, M.S. (2009b). 'Implementation of the MARPOL convention in Bangladesh. *Macquarie Journal of International and Comparative Environmental Law*, vol. 6, no. 1, pp. 51–82.

Karim, M.S. (2010a). Implementation of the MARPOL Convention in developing countries. *Nordic Journal of International Law*, vol. 79, no. 2, pp. 303–337.

Karim, M.S. (2010b). Environmental pollution from shipbreaking industry: International law and national legal response. *Georgetown International Environmental Law Review*, vol. 22, no. 2, pp. 185–240.

Karim, M.S. (2011). IMO mandatory energy efficiency measures for international shipping: The first mandatory global greenhouse gas reduction instrument for an international industry. *Macquarie Journal of International and Comparative Environmental Law*, vol. 7, no. 1, pp. 111–113.

Karim, M.S. (2015). *Prevention of Pollution of the Marine Environment from Vessels: The Potential and Limits of the International Maritime Organization*. Springer, Heidelberg.

Karim, M.S. (2018). *Shipbreaking in Developing Countries: A Requiem for Environmental Justice from the Perspective of Bangladesh*, Routledge, London.

Karim, M.S., & Alam, S. (2011). Climate change and reduction of emissions of greenhouse gases from ships: An appraisal. *Asian Journal of International Law*, vol. 1 no 1, pp. 131–148.

Lin, B., & Lin, C.-Y. (2006). Compliance with international emission regulations: Reducing the air pollution from merchant vessels. *Marine Policy*, vol. 30, no. 3, pp. 220–225.

Ringbom, H. (2015). Vessel-source pollution, in R. Rayfuse (ed.), *Research Handbook on International Marine Environmental Law*, Edward Elgar, Cheltenham, pp. 105–131.

Wolfrum, R. (1999). IMO interface with the law of the sea convention, in M.H. Nordquist & J.N. Moore (eds), *Current Maritime Issues and the International Maritime Organization*, Martinus Nijhoff Publishers, The Hague, pp. 223–236.

5
CONTROL AND PREVENTION OF MARINE POLLUTION FROM OFFSHORE HYDROCARBON AND MINERAL RESOURCES EXPLORATION AND PRODUCTION ACTIVITIES

Hossein Esmaeili

Introduction

Offshore hydrocarbon and mineral resources exploration and production are a major global economic development activity. It is estimated that the majority, or nearly all, of undeveloped petroleum resources and reserves in Africa, Europe, the Pacific, North America, and Latin America are offshore (World Energy Outlook, 2008). It is also anticipated that offshore hydrocarbon activities will be a major future economic development in the Arctic region (Hossain, Koivurova, & Zojer, 2014).

Offshore hydrocarbon development is risky for the marine environment as it requires the involvement of harmful substances for the exploration and exploitation of resources, and entails discharges and emissions. Further, accidental pollution, blowout and oil spills are significant environmental risks accompanying offshore hydrocarbon and mineral operations. The recent examples of major offshore accidents include the Montara Platform Blowout between the coasts of Australia and Indonesia in 2009 and the Deepwater Horizon oil spill off the Gulf of Mexico in 2010. In the first catastrophic incident, 250 kilometres Northwest from the Kimberly coastline of Western Australia, the Montara rig leaked for 74 days. The Deepwater Horizon leak continued for 87 days in 2010. Both incidents led to the involvement of several States, many multinational corporations, other legal entities, and a large number of individuals in significant international and domestic legal disputes.

The issue of the prevention and control of marine pollution from offshore petroleum and mineral resources operations has been the subject of international law, including global and regional legal instruments, and national law and policy responses. There have also been ad hoc regional and national legal and policy-based responses to major accidents, which have had significant international impacts.

This chapter will first review and examine the global international legal regime relating to marine pollution from offshore oil and gas activities (including binding and non-binding international instruments). Then, significant regional agreements and arrangements will be examined. National legal responses, including legal and policy-based responses to international accidents, particularly from Australia, will be reviewed and discussed. Finally, the effectiveness of existing global, regional and national frameworks will be analysed.

Background

Offshore oil and gas production has occurred for several decades. In the last two decades, however, significant technological advances have led to the possibility of exploring offshore oil and gas fields at water depths of up to three kilometres: 20 years ago, it was only possible to explore offshore fields at a depth of about one kilometre.

Offshore oil and gas production accounted for 30% of the world's total production in 2014, a significant increase from 20% in 1980. This growth is expected to continue. Further, considering that most oil and gas field discoveries were made offshore in the last decade, largely in deep-water Brazil, it is expected that offshore oil and gas production growth will continue to exceed the growth of onshore production (Brakenhoff, 2015).

The exploration of offshore hydrocarbon and other mineral resources, such as tin and offshore phosphate, may, however, have adverse impacts on marine ecosystems and biological resources.

Marine pollution is defined as 'the introduction by man, directly or indirectly, of substances or energy into the marine environment, including estuaries, which results or is likely to result in such deleterious effects as harm to living resources and marine life, hazards to human health, hindrance to marine activities, including fishing and other legitimate uses of the sea, impairment of quality for use of seawater and reduction of amenities'.[1]

Offshore hydrocarbon is the main problem for marine pollution, and it may cause severe biological and chemical changes to the ocean. Marine pollution is classified as a land-based source of pollution (Hassan, 2006). Two major threats to the marine environment are caused by pollution from seabed activities and dumping, and both of these sources of pollution are related to offshore exploration and production activities.

The first source of marine pollution can be identified as a result of offshore hydrocarbon exploration and exploitation activities, this may be caused by the process of operation (including the exploration and exploitation of offshore oil and gas), accidents and the disposal and decommissioning of offshore oil installations.

During the operational process, a number of stages are involved: surveying, exploration, development and operation (Patin, 1999). There are more than 800 chemicals and substances which may endanger the marine environment during the offshore oil and gas operations (Patin, 1999).

The second source of marine pollution, caused through the process of offshore oil and gas development and production, is accidents, largely involving offshore oil rigs, resulting in the discharge of petroleum into the sea. For example, in 2009, the Montara platform blowout between the coast of Australia and Indonesia resulted in the discharge of about 2,000 barrels of oil per day into the sea for nearly two and a half months (Australia. Montara Commission of Inquiry & Borthwick, 2010). Following the incident, a Montara Commission of Inquiry was established by the Australian government. The government responded to the Enquiry Report with a further report containing 100 findings and 105 recommendations for the government and regulators of Australian the offshore oil industry.[2]

Global legal regime

International regulations to prevent, reduce and control pollution of the marine environment arising from offshore oil and gas operations are subject to various international instruments such as global treaties, the rules of customary law, non-binding soft law provisions as well as domestic law provisions. There is no single and comprehensive treaty specifically regulating pollution from these operations. Significantly, the Law of the Sea Convention obligates Member States to adopt laws and regulations aimed at preventing, reducing and controlling the pollution of the marine environment arising from, or in connection with, seabed activities (which include activities for the exploration for and exploitation of offshore oil and gas resources).[3] It is also notable that international law principles relating to pollution from offshore hydrocarbon operations can be found in areas of international law such as dumping at sea, seabed activities, land-based sources of pollution and offshore pollution incidents (oil spills, collisions, oil rig blowouts, etc.). Likewise, some other areas of international environmental law, such as the carriage of oil at sea (by ships and pipelines) and collisions, may have certain laws and regulations which may be relevant to the operation of offshore oil and gas activities.

In examining the global legal regime relating to marine pollution from offshore hydrocarbon activities, we will discuss the relevant regulations of the Law of the Sea Convention (regulations relating to the control of pollution of the marine environment from seabed activities, land-based sources, dumping and vessels).

The Law of the Sea Convention

The Law of the Sea Convention, with 168 parties, is the most comprehensive international treaty, and one of the most influential global treaties relating to the protection of the marine environment. It also provides certain specific principles in relation to pollution from offshore oil and gas activities. Since the beginnings of the formulation of the Law of the Sea in the 1950s, and 1982 when the Law of the Sea Convention was concluded, and particularly since 1994, when the LOSC was entered into force, the Convention has significantly influenced the development of international environmental law with respect to the protection of the marine environment including pollution from offshore oil and gas activities. Given the widespread influences of the Law of the Sea Convention, particularly its rules on the protection of the marine environment, many States, international instruments and international legal scholars consider the Law of the Sea provisions on the protection of the marine environment as reflecting principles of customary international law.[4]

The relevant provisions of the Law of the Sea concerning protection and preservation of the marine environment are contained in Part XII of the Convention. This part includes 11 sections and includes Articles 192 to 237. The Convention acknowledges the sovereign right of States to exploit their natural resources but, at the same time, impose on them the duties to protect and preserve the marine environment.[5] This general obligation is followed by more detailed provisions of Article 194 which requires State parties to take measures to prevent, reduce and control pollution of the marine environment, including from 'installations and devices used in exploration or exploitation of the natural resources of the seabed and subsoil'.[6] The Convention treats pollution from offshore oil installations under pollution arising from seabed activities. Article 208 of the Convention obliges State parties to adopt laws and regulations in order to prevent, reduce and control pollution of the marine environment arising from or in connection with seabed activities and from artificial islands, installations and structures under the jurisdiction.[7] The provisions of Article 208 are complementary to provisions of Article 194(3)(c), which requires the State parties to take measures to prevent, reduce and control pollution of the marine environment from offshore oil installations (for details, please see Esmaeili, 2001).

The nature of the measures to be adopted by the coastal States with respect to offshore installations is unclear. Article 208 provides only general obligations for taking appropriate measures, including legal measures, to protect the marine environment from offshore activities relating to oil and gas production. Also, the coastal States may take measures and provide provisions for the protection of the environment within their national jurisdictions. This includes the territorial waters, the exclusive economic zone, and waters above the continental shelf. It should be noted that the 1994 Agreement on the Implementation of Part XI (The New York Agreement) states that any plan for exploration and exploitation of international seabed areas must be 'accompanied by an assessment of the potential environmental impacts of the proposed activities and by a description of a programme for oceanographic and baseline environmental studies in accordance with the rules, regulations and procedures adopted by the Authority'.[8] The Convention further obliges the State parties to cooperate on a global and regional basis and directly and through international organisations in order to formulate and elaborate international rules, standards and recommended practices and procedures for the protection and preservation of the marine environment.[9]

Article 235 of the LOSC holds State parties to the Convention responsible for the fulfilment of their international obligations in relation to the protection and prevention of the marine environment. The article provides that State parties shall be liable in accordance with international law.[10]

It has been said elsewhere (Esmaeili, 2001) that while the Law of the Sea Convention purported to establish a comprehensive global framework for protection of the marine environment, it lacks a developed procedure for the enforcement of its general provisions in relation to the protection of the marine environment from the exploration and exploitation of hydrocarbons from the sea. Unfortunately, about 35 years after the conclusion of the Convention, this is still the case. Nevertheless, there have been significant developments after the conclusion of the Law of the Sea Convention, particularly since the 1994 Agreement relating to the Implementation of Part XI. These include some reginal developments as well as considerable judicial and case developments by international tribunals including the International Tribunal for the Law of the Sea. For example the International Tribunal for the Law of the Sea, in an advisory opinion (Responsibilities and Obligations of States with Respect to Activities in the Area, 1 February 2011, ITLOS Reports 2011, p. 10) held that State parties and international organisations shall bear joint and several liability in relation to their failure to comply with the provisions of the Convention in particular Part XI when engaging in activities in the Area.[11] In addition, the advisory opinion held that the Precautionary Principle, as stated in Principle 15 of the Rio Declaration on Environment and Development 1992, should be applied by States which engage in offshore activities the Area.[12]

There are several other global treaties, which have regulations with respect to the protection of the marine environment in general, that may have specific provisions concerning control and prevention of marine pollution from offshore exploration and exploitation of natural resources.

The 1972 London Convention and its 1996 Protocol

The 1972 Convention on the Prevention of Marine Pollution by Dumping of Waste and Other Matter (London Convention) and its 1996 Protocol (London Protocol) oblige the parties at the Convention to promote the effective control of all sources of marine pollution and to take all practicable steps to prevent the pollution of the sea by the dumping of waste and other materials that may harm marine environment.[13] The Convention prohibits the contracting parties from the disposal and dumping of certain waste or materials such as crude oil and high-level radioactive waste.[14] However, certain other materials and waste may be dumped at sea with a prior special or general permit.[15] The Convention prohibits the dumping of waste and materials from offshore platforms, operating for exploration and exploitation of hydrocarbon and the disposal and dumping of offshore oil platforms without prior permission.[16] However, the disposal at sea of waste or other matter incidental to normal operations of platforms or vessels and their equipment is not included into the definition of prohibited dumping.[17] The London Protocol, which entered into force on 24 March 2006, built on and further modernises the principles of the London Convention. The Protocol widens the definition of dumping to include any storage of waste or other matter in the seabed and the subsoil from offshore platforms, and any abandonment, or toppling at site of platforms for the sole purpose of deliberate disposal.[18] The London Protocol embraces the precautionary principle which requires that

> appropriate preventative measures are taken when there is reason to believe that waste or other matter introduced into the marine environment are likely to cause harm even when there is no conclusive evidence to provide a causal relation between inputs and their affects.[19]

According to the International Maritime Organisation (IMO) an average of 500 million tonnes of permitted dredged materials are dumped annually in waters of countries which have signed the London Convention or London Protocol.[20] Further, the IMO states that the collaborative efforts among the contracting parties to the London Protocol have resulted in a significant decreasing of dumping of the disposal of several wastes.[21] The London Convention and its Protocol are specifically concerned with the disposal of waste and materials at sea. Given that one of the major sources of marine environmental pollution results from offshore oil activities and concerns the disposal of wastes, the London Convention and its Protocol, apart from the Law of the Sea Convention, are the most important international treaties relating to the protection of the marine environment concerning pollution from Offshore Hydrocarbon and Mineral Resources Exploration and Production Activities. However, it is notable that the London Convention and the London Protocol do not prohibit disposal at sea of wastes or other matter incidental to, or derived from, the normal operations of platforms or artificial structures and their equipment. This may mean that the effective protection of the marine environment from offshore oil and gas operation may require a specific instrument which can cover all aspects of marine pollution that may result from offshore oil operations including accidental incidents.

1990 OPRC and 1973 MARPOL

The 1990 International Convention on Oil Pollution Preparedness, Response and Cooperation (OPRC)[22] was concluded to develop measures to prevent pollution from ships. In March 2000 the Protocol on preparedness, response and cooperation to pollution incidents by hazardous and noxious substances was adopted.[23] This Convention covers pollution from offshore oil and gas installations and hence is the most specific international treaty that addresses the issue of pollution from offshore oil and gas operations. While the LOSC provides general obligations for contracting parties for the protection of the marine environment, and the London Convention and its Protocol are concerned with disposal of waste at sea, the OPRC provides specific provisions to protect the marine environment from oil pollution. The Convention covers oil pollution from offshore units, which means 'any fixed or floating or offshore instillation or structure engaged in gas or oil exploration, exploitation or production activities, or loading or unloading of oil'.[24] The Convention provides provisions in relation to oil pollution emergency plans, oil pollution reporting procedure, national and regional systems for preparedness and response, international cooperation in pollution response and research and development.[25] The OPRS is currently the most efficient international treaty concerning the protection of marine environment including from offshore oil and gas operations. (Esmaeili, 2001; Kashubsky, 2006).

The International Convention for Prevention of Pollution from Ships (MARPOL) was adopted in 1973 and its protocol was adopted in 1978.[26] The Convention and its protocol entered into force on 2 October 1983. In 1997 a protocol was adopted amending the Convention and adding a new annex that entered into force on 19 May 2005. MARPOL has been significantly amended in the last decades. While the Convention is primarily concerned with ships, it also applies to fixed offshore oil rigs. The Convention defines 'ship' as a 'vessel of any type whatsoever operating in the marine environment and includes hydrofoil boats, air-cushion vehicles, submersibles, floating craft and fixed or floating platforms'.[27] The Convention's regulations (in Annex I) are applicable to fixed or floating platforms, including drilling rigs, floating production, storage and offloading facilities used for the offshore production and storage of oil and floating storage units used for offshore storage of produced oil.[28] Further, the Convention requires fixed or floating offshore oil rigs when engaged in the exploration, exploitation and associated offshore processing of seabed mineral resources to comply with the requirement applicable to ships of 400 gross tonnage.[29] Every ship of 400 gross tonnage and above shall be provided with a tank or tanks of adequate capacity, having regard to the type of machinery and length of voyage, to receive the oil residues (sludge) which cannot be dealt with otherwise in accordance with the requirement of this annex (Annex I).[30]

International Convention on the Control of Harmful Anti-Fouling Systems on Ships 2001 (AFS Convention)

This treaty[31] is a more recent international instrument, which intends to prohibit and/or restrict the use of certain harmful materials on ships and offshore oil installations. The Convention was adopted in 2001 and entered into force 7 September 2010 and currently has over 70 parties. The Convention covers the application or the installation or use of harmful anti-fouling systems on ships and fixed or floating offshore oil and gas platforms.[32] The Convention prohibits the use of certain substances on ships and offshore installations such as organotin compounds, which act as biocides in anti-fouling systems from certain dates.[33] The treaty can be related to the international legal framework of the protection of the marine environment as well as the general protection of the earth environment. It covers certain areas which are related to areas subject of other international treaties such as the 1982 LOSC, the 1992 Convention on Biodiversity, the Basel Convention, climate change–related international instruments, and many other regional or international environmental treaties (Gipperth, 2009). Given that this treaty specifically covers offshore oil installations used in the exploration and exploitation of offshore hydrocarbon resources it is relevant to the broad area of control of marine pollution from offshore oil and gas activities. Nevertheless, its application is related only to the use of certain substances in ships and offshore oil rigs.

Draft international offshore oil rigs convention

For the exploration and exploitation of natural resources of the sea, various mobile and fixed offshore installations and crafts are used. Some of these installations may be treated as 'ships' for the purpose of some international treaties or domestic legislation and some others may be treated as artificial islands or other categories. In spite of an increasing number, as well as the growing commercial importance, of these installations there is no specific international treaty regulating various legal aspects of these installations. However, since 1977, there have been attempts to draft a convention on offshore installations. The Comite Maritime Internationale (CMI) drafted a Convention on Offshore Mobile Craft at a conference Rio de Janeiro, Brazil in 1977 (Rio Draft). This draft was considered again at the CMI conference in 1994 in Sydney. In this conference, a revised version of the Rio Draft was adopted known as the Sydney Draft. In the Sydney conference, a working group and a committee were established for further study and development of an international Convention on Offshore Units (White, 1999). However, the IMO legal committee, in their 83rd session, in 2001, removed the issue from its working programmes (Kashubsky, 2006). Nevertheless, the Canadian Maritime Law Association prepared a draft convention and presented to the CMI Units Working Group in 2001.[34] This draft convention covers a large number of legal issues relating to offshore installations and crafts such as ownership, registration, pollution, jurisdiction, salvage, decommissioning and occupational safety. It has been said that the Canadian draft fairly covers all types of offshore oil rigs and installations and applies to a range of important legal issues including some environmental aspects.

While international law extensively regulates shipping and navigation at sea in various international instruments, there is no international treaty relating to various types of offshore oil installations. Maritime law and shipping law are very traditional areas of international law. Offshore installations, used in exploration for and exploitation of hydrocarbon resources, deal with very similar international legal issues within the realms of navigation and maritime law. Also, similar environmental issues may be caused by offshore oil operations. An international treaty covering various legal aspects of offshore oil and gas installations, including effective regulations for the protection of the marine environment and prevention of serious international accidents, must be at the top of the agenda for international organisations.

Regional arrangements

Several regional treaties address the issue of pollution from offshore oil and gas activities. Indeed, regional treaties, in comparison with global conventions, cover the issue of pollution from oil installations in more detail and in a more effective way. Since early 1970 regional conventions addressed the issue of the prevention of marine pollution, including pollution from offshore oil and gas activities.

The 1974 Paris Convention for the Prevention of Marine Pollution from Land Based Sources is one of the earliest international treaties covering some aspects of marine pollution from offshore oil and gas operations. The Convention includes pollution from offshore oil and gas activities (through offshore artificial structures) in its definition of the 'pollution from land based sources'.[35] This Convention was amended by the Protocol of 26 March 1986. The Paris Convention and the Convention for the Prevention of Marine Pollution by Dumping from Ships and Aircraft, 1972, were replaced in 1992 by the Convention for the Protection of the Marine Environment of the North-East Atlantic (OSPAR Convention). The OSPAR Convention is the European treaty for the protection of the marine environment of the North Atlantic region. The Convention covers pollution from offshore sources, offshore installations and any vessel placed within the maritime area for the purpose of offshore activities. The Convention obliges contracting parties to prevent and eliminate pollution from offshore sources and prohibits the dumping of waste from offshore oil installations and the discharge or emissions of any substances that may damage the marine environment.[36]

Another European treaty is the Convention for the Protection of the Marine Environment of the Baltic Sea Area, which was adopted in Helsinki in 1992 and entered into force in 2000, replacing the 1974 Baltic Convention. This Convention covers marine pollution from land-based sources (including from offshore oil and gas activities and ships).[37] The Convention regulates discharges of oil and other matters during the exploration for and exploitation of offshore hydrocarbon resources.[38] The Convention requires State parties to remove from the marine environment all disused, abandoned or wrecked offshore oil rigs and to plug disused offshore oil wells.[39]

Three other regional conventions cover the Mediterranean Sea, the Persian Gulf and the Caspian Sea. The 1995 Barcelona Convention and its 1994 Madrid Protocol cover legal issues of hydrocarbon exploration and exploitation in the Mediterranean Sea. The Barcelona Convention[40] was adopted in order to protect the Mediterranean marine and costal environment and to reduce marine pollution whether land or sea based. The Convention and its Protocols provide rules and regulations and norms as well as legal grounds for institutional arrangements to address marine pollution in the Mediterranean Sea.[41] The Barcelona Convention has seven protocols addressing specific aspects of marine environment of the Mediterranean Sea. The protocols include the Land Based Sources and Activities Protocol and the Offshore Protocol (pollution from exploration and exploitation).[42] The Offshore Protocol, while specific to the Mediterranean region, is one of the most important international instruments specifically addressing marine pollution resulting from offshore exploration and exploitation of natural resources. According to the Protocol, all activities, including the construction of installations for the exploration and exploitation of oil and gas, should be subject of prior authorisation based on international standards and practice.[43] In order to ensure protection of the marine environment against exploration for and exploitation of offshore hydrocarbon resources, the Protocol covers issues such as harmful waste and substances, oil and oily mixtures, drilling fluids and cuttings, sewage, safety measures, contingency planning, decommissioning and removal of instillations and transboundary pollution.[44]

The 1975 Kuwait Convention[45] is concerned with the marine environment of the Persian Gulf, which is one of the most polluted seas in the world. The Persian Gulf is also an important offshore oil and gas-rich area of the world. The Convention includes four associated protocols including the 1990 Protocol for protection of the marine environment against pollution from land-based sources and 1989 Protocol on marine pollution resulting from exploration and exploitation of the continental shelf. The Convention established the Regional Organisation for Protection of Marine Environment (ROPME). Since its establishment the ROPME has made considerable contributions to the marine environment health of the Persian Gulf region (Nadim, Bagtzoglou, & Iranmahboob, 2008).

Another more recent regional convention for the protection of the environment, which also has a specific provision to protect the marine environment from offshore oil and gas operations is the 2003 Tehran Convention for the protection of the marine environment of the Caspian Sea.[46] The Caspian Sea is the largest landlocked lake on Earth and is rich in natural resources including hydrocarbon. The area has significant oil and natural gas reserves where offshore fields account for about 41% of the total Caspian crude oil and 36% of natural gas.[47] The area is significantly polluted by industrial, agricultural and radioactive pollution as well as from offshore oil and gas operations. The Tehran Convention is a regional treaty which is legally binding and is ratified by all five Caspian States.[48] There are four protocols to the Tehran Convention namely the Protocol on Conservation of Biological Diversity, the Protocol for the Protection of the Caspian Sea against Pollution from Land based Sources and Activities, the Protocol Concerning Regional Preparedness, Response and Cooperation in Combating Oil Pollution Incidents, and the Protocol on Environment Impact Assessment in a Transboundary Context.[49] The Convention requires parties to prevent, reduce and control pollution from land-based sources, seabed activities, vessels and pollution caused by dumping and introduction of invasive alien species.[50] The Convention defines 'vessel' to include platforms and other man-made offshore structures.[51] The Tehran Convention and its protocols lay down general requirements and institutional mechanisms for the protection of the marine environment of the Caspian Sea. It is fair to say that the Convention and its protocols cover extensively most legal issues arising from offshore hydrocarbon exploration and exploitation, which may adversely affect the marine environment of the region. Also the Convention incorporates certain principles such as the precautionary principle, the polluter-pays principle and the principle of access to information.[52] While the effectiveness of this Convention and its protocols in protecting the marine environment from pollution, particularly pollution resulting from offshore oil and gas operations, must be seen in practice, the Tehran Convention is a well-developed and comprehensive regional agreement and draws from UNEP's regional sea treaties to establish cooperation obligations and to provide provisions for dispute settlement (Sands & Peel, 2012).

There are also some other regional or international instruments, which have some provisions in relation to the protection of the marine environment from exploration for and exploitation of offshore hydrocarbon resources. These international instruments include some international treaties as well as instruments adopted by relevant maritime organisations such as IMO and UNEP.[53]

While there is no comprehensive international treaty in relation to the protection of the marine environment from offshore hydrocarbon operations, there are several well-developed regional arrangements in some offshore areas such as the Mediterranean Sea, the Persian Gulf and the Caspian Sea. Given that, at this stage, most offshore oil and gas exploration and exploitation are undertaken in the continental shelf off the coastal States, it seems that the majority of States prefer regional and bilateral treaties to cover pollution from offshore gas and oil operations.

National legal and policy response

States, particularly countries involved in significant offshore oil and gas activities, have enacted laws and policies to combat marine pollution resulting from exploration for and exploitation of offshore hydrocarbon sources.

In Europe, countries involved in offshore oil operations in the North Sea, while largely relying on international and regional treaties to combat marine oil pollution, have also developed policies and legislation to regulate oil drilling activities. However, most of the existing EU-legislation covers activities within the coastal State area of internal and territorial waters (Bosma, 2012).

In the Gulf of Mexico, marine oil pollution from offshore oil activities are regulated by various State jurisdictions involved in offshore oil activities in the area. The United States Government has a bureau within the Department of the Interior known as the Bureau of Ocean Energy Management, Regulation and Enforcement. Marine pollution caused by offshore oil activities is governed by the *Oil Pollution Act 1990*. The legislation regulates both oil transport facilities as well as offshore oil platforms used for exploration, drilling and production (Boyd, 2006).

Australia

The principal legislation in Australia governing offshore oil and gas exploration and production is the *Offshore Petroleum and Greenhouse Gas Storage Act 2006* (Cth). The legislation provides a regulatory framework for offshore petroleum exploration and recovery. The Act applies to the Australian territorial sea and extends seaward to the outer limits of the continental shelf. The regulatory system for offshore petroleum operations in Australia was the subject of intense scrutiny after the Montara platform accident. The Montara Commission of Inquiry highlighted the existing shortcomings and suggested legislative changes to improve safety and operational practices in Australian offshore areas. The report recommended regulatory reform by establishing a single independent regulatory body looking after safety as a primary objective, well integrity and environmental management.[54] In May 2012, the Minister for Resources and Energy introduced amendments into the parliament to modify the *Offshore Petroleum and Greenhouse Gas Storage Act 2006* (Cth). The amendment through the *Offshore Petroleum and Greenhouse Gas Storage Amendment (National Regulator) Act 2011* (Cth) created the National Offshore Petroleum Titles Administrator. The new administrator intends to produce better regulatory results to prevent accidents and to protect marine environment from offshore oil and gas activities (Chandler & Daintith, 2015).

International customary law

Besides international and regional treaties, international customary law may have a secondary role in creating binding principles for the protection of the marine environment including from offshore hydrocarbon operations. Since international environmental law and particularly protection of the marine environment is relatively of a recent origin. Customary international law principles in this area may not be clear. In the *Iron Rhine* Arbitration it was noted that it is debatable as to 'which environmental treaty law or principles have contributed to the development of customary international law'.[55] However, certain principles of law such as the principle of *sic utere tuo ut alienum non laedas* (A State's obligation in using its own territory in a manner not to damage other territories) may support a principle of customary international law relating to the protection of the marine environment. The principle of *sic utere tuo* has been referred to in many international instruments including the Charter of Economic Rights and Duties of States[56] and the Law of the Sea Convention.[57] In terms of international environmental law, this principle was referenced in the Principle 21 of the 1972 Stockholm Declaration on the Human Environment.[58] The principle was also referred to in a number of cases such as Corfu Channel[59] and the Nuclear Test cases.[60]

With the Award of the Arbitration Tribunal in the Trail Smelter Case, which arose out of a dispute between the United States and Canada in relation to emissions from a smelter suite situated in Canada causing damage in the State of Washington, the tribunal affirmed the principle that a State has no right to use or permit the use of their territory in such a manner as to cause injury to the territory of other States.[61] This award, decided in 1941, 'has come to represent a crystallising moment for international law, which has influenced subsequent developments in a manner that undoubtedly exceeds its true value as an authoritative legal determination' (Sands & Peel, 2012, p. 26).

It is arguable that, besides treaty obligations, the application of the principle of *sic utere tuo*, in light of developments (both in terms of international instruments and case law), indicates the existence of customary international law principles for States not to pollute the marine environment beyond their jurisdictions.

Major international offshore oil rig accidents

While a significant source of marine pollution is oil pollution caused by vessels, offshore oil rig accidents cause both marine pollution as well as complicated national and international legal issues with respect to oil pollution, civil liability and international responsibility. Since the 1960s there have been a large number of oil rig accidents in the world creating some of the worst offshore environmental disasters.[62] In recent years, there have been a number of oil rig accidents including the Montara Wellhead Platform in Australia (August 2009), Deepwater Horizon oil rig in the Gulf of Mexico (April 2010) and Chevron Nigeria Ltd oil rig which exploded in January 2012. The Deepwater Horizon oil rig accident is one of the worst environmental disasters in US history where 11 people were killed and millions of barrels of oil were discharged into the sea. This accident caused complex legal issues involving multiple parties in areas such as maritime law, common law, statutory law and international law (Richards, 2011; Sundaram, 2016). British Petroleum agreed in 2015 to pay 18.7 billion dollars to settle the Deepwater Horizon oil spill claims, which brought the settlement of all federal and State claims total costs to nearly 54 billion dollars (Gilbert & Kent, 2015).

The 2009 Montara oil rig accident involved an oil rig placed on Australian waters which leaked oil for 74 days[63] polluting part of the Indonesian Exclusive Economic Zone. The accident is described as 'the worst of its kind in Australia's offshore petroleum'.[64] The Montara oil rig disaster resulted in establishing a commission of inquiry and the government response to the Report of the Montara Commission of Inquiry[65] as well as a class action in the Federal Court of Australia for compensation for Indonesian seaweed farmers.

The increased number of offshore oil rig accidents and the pollution caused by these accidents has at some level promoted international activities for developing international instruments to deal with relevant legal issues including compensation. For example, it is proposed that 'there is an imperative need for an international convention to regulate the risks and consequences of existing and future offshore drilling activities' (Rares, 2012, p. 12).

Conclusion

Marine pollution, resulting from offshore hydrocarbon exploration and exploitation activities may be caused by offshore oil and gas operation or process or/and through the process, or by offshore accidents mainly involving offshore oil rigs discharging significant amounts of petroleum into the sea. While there is no single specific and comprehensive international treaty to control and prevent marine pollution from offshore hydrocarbon and mineral resources, this area is the subject of sporadic coverage by various international and regional treaties as well as international cases and national law and legislation. The 1982 Law of the Sea Convention, the 1972 London Convention, the 1990 OPRC and the 1973 MARPOL are the major international conventions which have certain provisions in relation to the protection of the marine environment from offshore oil and gas operations. None of these treaties are specifically adopted to combat and control marine pollution resulting from offshore hydrocarbon and mineral resources operations. However, each of those treaties has provided some relevant provisions that were discussed in this chapter. Regional treaties have more specifically covered the protection of the marine environment from offshore oil and gas activities. The regional arrangements in Europe, Mediterranean Sea, the Persian Gulf and the Caspian Sea have dealt with the issue of marine environment protection from offshore oil and gas activities in a more comprehensive manner.

In recent years, major international offshore oil rig accidents and significant discharge of oil into the marine environment has put oil rig accidents on the agenda of international law.

It seems that international law provisions in relation to offshore hydrocarbon and mineral resources exploration and exploitation are fragmented and sporadically covered in various international instruments. Given the increased offshore oil and gas activities in recent years and the prospect of further development in the future, an international treaty specifically for combating marine pollution from offshore oil and gas activities covering various legal aspects of offshore oil and gas installations may be suggested.

Notes

1 *Law of the Sea Convention*, Art 1(1)(4).
2 See Department of Resources, Energy and Tourism, *Final Government Response to the Report of the Montara Commission of Inquiry*, Commonwealth of Australia, 2011. See also, Tina Hunter, 'The Montara Oil Spill and the National Marine Oil Spill Contingency Plan: Disaster Response or Just a Disaster?' (2010) 24(2) *Australian and New Zealand Maritime Law Journal* 46; Michael G Faure, 'In the Aftermath of the Disaster: Liability and Compensation Mechanisms as Tools to Reduce Disaster Risks' (2016) 52(1) *Stanford Journal of International Law* 95; Tina Hunter, 'Offshore Petroleum Facility Incidents Post Varanus Island, Montara, and Macondo: Have we Really Addressed the Root Cause?' (2014) 38(3) *William & Mary Environmental Law and Policy* 585; and Simon Marsden, 'Regulatory Reform of Australia's Offshore Oil and Gas Sector After the Montara Commission of Inquiry: What About Transboundary Environmental Impact Assessment?' (2013) 15 *Flinders Law Journal* 41.
3 LOSC Art 208(1).
4 See the 1992 OSPAR Convention (Preamble to the Convention) which states that the relevant provisions in Part XII of the Law of the Sea Convention and, in particular, Article 197 are reflecting provisions of customary international law. See also Sands et al., 'Principles of International Environmental Law' (Cambridge, 3rd ed., 2012), 350.
5 The Law of the Sea Convention Article 193.
6 The Law of the Sea Convention, Article 194(3)(c).
7 The Law of the Sea Convention Article 208(1).
8 The 1999 Agreement to the Law of the Sea Convention, Annex, Section 7.
9 The Law of the Sea Convention, Article 197.
10 The Law of the Sea Convention, Article 235 (1).
11 Responsibilities and Obligations of States with Respect to Activities in the Area, 1 February 2011, ITLOS Reports 2011, p. 10, Question 2.

12 Rio Declaration on Environment and Development 1992, Principle 15, Question 3.
13 1972 Convention of the Prevention of Marine Pollution by Dumping of Waste and Other Matter, Article 1.
14 1972 Convention of the Prevention of Marine Pollution by Dumping of Waste and Other Matter, Article IV and Annex I.
15 1972 Convention of the Prevention of Marine Pollution by Dumping of Waste and Other Matter, Article IV and Annex II.
16 1972 Convention of the Prevention of Marine Pollution by Dumping of Waste and Other Matter, Article III.
17 1972 Convention of the Prevention of Marine Pollution by Dumping of Waste and Other Matter, Article III (1)(b)(i).
18 1996 Protocol to the Convention of Prevention of Marine Pollution by Dumping of Waste and Other Matter 1972, Article I (4).
19 1996 Protocol to the Convention of Prevention of Marine Pollution by Dumping of Waste and Other Matter 1972, Article 3 (1).
20 International Maritime Organisation, The London Protocol – What It Is And Why It Is Needed, London Protocol 1996, p. 1.
21 International Maritime Organisation, The London Protocol – What It Is And Why It Is Needed, London Protocol 1996, p. 3.
22 1990 International Convention on All Pollution Preparedness, Response and Cooperation, 30 ILM (1991) 733. In March 2000 State parties to the OPRC convention adopted a protocol on the OPRC aimed to establish national systems for preparedness and response and to provide a global framework for international cooperation in combating major incidents or threats of marine pollution specifically in relation to incidents involving hazardous and noxious substances. For the text of the Protocol see: https://cil.nus.edu.sg/rp/il/pdf/2000%20Protocol%20on%20PRC%20to%20Pollution%20Incidents%20by%20Hazardous%20Substances-pdf.pdf.
23 Protocol on Preparedness, Response and Co-operation to Pollution Incidents by Hazardous and Noxious Substances, 2000.
24 1990 International Convention on All Pollution Preparedness, Response and Cooperation, Article 2 (4).
25 1990 International Convention on All Pollution Preparedness, Response and Cooperation, Articles 4, 6, 7 and 8.
26 1973 International Convention for the Prevention of Pollution from Ships; Adoption 1973 Convention, 1978 (1978 Protocol), 1997 (Protocol – Annex VI); Entry into force: 2 October 1983 (Annexes I and II).
27 MARPOL Article 2(4).
28 MARPOL, Annex I, Regulation 39.
29 MARPOL, Annex I, Regulation 39.
30 MARPOL, Annex I, Regulation 12.
31 2001 International Convention On the Control of Harmful Anti-Fouling Systems on Ships, entered into force on 7 September 2010.
32 Articles 2(9) and 4.
33 Article 4 and Annex 1.
34 Draft Convention of Offshore Units, Artificial Islands and Related Structures Used in the Exploration for and Exploitation of Petroleum, and Seabed Mineral Resources 2001.
35 The 1974 Convention for the Prevention of Marine Pollution from Land based Sources, 4 June 1974, UKTS (1978) 64., Art 3 (c).
36 OSPAR Convention Articles 5, 3(1) and 4(1).
37 Convention for the Protection of the Marine Environment of the Baltic Sea Area which was adopted in Helsinki in 1992 and entered into force in 2000, Annex III, Article 6; Annex IV, Article 8 and Annex VI, Article 12.
38 Convention for the Protection of the Marine Environment of the Baltic Sea Area which was adopted in Helsinki in 1992 and entered into force in 2000, Annex VI, Regulations 4 and 5.

39 Convention for the Protection of the Marine Environment of the Baltic Sea Area which was adopted in Helsinki in 1992 and entered into force in 2000, Annex VI, Regulation 8.
40 Barcelona Convention for the Protection of the Marine Environment and the Coastal Region of the Mediterranean adopted in 1995. This Convention, previously called the Convention for the Protection of the Mediterranean Sea against Pollution, 1976, was adopted 16 February 1976 and entered into force 12 February 1978 (Barcelona Convention). This Convention was revised 10 June 1995.
41 For a study of the Barcelona Convention approach to marine pollution, see Suh-Yong Chung, Is the Convention-Protocol Approach Appropriate for Addressing Regional Marine Pollution?: The Barcelona Convention System Revisited (*Penn State Environmental Law Review*, vol 13:1, 2004) 85.
42 Protocol of the Mediterranean Sea against Pollution Resulting from Exploration and Exploitation of the Continental Shelf and the Seabed and its Subsoil (Offshore Protocol), 14 October 1994, entered into force on 24 March 2011.
43 Offshore Protocol, Article 4.
44 Offshore Protocol, Articles 9, 10, 11, 15, 16, 20, 26.
45 The Kuwait Regional Convention for Cooperation on the Protection of the Marine Environment from Pollution: Concluded in Kuwait, 24 April 1978, entered into force, 1 July 1979, 1140 UNTS 133.
46 The Framework Convention for the Protection of the Marine Environment of the Caspian Sea was adopted in Tehran, 4 November 2003, and entered into force 12 August 2006. It is available at www.tehranconvention.org/.
47 U.S. Energy Information Administration, 'Oil and natural gas production is growing in Caspian Sea region' (11 September 2013).
48 These are Russia, Azerbaijan, Kazakhstan, Turkmenistan, Uzbekistan and Iran.
49 The Protocol Concerning Regional Preparedness, Response and Co-operation in Combating Oil Pollution Incidents ('Aktau Protocol') (adopted in Aktau, Kazakhstan on 12 August 2011); The Protocol for the Protection of the Caspian Sea against Pollution from Land-based Sources and Activities ('Moscow Protocol') (adopted in Moscow, Russian Federation on 12 December 2012); The Protocol for the Conservation of Biological Diversity ('Ashgabat Protocol') (adopted in Ashgabat, Turkmenistan, on 30 May 2014).
50 Tehran Convention, Articles 7–12.
51 Tehran Convention, Article 1.
52 Tehran Convention, Articles 5, 17, 19 and 20.
53 See, for example, Convention on the Protection of the Black Sea against Pollution (adopted 21 April 1992, entered into force 15 January 1994); Convention for the Protection of the Natural Resources and Environment of the South Pacific (adopted 24 November 1986, entered into force 22 August 1990); Protocol for the Suppression of Unlawful Acts Against the Safety of Fixed Platforms Located on the Continental Shelf 1998 (adopted 10 March 1988, entered into force 1 March 1992); Protocol to Amend the International Convention on Civil Liability for Oil Pollution Damage 1969 (adopted 27 November 1992, entered into force 30 May 1996); Code of Conduct for the Construction and Equipment of Mobile Offshore Drilling UNITS 1989 IMO Assembly Resolution A649(16) (came into effect 1 May 1991); Guidelines and Standards for the Removal of Offshore Installations and Structures on the Continental Shelf and the Exclusive Economic Zone 1989 IMO Resolution A.672 (16).
54 Commonwealth of Australia, 'Report of the Montara Commission of Inquiry', June 2010, Chapter 4.
55 Award in the Arbitration regarding the Iron Rhine ('Ijzeren Rijn') Railway between the Kingdom of Belgium and the Kingdom of the Netherlands, decision of 24 May 2005, *Reports of International Arbitral Awards*, vol. XXVII 35–125, 58.
56 Article 30, UN Doc A/9559 (1974).
57 LOSC Article 194(2).
58 Principle 21 of the 1972 Stockholm Declaration on the Human Environment: 'States have in accordance with the Charter of the United Nations and principles of international

law ... responsibility to ensure that activities within their jurisdiction or control do not cause damage to the environment of other states or of areas beyond the limits of national jurisdiction'.
59 Corfu Channel (*United Kingdom of Great Britain and Northern Ireland v. Albania*) 1949, 22.
60 *Nuclear Tests Cases (Australia v France)*, ICJ, 1973, 106.
61 *Trail Smelter Case (United States, Canada)*, RIAA, vol. III 1905–1982.
62 For example, on 6 July 1988, Piper Alpha production platform exploded in the North Sea killing 165 crew members and resulted in significant marine pollution and financial losses of over 3.4 billion dollars: See 'Major Offshore Accidents of the 20th and 21st Century', *Arnold and Itkin LLP*, date accessed 10 February 2017, www.oilrigexplosionattorneys.com/Oil-Rig-Explosions/History-of-Offshore-Accidents.aspx.
63 Commonwealth of Australia, 'Final Government Response to the Report of the Montara Commission of Inquiry', 2001.
64 Commonwealth of Australia, 'Report of the Montara Commission of Inquiry', June 2010.
65 Commonwealth of Australia, 'Final Government Response to the Report of the Montara Commission of Inquiry', 2001.

References

Australia. Montara Commission of Inquiry & Borthwick, D. (Canberra, 2010). *Report of the Montara Commission of Inquiry*. Montara Commission of Inquiry.
Bosma, S. (2012). The regulation of marine pollution arising from offshore oil and gas facilities- an evaluation of the adequacy of current regulatory regimes and the responsibility of states to implement a new liability regime. *Australian and New Zealand Maritime Law Journal*, vol. 26, p. 89.
Boyd, J. (2006). Compensation for oil pollution damages: The American oil pollution act as an example for global solutions? *Prevention and Compensation of Marine Pollution Damage: Recent Developments in Europe, China and the US*, pp. 137–163.
Brakenhoff, R. (2015). *Outlook for offshore energy, Oil and Gas Financial Journal*, vol. 12, no. 4, Pennwell Corporation, Tulsa, OK.
Chandler, J., & Daintith, T. (2015). Offshore petroleum regulation after Montara: The new regulatory style. *Australian Resources and Energy Law Journal*, vol. 34, no. 1, p. 34.
Esmaeili, H. (2001). *The Legal Regime of Offshore Oil Rigs in International Law*. Routledge. London.
Gilbert, D., & Kent, S. (2 July 2015). BP agrees to pay $18.7 billion to settle Deepwater Horizon oil spill claims. *Wall Street Journal*.
Gipperth, L. (2009). The legal design of the international and European Union ban on tributyltin antifouling paint: Direct and indirect effects. *Journal of Environmental Management*, vol. 90, pp. S86–S95.
Hassan, D. (2006). *Protecting the Marine Environment from Land-Based Sources of Pollution: Towards Effective International Cooperation*. Ashgate Publishing, Ltd., Aldershot.
Hossain, K., Koivurova, T., & Zojer, G. (2014). Understanding risks associated with offshore hydrocarbon development. In *Arctic Marine Governance*. Springer, Berlin Heidelberg, pp. 159–176.
Kashubsky, M. (2006). Marine pollution from the offshore oil and gas industry: Review of major conventions and Russian law (Part I). *Maritime Studies*, vol. 2006, no. 151, pp. 1–11.
Nadim, F., Bagtzoglou, A.C., & Iranmahboob, J. (2008). Coastal management in the Persian Gulf region within the framework of the ROPME programme of action. *Ocean & Coastal Management*, vol. 51, no. 7, pp. 556–565.
Patin, S.A. (1999). *Environmental Impact of the Offshore Oil and Gas Industry*, Vol. 1, EcoMonitor Pub, East Northport, NY.

Rares, S. (2012). An international convention on off-shore hydrocarbon leaks. *Australian and New Zealand Maritime Law Journal*, vol. 26, p. 10.

Richards, R.K. (2011). Deepwater mobile oil rigs in the exclusive economic zone and the uncertainty of coastal state jurisdiction. *The Journal of International Business and Law*, vol. 10, no. 2, pp. 387–412.

Sands, P., & Peel, J. (2012). *Principles of International Environmental Law*. Cambridge University Press, Cambridge.

Sundaram, J. (2016). Offshore oil pollution damage: In pursuit of a uniform international civil liability regime. *Denning Law Journal*, vol. 28, pp. 66–108.

White, M. (1999). Offshore craft and structures: A proposed international convention. *Australian Mining & Petroleum Law Journal*, vol. 18, p. 21.

World Energy Outlook. (2008). International Energy Agency (OECD/IEA), IEA publications, 9, rue de la Federation, 75739 Paris Cedex 15.

6
CLIMATE CHANGE, OCEAN ACIDIFICATION AND THE MARINE ENVIRONMENT

Challenges for the international legal regime

Tavis Potts

Introduction

The oceans are vast, covering 71% of our planet, and are considered the common heritage of mankind. All living organisms rely upon the oceans to provide the fundamental ecosystem services that support life on earth. Human beings are connected to and benefit from oceanic systems using them as a means of transport, source of food, energy production, spiritual fulfilment, aesthetic enjoyment and space for coastal development. Every year the ocean absorbs approximately 25% of the carbon dioxide (CO_2) emitted by human economic activities. Despite the importance in providing a life support system and a range of critical ecosystem services, the oceans are under threat from human activities, the most concerning being the incidence of climate change driven by increased concentrations of CO_2 in the atmosphere.

Climate change is an existential threat to the health of ocean systems, biodiversity and the human communities that rely on marine ecosystem services. It is a threat that has driven unprecedented decades of scientific cooperation within the scientific institutions of the IPCC, resulting in an international political agreement and framework for action. Broad scientific consensus exists that the accumulation of CO_2 in the atmosphere (in addition to other climate forcing gases such as methane) pose an extremely serious threat to the stability of biosphere. Current scientific consensus through the International Panel on Climate Change (IPCC) highlights the following issues:

- The warming of the climate system is unequivocal and, since the 1950s, many of the observed changes are unprecedented over decades to millennia.
- Globally averaged land and ocean surface temperature data over the time scale of 1880 to 2012 shows an upwards warming trend of 0.85°C. Each of the last

three decades has been successfully warmer than the proceeding decade since 1850.
- Changes in extreme weather events have been observed since about 1950, including heat waves and heavy precipitation events.
- The ocean is storing most of the heat energy from the climate system. More than 60% of the net energy increase in the climate system is stored in the upper ocean (0–700 m) and 30% is stored in the ocean below 700 m.
- Arctic sea ice sheet has continually declined since initial observations in 1979, particularly in terms of the extent of the summer sea ice (minimum) which has declined every season.
- Global sea level is rising. The rate of sea level rise since the mid-19th century has been larger than the mean rate during the previous two millennia and between 1901 to 2010 global mean sea level rose by 0.19 metres.
- The atmospheric concentrations of human sourced greenhouse gases carbon dioxide (CO_2), methane (CH_4), and nitrous oxide (N_2O) have increased since 1750. In 2016 global concentrations of CO_2 exceeded 400 part per million, a globally significant milestone of the impact of climate change (IPCC, 2013).

What is ocean acidification?

Ocean acidification is a phenomenon resulting from increased concentrations of carbon dioxide (CO_2) in the atmosphereand the absorption of atmospheric carbon into marine systems. As the anthropogenic concentrations of carbon increase in the atmosphere, the ocean acts as a natural sink for carbon which in turn increases the acidity of waters. There is increasing evidence that acidification will drive major changes in species, communities and ecological systems. Ocean acidification is defined as the progressive increase in the acidity of the ocean over an extended period, which is distinct from short-term or local or intermittent acidification, which is driven by localised biogeochemical processes (e.g., upwelling, river discharges) (Laffoley & Baxter, 2012).

Since the industrial revolution, human beings have released over 500 billion metric tonnes of carbon into the atmosphere (Huttenhower et al., 2012) from the combustion of fossil fuels, deforestation, agriculture, cement production and transport. Records from monitoring stations such as Mauna Loa Observatory indicate the unprecedented levels of CO_2 in the atmosphere, reaching past the 400 ppm limit in 2016 in contrast to a natural range of 172–300 ppm over the past 800,000 years (Luthi et al., 2008). The oceans are a major sink for CO_2 and have absorbed between 24–33% of emissions during the past five decades (Bille et al., 2013). The absorption of carbon from the atmosphere into the ocean acts as a buffer for reducing the impacts of climate change but with the resulting effect of lowering of the pH in ocean waters. In areas such as the Californian current on the western seaboard of the United States, regional enhancement of acidification can occur due to an area that is naturally low in carbonate saturation with dire consequences for marine biodiversity (Gruber, 2012). While ocean acidification is not directly linked to climate change, additional sources of acidification can occur as a result of climatic changes, for example the dissolution of methane hydrates as a result of warming seas (Bille et al., 2013).

The absorption of CO_2 is a natural process within coupled ocean–atmosphere systems, with the production of a weak carbonic acid the result of CO_2 absorption (Bille et al., 2013). The chemical composition of seawater provides a natural buffer against acidification, but with the substantial increase of CO_2 in the atmosphere and consequent absorption, there are profound effects emerging on seawater carbonate chemistry (Raven et al., 2005). This leads to a lowering of the pH of seawater, and lowering the saturation state of the major shell-forming carbonate minerals such as calcite and aragonite, which in turn impacts the ecology and functioning of marine systems (Raven et al., 2005; Huttenhower et al., 2012; Bille et al., 2013). The surface waters of the oceans are naturally alkaline, with an average pH of 8.2 with regional variations due to geographical, chemical and seasonal factors. The current average pH is 8.1 and under current emissions scenarios is expected to drop to a pH of 7.8 (Feely, Doney, & Cooley, 2009). It is important to note that the pH scale is logarithmic and a pH decrease of one unit translates to a 10-fold increase in acidity. With the average pH of ocean surface waters having fallen by 0.1 units, this corresponds to a 26% increase in acidity from historical levels (IGBP, IOC, SCOR, 2013).

In a recent paper, Huttenhower et al. (2012) highlight how the trend in human-induced ocean acidification exceeds the level of natural variability by up to 30 times. Furthermore, it is demonstrated that the current rates of acidification at monitoring sites in the Atlantic and Pacific exceed those experienced during the last glacial termination by two orders of magnitude. Anthropogenic-driven acidification of the ocean over the past 250 years represents the largest such event in at least 55 million years of the Earth's history, and almost certainly the fastest of such changes in at least the past 300 million years (Royal Society, 2013). On average, the ocean is already almost 30% more acidic than it was prior to the 1750s (Harrould-Kolieb & Herr, 2012).

Impact of ocean acidification on species and ecosystems

Ocean acidification has drastic consequences for marine species and ecosystems and, in turn, undermines and erodes a number of services vital for human development (Royal Society, 2005). There is increasing scientific evidence, based on experiment and observation, about the impacts of acidification. Impacts can affect biological and physiological processes such as growth, reproduction, calcification and behaviour of marine species (Harrould-Kolieb & Herr, 2012). These impacts will affect species of ecological, commercial and cultural importance with consequent impacts on services and human welfare. This will depend on the extent of community reliance on species and systems prone to acidification in addition to the range on non-linear and indirect impacts that emerge as food webs and ecosystems (and their services) restructure and change.

Of particular concern is the emerging regional analyses that productive seas that are sites for upwelling may be particularly prone to acidification as deeper more acidic water moves into the coastal shelves where mixing occurs with carbon-rich waters (Laffoley & Baxter, 2015). This would have potential for large-scale ecological disruption in these highly productive regions that are major sources of food and could result in considerable social and economic impacts on seafood producers such as Peru or the small island States. Mathis et al. (2015) note recent studies in Alaska that indicate the vulnerability of Alaskan Pacific salmon to acidification through the decline in health of pteropods (marine snails) that form carbonate-based shells and are a key part of the food chain. This impact may affect marine food webs that support major fisheries such as salmon and Pollock in cold temperate waters. Coral reefs are particularly susceptible to the impacts of acidification. Both tropical and cold-water reefs are threatened by the increasing acidification of the oceans. As identified by Raven et al. (2005), coral reefs exist within an ecological envelope defined by temperature, light and aragonite saturation. To date over 30% of warm-water corals have disappeared since the 1980s due to the advancing impacts of climate change and warmer water temperatures. For example, it is of extreme concern that recent aerial surveys of the northern Great Barrier Reef in Australia, which are prone to extended warming of ocean waters, indicate that 80% of the reefs were seriously bleached, and in water surveys have confirmed 50% mortality in reefs (Normile, 2016). Increasing acidification from CO_2 absorption compounds the impacts from climate change and the pollution of coastal waters by lowering the aragonite saturation state of seawater and reducing the ability of corals, and other shell-forming species to form calcified structures.

The international legal response to ocean acidification

The international regime for protecting the oceans is advancing its scientific understanding of ocean acidification and developing responses for States to collectively manage impacts and build resilience. Acidification that is driven by CO_2 absorption is not covered by a specific body of environmental law but addressed *indirectly* by a number of legal instruments that predominantly support scientific and policy coordination. The most efficient response is to address the underlying driver, that is, the reduction of anthropocentric CO_2 within the mechanisms of the UN Framework Convention on Climate Change and additional mechanisms to combat pollution of the oceans. While carbon dioxide reduction is the most direct means to address acidification, there may be other legal mechanisms to treat CO_2 as an indirect source of pollution into the marine environment and hence strengthen the responsibility of States to address and reduce carbon emissions under the international climate framework. In addition, a number of obligations and mechanisms exist to improve the resilience of marine systems such as marine-protected areas in inshore and offshore marine environments. While such indirect measures do not directly address reduction of carbon pollution or acidification effects, it may strengthen the resilience of marine systems by building in the ecological flexibility to cope with state changes induced by cumulative pressures and multiple stressors. Recent explorations into 'polycentric' earth systems governance (Galaz, Crona, Österblom, Olsson, & Folke, 2012) highlight that multiple, overlapping and networked instruments and mechanisms at nested scales could be an effective response to issues such as ocean acidification. This is particularly salient in the context that the response to addressing acidification is not mapped onto one legal instrument or approach and crosses a number of legal, policy and scientific domains.

A strong scientific and policy consensus has emerged to address acidification through the leadership of the UN General Assembly (UNGA) in 2013. The Informal Consultative Process on Oceans and the Law of the Sea at its 14th meeting on July 2013 addressed the issue of ocean acidification in Resolution 68/70 in December 2013 (UNGA, 2013). The session examined the process and impacts of acidification and the opportunities and challenges to address acidification through legal means and scientific cooperation. The impact of acidification on Polar and coastal regions was emphasised as was the sensitivity of Small Island Developing States to acidification impacts through, for example, declines in the health of coral reef systems. Given the global nature of the problem, coordinated action at the global, regional, national and local levels was emphasised to minimise the impacts of ocean acidification. The UN General Assembly resolution (Res 68/70) in 2013 'encouraged States and competent international organisations and other relevant institutions, individually and in cooperation, to urgently pursue further research on ocean acidification, especially programmes of observation and measurement' (UNGA, 2014). A coordinated international approach on monitoring and observation would serve a number of important purposes including authoritative evidence on global changes in marine ecosystems to policy makers, the collation and analysis of global datasets on changes and system responses and improve the reliability of modelling and projections for future biogeochemical conditions (Newton, Feely, Jewett, Williamson, & Mathis, 2015). Institutions such as the Ocean Acidification International Coordination Centre (OA-ICC) emerged during this period (launched at Rio+20) to promote coordination, communication and capacity building within the scientific community and improve coordination between the scientific community, government and the general public (OA-ICC, 2010). Other institutions that enacted coordinated monitoring were launched during this period in response to a call for global action. The Global Ocean Acidification Observing Network was formed after two international workshops in 2012 and 2013 and involves over 30 nations observing, monitoring, data sharing and modelling of trajectories and impacts of acidification. The network aims to improve understanding of global ocean acidification conditions, improve understanding of the ecosystem response and exchange data on acidification and its impacts (Newton et al., 2015).

Further embedding of cooperation with the oversight of the UNGA has occurred in 2015 with action on ocean acidification being included in the UN Sustainable Development Goals. Goal 14.3 states (UN-DESA, 2015):

> *14.3 Minimize and address the impacts of ocean acidification, including through enhanced scientific cooperation at all levels.*

Inclusion as its own specific goal (14) substantially raises the status and profile of ocean acidification and the necessary UN coordination and reporting mechanisms that will be required to achieve it. In addition, the UN Goals are facilitating substantial political, social and economic partnerships and capacity to deliver the goals and the inclusion of acidification ensures it remains on the policy agenda and an area that is subject to social and technical innovation, engagement and partnership. Sub-goals within Goal 14 also relate to ocean acidification including building coastal and marine resilience (14.2); marine protected areas (14.4); increasing scientific knowledge, research capacity and transfer of marine technology (14.7) and enhancing conservation and sustainable use by implementing international law as reflected in UNLOS (14.7c).

The United Nations Convention on the Law of the Sea (LOSC)

Ocean acidification is not explicitly governed by international treaties. United Nations (UN) processes and international and regional conventions are beginning to include ocean acidification as a part of their evolving response to oceans governance (e.g., via the SDG goals noted previously) and to allocate resources to increased scientific and policy cooperation across a range of networks and initiatives.

The United Nations Convention on the Law of the Sea (UNCLOS) sets out the legal framework within which all activities in the oceans and seas must be carried out and is of strategic importance as the basis for national, regional and global action and cooperation in the marine sector. The 'Constitution for the Oceans' sets out the legal basis for delimitation of maritime jurisdiction, the sovereign rights in the maritime sphere, the rights and responsibilities of flag States, the right of transit through straits, the conservation of living resources and the protection of the environment, the status and access to resources beyond the limits of national jurisdiction and the settlement of disputes. While UNCLOS does not directly address climate change, carbon pollution or ocean acidification, elements of the text do relate to State responsibility for introducing pollution into the marine environment and arguably could constitute 'action by the backdoor' in addressing ocean acidification.

In Article 1(4) of UNCLOS, marine pollution is defined as

> the introduction by man, directly or indirectly, of substances or energy into the marine environment, including estuaries, which results or is likely to result in such deleterious effects as harm to living resources and marine life, hazards to human health, hindrance to marine activities, including fishing and other legitimate uses of the sea, impairment of quality for use of sea water and reduction amenities.

This definition covers the concept of the 'indirect pollution' of 'substances and energy in to the marine environment' that has a negative impact on health or the marine environment. Stoutenburg (2014) notes that the incidence of carbon pollution – both directly as a substance (pollutant) and indirectly in forcing a radiative effect in the form of climatic warming – can be considered as a pollutant under Article 1(4). In the context of carbon dioxide as an indirect pollutant causing an enhanced greenhouse effect, this can be considered as the 'addition of energy into the marine environment' that results in a range of negative impacts on the global commons. Stoutenburg notes that this interpretation was originally intended to cover the localised thermal pollution of marine waters (for example by the addition of warm water to marine environments from power stations). It is logical to assume that Article 1(4) is a flexible definition that is capable of adapting to new circumstances, such as the emission of CO_2 as both a driver of climate change and a driver of ocean acidification (Bille et al., 2013). Following this line of argument, CO_2 can readily be considered a direct pollutant that is causing acidification (Bille et al., 2013) in addition to the indirect impacts of climate warming.

On the assumption that CO_2 is considered a form of pollution, the provisions of UNCLOS Part XII 'Protection and Preservation of the Marine Environment' are relevant in strengthening controls over emissions. Part XII contains provisions and duties for States to protect the environment (Article 192), a sovereign right to exploit natural resources (Article 193) and an obligation to prevent, reduce and control pollution. Furthermore, Article 212 articulates that 'States shall adopt laws and regulations to prevent, reduce and control pollution of the marine environment from or through the atmosphere . . . taking into account internationally agreed rules, standards and recommended practices and procedures' and in Article 212[3] 'States, acting especially through competent international organisations or diplomatic conference, shall endeavour to establish global and regional rules, standards and recommended practices and procedures to prevent, reduce and control such pollution'. While this responsibility is vague in terms of the articulating a proposed instrument and mechanism, Article 212 is normative in that it places a duty on States to cooperate and adopt laws to reduce such pollution. The question of Article 212 effectiveness is explored comprehensively in Stoutenburg (2014) where it is noted that the Article does not directly impose actions on States to commit to reducing pollution but encourages them to adopt appropriate laws and other measures as necessary. The effect is twofold, acting as a mechanism to strengthen existing legal and regulatory engagement and compliance outside of UNCLOS in regimes such as the UN Framework Convention on Climate Change (UNFCCC) and the potential for States to use Article 212 to challenge other parties in upholding their commitments, although this is doubtful in terms of its effectiveness.

The Convention on Biological Diversity (CBD)

The CDB has been an active platform for the sharing of information on ocean acidification and a coordinating mechanism for action. The Convention was negotiated under the auspices of the United Nations Environment Programme and open for signature at the Rio Earth Summit in 1992, entering into force in 1993. The Convention is widely adopted with 196 parties at the Convention and 168 ratifications. The Convention establishes national sovereignty over natural resources and the common global commitment to halting the loss of biodiversity. Article 1 of the Convention states that its objective is 'the conservation of biological diversity, the sustainable use of its components and the fair and equitable sharing of the benefits arising out of the utilization of genetic resources' (CBD, 2016).

Initial concerns about ocean acidification were raised in the Conference of Parties (COP 9) in 2008, in particular the interactions between acidification, climate change and nutrient loading as multiple threats to inland water, coastal and marine biodiversity and the impacts upon marine habitats (particularly the threat to cold-water corals; CBD, 2009). A milestone was the production of a major scientific synthesis of the impacts of acidification by the CBD secretariat (CBD, 2009) that integrated a number of evidence streams concerning the impact on marine systems and links with climate and an updated scientific review in 2014 (Aze et al., 2014). Addressing ocean acidification, particularly in the context of the impacts upon biodiversity and ecosystem services, has become a significant policy priority for the CBD.

The Strategic Plan for Biodiversity 2011–2020 and the Aichi Biodiversity targets were adopted in 2010 by the parties to the Convention and provide an overarching framework for addressing biodiversity loss, not just within the CBD but across the UN system as a whole (Marques et al., 2014). While not binding upon parties, the targets provide a detailed and flexible framework for the implementation of national commitments under the convention, including the review of national biodiversity strategies and action plans. At its 10th meeting of the parties to the convention, Decision X/2 (CBD, 2010), the parties to the Convention agreed to implement the strategic framework and Aichi targets, including the development of additional indicators for monitoring progress and updating of national strategies in line with the Aichi targets. The mission of the strategy is:

> Take effective and urgent action to halt the loss of biodiversity in order to ensure that by 2020 ecosystems are resilient and continue to provide essential services, thereby securing the planet's variety of life, and contributing to human well-being, and poverty eradication. To ensure this, pressures on biodiversity are reduced, ecosystems are restored, biological resources are sustainably used and benefits arising out of utilization of genetic resources are shared in a fair and equitable manner; adequate financial resources are provided, capacities are enhanced, biodiversity issues and values mainstreamed, appropriate policies are effectively implemented, and decision-making is based on sound science and the precautionary approach.
>
> *(CBD, 2010)*

The Aichi targets, as a precursor and in a similar vein to the UN Sustainable Development Goals (although focused broadly on biodiversity and ecosystem services), establish specific targets to address biodiversity loss and conservation, sustainable use, sharing of benefits, participatory planning and capacity building. Strategic Goal B is the most relevant to ocean acidification and aims to 'Reduce the direct pressures on biodiversity and promote sustainable use'. The goal incorporates Target 10 which states:

> Target 10: By 2015, the multiple anthropogenic pressures on coral reefs, and other vulnerable ecosystems impacted by climate change or ocean acidification are minimized, so as to maintain their integrity and functioning.

This target stipulates that pressures from climate change and acidification should be minimised in order to maintain ecosystem integrity and functioning. The target elaborates a strategy where a range of anthropogenic pressures on coral reefs and vulnerable ecosystems are reduced: for example, pollution, sedimentation and unsustainable resource exploitation. Addressing the short- to medium-term pressures would build resilience and provide ecosystems time to adapt to pressures from climate change and acidification. Aichi Target 11 is also relevant and relates to protected areas. It states:

> By 2020, at least 17 per cent of terrestrial and inland water, and 10 per cent of coastal and marine areas, especially areas of particular importance for biodiversity and ecosystem services, are conserved through effectively and equitably managed, ecologically representative and well connected systems of protected areas and other effective area-based conservation measures, and integrated into the wider landscapes and seascapes.

Protected areas are a response to ecosystems that are predicted to experience degradation and impacts from acidification and climate change in addition to short-term and localised pressures from fishing and habitat destruction. Protection of marine biodiversity can enhance the resilience of species and habitats to climate change impacts (Micheli et al., 2012). MPAs have historically been implemented on an individual basis to address local stressors, more recently, MPA networks have been planned to achieve larger-scale conservation by protecting wider ecosystems.. An MPA network is intended to operate more effectively and comprehensively than individual MPA sites and over greater spatial scales (Hopkins, Bailey & Potts, 2016). However, there is little evidence of MPA sites within a network performing synergistically (Grorud-Colvert et al., 2014). A recent study by Hopkins et al. (2016) that interviewed MPA experts identified that the use of marine reserves may contribute to reducing the impacts of climatic disturbance by enhancing the resilience of populations and ecosystems. Current practice in MPA designation and management has generally failed to incorporate climate or acidification impacts, and future strategies, particularly in the context of the Aichi targets, would improve biodiversity protection. Hopkins et al. (2016) highlight that to incorporate climate change resilience in MPA design requires following ecological principles for good MPA network design, the inclusion of areas already showing signs of climate perturbation or areas having a mitigation potential (i.e., blue carbon) and the inclusion of strictly protected reserves to mitigate multiple pressures on habitats.

UN framework convention on climate change: the Paris Agreement

The primary effort to limit global emissions in the context of climate change and to reduce other secondary effects such as ocean acidification will occur through the UNFCCC. The recent UN Paris Agreement therefore represents the key political and legal process by which nations can identify, address and reduce carbon pollution. It is the key instrument in terms of mitigation of carbon dioxide and is supported by the adaptation efforts of other international instruments such as the CBD and scientific monitoring and cooperation as championed by the UNGA and aligned processes.

In 2015, 195 countries adopted the first truly global binding commitment to address human-induced climate change. This was the culmination of two decades of negotiation and planning via the UN Framework Convention on Climate Change and represents a substantial departure from the philosophy embedded within previous UNFCCC conferences and agreements that emphasised – and failed to deliver – a binding targetsand timetables-based approach (Clemencon, 2016). On 5 October 2016, the threshold for entry into force of the Paris Agreement was achieved and the Paris Agreement entered into force on November 2016..

The centralbinding aim of the Paris agreement is to strengthen the global response to climate change by keeping a global temperature rise to within 2°C above pre-industrial levels and to pursue efforts to limit the increase to 1.5 degrees. Article 2(a) of the Paris agreement aims to strengthen the global response by:

> Holding the increase in the global average temperature to well below 2°C above pre-industrial levels and pursuing efforts to limit the temperature increase to 1.5°C above pre-industrial levels, recognizing that this would significantly reduce the risks and impacts of climate change.
> *(UN Paris Agreement Article 2)*

The agreement commits nations to take stronger action concerning adaptation to the impacts of climate change. Article 2(b) states the intention to increase the capacity of nations to adapt to the impacts of climate change, improve climate resilience and pursue 'low greenhouse gas emissions' development while Article 2(d) identifies that future financial flows must be synonymous with low carbon and climate resilient development.

Despite an agreement on emissions reductions targets not agreed in Paris (e.g., in the form of 50%, 75%, 100% emissions cuts from a base year) there is general scientific agreement that the 1.5–2° ceiling in Article 2 indicates that emissions should be zero between 2060–2080 (Clemencon, 2016). The notion of setting binding targets based on historical fossil fuel emissions (i.e., from developed countries) has been removed in favour a flexible system of submitting national contributions. Article 4 of the agreement highlights that national emissions reductions and trajectories for developed and developing countries will be grounded on 'differentiated but common' responsibilities based on the overarching and legally binding limit of a global temperature rise of 2°. Article 4 notes:

> Parties aim to reach global peaking of greenhouse gas emissions as soon as possible, recognizing that peaking will take longer for developing country Parties, and to undertake rapid reductions thereafter in accordance with best available science, so as to achieve a balance between anthropogenic emissions by sources and removals by sinks of greenhouse gases in the second half of this century, on the basis of equity, and in the context of sustainable development and efforts to eradicate poverty.
>
> *(UN Paris Agreement Article 4)*

The central mechanism within the Paris agreement is through governments submitting 'nationally determined contributions' (NDCs). Article 4(2) indicates that 'Each Party shall prepare, communicate and maintain successive nationally determined contributions that it intends to achieve. Parties shall pursue domestic mitigation measures, with the aim of achieving the objectives of such contributions'. These contributions, while in themselves not binding (although the process of submitting, verifying and communicating is), aim to increase in ambition and effectiveness over time. Article 3 states 'Each Party's successive nationally determined contribution will represent a progression beyond the Party's then current nationally determined contribution and reflect its highest possible ambition'. In 2018 Parties to the agreement will review the current status of pledges in the context of meeting the objectives of the agreement and will review NDCs every five years (Article 4[9]).

A critical question is the ramification of the UN Paris Agreement for the health of the oceans. As the primary mechanism for the mitigation of climate change and carbon reduction the Paris Agreement and the associated mechanisms of the UNFCCC are the main response of the international community in addressing the impacts of ocean acidification. In a recent *Nature* article Magnan et al. (2016) discusses the implications of the Paris Agreement for the oceans. Citing the outputs from analysis such as the Climate Scoreboard (Climate Interactive, 2016) they note that current national pledges will not be sufficient to meet the agreed 2° target. Under the scenarios and trajectories of national pledges in the model, current pledges are insufficient and will result in a 3.5° warming with dramatic consequences for ocean health. Magnan et al. (2016) identify that impacts associated with the 3.5° scenario (i.e., the sum of current pledges) locks in serious cumulative impacts on the oceans. For example, under the 3.5 scenario, surface ocean pH would drop by –0.34 units from the pre-industrial level, an increase in acidity of the order of 150–200% with severe impacts on marine species including warm-water corals, pteropods, bivalves, fish and krill and the multitude of services they provide (Magnan et al., 2016).

From an ocean health and acidification perspective, the current trajectory established by the aggregated national contributions under the Paris Agreement will continue to deteriorate ocean systems and their services. However, it is important to note that these initial pledges – if implemented – do provide a positive signal of deviation from the business-as-usual scenario and a turning point for global action on carbon. What is critical is that the parties to the convention continue be ambitious in national pledges and associated actions to restrict carbon emissions and bring the emissions trajectory and temperature increase under the 2° target. This is the aforementioned objective of the convention, and, in order to deliver the (under) 2° target, significant additional pledges and implementation will be required in the coming years of Paris agreement negotiations. The Paris Agreement establishes the policy architecture to achieve this, but it is fundamentally based on international cooperation and political commitment to a low or no carbon economy.

Conclusion

No legal instrument directly addresses ocean acidification in terms of its causes and its impacts on the marine ecosystem. The response from the legal perspective has been diverse, with differing instruments addressing different elements of the acidification problem. In terms of reducing carbon dioxide, the primary approach is via the UN Framework Convention on Climate Change and the Paris Agreement. The agreement represents an ambitious step change in the global response to climate change and emissions reductions, but the challenge will be ensuring that all parties to the convention implement current pledges and continue to upscale their ambitions to limit warming to under 2° C. While the UN Law of the Sea Convention plays an indirect role in addressing carbon pollution, its provisions under Article 212 could play a potentially reinforcing and strengthening role in regards to the delivery of the Paris agreement as the primary means of addressing the driver of acidification. The cooperative and agenda-setting instruments of the UN General Assembly play a significant role in building civil society engagement and coordination on understanding and addressing ocean acidification, supporting large-scale international monitoring initiatives that provide the scientific evidence and basis for action. The recent SDGs and the specific inclusion of ocean acidification as a sub-goal within this process further illustrates the priority given to addressing this issue. In terms of adaptation to increasing ocean pressures, the Convention on Biodiversity provides Member States with the knowledge and process to ensure that marine systems are resilient and are able to cope with increasing multiple threats. Continued implementation of the Aichi targets in parallel to the SDGs, including the development of marine protected areas and a focus on vulnerable marine systems, aim to improve resilience in the face of system change. No single approach can deal with the catastrophic impacts of ocean acidification caused by excessive emissions of carbon dioxide into Earth's atmosphere. It is a multifaceted problem that is affecting coastal and marine systems and will continue to grow in threat over coming decades. The positive outcome is that the instruments and knowledge that are needed to reduce the drivers and adapt to change are advancing and there is an increasing capacity and willingness amongst global actors to halt acidification and protect our common marine heritage.

References

Aze, T., Barry, J., Bellerby, R.G., Brander, L., Byrne, M., Dupont, S., . . . Hauton, C. (2014). An updated synthesis of the impacts of ocean acidification on marine biodiversity (CBD Technical Series; 75). Secretariat of the Convention on Biological Diversity.

Bille, R., Kelly, R., Biastoch, A., Harrould-Kolieb, E., Herr, D., Joos, F., Kroeker, K., Laffoley, D., Oschlies, A., & Gattuso, J. (2013). Taking action against ocean acidification: A review of management and policy options. *Environmental Management*, vol. 52, pp. 761–779.

Clemencon, R. (2016). The two sides of the Paris climate agreement: Dismal failure or historic breakthrough? *Journal of Environment & Development*, vol. 25, no. 1, pp. 3–24.

Convention on Biological Diversity (CBD). (2009). Scientific synthesis of the impacts of ocean acidification on marine biodiversity. Montreal, Technical Series No. 46, 61pp.

Convention on Biological Diversity (CBD). (2010). Decision adopted by the conference of the parties to the convention on biological diversity at its 10th Meeting. X/2. The strategic plan for biodiversity 2011–2020 and the Aichi biodiversity targets, www.cbd.int/doc/decisions/cop-10/cop-10-dec-02-en.pdf.

Convention on Biological Diversity (CBD). (2016). Text of the convention, www.cbd.int/convention/text/.

Feely, R., Doney, S., & Cooley, S. (2009). Ocean acidification: Present conditions and future changes in a high-CO_2 world. *Oceanography*, vol. 22, no. 4, pp. 36–47.

Galaz, V., Crona, B., Österblom, H., Olsson, P., Folke, C. (2012). Polycentric systems and interacting planetary boundaries – Emerging governance of climate change – Ocean acidification – Marine biodiversity. *Ecological Economics*, vol. 81, pp. 21–32.

Grorud-Colvert, K., Claudet, J., Tissot, B.N., Caselle, J.E., Carr, M.H., Day, J.C., . . . Walsh, W.J. (2014). Marine protected area networks: Assessing whether the whole is greater than the sum of its parts. *PloS one*, vol. 9, no. 8, p. e102298, doi: 10.1371/journal.pone.0102298.

Gruber, N., Hauri, C., Lachkar, Z., Loherm D., Frolicher, TL., Plattner, GK. (2012). Rapid progression of ocean acidification in the California Current System. Science, vol 337 (6091), pp.220-223.

Harrould-Kolieb, E., & Herr, D. (2012). Ocean acidification and climate change: Synergies and challenges of addressing both under the UNFCCC. *Climate Policy*, vol. 12, no. 3, pp. 378–389.

Hopkins, C.R., Bailey, D.M., & Potts, T. (2016). Perceptions of practitioners: Managing marine protected areas for climate change resilience. *Ocean & Coastal Management*, vol. 128, pp. 18–28.

Huttenhower, C., Gevers, D., Knight, R., Abubucker, S., Badger, J.H., Chinwalla, A.T., . . . Giglio, M.G. (2012). Structure, function and diversity of the healthy human microbiome. *Nature*, vol. 486, no. 7402, p. 207.

IGBP, IOC, SCOR. (2013). Ocean Acidification Summary for Policymakers – Third Symposium on the Ocean in a High-CO2 World. *International Geosphere-Biosphere Programme*, Stockholm, Sweden.

International Panel on Climate Change (IPCC). (2013). Summary for policymakers, in T.F. Stocker, D. Qin, G.K. Plattner, M.M. Tignor, S.K. Allen, J. Boschung, . . . P.M. Midgley (eds), *Climate Change 2013: The Physical Science Basis. Contribution of Working Group to the Fifth Assessment Report of the Intergovernmental Panel on Climate Change*. Cambridge University Press, Cambridge.

Laffoley, D., & Baxter, J. (Eds.) (2012). *Ocean Acidification: The Knowledge Base 2012. Updating What We Know About Ocean Acidification and Key Global Challenges*. European Project on Ocean Acidification (EPOCA), UK Ocean Acidification Research Programme, (UKOA), Biological Impacts of Ocean Acidification (BIOACID) and Mediterranean Sea

Acidification in a Changing Climate (MedSeA), www.oceanacidification.org.uk/pdf/IOA_ KnowledgeBase-pdf.pdf.

Laffoley, D., & Baxter, J. (2015). *Tackling Ocean Acidification – Improving Prospects By Planning Ahead*. Ocean Acidification International Reference User Group.

Luthi, D., Le Floch, M., Bereiter, B., Blunier, T., Barnola, J., Siegenthaler, U., Raynaud, D., Jouzel, J., Fischer, H., Kawamura, K., & Stocker, T. (2008). High-resolution carbon dioxide concentration record 650,000–800,000 years before present. *Nature*, vol. 453, pp. 379–382.

Magnan, A., Colombier, M., Billé, R., Joos, F., Hoegh-Guldberg, O., Pörtner, H.O., . . . Gattuso, J.P. (2016). Implications of the Paris agreement for the ocean. *Nature Climate Change*, vol. 6, no. 8, pp. 732–735.

Marques, A., Pereira, H.M., Krug, C., Leadley, P.W., Visconti, P., Januchowski-Hartley, S., Krug, R., Alkemade, R., Bellard, Cheung, W., Christensen, V., Cooper, H.D., Hirsch, T., Hoft, R., van Kolck, J., Newbold, T., Noonan-Mooney, K., Regan, E.C., Rondinini, C., Sumaila, U.R., Teh, L.S., Walpole, M. (2014). A framework to identify enabling and urgent actions for the 2020 Aichi Targets. Basic and Applied Ecology, vol 15, no 8, pp. 633–638.

Mathis, J., Cooley, S., Lucey, N., Colt, S., Ekstrom, J., Hurst, T., Hauri C, Evans W, Cross, J., & Feely, R. (2015). Ocean acidification risk assessment for Alaska's fishery sector. *Progress in Oceanography*, vol. 136, pp. 71–91.

Micheli, F., Saenz-Arroyo, A., Greenley, A., Vazquez, L., Montes, J.A.E., Rossetto, M., & De Leo, G.A. (2012). Evidence that marine reserves enhance resilience to climatic impacts. *PloS one*, vol. 7, no. 7), p. e40832, doi: 10.1371/journal.pone.0040832.

Newton, J.A., Feely, R.A., Jewett, E.B., Williamson, P., & Mathis, J. (2015). *Global Ocean Acidification Observing Network: Requirements and Governance Plan*, www.goa-on.org/docs/GOA-ON_plan_print.pdf.

Normile, D. (2016). Survey confirms worst-ever coral bleaching at Great Barrier Reef. *Science*, www.sciencemag.org/news/2016/04/survey-confirms-worst-ever-coral-bleaching-great-barrier-reef.

Ocean Acidification International Coordination Centre (OA-ICC). (2010). *About the Project*, www.iaea.org/ocean-acidification/page.php?page=2178.

Raven, John. (2005). *Ocean Acidification Due to Increasing Atmospheric Carbon Dioxide*, The Royal Society, London, www.royalsoc.ac.uk.

Stoutenburg, J. (2014). Through the back door: The limits of the UN law of the sea conventions usefulness as a tool to combat climate change, in C. Schofield, S. Lee, K. Moon-Sang (eds), *The Limits of Maritime Jurisdiction*, Martinus Nijhoff Publishers, The Netherlands.

UN General Assembly (UNGA). (2013). Sixty-eighth session Oceans and the law of the sea – Report on the work of the United Nations Open-ended Informal Consultative Process on Oceans and the Law of the Sea A/68/159. July 2013, www.un.org/depts/los/consultative_process/consultative_process.htm.

UN General Assembly (UNGA). (2014). 68th Session. Resolution adopted by the General Assembly on 9 December 2013 68/70. Oceans and the law of the sea. A/Res/68/70, www.un.org/en/ga/search/view_doc.asp?symbol=A/RES/68/70.

UN Division of Social and Economic Affairs (UN-DESA) 2015. Sustainable Development Goal 14. Division for Sustainable Development Goals, https://sustainabledevelopment.un.org/sdg14

7

MARINE SPATIAL PLANNING AND THE NEW FRONTIERS OF MARINE GOVERNANCE[1]

Niko Soininen and Daud Hassan

Introduction

The perception of marine areas and resources has evolved over time from limitless to limited. The limitations are apparent in the face of a growing need for marine space, natural resources[2] such as food, minerals, energy and genetics as well as ecosystem services,[3] such as transportation, disease management, climate regulation, spiritual fulfilment and aesthetic enjoyment provided by the marine environment. The paramount importance of the marine environment has not translated into effective governance frameworks as the loss of marine biodiversity is increasingly impairing the ocean's ability to produce seafood, resist diseases, filter pollutants, maintain water quality and recover from perturbations such as overfishing and climate change (Craig, 2012; Crowder et al., 2006; Hall, 2005; Pew Oceans Commission, 2003; US Commission on Ocean Policy, 2004). Over the past 50 years, humans have changed ecosystems, including marine ecosystems, more rapidly and extensively than in any comparable period in human history (World Resources Institute, 2005). All these indicate that there is a pressing need to develop global, regional and national governance frameworks further in order to protect and preserve the marine environment.

In tandem with the decline of the marine environment, there is a need for increasingly effective utilisation of marine space, resources and ecosystem services to sustain the blue economy and to accumulate blue growth. Over the past decades, sea uses have increased significantly due to the emergence of new maritime zones established by the Law of the Sea Convention[4] as well as the discovery of new resources. Sea uses have also increased because of increased technological capabilities of coastal States. For example, within the European Union blue growth has been adopted as one of the central pillars of the Union's marine policy.[5] This will likely translate into challenges for improving the ecological condition of the marine environment simultaneously with increased environmental pressure from aquaculture, shipping, production of renewable and non-renewable energy, and extraction of minerals, to name but a few. The finite nature of marine space and resources is causing conflicts among human uses (human/human conflicts) as well as conflicts between human uses and the environment (human/environment conflicts).

Both the protection and the intensified use of the marine areas and resources are facing serious problems stemming from the fragmentation of marine governance. The governance framework is vertically fragmented on international, regional, national and local levels. Furthermore, fragmentation is visible horizontally as different sectors such as shipping, natural resources, national security and protection of the environment are often scattered between sectoral institutions on international, regional and domestic levels alike (Platjouw, 2016). Without a coherent picture of the normative contents of steering mechanisms and a real dialogue between sectoral institutions, there is little chance of significantly improving the ecological condition of the marine environment or increasing effectiveness in the utilisation of marine space and resources.

Marine Spatial Planning (MSP)[6] is a relatively new instrument designed to aid in answering all the three problems raised previously. According to a popular description, MSP is 'a process of analysing and allocating parts of three-dimensional marine spaces (or ecosystems) to specific uses or objectives, to achieve ecological, economic, and social objectives that are usually specified through a political process'.[7] Forward-looking planning can supplement or even replace *ad hoc* systems of decision-making and regulation (Crowder & Norse, 2008; Ehler & Douvere, 2009). What MSP is promising, then, is a new process, which takes into account all the sectors of marine governance and allocates marine space both geographically and temporally for different purposes that are deemed politically desirable.[8] MSP allows both high level of environmental protection as well as a wide range of human activities, and emphasises coordinated networks of national, regional and global institutions.

The aim of this chapter is first to analyse the core elements of MSP, namely integration, spatiality and adaptivity. It then proceeds to analyse its potential for addressing the problems of declining environmental conditions, increasing uses and fragmentation of governance in European and Australian contexts. The chapter concludes with some cautionary notes and a call for balancing the promises and threats of MSP.

Basic elements of marine spatial planning

MSP is often defined as a holistic and integrated process, which aims at *identifying*, *allocating*,[9] and *reconciling* ecologically, economically and socially important uses of marine space.[10] The identification of different uses is required in order to avoid unnecessary conflicts, to acquire information of what resources are to be allocated, and to scope the interests that need reconciling.[11] Allocation and reconciliation are required for the reason that the outputs of the marine environment are limited, and the marine environment cannot usually meet all of the conflicting needs simultaneously without management.[12] In some cases, this means solving a priori conflicts by adjusting the activities in conflict so that they could coexist. In severe conflicts between uses, however, one has to resort to spatially separating the conflicting interests so that they would not interfere with each other (Young et al., 2007).

Marine spaces have been allocated for different purposes, such as shipping routes, cables, pipelines and marine protected areas for the greater part of the 20th century.[13] Similarly, all the tools that are required to implement a marine spatial plan – mainly zoning, environmental impact assessment and environmental permitting – are widely utilised. It should be underlined that MSP cannot replace other governance mechanisms, but rather it complements them and gives them a more temporal dimension and a strategic, as well as an anticipatory, nature. In a long-term evaluation, it is paramount to understand how ecosystems and different human uses of the marine environment interact and change over time (Crowder & Norse, 2008; Ehler & Douvere, 2009). Since species, habitats, populations, oil and gas deposits, sand and gravel deposits and sustained winds are all distributed in various places on a variety of timescales, they require strategic, integrated and coherent management to secure sustainable growth, and to preserve coastal and marine ecosystems for the future generations.

In its coordinating function, MSP operates as a mechanism for addressing horizontal fragmentation of marine governance. Ehler and Douvere (2009) have stated that fragmentation in governance could potentially lead to a regulatory chaos if multiple authorities regulate different aspects of the same marine space 'while pursuing individual and often conflicting priorities' (p. 93). Any sector-by-sector, case-by-case marine management system lacks the ability to facilitate coordinated responses to the aforementioned human/human or human/environment conflicts. MSP is designed to coordinate different governance tools and bring sectoral authorities to plan the use of marine areas.

Addressing vertical fragmentation, MSP has also been associated with delivering better regulation, implementing multiple legal principles of international environmental law – such as the precautionary principle[14] and the polluter-pays principle[15] – and enabling compliance with international, regional and national obligations (Gilliland & Laffoley, 2008). MSP has a central coordinating function for which it can bring disjointed decision-making regimes under one umbrella (Heinrichs, 2007).

MSP can be seen as implementing Ecosystem Based Management (EBM),[16] which 'considers the entire ecosystem, including humans. The goal of ecosystem-based management is to maintain an ecosystem in a healthy, productive and resilient condition so that it can provide the goods and services humans want and need' (Ehler & Douvere, 2009, p. 24). Within the Convention on Biological Diversity (CBD),[17] EBM is defined as a 'strategy for the integrated management of land, water and living resources that promotes conservation and sustainable use in an equitable way'.[18]

In order for the goals of EBM to be achieved in marine areas, integrated management systems are needed, which allow for a vast amount of information from different sectors to be taken into account when deciding whether a certain action in a certain area should be allowed or not (Douvere, 2008; Douvere, Maes, Vanhulle, & Schrijvers, 2007; Ehler & Douvere, 2009; Young et al., 2007). The idea behind EBM is to move away from traditional single sector–based strategies of environmental governance (Slocombe, 1993).

In line with EBM, addressing horizontal and vertical fragmentation can only take place if all the different interests regarding the protection and use of marine areas and resources are taken seriously and included in the planning. MSP should not be viewed purely as either an instrument of environmental protection or as an instrument advancing economic or social interests.[19] Seeking to reconcile diverse objectives is a necessary precondition of achieving integration. For this reason, MSP has to be understood as addressing environmental, social and economic interests simultaneously. The rationale of this thinking is to enable maximum utilisation as well as maximum protection of biodiversity and ecosystems simultaneously (Jay, 2010). Seeing MSP as purely an instrument for advancing economic or environmental interests would turn a blind eye on MSP's greatest strengths in addressing the fragmentation of marine governance.

It is true that many MSP systems have close (past or present) linkages to conservation (for instance, marine protected areas), but marine zoning within MSP can also be used for economic purposes.[20] As Holling (2000) has noted:

> [s]ustainable designs driven by conservation interests often ignore the needs for an adaptive form of economic development that emphasizes human economic enterprise and institutional flexibility. Those driven by economic and industrial interests often act as if the uncertainty of nature can be replaced with human engineering and management controls, or be ignored all together. These are not wrong, just too partial.

Illustrating this, MSP is often used as a vehicle for supporting sustainable Blue Economy.[21] Since climate change is placing increasing pressure on the coastal regions causing population displacement,[22] the question is raised as to what extent these areas will retain their residential and economic value in the decades and centuries to come. MSP can be used to actively promote disadvantaged areas and ensure more equitable access to marine resources and the benefits arising from therein. Again, the siting of key industries can be a means for steering development, for instance in rural or structurally weak areas of coast and coastal hinterland. Indirectly, MSP can also be used to facilitate urban regeneration, such as that of former port areas (Heinrichs, 2007).

MSP aims to boost economic growth and prosperity of a State, as well as the opportunity for employment (Backer et al., 2012). It encourages investment by instilling predictability, transparency and clearer rules, it increases coordination between the administrations of a State and increase cross-border cooperation and it protects the environment through early identification of impacts and opportunities for multiple uses of marine space.[23] MSP provides a means of visualising future trends and demands and provides a framework for responding to these. In line with market demands, this can ensure better access to markets, for instance by providing transport connections, links to other countries, or supporting the development of ports as a key for future competitiveness. The establishment of maritime industry clusters on the mainland and on the coast is also a good example of this (Heinrichs, 2007). Indeed, MSP is equally important for its social, economic and environmental dimensions.

Spatiality of marine planning

Marine spatial plans usually consist of two parts. First, a textual formulation of the important goals, priorities and principles of the plan, reasons for adopting the plan and guidance for the interpretation of the plan. Second, it can include a map, which indicates the spatial distribution of different activities.[24] A key aspect of MSP is that it is place-based or area-based, which means that it covers only a certain geographical area and does not concentrate on a certain sector – such as aquaculture or renewable energy – or on a particular environmental problem as a whole (Agardy, 2010; Ehler & Douvere, 2009). Some claim that such place-based measures can aid in targeting economic and ecological goals simultaneously. According to Craig: 'the quest for a more holistic approach to ocean governance leads naturally to an increased use of place-based management' (Arkema, Abramson, & Dewsbury, 2006; Craig, 2012).

There are generally four types of zones in marine spatial planning: 1) General Use Zones: areas in which all activities are allowed as long as they are permitted by law and fulfil some legal requirements such as permitting and environmental impact assessment; 2) Targeted Management Zones: areas in which some restricted activities and uses are allowed, so that overlapping activities and uses may occur; 3) Exclusive-Use Zones: areas to be used for a specific type use only, although certain activities such as aquaculture, gas pipelines and production renewable energy could take place in the zone if they are compatible with the main purpose of the zone; and 4) Restrictive-Access Zones: areas to which access is highly restricted for adequate protection of certain sectoral uses of the area (unique ecological habitat, military use).[25] From a legal perspective these zones are usually located in coastal State's territorial waters or the Exclusive Economic Zone, giving the State the legal competence to draft, implement and enforce a marine spatial plan (Maes, 2008).

Until recently, the idea of spatial planning, let alone zoning, was mainly thought of as a terrestrial instrument. This has been closely related to the basic purposes of spatial planning in controlling the development and use of (terrestrial) space. This control has usually been based on land ownership and parcelling of land by visible and accurate boundaries (Jay, 2010). Furthermore, terrestrial planning has often had the objective of making organised construction and settlement possible. The marine environment, by its very nature, resists all the aforementioned basic elements of terrestrial planning (Jay, 2010). However, with the present prospects of major offshore wind farms, as well as of renewable marine energy, spatial planning on marine areas is starting to share more and more elements with the terrestrial land-use planning.[26] From a legal perspective, the Law of the Sea Convention – recognising certain rights of the coastal States and creating legally binding maritime zones – has been responsible for bridging the gap between terrestrial and marine spatial planning by eliminating some of the key problems of spatial planning in marine areas (Maes, 2008).

On the other hand, the unique characteristics of marine space differentiate it somewhat from terrestrial planning.[27] In the view of the Commission of the European Union, 'MSP does not replicate terrestrial planning at sea, given its tri-dimensionality and the fact that the same sea area can host several uses provided they are compatible'.[28] In contrast to terrestrial spatial planning, the nature of the marine environment offers different possibilities for accomplishing reconciliation between different interests – even within the same marine space. This is made possible by the three-dimensional and temporal allocation of activities as well as the compatibility between certain interests to exist in the same area spatially and temporally.

Balancing adaptivity and certainty

MSP is commonly seen as being highly customisable and responsive to environmental and social change (Young et al., 2007). This translates to adaptive management, which is usually taken to mean 'managing according to plan by which decisions are made and modified as a function of what is known and learned about the system, including information about the effect of previous management actions' (Parma, 1998, 26). To balance the notion of adaptivity, predictability and stability are also central features of any marine spatial plan, creating a familiar tension between the flexibility and certainty of governance (Craig, 2010, Craig, 2012; Hill, 2012; Pardy, 2008; White House Council on Environmental Quality, 2010).[29]

The need for adaptive marine spatial planning stems from a frustration towards traditional legal instruments that have been unsuccessful in resolving large-scale and complex environmental problems. Johnson, for instance, has argued that traditional regulatory methods creating permanent legal rights and obligations have been effective in solving problems in which the management system has been clear in its goals and focused on problems that could be solved by scientific or technological means. Quite the opposite, they have not been that successful in managing uncertainties and complex environmental problems, such as non-point source pollution or climate change (Bosselmann, Engel & Taylor, 2008; Brunner & Clark, 1997; Hill, 2012; Johnson, 1999).[30] In order to respond to these challenges, Agardy has stated that MSP 'is likely to be dynamic, with zones moving year to year or even seasonally in some cases' (Agardy, 2010, 13. See also Craig, 2012, 109.).[31]

Simultaneously with the need for more adaptivity to safeguard the ecological functioning of the marine environment, there is a need for increased certainty in marine spatial planning to facilitate the allocation of marine space for different uses such as aquaculture and the production of renewable energy.[32] These developments require permanent structures in the sea, which have to be sufficiently protected against frequent changes in the management of the marine area in question. For this reason MSP should provide increased certainty and boost investor confidence in regulatory processes and decision-making, especially if coupled with tools such as licencing (Heinrichs, 2007). Without adequate checks and balances for adaptivity, private investors will have little interest in sustaining blue growth no matter how compelling the political will to improve the different uses of the marine area would be.

Upholding an element of certainty gains strong support from the rule of law as well. One of the basic aspects widely accepted and inherent in any developed legal system is that the contents of the system do not change frequently, facilitating awareness among legal actors of the contents of their rights and obligations at any given time (for instance, Fuller, 1969).[33] For this reason, it is paramount that all the relevant stakeholders have access to the planning process and that there are clear procedural safeguards, for example, on how often and to what extent the marine spatial plan can be adapted to changed circumstances.

The European Union framework for MSP

Policy developments leading to the adoption of MSP in the EU

In 2006, the European Commission in its Green Paper on Maritime Policy emphasised the importance of sustainable development, mainly the importance of competitiveness and growth of the maritime industry, increasing employment and sustainable use of marine resources (Blue Growth), protection of marine environment and mitigation of and adaption to climate change.[34] It further emphasised the importance of a stable regulatory framework in the form of strategic spatiality as a way forward to implement these policy goals. The Commission stated that, marine spatial planning should be ecosystem based and this regulatory framework should also be connected to licencing or other means of 'promoting or placing restriction on maritime activities'.[35] This emphasis on MSP as an implementation mechanism for sustainable development gained further support in the Blue Book of the Commission in which it stated that MSP is one of the key instruments in implementing Integrated Maritime Policy (IMP) in the EU.[36]

After the Green Paper and the Blue Book, the Commission drafted a roadmap for the implementation of MSP in the EU. The European Commission justified an EU-wide approach to MSP with creating coherence and integration between sectoral planning. This in turn would help in addressing the problems acknowledged in the Green Paper mentioned previously.[37] The aim of the roadmap was to facilitate MSP developments in the Member States, encourage implementation of MSP and stimulate a EU-wide debate on the development of MSP (Schäfer, 2009).

After the roadmap, the Commission emphasised that the implementation of MSP would remain with the Member States. This would, however, be supported by EU-wide coordination of MSP to secure 1) the efficiency of MSP; 2) the implementation of EU's Blue Growth strategy by increasing legal certainty, predictability and transparency of marine planning; 3) the effective implementation of EU-legislation already in place and 4) knowledge and expertise sharing.[38] Following these policy developments, the Commission gave a proposal on a new MSP-directive in the spring of 2013.[39] The directive (MSPD)[40] was adopted in July 2014 and came into force in September the same year.

Integration, spatiality and adaptivity in the European Marine Spatial Planning framework

The MSP-directive is one of the legal instruments designed to implement Integrated Maritime Policy in the EU. It is aimed at achieving sustainable growth and development of marine areas and sustainable use of its resources (Art. 1). Consistent with integrative ideals, the directive aims at economic growth and better quality of the environment simultaneously.[41] By way of doing this, marine spatial planning has also been endorsed and encouraged in different sectors (or pillars) of the Integrated Maritime Policy.[42] As its environmental pillar, the Marine Strategy Framework Directive (MSFD)[43] sets certain obligations to the Member States, e.g., for the Programmes of Measures aimed at implementing the overall aim of good marine environmental status by 2020 in the EU (MSFD Art. 13(2)). One of the instruments to be considered in the Programme is the spatial and temporal distribution of marine activities.

Presently it seems that the obligations set for the Member States in MSPD are mainly procedural. This means that the requirements of the directive can be met by setting up a rather loose framework for planning, and the requirements for the plan itself can be fulfilled on a quite abstract level of planning. Much is left to the discretion of the Member States. This means that the directive does not oblige the Member States to develop and implement a detailed system of planning, coupled with marine zoning, environmental impact assessment and a permit system.[44] In other words, there is no strict obligation in the directive to integrate different sectors and instruments of marine governance under the umbrella of MSP.[45] At first sight it seems that the directive contains hardly any legal mechanisms for implementing its integrative aims.[46]

Despite the discretion left to the Member States in how to implement MSP on a national level, one can argue that the MSPD does set certain minimum requirements for integration.[47] First, the integrative objectives set in the directive should have an effect on the drafting and implementation of MSPs in the Member States. Under Art. 5 of MSPD, Member States must, *inter alia*, consider economic, social and environmental aspects of MSP and shall aim to contribute to the sustainable development of energy sectors at sea, of maritime transport, and of the fisheries and aquaculture sectors, and to the preservation, protection and improvement of the environment, including resilience to climate change impacts.

The substantive obligation to integrate sectoral policies within the MSP are further strengthened by Art. 6, which stipulates that Member States shall establish procedural steps to reach the aims set in the directive. These procedural steps must take into consideration several substantive requirements. In line with Art. 6(1) of the MSPD, this process shall:

- take into account land-sea interactions;[48]
- take into account environmental, economic and social aspects, as well as safety aspects;
- aim to promote coherence between maritime spatial planning and the resulting plan or plans and other processes, such as integrated coastal management or equivalent formal or informal practices;
- ensure the involvement of stakeholders in accordance with Article 9;
- organise the use of the best available data in accordance with Article 10;
- ensure trans-boundary cooperation between Member States in accordance with Article 11; and
- promote cooperation with third countries in accordance with Article 12.[49]

Interestingly, the draft directive[50] (Art. 7(1)) stated that an MSP must also contain at least marine interests such as shipping, fishing, nature conservation. This formulation was softened significantly in the directive.[51] Under Art. 8(2) of MSPD, the interests included in the temporal and spatial allocation of MSP *may* include the following: aquaculture areas; fishing areas; installations and infrastructures for the exploration, exploitation and extraction of oil, gas and other energy resources minerals and aggregates and the production of energy from renewable sources; maritime transport routes and traffic flows; military training areas; nature and species conservation sites and protected areas; raw material extraction areas; scientific research; submarine cable and pipeline routes; tourism and underwater cultural heritage.[52] Even though there are no specific obligations as to what interests must be integrated and considered in the plan, Member States have an obligation – when considering obligations set in Art. 5 and 6 – to show that the planning process has included all the relevant interests in the marine area. The Member States are then free to balance marine interests as they see fit in the confinements of international and EU law.

Despite certain procedural efforts towards integration, the issue of multi-level sectoral governance remains an issue untouched by the directive. Art. 4(3) of MSPD states that national MSPs shall be developed and produced in accordance with institutional and governance levels determined by the Member States. The directive does not harmonise the scale or level of planning which can have a negative effect on the overall level of integration of sectoral policies and cooperation between Member States.[53] This has a negative potential of undermining the advantages identified with MSP in the beginning of this chapter.[54]

The directive is also problematic in terms of spatiality. Under Art. 8(1) of the directive, the Member States are under an obligation to identify the spatial and temporal distribution of marine activities in their marine waters. Furthermore, Art. 3(1) stipulates that each Member State shall establish and implement a marine spatial plan. However, when comparing the draft directive[55] to the adopted directive, one can see that the obligations relating to the spatial scale of the planning have been dropped from the final directive. Art. 7 of the draft directive stated that 'Maritime spatial plans shall contain at least a mapping of marine waters which identifies the actual and potential spatial and temporal distribution of all relevant maritime activities'. In the adopted directive, this formulation was changed to read: 'When establishing and implementing maritime spatial planning, Member States shall set up maritime spatial plans which identify the spatial and temporal distribution of relevant existing and future activities and uses in their marine waters'.[56] The biggest difference between the two formulations is that the Member States *do not* have an obligation to produce *a map* of activities in the marine areas. This can severely cripple the spatial strengths of MSP in the EU.

Another important limitation in terms of spatiality and integration becomes clear when comparing the scope and applicability of the final and draft directives. According to the directive proposal Art. 2(1), the directive was to be applied to coastal zones as well as marine waters. The proposed scope of the directive would have undoubtedly supported increased integration within the land-sea interface. Despite these benefits, the scope was considerably narrowed down in the adopted directive. According to Art. 2(1), MSPD shall apply only to marine waters, not to coastal waters. This restriction of scope leaves one important element of MSP outside the scope of its application and limits the EU-wide application of MSP mostly to the outer edges of Territorial Waters, and to the Exclusive Economic Zone.[57]

Despite the aforementioned shortcomings, MSPD sets legally binding obligations to the Member States in terms of the process leading to a Europe-wide adoption of MSP.[58] This means that the Member States had to transpose the requirements of the MSPD into their national legislation by 18.9.2016 (Art. 15(1)). By that date, relevant authorities had to be identified and reported to the European Commission. National marine spatial plans have to be in place by 31 March 2021 at the latest.

After the adoption and implementation of a national MSP, the plans must be reviewed at least every 10 years (MSPD Art. 6(3)). This provision sets a minimum requirement for adaptivity, which is generally seen as an important characteristic of MSP. The provision does not prevent Member States from adapting MSPs more frequently. The interval for adaptivity was first set to six years in the directive proposal, but it was then lengthened in the adopted directive to 10 years. One of the reasons for this can be seen in the Committee of the Regions' opinion which preferred to remove a strict timeline for adaptivity altogether.[59] In its final form, the directive ended up with a strict timeline for revision, setting the minimum standard for the adaptivity of the plans and increasing certainty as to how often the plans are re-evaluated. In times of increasingly rapid environmental change, it may prove to be too long of an interval. The 10-year interval sets, however, only an obligation for minimum harmonisation, meaning that the Member States are free to adopt shorter intervals for re-evaluating their marine spatial plans.

MSP in the Great Barrier Reef Marine Park

One of the pioneer examples of MSP is the Great Barrier Reef Marine Park (GBRMP) in Australia.[60] The total area of GBRMP is 344,400 km^2.[61] The GBRMP is one of the largest, richest and most diverse marine ecosystems in the world. The reef spans a length of 2,300 kilometres along two-thirds of the East Coast of Queensland and represents about 10% of the world's coral reef areas.[62]

The GBRMP 'brings billions of dollars in Australian economy each year, and supports more than 50 000 jobs'.[63] The catchment area adjacent to the Reef comprises 22% of the Queensland's land area.[64]

There are more than 70 traditional owner groups along the Reef coast and their custodianship extends to marine resources and the sea and islands.[65] Due to its natural as well as historical significance, the Park has been included in World Heritage list since 1981.

The adoption of the *Great Barrier Reef Marine Park Act* 1975 (Cth) (hereinafter the *Marine Park Act*) is a significant milestone in that it provides a strong legislative basis for the protection and management of marine and coastal resources in the Reef region.[66] In addition, various plans and policy guidelines such as the 2006 Review of Marine Park Act, the 2009 Great Barrier Reef Intergovernmental Agreement and GBRMP Outlook Reports and Implementation Systems and arrangements in accordance with the *Marine Park Act* to manage the GBRMP and to provide better protection of the ecosystem in the Region.

The *Marine Park Act* provides a special regime of conservation and multiple use of the Reef which 'includes spatial management of a large marine ecosystem through zoning with powers to deny, or impose limiting conditions on, use of or entry to all part of marine commons with in the Marine Park'.[67]

A comprehensive and adaptive spatial panning system exists to manage and protect the GBRMP. Spatial Planning is one of the cornerstones of the GBRMP's management strategy to maintain the biological diversity and ecological systems that create the marine park and to manage the impacts of increasing recreation and expanding tourist industry and to manage the impacts of risks of pollution and shipping. Zoning in the GBRMP is a legislative instrument in its own right as well as being the key to its planning.[68]

Given the dynamic nature of the marine environment as well as to measure the effectiveness of the management plan, the whole management process in the GBRMP is under constant governmental review for any future changes to the process based on the *Outlook Report* published every five years. The *Report* is peer reviewed by at least three qualified persons. It contains the current environmental status of the Reef and the effectiveness of the management plans. All assessment objectives are framed on the basis of environmental impact and risks to the ecosystem in the region. Assessment of current biodiversity, current condition of ecosystem health, current risk to ecosystem and current as well as future environmental, economic and social values of the region are contained in the assessment report.[69]

Under the current management regime, it is likely that the ecosystem of the Great Barrier Reef will survive better under the pressure of accumulating risks than most of the ecosystems around the world.[70] The Great Barrier Reef's approach could be an ideal example from a strong conservation perspective. It could be a very useful approach at the national level where no jurisdictional complexities limit MSP.

Conclusion

Marine Spatial Planning is a way forward in effective marine governance as it includes integrated, strategic, area-based and participatory measures. These measures on the one hand allow adaptivity in the governance of marine space, and on the other provide a permanent institutional structure with some predictability. Despite its shortcomings, the EU MSP Directive sets a legally binding obligation for the Member States to adopt MSP across Europe. The Directive requires transboundary cooperation and contains some elements of sectoral integration. The directive also contains a modest notion of adaptivity with its 10-year renewal interval. Overall, the MSP Directive should be seen as the first EU-wide step towards integrated marine governance, nothing more. Harmonising some of the core procedural elements for a EU-wide MSP framework is a good place to start.

In some contrast to its EU counterpart, MSP in the Great Barrier Reef Marine Park provides a strong legislative basis for the protection and management of marine and coastal resources in the Reef region. The Marine Park Act provides a legal framework for the conservation and multiple use of the Reef, which is comprehensive and adaptive in protecting and managing the GBRMP. Also, the Marine Park Act provides mechanisms for constant governmental review for any feature changes to the process based on Outlook Report to make it more adaptable. The assessment and review systems in the Great Barrier Reef areunique features supporting the effectiveness of MSP. In this way, the Great Barrier Reef regulatory system has still many lessons to teach for developing MSPs across the globe.

Notes

1 Parts of this chapter have been adapted from Hassan, Daud, Kuokkanen, Tuomas & Soininen, Niko (2015) *Transboundary Marine Spatial Planning and International Law* (Earthscan/Routledge), Ch. 1, 4, 9 and Soininen, Niko (2012) 'Marine Spatial Planning as an Instrument of Reconciliation' International Environmental Law and Diplomacy Review.
2 Marine resources may be classified into three categories: chemical (materials dissolved in the water); biological (living resources) and geological (minerals that are found on or beneath the ocean floor). See Jones (1972, p. 71).
3 Ecosystem services include 'provisioning services' such as food, freshwater, fibre, biochemicals, genetic resources; 'regulating services' such as climate regulation, disease regulation, water regulation, water purification, pollination; 'cultural services' such as recreation and tourism, as well as spiritual and religious, aesthetic, inspirational, and educational benefits; and 'supporting services' such as soil formation, nutrient cycling, and primary production. See World Resources Institute (2005).

4 United Nations Convention on the Law of the Sea, Montego Bay, 10 December 1982, in force 16 November 1994, 21 International Legal Materials (1982) 1261.
5 See COM (2012) 494, final; COM (2014) 254, final/2.
6 Most commonly, MSP is referred to as marine spatial planning but the Commission of the European Union, for instance, uses the concept of maritime spatial planning to refer to the same instrument. See, for instance, COM (2008) 791 final 25 November 2008. 'Roadmap for Maritime Spatial Planning: Achieving Common Principles in the EU' p. 2: 'The term maritime spatial planning is favoured over marine spatial planning to underline the holistic cross-sectoral approach of the process'. See also European Commission, Maritime Spatial Planning, available at <http://ec.europa.eu/maritimeaffairs/policy/maritime_spatial_planning/index_en.htm> (visited 9 January 2013). See also on the conceptual differences between the EU and other parts of the world, Backer (2011) p. 280.
7 UNESCO, 'Marine Spatial Planning Initiative, Marine Spatial Planning (MSP)', available at <www.unesco-ioc-marinesp.be/marine_spatial_planning_msp> (visited 5 February 2013).
8 Although the history of MSP can be traced back to the 1970s, the modern era of MSP can be seen to have begun at the 2002 World Summit on Sustainable Development in Johannesburg. See Douvere (2008), pp. 762–771. See also Ehler & Douvere (2009) pp. 79–80; and Plan of Implementation of the World Summit on Sustainable Development, UN Doc. A/CONF.199/20 (2002), para. 31(c). At the moment, MSP is being used for the governance of marine areas in several countries throughout the world, for instance in Australia, Belgium, Germany, Norway, Sweden, Finland, the Netherlands, the United Kingdom, Canada, the United States and China. For a more comprehensive list of MSP systems throughout the world, see UNESCO, 'Marine Spatial Planning Initiative, MSP around the world', available at <www.unesco-ioc-marinesp.be/msp_around_the_world> (visited 5 February 2013).
9 EC COM (2008) 791 final, p. 9: 'MSP operates within three dimensions, addressing activities (a) on the seabed; (b) in the water column; and (c) on the surface. This allows the same space to be used by different purposes. Time should also be taken into account as a fourth dimension, as the compatibility of uses and the "management need" of a particular maritime region might vary over time'.
10 Ehler & Douvere (2009).
11 See for instance, Maes, Schrijvers, & Vanhulle (2005). The working group first identified the present uses of the marine environment in a certain area and then analysed the impacts that each individual use has on the marine environment; they also laid out different scenarios of how the competing interests relating to the use of ocean space could be reconciled and the conflicts between those interests alleviated and solved.
12 Ehler & Douvere (2009). For instance, in the Belgian part of the North Sea, studies showed that the need for the marine space was almost three times larger than the available space. See Maes et al. (2005).
13 In this way MSP has a long history in international environmental law, see Kuokkanen (2015).
14 According to Art. 15 of the Rio Declaration on Environment and Development, Rio de Janeiro, 3–14 June 1992, the precautionary principle can be taken to mean the following: 'Where there are threats of serious or irreversible damage, lack of full scientific certainty shall not be used as a reason for postponing cost-effective measures to prevent environmental degradation'.
15 The polluter-pays principle is defined in the OECD Recommendation of the Council on the Guiding Principles concerning International Economic Aspects of Environmental Policies (26 May 1972 – C(72)128) in the following way: 'This principle means that the polluter should bear the expenses of carrying out the above-mentioned measures decided by public authorities to ensure that the environment is in an acceptable state. In other words, the cost of these measures should be reflected in the cost of goods and services which cause pollution in production and/or consumption. Such measures should

not be accompanied by subsidies that would create significant distortions in international trade and investment'.
16 See Gilliland & Laffoley (2008) pp. 787–796. Pardy (2003) pp. 675–692 has been quite critical of the claim that ecosystems have to be managed instead of left to their own devices. While the present authors agree with Pardy on the notion that ecosystem management is a policy choice and that not every ecosystem should be managed, the author swould like to point out that modern ecosystem management instruments are constructed in a way that allows some areas to be preserved (or maintained in a natural state of non-equilibrium) and other areas to be used more heavily for human purposes. This can be seen especially well in the place-based management instruments designed for marine areas, such as marine spatial planning. Ecosystem management can be a tool of management or non-management.
17 Convention on Biological Diversity, Rio de Janeiro, 5 June 1992, in force 29 December 1993, 31 International Legal Materials (1992) 822, <www.biodiv.org>.
18 See CBD, 'Ecosystem Approach', available at <www.cbd.int/ecosystem/> (visited 28 January 2013). The objectives of the Convention are presented in Article 1: 1) conservation of biological diversity, 2) sustainable use of its components, and 3) fair and equitable sharing of benefits rising out of the utilisation of genetic resources.
19 See COM (2008) 791 final 25 November 2008. 'Roadmap for Maritime Spatial Planning: Achieving Common Principles in the EU', at 2: 'Objective [of the MSP] is to balance sectoral interests and achieve sustainable use of marine resources'. The Commission of the European Union is currently preparing a directive for an EU-wide framework of the MSP. See also Ehler & Douvere (2007) p. 7; Agardy (2010); Hassan (2013) p. 260.
20 See Agardy (2010) p. 18: 'zonation may also be based on a kind of conservation-in-reverse process, whereby areas not needing as much protection or management as others would be highlighted. Such high-use zones could be "sacrificial" areas, already so degraded or heavily used that massive amounts of conservation effort would not be cost-effective, or they might be areas determined to be relatively unimportant in an ecological sense'.
21 The Concept of Blue Economy, which integrates and is inclusive of Green Economy, has been introduced by Awni Behnam (President, International Ocean Institute and former UN Assistant Secretary General). Blue economy is mainly an ocean-based economy and it approaches sustainable development from ocean to land holding that the land is the continuation of the Sea, which is different from the traditional approach of sustainable development, a land-locked vision that looked from land to the ocean space as if it were an endless horizon. According to him 'most countries' Gross Domestic Product (GDP) is contributed largely from activities in coastal areas (shipping, tourism, fisheries, aquaculture, energy, national defense, etc.). All these factors have to be integrated into holistic and collective governance architecture just as their value added is interconnected. Blue Economy may be characterised by the recognition of the interdependence of and the necessity for the integration of all stakeholders and actors in this area. Therefore, Blue Economy, defined as living with the ocean and from the ocean in a sustainable relationship, is the transition toward a human–ocean centred relationship where humankind coexists with the ocean and from the ocean in a sustainable way. See Behnam (2012) pp. 4–6, www.ioinst.org/index.php?option=com_phocadownload&view=category&download=319:1012-from-unclos-to-rio-20-and-the-ocean-compact-Behnam2012&id=47:ioinforma2012&Itemid=60, accessed 28 December 2013; Behnam, Awni (2007) 'Biodiversity of the Ocean, A Question of Governance' (IOI Proceedings of PIM XXXII, Malta).
22 The World Ocean Review warns that 'without doubt sea level will rise slowly at first, speeding up and continuing beyond the 21st century. Gradually many coastal areas will become uninhabitable. People will lose their homes and part of their culture'. According to this report more than one billion people, most of them in Asia, are threatened of displacement. See World Ocean Review (2010), vol. 1, p. 73, http://worldoceanreview.com/en/, accessed 27 December 2013.

23 Maritime Affairs, 'Maritime Spatial Planning', European Commission, http://ec.europa.eu/maritimeaffairs/policy/maritime_spatial_planning/index_en.htm, accessed 27 December 2013.
24 For a good overview of planning and spatial planning in general and their relationship to MSP, see Backer (2011, pp. 280–281). MSP is often confused with ocean zoning or other already existing governance instruments, or is mistakenly thought to replace some or all of the existing instruments of governance, see Agardy (2010) p. 13:'Though zoning is one of the central components of MSP, contrary to the public perception, the two are not one and the same'. However, Agardy has argued that any MSP-system not using zoning as an implementation mechanism 'is not taking advantage of the power of ocean zoning as a problem-solving tool'. To Agardy, zoning represents the concrete implementation of the aims set in MSP. See ibid. p. 14. See, on the misconceptions related to marine zoning, ibid. p. 34.
25 See the synthesis report of a project known as 'Baltic Sea Management – Nature Conservation and Sustainable Management of the Ecosystem through Spatial Planning' The project is also known as the Balance project and was partly funded by the EU through its regional development fund. Running from 2005–2007, and coordinated through the Balance secretariat located in Copenhagen, Denmark, its main aim was to develop adequate management tools based on spatial planning and transnational and cross-sectoral cooperation for Baltic Sea governance. For additional details, see <www.balance-eu.org>. See also Merrie (2010, p. 10).
26 Jay, S. (2010) pp. 173–192. The building of wind farms has been one major driver behind the development of MSP in many of the European Countries, see UNESCO, 'MSP around the World', available at <www.unesco-ioc-marinesp.be/msp_around_the_world> (visited 13 June 2013). On specific wind farm projects, see for instance Schoukens, Cliquet & Maes (2012) pp. 304–312.
27 In addition, Peel & Lloyd (2004) argued that one must be careful when contemplating the transfer of terrestrial planning instruments to marine environments, stating that '[t]here is little evidence that land-based policy solutions will readily transfer offshore'.
28 COM (2008) 791 final, p. 10.
29 See White House Council on Environmental Quality (2010). Final Report of the Ocean Policy Task Force (2010), available at www.whitehouse.gov/files/documents/OPTF_FinalRecs.pdf. See also Craig (2012) p. 109:'one of the tensions in promoting place-based management for the oceans is how to balance the desire for predictability and stability with the knowledge that human needs and desires will change over time'. On a general level, see also Hill (2013), pp. 41–44; Pardy (2008), pp. 351–353.
30 Johnson (1999). See also Brunner & Clark (1997) pp. 48–58; Hill (2012) p. 9. Bosselmann, Engel & Taylor (2008) p. 4, have also recognised these problems in assessing tensions between present forms of governance and sustainability. Mainly, these tensions manifest in the failure of present forms of governance to answer increasing complexities and the magnitude of environmental problems.
31 Craig (2012) p. 109, has been quite sceptical whether the adaptability suggested by Agardy is possible. Craig states that the dynamic changes to marine zones are 'likely to be limited' due to a 'lengthy and contentious process' in drafting the zones. In addition, the legal instruments by which the zoning system is created may be quite cumbersome not allowing swift changes to the zones.
32 This has been emphasised by the European Commission, see COM (2010) 771, p. 1.
33 Fuller (1969) has persuasively argued that legal norms must have a degree of stability in order for the legal system to function properly.
34 COM (2006) 275, final, Volume II – Annex. Green Paper. Towards a future Maritime Policy for the Union: A European vision for the oceans and seas, pp. 3–21. The key drivers on a more concrete level are maintaining and improving biological diversity and blue growth with a close connection to renewable energy, such as offshore wind, see Maes (2012). Available at: www.omgevingsrecht.be/sites/default/files/habtitat1213122012/20121213-08.pdf, accessed on 15.10.2014.

35 COM (2006) 275, final, Volume II – Annex. Green Paper. Towards a future Maritime Policy for the Union: A European vision for the oceans and seas, p. 34.
36 COM (2007) 575, final. Communication from the Commission to the European Parliament, the Council, the European Economic and Social Committee and the Committee of the Regions. An Integrated Maritime Policy for the European Union, p. 6. IMP includes policy areas such as renewable marine energy, fisheries, transportation and the protection of the marine environment. One of the operational objectives of the Regulation concerning a programme of support for the IMP (Regulation No 1255/2011 of the European Parliament and of the Council of 30 November 2011 establishing a Programme to support the further development of an Integrated Maritime Policy, OJ L 321, 5.12.2011, p. 1.) is to promote cross-sectoral tools, such as marine spatial planning (Art. 2(b)). The importance of cooperation between member states is further emphasised in Art. 3(2)(b) of the Regulation.
37 COM (2008) 791, final. Communication from the Commission. Roadmap for Maritime Spatial Planning: Achieving Common Principles in the EU, pp. 2–3.
38 COM (2010) 771, final. Communication from the Commission to the European Parliament, the Council, the European Economic and Social Committee and the Committee of the Regions. Maritime Spatial Planning in the EU – Achievements and Future Development, pp. 2–3.
39 COM (2013) 133, final. Proposal for a directive of the European Parliament and of the Council establishing a framework for maritime spatial planning and integrated coastal management.
40 Directive 2014/89/EU of the European Parliament and of the Council of 23 July 2014 establishing a framework for maritime spatial planning, OJ L 25, 28.8.2014, p. 135.
41 This point of view can partially be criticised in the sense that the MSP directive can be seen as deteriorating the status of marine environmental protection by shifting the viewpoint from a hard conception of sustainability to a weak one. The gist of the argument is that the adoption of multiple goals in MSP (environmental protection and economic development) simultaneously will erode prior levels of environmental protection in the EU. See Qiu & Jones (2013) pp. 182–189. Interestingly, similar argument was voiced in the Opinion of the European Economic and Social Committee on the 'Proposal of the Directive of the European Parliament and of the Council establishing a framework for maritime spatial planning and integrated coastal management', OJ C 341, 21.11.2013, p. 69. The Committee saw that it would be better to wait for the existing EU legislation to reach its full potential before adding a new regulative layer in the form of an MSP-directive. While these arguments have some merit, I would be inclined to argue that the MSP directive places mostly procedural obligations for the implementation of the MSFD, which do not necessarily convey in them the ability to weaken the level of marine environmental protection. It is up to the Member States to deliberate how different substantive sectoral policies will be made compatible with the overall aim of good marine environmental condition. In this sense, MSP is a blank tool for the implementation of other policies.
42 In the drafting process, the European Economic and Social Committee posed a question as to how the proposed MSP directive would be coordinated with other EU legislation, such as the Habitats Directive (Directive 92/43/EEC of the European Council of 21 May 1992 on the conservation of natural habitats and of wild fauna and flora, OJ L 206, 22.7.1992, p. 7). See Opinion of the European Economic and Social Committee on the 'Proposal of the Directive of the European Parliament and of the Council establishing a framework for maritime spatial planning and integrated coastal management', OJ C 341, 21.11.2013, p. 69.
43 Directive 2008/56/EC of the European Parliament and of the Council of 17 June 2008 established a framework for community action in the field of marine environmental policy (Marine Strategy Framework Directive), OJ L 164, 25.6.2008, p. 19.
44 These requirements usually follow from other EU-level obligations.

45 In this sense it seems that the EU-level MSP framework is still quite far from the ideal characteristics of MSP discussed in section 1.
46 The Committee of the Regions, in its opinion on the proposed MSP directive, stated that the directive should not include substantive elements and that in its suggested form it was in breach of the proportionality principle, see Opinion of the Committee of the Regions on Proposed directive for maritime spatial planning and integrated coastal management, OJ C 356, 5.12.2013, p. 124.
47 However, taking into account the preamble of the directive, one could argue that there are no substantive requirements in the directive. In the preamble of MSPD it is stated that the directive does not set substantive obligations on marine spatial planning as these issues are for the most part left to national discretion. See MSPD, preamble 9–11.
48 With regard to taking into consideration land sea interactions, the directive states the possibility of complementing MSP with Integrated Coastal Management, see art. 7 of the MSPD.
49 In the legislative process, the European Economic and Social Committee was of the opinion that none of these requirements could be implemented ' – – in the absence of genuine cooperation the Member States and with third countries, given that maritime areas are, by their very nature, open and constantly interacting.' Opinion of the European Economic and Social Committee on the 'Proposal of the Directive of the European Parliament and of the Council establishing a framework for maritime spatial planning and integrated coastal management', OJ C 341, 21.11.2013, p. 69.
50 COM (2013) 133, final. Proposal for a directive of the European Parliament and of the Council establishes a framework for maritime spatial planning and integrated coastal management.
51 This was also the proposal of the Committee of the Regions, see Opinion of the Committee of the Regions on Proposed directive for maritime spatial planning and integrated coastal management, OJ C 356, 5.12.2013, p. 130.
52 This was the opinion of the Committee of the Regions as well, see Opinion of the Committee of the Regions on Proposed directive for maritime spatial planning and integrated coastal management, OJ C 356, 5.12.2013, p. 126. The Committee 'underlines that MSP must be developed as a neutral planning tool which incorporates a certain level of flexibility to accommodate appropriate policy processes for diverse marine environments; further calls for clarity on the scope of the ecosystem-based approach of the draft Directive as there will need to be a balance between economic development and environmental protection; rejects therefore the setting of "top-down" priorities and minimum requirements for management plans and using MSP as an instrument to ensure implementation of sector specific policy objectives'.
53 The problem of scale is further impeded by a very wide definition of MSP in Art. 3(2) of the MSPD: '"maritime spatial planning" means a process by which the relevant Member State's authorities analyse and organise human activities in marine areas to achieve ecological, economic and social objectives'.
54 See, on these advantages, Chapter 1 of this volume.
55 COM (2013) 133, final. Proposal for a directive of the European Parliament and of the Council establishing a framework for maritime spatial planning and integrated coastal management.
56 National security and defense issues are excluded from the planning process (Art. 2(2)). Understandably, land-locked countries in the EU are excluded from the obligations set in the directive (Art. 15(4)).
57 MSPD does not alter the international legal framework forming the background of any MSP or affect national land-use planning which may include coastal areas (Art. 2(3) and 2(4)). See on this international legal background, chapter 4 and 5 of this book. The reason for leaving ICM out of the adopted directive was that legislating on ICM was seen to belong to the competence of the Member States, see Opinion of the Committee of the Regions on Proposed Directive for Maritime Spatial Planning and Integrated Coastal

Management, OJ C 356, 5.12.2013, pp. 130–131. On the contrary, the European Economic and Social Committee was of the opinion that the integration of marine, coastal and even terrestrial planning would be a welcome development taking into consideration that a considerable amount of marine pollution is caused by land-based pollution, see Opinion of the European Economic and Social Committee on the 'Proposal of the Directive of the European Parliament and of the Council establishing a framework for maritime spatial planning and integrated coastal management', OJ C 341, 21.11.2013, p. 68.
58 See MSPD, preamble 9–11.
59 See Opinion of the Committee of the Regions on Proposed Directive for Maritime Spatial Planning and Integrated Coastal Management, OJ C 356, 5.12.2013, pp. 129–130. European Economic and Social Committee on the other hand emphasised the importance of MSPs adaptivity, see Opinion of the European Economic and Social Committee on the 'Proposal of the Directive of the European Parliament and of the Council establishing a framework for maritime spatial planning and integrated coastal management', OJ C 341, 21.11.2013, p. 68.
60 The GBRMP was established by the Great Barrier Reef Marine Park Act 1975 (Cth). Its control and development are basically governed through the Great Barrier Reef Marine Park Authority (the Park Authority).
61 See UNESCO-IOC-Marine Spatial Planning Initiative, at www.unesco-ioc-marinesp.be/spatial_management_practice/australia_great_barrier_reef.
62 The 2009 Great Barrier Reef Marine Park Outlook Report p. 1.
63 The 2009 Great Barrier Reef Marine Park Outlook Report p. 1.
64 The 2006 Review of the Marine Park Act p. 8.
65 Ibid.
66 Hassan (2013, pp. 259–260).
67 Kenchington & Day (2011, p. 271).
68 Great Barrier Reef Marine Park Act 1975 (Cth), Act No 85 of 1975 (as amended up to 2011). Zoning plans are legislative instruments – Art. 35D.
69 S54(3).
70 The 2009 Great Barrier Reef Marine Park Outlook Report, pp. ii and 20.

References

Agardy, T. (2010). *Ocean Zoning: Making Marine Management More Effective*, London: Earthscan.
Arkema, K.K., Abramson, S.C. & Dewsbury, B.M. (2006). Marine ecosystem-based management: From characterization to implementation. *Frontiers in Ecology and the Environment*, vol. 4, no. 10, pp. 525–532.
Backer, H., Frias, M., Bergström, U., Fredricsson, C., Fredriksson, R., Hämäläinen, J., . . . Lehto, S. (2012). *Planning the Bothnian Sea-Key Findings of the Plan Bothnia Project*, Finepress, Turku.
Bosselmann, Klaus, Engel, Ron & Taylor, Prue. (2008). Governance for Sustainability – Issues, Challenges, Successes. IUCN Environmental Policy and Law Paper No. 70, IUCN, Gland, Switzerland.
Brunner, R.D. & Clark, T.W. (1997). A practice-based approach to ecosystem management. *Conservation Biology*, vol. 11, no. 1, pp. 48–58.
Craig, R.K. (2010). 'Stationarity is Dead' – long live transformation: Five principles for climate change adaptation law. *Harvard Environmental Law Review*, vol. 34, pp. 9–73.
Craig, R.K. (2012). *Comparative Ocean Governance: Place-Based Protections in an Era of Climate Change*, Edward Elgar, Cheltenham.
Crowder, L. & Norse, E. (2008). Essential ecological insights for marine ecosystem-based management and marine spatial planning. *Marine Policy*, vol. 32, no. 5, pp. 772–778.

Crowder, L.B., Osherenko, G., Young, O.R., Airamé, S., Norse, E.A., Baron, N., ... Langdon, S.J. (2006). Resolving mismatches in US ocean governance. *Science*, vol. 313, no. 5787, p. 617.
Douvere, F. (2008). The importance of marine spatial planning in advancing ecosystem-based sea use management. *Marine Policy*, vol. 32, no. 5, pp. 762–771.
Douvere, F., Maes, F., Vanhulle, A. & Schrijvers, J. (2007). The role of marine spatial planning in sea use management: The Belgian case. *Marine Policy*, vol. 31, no. 2, pp. 182–191.
Ehler, C. & Douvere, F. (2009). *Marine Spatial Planning: A Step-By-Step Approach Toward Ecosystem Based Management*, UNESCO/IOC, Paris.
Fuller, L.L. (1969). *The Morality of Law*, Yale University Press, New Haven and London.
Gilliland, P.M. & Laffoley, D. (2008). Key elements and steps in the process of developing ecosystem-based marine spatial planning. *Marine Policy*, vol. 32, no. 5, pp. 787–796.
Hall, S.J. (2005). US ocean policy: A blueprint for the future. *Environment: Science and Policy for Sustainable Development*, vol. 47, no. 2, pp. 41–43.
Hassan, Daud. (2013). The Great Barrier Reef-Maritime Spatial Planning. *Environmental Policy and Law*, vol. 43, no. 4–5, pp. 259–269.
Heinrichs, B. (2007). Plan coast-contribution to maritime spatial planning, paper presented at 4th International Plan Coast Conference, Berlin, 21 November 2007.
Hill, M. (2012). *Climate change and water governance: Adaptive capacity in Chile and Switzerland*. Springer Science & Business Media, Dordrecht.
Holling, C.S. (2000). Theories for sustainable futures. *Conservation Ecology*, vol. 4, no. 2.
Jay, S. (2010). Built at sea: Marine management and the construction of marine spatial planning. *Town Planning Review*, vol. 81, no. 2, pp. 173–192.
Johnson, B. (1999). The role of adaptive management as an operational approach for resource management agencies. *Conservation Ecology*, vol. 3, no. 2.
Jones, E.B. (1972). *Law of the Sea: Oceanic Resources*, Southern Methodist University Press, Dallas.
Kenchington, R.A. & Day, J.C. (2011). Zoning, a fundamental cornerstone of effective Marine Spatial Planning: lessons learnt from the Great Barrier Reef, Australia, *Journal of Coastal Conservation*, vol. *15(2)*, pp. 271–278.
Kuokkanen, Tuomas (2015). Marine Spatial Planning in International Law Before MSP. In Daud Hassan, Tuomas Kuokkanen & Niko Soininen (eds.): Transboundary Marine Spatial Planning and International Law, Routledge, London, pp. 23–41.
Maes, F. (2008). The international legal framework for marine spatial planning. *Marine Policy*, vol. 32, no. 5, pp. 797–810.
Maes, F., Schrijvers, J., & Vanhulle, A. (2005). A flood of space. Towards a spatial structure plan for the sustainable management of the North Sea, Gaufre project publication. Available at: http://www.belspo.be/belspo/organisation/publ/pub_ostc/MA/GaufreZVR_en.pdf, accessed 23 May 2018.
Merrie, A. (2010) Managing the Marine Mosaic: A Briefing on Marine Spatial Planning with an Ecosystem Approach. Annual Report, Spatial Planning Stockholm Resilience Centre, Stockholm.
Pardy, B. (2003). Changing Nature: The Myth of the Inevitability of Ecosystem Management, *Pace Environmental Law Review*, vol. 29, pp. 675–692.
Pardy, B. (2008). The Pardy-Ruhl Dialogue on ecosystem management part V: Discretion, complex-adaptive problem solving and the rule of law. *Pace Environmental Law Review*, vol. 25, p. 341.

Parma, A.M. (1998). What can adaptive management do for our fish, forests, food, and biodiversity? *Integrative Biology: Issues, News, and Reviews*, vol. 1, no. 1, pp. 16–26.
Peel, D., & Lloyd, M.G. (2004). The social reconstruction of the marine environment: Towards marine spatial planning? *Town Planning Review*, vol. 75, no. 3, pp. 359–378.
Pew Oceans Commission. (2003). America's living oceans: Charting a course for sea change, www.pewtrusts.org/uploadedFiles/wwwpewtrustsorg/Reports/Protecting_ocean_life/env_pew_oceans_final_report.pdf.
Platjouw, F.M. (2016). *Environmental Law and the Ecosystem Approach: Maintaining Ecological Integrity Through Consistency in Law*, Routledge, London.
Qiu, W. & Jones, P.J.S. (2013). The emerging policy landscape for marine spatial planning in Europe, *Marine Policy*, vol. 39, pp. 182–190.
Schäfer, N. (2009). Maritime spatial planning: The roadmap. Presentation in the HELCOM MSP Workshop in Helsinki 27–29 January 2009.
Slocombe, D.S. (1993). Implementing ecosystem-based management. *BioScience*, vol. 43, no. 9, pp. 612–622.
US Commission on Ocean Policy (2004). An ocean blueprint for the 21st century, final report of the U.S. commission on ocean policy to the president and congress, Washington, DC.
White House Council on Environmental Quality (2010). Final report of the ocean policy task force, Available at: www.whitehouse.gov/files/documents/OPTF_FinalRecs.pdf.
World Resources Institute (2005). Millennium Ecosystem Assessment: Summary for Decision-Makers. Available at: http://www.wri.org/publication/millennium-ecosystem-assessment, accessed 27 December 2013.
Young, O.R., Osherenko, G., Ekstrom, J., Crowder, L.B., Ogden, J., Wilson, J.A., . . . Halpren, B.S. (2007). Solving the crisis in ocean governance: Place-based management of marine ecosystems. *Environment: Science and Policy for Sustainable Development*, vol. 49, no. 4, pp. 20–32.

PART III
Conservation and management of marine living resources

PART III

8
CONSERVATION OF MARINE LIVING RESOURCES AND FISHERIES MANAGEMENT

Daud Hassan and Emdadul Haque

Introduction

The extensive maritime spaces and their associated coastal zones are critically important to sustaining life on Earth. Coastal and ocean areas are the drivers for the global economy and play a crucial and increasingly important role in global food security. These areas are therefore of critical importance across scales, from the global to the regional, at national and sub-national coastal community levels especially, in terms of marine living resources and fisheries management. The oceans are, however, also increasingly under threat, notably as a result of enhanced competition for coastal and marine resources, coupled with increasingly intense and diverse uses, which often occur in coincident maritime spaces leading to a threat to the sustainability of those resources.

The aim of this chapter is to critically evaluate the applications and shortcomings of the current regimes for fisheries resources management in a sustainable manner. In this context, the United Nations Convention on the Law of the Sea (UNCLOS),[1] the 1995 Fish Sticks Agreement (FSA)[2] and other international law and policies relating to fisheries management will be analysed. Various obstacles and challenges present in the current fisheries resources management regime that could be identified as posing an obstacle to effective conservation and management due in particular to climate change will be highlighted in the paper. Applications of management principles, vulnerability, adaptive capacity and mitigation measures of the current regimes will be considered in this respect. Exploring the reasons for weaknesses in current arrangements, the chapter will suggest an effective and rational cooperative regime for sustainable fisheries resources management.

World ocean and its fisheries resources

The ocean is one of the Earth's most valuable natural resources. It occupies 71% of the Earth's surface. It is, thus, possible to argue that it is more appropriate to label it being planet Ocean rather than planet Earth.

The ocean is a source of food, energy and minerals, and it has apparently also increasingly become a source of natural medicine; it regulates the Earth's climate and hosts the greatest diversity of life and ecosystems; it is a provider of economic, social and aesthetic services to humankind (Ryabinin & Tang, 2017). Among these services, marine living resources including fisheries and marine genetic resources (MGRs)[3] are of particular importance. The ocean provides many types of fish including highly migratory species,[4] anadromous stocks, catadromous species and pelagic fishes. Marine living resources also include marine mammal like sea turtles, whales, seals and sea lions, dolphins and porpoises etc.[5] The connection to the oceans and livelihoods is deeply intertwined. It is estimated that marine fisheries support, directly or indirectly, more than 200 million people globally.[6]

Climate change and its impact on marine living resources

The ocean has a natural ability to buffer the atmosphere and the ocean surface is in a state of equilibrium with the atmosphere with respect to CO_2 and heat. As concentrations of either increase in the atmosphere, they increase in the ocean as well. These increases change the physical and chemical properties of the ocean and affect several oceanic processes (Herr & Galland, 2009).

On the other hand, the Earth's climate has always changed, alternating ice ages and interglacial periods have shaped the living world. The contemporary human activities, through the emission of greenhouse gases, are the new engine of the evolution of the climate system. The speed of contemporary climate change seems unprecedented and exceeds the natural adaptive capacity of many living organisms (Simard, Laffoley, & Baxter, 2016).

Oceanic climatological changes have a profound effect on life in the oceans. They particularly involve range shifts towards the poles, causing an overall decrease in biodiversity at the equator and the tropics, and an increase in biodiversity at higher latitudes (Simard et al., 2016). Climate-related changes in ocean ecosystems such as warming oceans, increasing acidification and rising seas can affect the distribution and abundance of marine species and thereby impact the people and communities that depend on them.[7]

The ocean absorbs between one fourth and one half of all anthropogenic CO_2 emissions.[8]

While absorption of CO_2 by the ocean slows the atmospheric greenhouse effect, it puts marine and thus human life at risk. Dissolved CO_2 lowers the ocean's pH and leads to acidification (Herr & Galland, 2009). A doubling of the atmospheric CO_2 concentration, which could occur within the next 50 years, would cause a velocity of change to marine chemistry and subsequent extinction events not seen for 65 million years (Mcleod et al., 2008). Experiments show that ocean acidification affects ocean physics by reducing sound absorption and allowing sound to travel much further (Hester, Peltzer, Kirkwood, & Brewer, 2008). This reduced absorption causes ambient sound levels to rise significantly, harming marine life.

According to the latest climate change report card released by the Marine Climate Change Impacts Partnership (MCCIP), ocean acidity has increased by 30% in the last 200 years, which has serious implications for marine ecosystems with changes in plankton, fish distribution and species composition in the ocean; in the last decade there has been a 35% decrease in Arctic sea ice and a 15% reduction in winter sea ice, leading to changes in habitats and ecosystems.[9]

For millennia, we have fished. And with continued increases in human population numbers, improvements in fishing technologies and the globalisation of seafood markets, we have achieved levels of industrialised fishing that the ocean cannot support. As a direct result of human fishing pressure, several species have become commercially, ecologically or biologically extinct (Jackson et al., 2001) and large predatory fishes have decreased by 90% (Myers & Worm, 2003). This loss of biodiversity and biomass threatens the ocean's ability to continue providing food and other ecosystem services to billions of people around the world (Worm et al., 2006). Added pressure from a changing climate and changing ocean increase the impacts of fisheries on marine biodiversity and ecosystems, and fishing decreases a system's resilience to change (Planque, et al., 2010). Seventy-nine percent of the world's marine fish stocks are now fully exploited, over-exploited, depleted or recovering.[10]

Marine pollution is a serious problem that affects all marine organisms and ecosystems, no matter how remote. Beaches on tiny islands in the middle of the Pacific thousands of kilometres from the nearest major population centre can be covered with plastic. Tissues in marine mammals that live in the Arctic, far from any factories, contain some of the highest levels of industrial pollutants of any animals on the planet (Herr & Galland, 2009).

Mangroves are highly productive ecosystems providing numerous goods and services that include supporting fisheries, maintaining and improving water quality and providing coastal protection and carbon sequestration. Mangroves have been estimated to provide at least US$1.6 billion per year in ecosystem services worldwide. Approximately 67% of global mangroves have been lost in the past century to coastal development, aquaculture, pollution and other human activities.[11]

Again, the increasing sea level rise due to greenhouse gases emission will permanently flood and reconfigure present-day coastal ecosystems which will have profound consequences on marine living resources and thus on human societies.[12]

Current regimes for conservation fisheries resources management

From time immemorial, humans have closely interacted with oceans mainly for two reasons: navigation and fishing. These two reasons again serve one common purpose, human livelihood. Therefore, oceans and its resources, particularly fisheries resources, are an inseparable part of human existence and development. This might be the reason that the international commons, when they first started growing as a community, put their best efforts in codifying law regarding control and management of the oceans and their resources (Haque, 2016). The latest development as to that effort is UNCLOS. Prior to UNCLOS, there were also some responses which lacked development.

International legal responses prior to UNCLOS

Prior to the 19th century, the world's oceans were considered an endless waste bin, regarded too vast for overuse. No meaningful regime with respect to fisheries resources management was developed at this stage. However, some conventions such as the Bi-Lateral Fisheries Agreements between Norway, Sweden, Netherlands, Germany and the Great Britain, and the North Sea Fisheries Convention 1881 between Belgium, Denmark, France, Germany and the Great Britain, were adopted to deal with fisheries resources. Rather than conservation measures they focused on enforcement and perceived overfishing close to coasts. In the beginning of the 20th century, research and investigations relating to marine living resources were promoted and encouraged by the International Council for the Exploration of the Sea (ICES), 1902. The ICES formalised the 1964 ICES Convention and brought an important development in International Law on Marine Living Resources. A number of Conventions with respect to fisheries were adopted after the Second World War such as the 1949 North West Atlantic Fisheries Convention, which focused on maximum sustained catch and the 1949 US–Mexico Agreement Relating to the Establishment of an International Commission for the Scientific Investigation of Tuna, which focused on maximum reasonable utilisation. But no formula for the size of permissible catch or over-exploitation of marine living resources was prescribed at this stage. Because of unsatisfactory arrangements of fisheries resources management, a special conference entitled the International Technical Conference on the Conservation of the Living Resources was assembled in Rome in 1955 under the auspices of the International Law Commission (ILC). A number of important issues were considered in the conference, which included the following: objectives of fishery conservation, types of scientific information and conservation measures applicable in fishery conservation programme and international conservation problems and appropriate measures to resolve them (Amador, 1959). However, the conference stressed on international cooperation for the conservation of high seas fisheries without prescribing appropriate methodology for conservation. As a result, fisheries remained unregulated and therefore tend to become over-exploited. Based on the recommendation of this Technical Conference, the ILC prepared draft articles for the 1958 Geneva Conference on the Law of the Sea, which was largely incorporated into the Convention on Fishing, and the Conservation of the Living Resources of the High Seas 1958 (hereinafter 1958 Convention).[13] The 1958 Convention defined conservation of the living resources of the high seas and imposed obligations upon States in terms of harvesting and conservation of fisheries.[14] Some of the provisions of the 1958 Convention are directed toward the implementation of conservation measures individually, cooperatively as well as unilaterally.[15] Special interests of coastal States in the fisheries adjacent to their waters are recognised, and the Convention provides that other States fishing in such areas of the high seas cannot implement their own conservation measures which are opposed to those of the coastal States (CS).[16] In this circumstance a duty to enter into negotiations to conclude cooperative measures are included in Art. 6 of the Convention. Article 9 of the Convention contains provisions on settlement of disputes. This Convention was not related to internal or territorial waters fishing, but provisions relating to fisheries conservation and management were significant. The 1958 Convention completed the groundwork for the conservation of living resources in the sea, however, the Convention failed to achieve support by State parties due to some reasons which included the following: lack of conservation standards, weak enforcement mechanisms and undefined jurisdictional responsibility of coastal States' preferential position with respect to high seas adjacent to their waters. Although it failed to provide satisfactory conservation measures as its provisions lacked guidance and scientific advice, the 1958 Convention provided the basis for fisheries resources management.[17] In the 1970s new beginnings in the protection and management of world resources was observed. The Stockholm Declaration[18] and a range of the international instruments were concluded and improved the management regime for the protection of the natural environment substantially, however, there was no notable development with respect to fisheries resources management before the 1980s.

UNCLOS and its response to conserving marine living resources and fisheries management

In 1982, after a decade-long negotiation, the international community adopted the UNCLOS, the most comprehensive international treaty to date governing the world oceans and their resources, which in essence is referred to as the 'Constitution of the Oceans'.[19] UNCLOS basically divided the ocean spaces in two fundamental categories: areas under national jurisdiction (AWNJ)[20] and areas beyond national jurisdiction (ABNJ).[21] Articles 61 to 67 of UNCLOS provide rules regarding the conservation and utilisation of resources and fisheries management at AWNJ, while Articles 88, 116 to 120 provide the same at ABNJ. Besides UNCLOS, international legal and policy instruments of particular relevance include the UN Fish Stocks Agreement, and the FAO International Guidelines for the Management of Deep-sea Fisheries in the High Seas (FAO Deep-sea Fisheries Guidelines).[22]

Laws regulating conservation living resources and fisheries management at AWNJ

The UNCLOS made a notable change by establishing the Exclusive Economic Zone (EEZ) which gives coastal States exclusive jurisdiction up to 200 nautical miles from their shores.[23] The adoption of the EEZ in the UNCLOS framework has placed 90% of world fisheries under domestic jurisdiction (Franckx, 2006) and increased potential for rational and sustained use of fisheries resources.

Articles 61–73 of UNCLOS set out various rights and duties of a coastal State (hereinafter referred to as CS) with respect to the conservation and management of marine living resources. However, Articles 61 and 62 of the UNCLOS contain main provisions with respect to fisheries management in the EEZ, these provisions are supplemented b several several other articles for the management arrangements of overall living resources in the sea. These include management of straddling stocks (Article 63), highly migratory species (Article 64), anadromous species (Article 66), catadromous species (Article 67) and marine mammals (Article 65).

Article 56(1) of UNCLOS gives CS rights to explore, exploit and manage fish stocks within the EEZ. Article 61 of UNCLOS also imposes certain duties on CS. These include the following: CS must establish the total allowable catch (TAC);[24] CS must also implement conservation and management measures which counters over-exploitation.[25] With specific reference to management and conservation measures, the UNCLOS emphasises that harvested stocks must be maintained or restored at certain levels. In this respect Article 61(3) of the UNCLOS provides:

> measures shall ... be designed to maintain or restore population to harvested species at levels that can produce the maximum sustainable yield, as qualified by relevant environmental and economic factors, including the economic needs of coastal fishing communities and the special requirements of developing States, and taking into account fishing patterns, the interdependence of stocks and any generally recommended international minimum standards, whether sub-regional, regional or global.[26]

Article 62 of UNCLOS 'substantiates the nature of the rights provided by article 61, and confirms that a CS has wide range of methods open to it to meet its management objectives'.[27] UNCLOS expressly requires CS to promote the optimum utilisation of living resources in its EEZ.[28] It also provides that CS should give access to foreign States where a CS lacks capacity to harvest the entire allowable catch.[29] However, in terms of access to surplus foreign States, the UNCLOS emphasises certain issues, which include these:

> [S]hall take into account all relevant factors, including, *inter alia*, the significance of living resources of the area to the economy of the CS and its other national interest, the provisions of articles 69 and 70, the requirements of developing states in the sub-region or region in harvesting part of the surplus and the need to minimize economic dislocation in states whose nations have habitually fished in the zone or which have made substantial efforts in research and identification of stocks.[30]

This article also provides that where there is shared stock between two EEZs, CS of those EEZs should seek, either directly or through appropriate sub-regional or regional organisations, to agree upon measures necessary for the conservation of these stocks in the adjacent area.[31]

Laws regulating conservation living resources and fisheries management at ABNJ

Nearly two thirds of the oceans are beyond any State's territorial sovereignty or jurisdiction.[32] The high seas and the deep seas are two distinct areas of the oceans that are home to unique marine wildlife that are beyond national jurisdiction. Since these resources do not belong to any one State, they are subject to international law. While the UNCLOS provides the fundamental and overarching legally binding framework for fisheries management in ABNJ, the UN Fish Stocks Agreement elaborates on requirements for the conservation and management of straddling fish stocks and highly migratory fish stocks, particularly in the high seas. The FAO Deep-sea Fisheries Guidelines addresses and provides policy directions on various issues raised in the UNGA resolutions (e.g., UNGA Res. 61/105) in relation to deep-sea fisheries.[33]

Articles 116 to 120 of UNCLOS provide the legal framework on conservation of living resources and fisheries management in the high seas.

Article 116 reinforces the State's duty of cooperation as expressed in article 63(2), Article 117 establishes a duty on States to take measures for their respective nationals as may be necessary for conservation, and to cooperate with other States to reach the same issue, and Article 119 provides a theoretical basis for the management of high seas fisheries in the same manner as used for the EEZ. Whereas Article 116 of UNCLOS approves the right of all States to engage in fishing on the high seas subject to the rights and duties as well as the interests of coastal States provided for EEZ, *inter alia*, in Article 63 and articles 64 to 67,[34] it, in fact, recognises the necessity of conserving and managing the 'transboundary' or 'shared' fish stocks.[35]

Due to the flexible nature of the UNCLOS, further adjustments of these provisions were not ruled out, and, one year after the UNCLOS came into force, the Agreement for the Implementation of the Provisions of the United Nations Convention on the Law of the Sea of 10 December 1982 Relating to the Conservation and Management of Straddling Fish Stocks and Highly Migratory Fish Stocks[36] (hereinafter Fish Stock Agreement) was implemented.

With the need for more effective enforcement measures for the conservation and management of straddling and highly migratory fish stocks, the Preamble of the Fish Stock Agreement indicates that the management of high seas fisheries is inadequate in many areas, which include the following:

> some resources are over utilized, there are problems of unregulated fishing, problems of over capitalization, excessive fleet sizes, vessel re-flagging in order to escape regulatory controls, insufficiently selective fishing gear, unreliable databases and a lack of sufficient cooperation between States.[37]

On the basis of principles 4 and 15 of Rio Declaration and Para 17.21 of Agenda 21 of United Nations Conference on Environment and Development (UNCED), 1992,[38] the Fish Stocks Agreement intends to ensure the long-term conservation and sustainable use of straddling fish stocks and highly migratory fish stocks through effective implementation of fisheries-related provisions of the UNCLOS.[39] The Agreement contains general principles of stock management and obliges CS to utilise the principles by adopting measures to ensure the long-term sustainability of straddling fish stocks and highly migratory fish stocks and promoting the objective of their optimum utilisation.[40] It incorporates the precautionary approach and the ecosystem approach to the conservation, management and exploitation of fish stocks in waters both within AWNJ and ABNJ.[41]

The Fish Stocks Agreement is the first international fishery convention that explicitly mentions a precautionary approach for fisheries resources management. It requires that States shall be more cautious when information is uncertain, unreliable or inadequate and that the absence of adequate scientific information shall not be used as a reason for postponing or failing to take conservation and management measures.[42] When new or exploratory fisheries are being undertaken, the Agreement also obliges States to take special precaution providing that States shall adopt as soon as possible cautious conservation and management measures, including catch limits and effort limits.[43] Importantly the Agreement has laid down the way of implementation of precautionary approach.[44]

The Fish Stocks Agreement emphasises the compatibility of conservation and management measures. In terms of determining this issue the Agreement obliges States to take into account various matters in accordance with the UNCLOS which include: biological unity and other biological characteristics of the stocks and the relationship between the distribution of the stocks; the fisheries and the geographical particularities of the region concerned; and ensure that such measures do not result in harmful impact on the living marine resources as a whole.[45] It provides more stringent obligation on the flag State to fish on high seas.

The Agreement contains stronger dispute settlement provisions than the UNCLOS.[46] In terms of procedures for the settlement of disputes, it states that 'the provisions relating to the settlement of disputes set out in Part XV of the Convention apply mutatis mutandis to any dispute between States Parties to this Agreement concerning the interpretation or application of a sub-regional, regional or global fisheries agreement relating to straddling fish stocks or highly migratory fish stocks to which they are parties, including any dispute concerning the conservation and management of such stocks, whether or not they are also parties to the Convention'.[47]

The Jakarta Mandate on Marine and Coastal Biological Diversity, which is based on the recommendations of the Subsidiary Body on Scientific, Technical and Technological Advice (SBSTTA),[48] has adopted five thematic areas which include: sustainable use of coastal and marine living resources; integrated marine and coastal zone management; and marine and coastal protected areas. The necessity for application of the precautionary approach was also repeated in the mandate. However, in terms of the management of marine and coastal living resources, the Mandate's application is limited to within the EEZ.

Soft law including the 1995 FAO Code of Conduct for Responsible Fisheries[49] and the 1995 Kyoto Declaration and Plan of Action on the Sustainable Contribution of Fisheries to Food Security have encouraged States to undertake strategies and policies for fisheries resources management and urge States to utilise fishing techniques and practices that could reduce the impact on the ecosystem.[50] However, they are voluntary in nature and therefore unable to establish any legal rights or obligations upon States. They have the same legal status as other non-binding instruments.

The FAO International Guidelines for the Management of Deep-sea Fisheries in the High Seas (hereinafter FAO Deep Sea Fisheries Guideline) provide recommendations on governance frameworks and management of deep-sea fisheries with the aim to ensure long-term conservation and sustainable use of marine living resources in the deep sea and to prevent significant adverse impacts on vulnerable marine ecosystems (VMEs).[51] The FAO Deep-sea Fisheries Guidelines include criteria for identifying VMEs and assessing potential impacts of bottom fishing in order to facilitate the adoption and implementation of conservation and management measures by RFMO/As and flag States.[52]

The guidelines also set out a framework for data collection, assessments and monitoring, control and surveillance. All management measures taken by States or Regional Fisheries Management Organizations and Arrangements (RFMO/As) should be in compliance with other international instruments for the management of deep-sea fisheries and should be based on the precautionary approach and the ecosystem approach to fisheries.[53]

They also call on States to cooperate through RFMO/As and/or establish and strengthen RFMO/As to this end. While RFMO/As are given a central place in the management of these fisheries, the Guidelines also offer advice on interim measures that may be taken in areas where no competent RFMO/As exist or where an RFMO/A is in the process of developing the range of policies and measures required for effective management of deep-sea fisheries.[54]

Protection and preservation of the marine environment and fisheries resources

Part XII of the UNCLOS provides provisions about the protection and preservation of the marine environment, which, without targeting any particular resources, are applicable, generally. However, as far as the marine environment is concerned, it has an inevitable impact on its resources, and thus on marine fisheries resources as well.

Article 194 (5) of the UNCLOS contains a presumption of management of fisheries resources. It provides: 'the measures taken in accordance with this Part shall include those necessary to protect and preserve rare or fragile ecosystems as well as the habitat of depleted, threatened or endangered species and other forms of marine life.'[55]

However, it allows States wide discretion in performing duties by including reference to the use of 'best practicable means' and 'in accordance with their capabilities'[56] in terms of fisheries resources management. The insertion of those words has given States a licence to be reluctant in relation to their responsibility for taking adequate measures in this respect. It introduces an uncertain standard for fisheries resources management.

Article 197 of UNCLOS obliges States to consider international and regional cooperation for marine environmental protection. However, it is without significant normative content and tends to demonstrate that UNCLOS does not require States to take effective measures for living resources management.

Rather than imposing additional requirements to cooperate or consult, these provisions do not represent any important progress with respect to the effective management of fisheries resources. Questions remain as to the positive obligation to cooperate and to the nature and extent of duty to cooperate.

UNCLOS provides the legal basis to implement the management principles of the sustainable development of marine and coastal environment and resources (Tsamenyi, 1997). However, it does not itself provide a framework for the management of fisheries resources. The UNCLOS does not give guidance to States on how to govern oceans and coastal areas in an integrated manner, or how to deal with the effects of one use on other uses, or how to bring ocean and coastal management together.[57] The concept of the precautionary principle has not been explicitly enshrined in UNCLOS. Provisions regarding the polluter-pays principle is absent in UNCLOS.[58]

UNCLOS gives CS their rights to adopt laws and policies in ice covered areas to protect the environment from pollution and other activities, which could disturb the ecological balance of the polar regions. Article 234 states that

> Coastal States have the right to adopt and enforce non-discriminatory laws and regulations for the prevention, reduction and control of marine pollution from vessels in ice-covered areas within the limits of the exclusive economic zone, where particularly severe climatic conditions and the presence of ice covering such areas for most of the year create obstructions or exceptional hazards to navigation, and pollution of the marine environment could cause major harm to or irreversible disturbance of the ecological balance. Such laws and regulations shall have due regard to navigation and the protection and preservation of the marine environment based on the best available scientific evidence.

It is an important article as it has relevance with respect to Arctic fisheries resources management. It provides a stimulus for CS to develop their laws in area of pollution control and it also provides a legal basis for the integration of laws and policies for the protection of Arctic marine environment. However, it is too general and broad to provide useful guidance to States for fisheries resources management. It has been drafted in such terms that it gives no specific content to the underlying obligation of due diligence. Vague or imprecise language is used in relation to the obligation to the protection and preservation of the marine environment and in terms of the 'best available scientific evidence'. The article is far from satisfactory and does not have much of a practical effect with respect to fisheries resources management.

An effective marine environmental dispute settlement system is important to encourage development of appropriate marine and coastal environmental standards. Specific exclusion of conservation and management issues from UNCLOS compulsory dispute settlement system stifles any chance of judicial development in terms of the management and conservation of fisheries resources.

Effective conservation and management of fisheries resources: existing legal framework and challenges

The formulation and adaption of UNCLOS was an outcome of the continuous effort and will of the international community towards codifying customary rules of the international law of the sea (mainly customary laws on maritime jurisdiction and delimitation) and to adopt some progressive development in conserving oceans' environments and their resources as well as governing oceans' activities in a sustainable manner (Haque, 2016). The progressive development part of UNCLOS seemingly provided significant basis for such shortcomings. These shortcomings lie not in the formulation of UNCLOS, rather in the scope of its framework. There are two main reasons of such shortcomings: first, the limitation of the framers to foresee the upcoming changes in scientific development, socio-economic status, ecology and climate. Such changes mostly refer to the natural changes to which some human activities are responsible to act with. Second, the lack of legal and policy framework in addressing, controlling and managing the increasing dependency and growing human activities in the oceans. Here in this chapter the lack of legal and policy framework of UNCLOS will be of particular relevance.

These provisions of the UNCLOS intend to change the philosophy of fisheries exploitation and ownership of fishing vessels patterns through the exploitation of resources in the EEZ in a rational and sustainable manner and considering maximum sustainable yield (MSY) for fishing. However, these provisions are not free of shortcomings.

UNCLOS has not imposed any restrictions on coastal States to deal with the fisheries in the territorial Sea. It even does not recommend any sub-regional, regional or international minimum standard of TAC or MSY rather left a large degree of discretion to the coastal states in deciding the TAC and the MSY as long as it does not lead to over-exploitation.[59] Obviously, the limit of the TAC and MSY may vary from place to place depending on prevailing environment. Given this identified gap in UNCLOS, '(e)ach state can seek to qualify the MSY in manner best fitting its individual circumstances'.[60] Relevant environmental and economic factors as qualifications give a coastal State to exercise its power at any size of allowable catch legitimately.[61] Also a CS can decide what constitutes surplus and thus regulate who gets to fish in their EEZ. Right to levy fees, which in turn means that the right to access surplus can amount to simply the right to purchase stock at an open market. All these discretions create a scope for coastal States to demonstrate a greater readiness to claim their rights than to accept their obligations. This could severely undermine proper accountability for the management of marine fisheries in a rational manner.

UNCLOS does emphasise that coastal States take necessary conservation and management measures for the maintenance of the living resources, so that the level of their reproduction may not be endangered or seriously threatened; this empowered the coastal States to establish laws and regulations in this regard, but it failed to provide any international minimum standard to this effect. Absent such standard, power to determine such conservation and management measures in fact lies with the coastal State, which demonstrates the lack of an international approach to set an accorded international governing pattern as the solemn expression of the will of the international commons.[62] Again, in determining the conservation measures, a coastal State has an obligation to consider the 'best scientific evidence' available to it.[63] Unfortunately, UNCLOS does not provide any definition of 'best scientific evidence'. Rather it stressed that the coastal States and competent or appropriate international organisations irrespective of their sub-regional, regional or global character to cooperate to these ends.[64] UNCLOS also urge CS to enter into cooperative arrangements with other States whose interests may be specifically affected by the harvesting of certain categories of stocks which include straddling stocks, highly migratory species, anadromous species, catadromous species and marine mammals.[65] In terms of cooperation between States, the role of regional and sub-regional organisations have been referred to in the UNCLOS.[66] Even in absence of such organisations, Article 64 of UNCLOS urges States to establish them.[67] What is striking is that these provisions, without making any reference to any international organisation, left all powers to the States to take measures or to cooperate with other States for the conservation of the living resources of the high seas, and emphasised establishing sub-regional or regional fisheries organisations for this purpose,[68] which is not compatible with the spirit of UNCLOS itself. Because none of the marine spaces and its resources attributes the character of *res nullius*, they lie either within national jurisdiction or within international jurisdiction. If UNCLOS established the International Seabed Authority (ISA) to govern the Area as the common heritage of mankind, likewise, UNCLOS must establish an international organisation to conserve and manage marine living and fisheries resources lying with ABNJ since they are also inevitable for the survival of mankind. Again, the persistent emphasis to cooperate in managing transboundary fish stock is not easy.[69] UNCLOS does not provide any principle or standard of such cooperation, which makes this issue optional for the States.

Although Article 68 of the UNCLOS specified provisions regarding sedentary species, but referred to its definition in Article 77(4) and, therefore, projected its application within the area of continental shelf (4).[70] Thus, the conservation and management of this type of resources may involve areas beyond EEZ (200 nm) and may fall within the water column of the high seas, but within AWNJ since the extent of a coastal State's continental shelf (based on its geographical, geological and geomorphological circumstances) may extend up to 350 nm or 100 nautical miles from the 2,500-metre isobath.[71] Again, such species may inhabit in areas beyond national jurisdiction. Interestingly, UNCLOS does not provide any clear provision as to how the States should conserve and manage this type of resources both within and beyond national jurisdiction.[72] It also remains silent as to whether these living resources should be considered as Common Heritage of Mankind. This creates a back-lock in the UNCLOS legal framework.

There are currently gaps in the international legal framework that exists around the use of MGRs. Different legal instruments exist which are related to marine biodiversity and access and benefit sharing (ABS) (Greiber, 2011). These include the Convention of Biological Diversity (CBD)[73] and its Nagoya Protocol.[74] The International Treaty on Plant genetic resources for food and agriculture (ITPGRFA)[75] is also a useful model applicable to plant genetic resources. However, these agreements place a greater emphasis on the protection of terrestrial genetic resources compared to marine genetic resources. In fact, marine genetic resources that lie beyond the national jurisdiction are not covered under these agreements. There is currently a lack of a specific legal instrument to regulate their use. However, the UNCLOS does not provide guidance on marine genetic resources. Hence, marine genetic resources located in places beyond national jurisdiction can be considered unregulated.

UNCLOS provides no provision for the conservation and management of MGRs. The reason might be that UNCLOS was adopted before the potential identification of microbial life in the oceans and the commercial uses of marine genetic resources were known. Most of the MGRs development to date occurred within EEZ, although many come from ABNJ.[76] It is assumed that the demand of MGRs from ABNJ is increasing at a fast pace. Therefore, the mechanism for its conservation and management is of importance. The existing conventional provisions for EEZ may be applied for MGRs from EEZ. But, absent the legal provisions, conservation and management of MGRs from ABNJ has become a big challenge for the effective application of UNCLOS. In terms of marine genetic resources, UNCLOS does not provide any single provision as to whether the 'common heritage of mankind' principle relates and applies to these resources (McGarry, 2011) because MGRs from ABNJ may share high similarity with that from AWNJ (Jianming, n.d.)

It has established a framework for the cooperation of States in terms of fish stocks management.[77] The adoption of the UN Fish Agreement was pivotal in improving international coordination in the establishment and fixing the responsibilities of regional and sub-regional fisheries management organisations and arrangements. This Agreement provides the formula for the functions of sub-regional and regional fisheries management organisations (RFMOs)[78] and arrangements, and the obligation of States in such organisations and arrangements and thus strengthened the arrangements of conservation and management of fish stocks.[79] It can be attributed that while the Fish Stocks Agreement provides the framework, RFMOs are the implementing mechanisms. But what is striking, UNCLOS does not provide any standard to measure competency or appropriateness of such organisations. There is a lack of effective linkage between national, regional and international conservation measures, and management response to transition phase is insufficient. Generally real commitment for regional management fisheries is still far away (Hassan, 2009). One might speculate that UNCLOS impliedly but deliberately avoided any accorded international approach in terms of forming any international organisation with the mandate to regulate, control and supervise the conservation of marine living resources and fisheries management.

Moreover, it also sets out the framework for international cooperation in fisheries compliance and enforcement and outlined the procedures for boarding and inspection.[80] The final component of the international compliance and enforcement framework involves port States, which is laid out in Article 23.[81] This provision goes beyond the UNCLOS in that it is perhaps the first occasion in which port State obligations are associated with the monitoring and control of fishing vessels to ensure compliance with measures. The Agreement also provides that State parties are liable in accordance with international law for damage or loss attributable to them in regards to this Agreement.[82] In the conservation and management of straddling fish stocks and highly migratory fish stocks on the high seas, this Agreement provides the factors to be considered in the determination of the nature and extent of the rights of a participating State in RFMOs and encourages and facilitates participation of developing States in RFMOs and assists particularly the least-developed and small island developing States to enable them to participate in high seas fisheries.[83]

All the relevant provisions of UNCLOS and of the Fish Stocks Agreement constitute an important contribution to the conservation and management of fish stocks. In some instances, it provided new principles, strategies and developments and brought significant change in the philosophy of conservation and management of fisheries resources as well as to the development of international fisheries law. However, no explicit reference has been made with respect to integrated coastal zone management and to the polluter-pays principle in the Agreement, although these management principles are useful for the sustainable management of fisheries resources as they advocate unifying policy components across the board to achieve comprehensiveness, aggregation and consistency and rational use of scarce resources respectively.[84] There is no explicit provision with respect to living resources management in ice-covered areas. Again, this Agreement can be seen as biased towards the fishing interests of coastal States whose waters lie adjacent to the high seas. Although the 'preferential fishing rights' of the coastal States have been supported both by the jurists and publicists,[85] an abstract examination of the coastal States' interests to marine living resources would find support to this idea that due to their of relevant importance for the survival of the mankind as a whole as well as for their equitable distribution amongst the intra and inter generations, such preferential character of the coastal States fishing rights should not be bifurcated from the common interest. Evidently UNCLOS and its umbrella legal framework like the Fish Stocks Agreement failed to uphold the direct control of the international commons on managing such resources, rather it left it on the will of the coastal States and other States and organisations involved in such fishing. This is a significant lack of UNCLOS to be considered as a comprehensive convention. Obviously, resources for their extinguishable nature are not granted, and hence their conservation and management are of particular importance for their sustainability. Here, we should be mindful that one small step into marine space, without following any internationally agreed or approved given standard, may bring giant negative impact for mankind.[86]

The concept of MPA emerged in the 1980s as a tool for managing and protecting the marine environment and biodiversity in exercising sovereign rights in areas under national jurisdictions.[87] For the last two decades, the nature and designation of MPA has undergone a process of rapid change (Beatriz, 2017). As a result, replacing MPA, a new concept, Marine Spatial Planning (MSP), has been developed and international attention is growing in its favour. The nature of MSP is more inclusive; it advocates and promotes an ecosystem-based ocean governance system in an integrated and sustainable manner (Hassan, Kuokkanen, & Soininen, 2015). MSP, in its approach to marine conservation, claims its extension and application to areas beyond national jurisdiction, the high seas and the Area. UNCLOS does not have any specific provision that approves the application of such an inclusive concept.

Articles 192 and 194 of UNCLOS mainly focuses on State's obligation to undertake individual or joint measures to prevent, reduce and control pollution of the marine environment in areas under States' jurisdiction or control although softly emphasised to 'protect and preserve rare or fragile ecosystems as well as the habitat of depleted, threatened or endangered species and other forms of marine life'.[88] One might find this soft emphasis as UNCLOS's approval to the application of measures to prevent or control pollution of the marine environment in areas beyond national jurisdiction (ABNJ), but that is not the fact at all (Beatriz, 2017). Provisions regarding the adoption and enforcement of applicable international rules, regulations and standard to prevent, reduce and control marine pollution as specified in Articles 207–222 has scant guidance for the States in its formulation. It does not provide answers as to what are the applicable international rules and standards relating to the prevention, reduction and control of pollution, rather it only emphasised taking into account internationally agreed rules, standards and recommended practices and procedures. This lacuna raises question as to the effectiveness of UNCLOS to ensure a standard of international practice relating to the prevention, reduction and control of pollution. [89] Again, in terms of obligations under other conventions on the protection and preservation of the marine environment, States which have concluded special conventions and agreements earlier and intending to conclude agreements in furtherance of UNCLOS are to act and proceed in a manner consistent with the general principles and objectives of UNCLOS.[90] Strikingly, although compliance with the general principles as set forth in UNCLOS has been emphasised, UNCLOS, in essence, does not provide any range or reference to such general principles.[91]

Article 235 of UNCLOS provides provisions empowering the States to apply their national legislation for prompt and adequate compensation or other relief in respect of damage caused by the pollution of the marine environment by natural or juridical persons under their jurisdiction.[92] But it does not even provide any legal tool for measuring the gravity or degree of marine pollution as well as possible legal remedies to that effect; it also lacks any sort of standard for accounting and imposing penalties, compensations etc. for non-fulfilment of the international obligation imposed on the States.[93] Again, the general provisions, as stipulated in Article 237, with regard to obligations under other conventions on the protection and preservation of the marine environment are so flexible and accommodative that it makes an identity and applicability crisis for UNCLOS itself.[94]

What is striking, in terms of environment pollution and biodiversity conservation and preservation in ABNJ, is that UNCLOS lacks any provision as to defining and clarifying the *locus standi* or international legal personality of persons, States or international organisations competent to file cases against the persons, ships, organisations or States responsible for such pollution. Even if the marine pollution caused by a coastal State in areas under its national jurisdiction are found to be having a fatal transboundary effect on the marine environment, affecting severely the living and non-living resources of the other coastal States, UNCLOS is also quiet in this regard.

In the context of conserving and preserving marine biodiversity beyond national jurisdiction (BBNJ), the legal framework of UNCLOS significantly lacks a definitive approach (McGarry, 2017). This ultimately affects the sustainable management of the fishery resources in the high seas and Area as well. In terms of climate change–induced environmental hazards, whether it causes within or beyond national jurisdiction, how the States should act or control oceanic activities to combat such climate change and its impact on oceanic environment and its living resources, UNCLOS is quite silent in this regard. Thus, in terms of conservation and preservation of the oceans and their resources, it lacks an actual ecosystem-based approach, rather it mostly advocates a precautionary approach (McGarry, 2017). Climate change strategies have been tailored to address controlling atmospheric pollution; however, they are not sufficient to address the challenges of fisheries resources management adequately. This requires more appropriate and concrete functions and techniques of fisheries resources management. An enhanced cooperative arrangement could be a way forward in this respect (Hassan, 2009).

Traditional fisheries management – based on single species – has proved to be inadequate to sustainably manage living resources, due to the highly complex structure of marine ecosystems (Pinto, 2012). Recent developments in marine scientific research have indicated that the ecosystem-based approach, which takes into consideration the interdependence among species and their habitats, is the most appropriate way to sustainably manage marine living resources. Shifting from a single-species approach to an ecosystem-based fisheries management (EBFM) in areas beyond national jurisdiction (ABNJ) is extremely important, because species occurring in these regions are often more vulnerable to collapse than coastal species due to their biological characteristics (Pinto, 2012).

By applying modern technology, new opportunities could be opened up due to climate–changing circumstances. Therefore, the possibility of extensive/overfishing in a higher rate from the area by distant fishing States cannot be ruled out. (Hassan, 2009). These changes could create new issues and challenges in fisheries resources management, particularly in relation to straddling and highly migratory species in the high seas. Emerging activities regarding fishing warrant a more coordinated and integrated strategic approach including more effective cooperative management and enforcement measures to address fisheries resources adequately (Hassan, 2009).

Sustainable fisheries resources management: proposal for an effective and cooperative regime

In view of previous discussion, it can be perceived that that the framer of the UNCLOS, for understandable reasons, could not consider or failed to foresee many important issues related to the conservation and management of the marine living resources and as such, despite being a comprehensive international legal instrument, UNCLOS exhibits significant lacking to that regard in terms of its scope, applicability and binding effect, and thus its effectiveness as the constitution of the ocean is at stake. The increasing use of the oceans, and thus the enhanced opportunities and threats related to the oceans, in effect pushes the limits of UNCLOS from both legal and technical perspectives.[95] Therefore, there is growing pressure for a comprehensive global regime to better address the conservation and sustainable use of marine biological diversity of areas beyond national jurisdiction, as the world has recognised the opportunities that sustainable, ocean-based economies provide while also expressing concern about the increasing deterioration of the ocean, and the resulting negative impacts on sustainable development. Pollution, the destruction of marine habitats, overfishing and the impacts of climate change are among the major drivers of the ocean's decline.[96]

Therefore, any new development in this field of international law cannot bring any effective solution, leaving these issues unconsidered. This might be the reason that the international community fixed and declared 17 Sustainable Development Goals (SDGs) and 169 targets to protect the planet from degradation, including through sustainable consumption and production, sustainably managing its natural resources and taking urgent action on climate change, so that it can support the needs of the present and future generations.[97] Goal 14 of SDGs (hereinafter SDG14) particularly stressed on the conservation and sustainable use of the oceans, seas and marine resources for sustainable development and fixed some targets to achieve that goal by 2030.[98] However, conceivably, UNCLOS provided the primary basis of international legal framework on the conservation and management of marine living resources, and thus can necessarily be considered as the starting point of international law in this regard. Through fixing SDG14, the international community projected their consensual commitment to undertake necessary steps for developing an effective measure for conservation and sustainable use of marine fisheries resources.[99] But, a comprehensive international legal framework on the conservation of marine living resources and fisheries management is still missing. Taking in account this lack, in 2004, the General Assembly of the United Nations established the Ad-Hoc Open ended Informal Working Group to study issues relating to the conservation and sustainable use of marine biological diversity beyond areas of national jurisdiction.[100] Based on the recommendation made by this Working Group, the General Assembly, on 19 June 2015, adopted a resolution deciding the development of an international legally binding instrument under the United Nations Convention on the Law of the Sea on the conservation and sustainable use of marine biological diversity of areas beyond national jurisdiction; and established, prior to holding an intergovernmental conference, a preparatory committee, to make substantive recommendations to the General Assembly on the elements of a draft text of an international, legally binding instrument under the Convention.[101] The preparatory Committee on its fourth session, held in New York on 10–21 July 2017 finalised its report and submitted it to the General Assembly.[102] The Preparatory negotiations mainly focused on a package of issues including four main areas for the treaty, namely marine genetic resources, including questions on the sharing of benefits, area-based management tools, including marine-protected areas, environmental impact assessments, capacity building and the transfer of marine technology.[103]

Based on this report, the General Assembly is now to convene an intergovernmental conference to consider the recommendations of the Preparatory Committee on the elements and to elaborate the text of an international, legally binding instrument under UNCLOS. Notably, in the report, the Preparatory Committee mainly addresses issues related to the biological biodiversity of areas beyond national jurisdiction. But, this has also created an opportunity to adopt a comprehensive, international, legally binding instrument under the scope of UNCLOS for governing the conservation and management of the marine living resources and marine environment in areas both within and beyond national jurisdiction. Bearing this in mind, this paper intends to make some proposals as follows:

- The proposed international legal instrument regarding conservation of marine living resources and fisheries management would be adopted under the scope of UNCLOS and it would have legally binding force. It should be kept in mind that the existing international legal arrangement as laid down in UNCLOS is more persuasive than binding.
- The legal instrument would differentiate between measures and standards for living resources including fisheries and marine genetic resources lying in areas within and beyond national jurisdiction as well as for transboundary or shared fish stocks. Such measures would be specific or of expressed international minimum standard, and would be set out on a case-by-case basis, relying on the geographical and material scope of particular the marine space. In so deciding,

uniqueness, rarity, special importance for threatened, endangered or declining species or habitats, vulnerability, biological diversity and productivity, sensitivity, dependency, economic and social factors of that marine space can be considered.
- The legal instrument would set out a relationship between measures under the instrument and measures under existing under relevant instruments, frameworks and relevant global, regional and sectoral bodies for the purpose of coherence and coordination of efforts.
- Without prejudice to the sovereign jurisdiction and sovereign rights of the States to exploit their natural resources, the legal instrument would set out an international minimum standard of TAC or MSY of marine living resources, including fisheries and marine genetic resources both for areas within and beyond national jurisdiction. It would also set out specific measures to prevent, reduce and control pollution of the marine environment including pollution from land-based sources, from seabed activities subject to national jurisdiction, from activities in the Area, from dumping, from vessels and from or through the atmosphere.
- The legal instrument would specifically set out an international minimum standard for conservation, protection and preservation of the marine environment for areas both within and beyond national jurisdiction. It would also set out provisions prohibiting the transformation of one type of pollution into another, consistent with the Convention.
- The legal instrument would set out specific obligations to conduct environmental impact assessments for the States to assess the potential effects of planned activities under their jurisdiction or control in areas both within and beyond national jurisdiction.
- In terms of setting out general principles, approaches, measures or standards, the legal instrument would consider the following: climate change, sustainable development, marine spatial planning or ecosystem-based management approach, precautionary approach, integrated approach, relevant stakeholder engagement, science-based approach using the best available scientific information and knowledge, including traditional knowledge and area-based management tools[104] including MPA and MSP etc.[105]
- The legal instrument would establish a legal framework on rules regulating the relation between States, RFMOs and the UNCLOS, and would set out the minimum limit of cooperation between States and RFMOs.
- The legal instrument would set out provisions making the instrument of an inclusive character in that it would be capable to absorb any measure or principle needed in future to meet the challenge for that time.
- The legal instrument would promote international cooperation and coordination at all levels, including North-South, South-South and triangular cooperation, and fix the extent of cooperation between States and RFMOs.
- The legal instrument would address the objectives of capacity building and the transfer of marine technology in supporting the achievement of the

conservation and sustainable use of marine biological diversity of areas beyond national jurisdiction by developing and strengthening the capacity of States, which may need and request it, particularly in developing States, in accordance with Article 266, paragraph 2, of the Convention, and in assisting them in fulfilling their rights and obligations under the instrument.
- This legal instrument would set out provisions to build a shared information system, based on trustworthy, science-based data, from all parts of the world's ocean.[106]
- The instrument would recognise the importance of ocean literacy for all and set out provisions for building a civic relationship with the ocean. Because the ocean and humans are inextricably interconnected, and ocean life shapes the features of Earth, such civic relation is of particular importance.[107]
- The legal instrument would ensure effective enforcement mechanisms with regard to the compliance of provisions provided in the instrument as well as in the UNCLOS.
- Without prejudice to Article 235 of the UNCLOS, the legal instrument would address specific provisions relating to responsibility and liability. In this regard, it would create a list of applicable principles, including the polluters-pay principle, for any damage caused by the pollution of the marine environment, and would set out provisions making the instrument flexible to adopt any future development in this regard.
- Without prejudice to such responsibility and liability, the legal text would stipulate provisions empowering any State or competent international, or regional or sub-regional, organisation the *locus standi* to bring any case before the international courts and tribunals established under UNCLOS for any unauthorised exploitation of marine living resources, including fisheries and MGRs, as well as for marine pollution having severe damaging effect on the conservation and sustainability of any particular marine living resource including fisheries and MGRs (this is more like public interest litigation [PIL]). Besides, a criminal case being brought before the International Criminal Court since, such damage can be seen as a crime against the environment and thus against mankind, in the sense that it could be argued that it is damaging the surviving factor for mankind.[108]
- Like the International Seabed Authority established under UNCLOS to govern the Area and its resources, this instrument would establish an international organisation (possible name of this organisation could be the High Sea Authority [HSA] or the United Nations Marine Living and Fisheries Resources Organisation [UNMALFRO]) for governing, monitoring, controlling and managing the conservation and sustainable use of all types of marine living resources including marine genetic and fisheries resources, as well as biological diversity and marine environment both within and beyond national jurisdiction. This international organisation might be comprised of four different bodies: a decision-making body, a scientific or technical body, an advisory and enforcement body and a secretariat.

- With regards to MGRs lying beyond 200 nm, the legal text, due to their location and habitats, should consider them as part of the Common Heritage of Mankind regime. The ISA should obtain an environmental impact assessment report from the organisation set under this legal instrument before issuing any licence towards the exploitation of such MGRs.
- Without any prejudice to the rights of the States and other competent international legal persons or organisations, the international organisation set out under this instrument would be competent to take notice of any sort of violation or non-compliance with any of the international principles, measures or standards set out in the instrument with regard to MSY, TAC and the conservation and preservation of marine diversity.
- Without prejudice to the dispute settlement provisions as set out in Part XV of the UNCLOS, this legal text would set out the obligation to settle disputes by peaceful means as well as the need to cooperate to prevent disputes.
- In the context of non-compliance, and where necessary, this organisation should be endorsed with the authority to initiate legal actions against the actor responsible for non-compliance.

The United Nations has proclaimed a Decade of Ocean Science for Sustainable Development (2021–2030) to gather ocean stakeholders worldwide behind a common framework that will ensure that ocean science can fully support countries in the achievement of the SDG 14 on the ocean.[109]

As mandated by the UN General Assembly, the Intergovernmental Oceanographic Commission (IOC) of UNESCO will coordinate the decade's preparatory process, inviting the global ocean community to plan for the next 10 years in ocean science and technology to deliver, together, the ocean we need for the future we want.[110] The international community may consider negotiating and adopting a comprehensive, legally binding agreement under UNCLOS to better address the issues regarding the conservation of marine living resources and fisheries management. UNCLOS, indeed, proved itself accommodating and approving in its further development without invoking any amendment procedure (Haque, 2016). Moreover, a new Ocean Conference may be convened to address the negotiation and adoption of a legally binding agreement for conserving and preserving marine living resources.

Conclusion

The planet we live in is more ocean than earth. We have one ocean in our one earth. The ocean provides the most important services for the betterment and survival of humankind. Marine living resources including fisheries resources are of particular relevance. In order to conserve and ensure the sustainable use of such marine resources, the existing international legal framework, despite the utmost effort of the international community, proves to be inadequate. Encouragingly, the existing legal framework provides flexibility to accommodate any upcoming development in this part of international law. Taking this opportunity, the international community, once again, agreed to establish a comprehensive and legally binding international legal framework on the conservation and management of marine living resources including fisheries and marine genetic resources. At this stage, the international community should consider this issue as a whole, irrespective of the area within and/or beyond national jurisdiction. To that effect, the proposal made in this chapter can be worthy of consideration.

Notes

1 United Nations Convention on Law of the Sea, opened for signature 10 December 1982, 1833 UNTS 397 (entered into force 16 November 1994) [hereinafter referred to as UNCLOS].
2 Agreement for the Implementation of the Provisions of the United Nations Convention of the Law of the Sea of 10 December 1982 Relating to the Conservation and Management of Straddling Fish Stocks and Highly Migratory Fish Stock, Opened for signature 4 December 1995, [2001] ATS 8, 34 ILM 1542 (1995) (entered into force 11 December 2001).
3 There is no universally accepted definition for marine genetic resources (MGRs). The definition provided in Article 2 of the Convention on Biological Diversity (CBD) and Nagoya Protocol could be the starting point where MRRs defined as genetic material of actual or potential value (while genetic material is any material of plant, animal, microbial or other origin containing functional units of heredity). CBD's Nagoya Protocol is limited to genetic resources over which States have sovereign rights. There are 0.7 to 1.0 million marine species, 2,000 new species are described per year. Many MGRs are of actual or potential interest for biotechnology. Marine genetic resources are likely to be useful for the development of new drugs, compounds, for use in food and industrial process, among others. For both pharmaceutical companies and researchers, this offers an opportunity to engage in marine bioprospecting, searching for new genes and biomolecules of plants and animals located in oceans. MGRs are used in producing industrial enzymes like deep vent DNA polymerase, antifreeze protein; prescription drugs like pain killers, cancer drugs, omega 3 supplements; nutraceuticals and cosmeceuticals like eye cream, anti-wrinkle cream. Global market of MGRs worth approximately US $1.5 trillion in 2016. See generally Jianming Chen, Basics of Marine Genetic Resources <www.un.org/Depts/los/biodiversityworkinggroup/workshop1_chen.pdf>; Marjo Vierros, Marine Genetic Resources-Current Uses and Schemes for benefit-sharing (UNU-IAS) <https://globaloceanforumdotcom.files.wordpress.com/2016/03/mgr-and-bioprospecting-vierros.pdf>.
4 A list of highly migratory fish is provided in Annex I of UNCLOS.
5 NOAA Fisheries <www.fisheries.noaa.gov/welcome>.
6 First UN Oceans Conference Concludes with Call to Action <www.unaa.org.au/2017/06/first-un-oceans-conference-concludes-with-call-to-action/>.
7 Climate, NOAA Fisheries <www.fisheries.noaa.gov/topic/climate>. As examined, due to climate change, some species, populations, communities or habitats will move, disappear, or decrease drastically; they will be replaced by others, indigenous, migrant or non-native species that will eventually prosper. These bio-geographical changes will lead to a global reorganisation of the distribution and abundance of the species, and will be highly variable in time and space. Simard, F., Laffoley, D. and J.M. Baxter (editors), Marine Protected Areas and Climate Change: Adaptation and Mitigation Synergies, Opportunities and Challenges (Gland, Switzerland: IUCN, 2016) 13.
8 Keeling, R.F. (2005). Comment on 'The Ocean Sink for Anthropogenic CO_2 ', Science, 308(5729): 1743c; IPCC (2007) Climate Change 2007: Synthesis Report. Contribution of Working Groups I, II and III to the Fourth Assessment Report of the

Intergovernmental Panel on Climate Change. Core Writing Team Pachauri, R.K & Reisinger, A. (eds.) IPCC, Geneva, Switzerland. 104pp; Sabine, C.L. et al. (2004) The Oceanic Sink for Anthropogenic CO2, Science 305(5729): 367–371.
9 Marine Ecosystems and Climate Change: The Bigger Picture <www.iucn.org/content/marine-ecosystems-and-climate-change-bigger-picture>. See also IOC-UNESCO and UNEP (2016). Open Ocean: Status and Trends, Summary for Policy Makers. United Nations Environment Programme (UNEP), Nairobi.
10 FAO (2009) The State of World Fisheries and Aquaculture 2008. Food and Agriculture Organization of the United Nations. Rome. 178pp.
11 Communities of Ocean Action: Sustainable Fisheries <https://oceanconference.un.org/coa/SustainableFisheries>.
12 See Marjo Vierros, Marine Genetic Resources-Current Uses and Schemes for benefit-sharing (UNU-IAS) https://globaloceanforumdotcom.files.wordpress.com/2016/03/mgr-and-bioprospecting-vierros.pdf. See also IOC-UNESCO and UNEP (2016). Open Ocean: Status and Trends, Summary for Policy Makers. United Nations Environment Programme (UNEP), Nairobi, 8. In the last 30 years, tide gauges and satellite altimetry measures reveal a global sea level rise of approximately 3 mm/year (the 20th-century average was 1.7 mm/year), integrating the effects of expansion from warming and additional ocean mass from melting land ice. Important regional effects are observed with sea level variations going from negative values over the Eastern Pacific to about four times the mean global value in the Indonesia–Philippines area. In a warming earth, sea level will most likely rise for over 95% of the global ocean with areas near glaciers and ice sheets very likely to experience sea level fall (because land rises with the reduced weight of melting ice) by 2100. Greenhouse gases in the last 200 years have committed us to millennia of sea level rise.
13 Geneva Convention on Fishing and the Conservation of the Living Resources of the High Seas, 1958, entered into force 20 March 1966., UNTS 285.
14 Articles 1 and 2 of Geneva Convention. Art. 2 of the Convention provides the following: as employed in this Convention, the expression 'conservation of the living resources of the high seas' means the aggregate of the measures rendering possible the optimum sustainable yield from those resources so as to secure a maximum supply of food and other marine products. Conservation programmes should be formulated with a view to securing in the first place a supply of food for human consumption.
15 Articles 3–7 of Geneva Convention.
16 Art 6 of Geneva Convention; See also Kaye SM, International Fisheries Management (Kluwer Law International, 2001) at 71.
17 Management methodology drew heavily from the technical Conference report 1955. Herrington WC, 'The Convention on Fisheries and Conservation of Living Resources: Accomplishments of the 1958 Geneva Conference' in Alexander LM (ed) The Law of the Sea: Offshore Boundaries and Zones (Columbus: Ohio State University Press, 1967) 29.
18 United Nations Conference on Human Environment 1972, 11 ILM vol 11 (1972) 1416.
19 See generally, United Nations, A Constitution for the Oceans: Remarks of Tommy T.B. Koh of Singapore, President of the Third United Nations Conference on the Law of the Sea <www.un.org/Depts/los/convention_agreements/texts/koh_english.pdf > (hereinafter Koh, 'Constitutioin for the Oceans'); The Text of the Convention and the Final Act of the Conference, UN Publication, Sales No. E.83.V.5 (1983).
20 Areas under national jurisdiction (AUNJ) include internal waters, territorial sea and exclusive economic zone and continental shelf.
21 Areas beyond national jurisdiction (ABNJ) include high seas and the Area (Common Heritage of Mankind).
22 FAO International Guidelines for the Management of Deep-sea Fisheries in the High Seas, FAO Fisheries and Aquaculture Department, Rome, updated 30 April 2013. <www.fao.org/fishery/topic/166308/en>.
23 The EEZ has been considered to be a dividing line between the coastal state's sovereign rights and jurisdiction on the one hand and the freedom of fishing on the other. (Franckx E, 'The 200 mile Limit: Between creeping Jurisdiction and Creeping Common

146 Daud Hassan and Emdadul Haque

      Heritage' 48 (2005) German Yearbook of International Law, Biodiversity and Conservation of Fisheries at 119).
24 Article 61(1) of UNCLOS.
25 Article 61(2) of UNCLOS.
26 Article 61(3) of the UNCLOS. Churchill and Lowe define MSY as follows: 'A stock which is not fished at all will tend to remain at maximum size, and natural mortality and reproduction will balance out. Once the stock begins to be fished, however, its size will decrease. To recover its losses, the stock then starts growing at a rapid rate in an attempt to reach its original level. This rate of increase is greatest when a stock has been reduced to a particular size (which varies from stock to stock). It is at this level, which is known as the maximum sustainable yield'. Churchill RR and Lowe AV, The Law of the Sea (Manchester University Press, 1999 at 282. See also Kaye SM, International Fisheries Management (Kluwer Law International, 2001) at p. 100.
27 Kaye SM, International Fisheries Management (Kluwer Law International, 2001) at p. 104.
28 Article 62(1) of the UNCLOS.
29 Article 62(2) of the UNCLOS.
30 Article 62(3) of the UNCLOS. Other relevant considerations include the rights of landlocked and geographically disadvantaged states, developing States, issues in accessing surplus and States with close connections in fishing or research interests in the EEZ.
31 Article 62(4) of the UNCLOS.
32 Charlotte Salpin, Marine Genetic Resources and the Law of the Sea (DOALOS, United Nations, 2013) <www.marinebiotech.eu/sites/marinebiotech.eu/files/public/images/conference/presentations/04SalpinCharlotte.pdf>.
33 Fisheries Management in the Areas Beyond National Jurisdiction (FAO, Rome) <www.fao.org/3/a-i5565e.pdf >).
34 The terms 'occur within the exclusive economic zones of two or more coastal States', 'occur both within the exclusive economic zone and in an area beyond and adjacent to the zone', 'both within and beyond the exclusive economic zone', 'fishing beyond the outer limits of the exclusive economic zone', 'through the exclusive economic zone of another state' used in Articles 63–67 of UNCLOS in fact refer the character of transboundary or shared fish stock.
35 There is not a uniform agreement on the categorisation of these fish stocks. While there is no disagreement on the definitions of straddling, highly migratory and discrete high seas stocks, what we might refer to as a second school of thought prefers to use the term 'transboundary stocks' as the generic term, and to use the term 'shared stocks' to denote those fish stocks crossing the EEZ boundary of one coastal State into the EEZ(s) of one, or more, other coastal States. The term 'shared fish stocks' is understood by FAO (see, in particular, the FAO, Code of Conduct for Responsible Fisheries, Article 7 (FAO, 2003b)) to include the following:

- fish resources crossing the EEZ boundary of one coastal State into the EEZ(s) of one, or more, other coastal States/transboundary stocks;
- highly migratory species, as set forth in Annex 1 of the 1982 UN Convention on the Law of the Sea (UN, 1982), consisting, primarily, of the major tuna species (being highly migratory in nature, the resources are to be found, both within the coastal State EEZ, and the adjacent high seas);
- all other fish stocks (with the exception of anadromous/catadromous stocks) that are to be found, both within the coastal State EEZ and the adjacent high seas–straddling stocks; and
- fish stocks to be found exclusively in the high seas – discrete high seas fish stocks. See Gordon Munro, Annick Van Houtte and Rolf Willmann, The conservation and management of shared fish stocks: legal and economic aspects (FAO Fisheries Technical Paper 465, Rome, 2004) <www.fao.org/docrep/007/y5438e/y5438e05.htm#TopOfPage>.

36 Fish Stocks Agreement, *supra* note 2.
37 Freestone D, Implementing Precaution Cautiously: The Precautionary Approach in the Straddling and Highly Migratory Fish Stocks Agreement', in Hey E (ed), Developments in International Fisheries Law (Kluwer Law International, 1999) at 313.
38 Principle 4 of the Rio Declaration provides: In order to achieve sustainable development, environmental protection shall constitute an integral part of the development process and cannot be considered in isolation from it. Principle 15 provides: Where there are threats of serious irreversible damage, lack of full scientific certainty shall not be used as a reason for postponing cost-effective measures to prevent environmental degradation.
39 Article 2 of the Fish Stocks Agreement.
40 Article 5(a) of the Fish Stocks Agreement.
41 An ecosystem is a functional unit of physical and biological organisation with characteristic trophic structure and material cycles, some degree of internal homogeneity, and recognisable boundaries. (Odum E, 'The emergence of Ecology as a New Integrative Discipline', (1977) 195 Science 1289. The ecosystem management was advocated in the 1984 FAO Strategy for Fisheries Management and Development and also reflected in the Code of Conduct (particularly art. 6). For details see Kaye SM, International Fisheries Management (Kluwer Law International, 2001) 269–281.
42 Art 6(2) of the Fish Stock Agreement.
43 Hayashi M, The Straddling and Highly Migratory Fish Stocks Agreements in Hey E (ed) Developments in International Fisheries Law (Kluwer Law International, 1999) 60.
44 Article 6(3) of the Fish Stocks Agreements.
45 Art. 7 of the Fish Stocks Agreements.
46 Article 28 of the Fish Stocks Agreement.
47 Article 30(2) of the Fish Stocks Agreement.
48 An organ of the Convention on Biological Diversity 1992 (1992) ILM 818. Since 1994 the SBSTTA began a series of meetings that resulted in development of the Jakarta Mandate on Marine and Coastal Biological Diversity (Goote MM, 'Convention on Biological Diversity-The Jakarta Mandate on Marine and Coastal Biodiversity', (1997) 12 International Journal of Marine and Coastal Law, 377–378.
49 FAO, Code of Conduct for Responsible Fisheries (FAO, Rome 1995).
50 For details see Art. 6 of the code and principle 9 of the Declaration. Article 6 is the core of the code – it sets out a series of general principles from which the rest of the code is derived.
51 FAO International Guidelines for the Management of Deep-sea Fisheries in the High Seas, updated 30 April 2013 <www.fao.org/fishery/topic/166308/en>.
52 Fisheries Management in the Areas Beyond National Jurisdiction (FAO, Rome) <www.fao.org/3/a-i5565e.pdf >.
53 FAO International Guidelines for the Management of Deep-sea Fisheries in the High Seas, updated 30 April 2013 <www.fao.org/fishery/topic/166308/en>.
54 FAO International Guidelines for the Management of Deep-sea Fisheries in the High Seas, updated 30 April 2013<www.fao.org/fishery/topic/166308/en>.
55 Article 194(5) of the UNCLOS.
56 Article 194(1) of the UNCLOS.
57 Cicin-Sian, B and Knecht RW, Integrated Coastal Zone Management-Concept and Practice (Inland Press, Washington DC, 1998) 72.
58 The adoption of management principles in marine environmental resource planning and implementation in Chapter 17 of Agenda 21 is in recognition that current sectoral approaches are inadequate for resource management. See Tsamenyi BM, 'Mechanisms for Integrated Resource Management', Paper presented in 29th Annual Conference of the Law of the Sea Institute, Denpasar, Bali, 19–22 June 1995 at 22.
59 Article 61 (2)–(3) of the UNCLOS.
60 Kaye SM, International Fisheries Management (Kluwer Law International, 2001) at 101.

61 Churchill RR and Lowe AV, The Law of the Sea (Manchester University Press, 1999) at p. 289.
62 Article 61 (2), 61 (4), 62 (4) of the UNCLOS.
63 Article 61(2) of the UNCLOS.
64 Articles 61 (1), 61 (5), 63(2), 64,65, 66, 67 and 118 of the UNCLOS.
65 Kaye SM, International Fisheries Management (Kluwer Law International, 2001) 110.
66 Article 63(2) states:

> Where the same stock or stocks of associated species occur both within the exclusive economic zone and in the area beyond and adjacent to the zone, the coastal State and the States fishing for such stocks in the adjacent area shall seek, either directly or through appropriate sub-regional or regional organizations, to agree upon the measures necessary for the conservation of these stocks in the adjacent area.

67 Article 64(1) states:

> The coastal State and other States whose nationals fish in the region for the migratory species listed in Annex I shall cooperate directly or through appropriate international organizations with a view to ensuring conservation and promoting the objective of optimum utilization of such species throughout the region, both within and beyond the exclusive economic zone. In regions for which no appropriate international organization exists, the coastal State and other States whose nationals harvest these species in the region shall cooperate to establish such an organization and participate in its work.

68 Article 118 of UNCLOS states:

> States shall cooperate with each other in the conservation and management of living resources in the areas of high seas. States whose nationals exploit identical living resources, or different living resources in the same area, shall enter into negotiations with a view to talking the measures necessary for the conservation of the living resources concerned. They shall, as appropriate, cooperate to establish sub-regional or regional fisheries organizations to this end.

69 Because the theory of cooperation is to be seen as a theory of bargaining, it is assumed that each party is motivated by self-interest alone. If the parties agree to cooperate, it is because each is convinced that it can gain more from cooperation, than it could by engaging in competitive behaviour. Again, numbers are important for cooperation. Once the number of players exceeds two, the analysis becomes much more complex. See Gordon Munro, Annick Van Houtte and Rolf Willmann, The conservation and management of shared fish stocks: legal and economic aspects (FAO Fisheries Technical Paper 465, Rome, 2004) <www.fao.org/docrep/007/y5438e/y5438e05.htm#TopOfPage>.
70 Article 77(4) of UNCLOS states:

> The natural resources referred to in this Part consist of the mineral and other non-living resources of the seabed and subsoil together with living organisms belonging to sedentary species, that is to say, organisms which, at the harvestable stage, either are immobile on or under the seabed or are unable to move except in constant physical contact with the seabed or the subsoil.

71 Article 76(5) of the UNCLOS.
72 Because the conservation and management provisions regarded to the living resources within EEZ are not applicable for the sedentary species. As Article 68 of the UNCLOS states:

> This Part does not apply to sedentary species as defined in article 77, paragraph 4.

73 Convention on Biological Diversity, Rio de Janeiro, opened for signature 5 June 1992, entry into force 29 December 1993, UNTS vol 1760, 76 <https://treaties.un.org/doc/Treaties/1992/06/19920605%2008-44%20PM/Ch_XXVII_08p.pdf>.

74 *Nagoya Protocol on Access to Genetic Resources and the Fair and Equitable Sharing of Benefits Arising from their Utilization to the Convention on Biological Diversity* (Secretariat of the Convention on Biological Diversity, United Nations Environmental Programme, Canada, 2011) <www.cbd.int/abs/doc/protocol/nagoya-protocol-en.pdf>.
75 International Treaty on Plant Genetic Resources for Food and Agriculture, FAO, Rome, opened for signature 3 Nov 2001, entry into force 29 June 2004, UNTS vol 2400, 303 <https://treaties.un.org/doc/Publication/UNTS/Volume%202400/v2400.pdf>.
76 While there is good future potential for MGRs from ABNJ, realising their actual value may take a long time. Marjo Vierros, Marine Genetic Resources-Current Uses and Schemes for benefit-sharing (UNU-IAS) https://globaloceanforumdotcom.files.wordpress.com/2016/03/mgr-and-bioprospecting-vierros.pdf; Regulating marine genetic resources in areas beyond national jurisdiction <www.abs-canada.org/news/regulating-marine-genetic-resources-in-areas-beyond-national-jurisdiction/>.
77 Article 8 of the Fish Stocks Agreement.
78 For example, Inter-American Tropical Tuna Commission, International Commission for the Conservation of Atlantic Tunas, Indian Ocean Tuna Commission, Commission on the Conservation of Southern Bluefin Tuna, Western and Central Pacific Fisheries Commission etc. There are regional fisheries bodies (RFB) which are also working under the umbrella of FAO. For example, General Fisheries Commission for the Mediterranean (GFCM), Bay of Bengal Programme Inter-Governmental Organization (BONP-IGO) etc. See Regional Fisheries Bodies, FAO Fisheries and Aquaculture Department <www.fao.org/fishery/rfb/search/en>. It is true that international concern arises from overfishing and the illegal, unreported and unregulated (IUU) fishing activity gave impetus to the work of international fisheries organisations and led to the negotiation of international fisheries instrument built upon UNCLOS.
79 Article 9 and 10 of the Fish Stocks Agreement.
80 Articles 19–23 of the Fish Stocks Agreement. The framework first provides for the obligations of the flag State to enforce where contraventions occur, to investigate when required, and to take appropriate action against its flagged vessel and masters or officers on such vessels; second, international cooperation in enforcement is called for. All States are obliged to cooperate either directly or through sub-regional or regional fisheries management organisations or arrangements to ensure compliance with measures.
81 Article 23 of the Fish Stocks Agreement.
82 Article 35 of the Fish Stocks Agreement.
83 Articles 24 and 25 of the Fish Stocks Agreement.
84 For details see Hassan D, Protecting the Marine Environment from Land Based Sources of Pollution: Towards Effective International Cooperation, (Ashgate Publishing Ltd, 2006) 53 &62–63.
85 The ICJ, in the Fisheries jurisdiction case, held that under customary international law a coastal state with a special dependence on fishing for its economic livelihood in certain situations had preferential fishing rights to high seas fishery resources adjacent to its waters. See generally Fisheries Jurisdiction (United Kingdom v Iceland) [1974] ICJ Rep 3, [55]-[58]; Fisheries Jurisdiction (Federal Republic of Germany v Iceland) [1974] ICJ Rep 175; Eminent publicist Crawford opines that 'the concept of preferential fishing rights seems to have survived in customary law despite its absence from UNCLOS'. See generally Crawford, Brownlie's Principles of Public International Law, 275; Churchill and AV Lowe, 285. According to Burke, both UNCLOS and the Fish Stocks Agreement contains several provisions which appear to favour the interests of coastal States. See William T Burke, 'Highly Migratory Species in the new law of the sea' (1984)14 (3) Ocean Development and International Law 273–314, 278.
86 Marine spaces, by their nature, are of international character, no matter whether they are within or beyond national jurisdiction. Since water knows no fence and it is not possible to divide the ocean's water according to the delimitation line as decided amongst the coastal states, therefore, the planet Earth retains only one ocean. Hence, any activity against the ocean environment may have a sub-regional, regional or global impact.

87 Marine areas under national jurisdiction refer to marine spaces under territorial sea, exclusive economic zone, continental shelf.
88 Articles 192 and 194 of UNCLOS.
89 Articles 207–222 of UNCLOS.
90 Article 237 of UNCLOS.
91 Ibid.
92 Article 235 of UNCLOS.
93 Article 235 of UNCLOS.
94 Article 237 of UNCLOS.
95 Countries agree to recommend elements for a new treaty on marine biodiversity of areas beyond national jurisdiction, <www.un.org/sustainabledevelopment/blog/2017/07/countries-agree-to-recommend-elements-for-new-treaty-on-marine-biodiversity-of-areas-beyond-national-jurisdiction/>.
96 Countries agree to recommend elements for a new treaty on marine biodiversity of areas beyond national jurisdiction, <www.un.org/sustainabledevelopment/blog/2017/07/countries-agree-to-recommend-elements-for-new-treaty-on-marine-biodiversity-of-areas-beyond-national-jurisdiction/>.
97 Transforming our World: The 2030 Agenda for Sustainable Development, 2 <www.un.org/pga/wp-content/uploads/sites/3/2015/08/120815_outcome-document-of-Summit-for-adoption-of-the-post-2015-development-agenda.pdf>. See also Sustainable Development Goals, <https://sustainabledevelopment.un.org/topics/sustainabledevelopmentgoals>.
98 Sustainable Development Goals, <https://sustainabledevelopment.un.org/topics/sustainabledevelopmentgoals>.
99 Target 14.4 of the SDG14 states:
   By 2020, effectively regulate harvesting and end overfishing, illegal, unreported and unregulated fishing and destructive fishing practices and implement science-based management plans, in order to restore fish stocks in the shortest time feasible, at least to levels that can produce maximum sustainable yield as determined by their biological characteristics.
   See Sustainable Development Goals, <https://sustainabledevelopment.un.org/topics/sustainabledevelopmentgoals>.
100 Oceans and the Law of the Sea, UN doc. A/RES/59/24, 17 November 2004 <https://documents-dds-ny.un.org/doc/UNDOC/GEN/N04/477/64/PDF/N0447764.pdf?OpenElement>.
101 Development of an international, legally binding instrument under the United Nations Convention on the Law of the Sea on the conservation and sustainable use of marine biological diversity of areas beyond national jurisdiction, UN Doc. A/Res/69/292, 19 June 2015 <https://documents-dds-ny.un.org/doc/UNDOC/GEN/N15/187/55/PDF/N1518755.pdf?OpenElement>.
102 Report of the Preparatory Committee established by General Assembly resolution 69/292: Development of an international legally binding instrument under the United Nations Convention on the Law of the Sea on the conservation and sustainable use of marine biological diversity of areas beyond national jurisdiction, UN Doc. A/AC.287/2017/PC.4/2, 31 July 2017 <www.un.org/ga/search/view_doc.asp?symbol=A/AC.287/2017/PC.4/2>.
103 See generally, Report of the Preparatory Committee established by General Assembly resolution 69/292: Development of an international legally binding instrument under the United Nations Convention on the Law of the Sea on the conservation and sustainable use of marine biological diversity of areas beyond national jurisdiction, UN Doc. A/AC.287/2017/PC.4/2, 31 July 2017 <www.un.org/ga/search/view_doc.asp?symbol=A/AC.287/2017/PC.4/2>; Countries agree to recommend elements for new treaty on marine biodiversity of areas beyond national jurisdiction, <www.un.org/sustainabledevelopment/blog/2017/07/countries-agree-to-recommend-elements-for-new-treaty-on-marine-biodiversity-of-areas-beyond-national-jurisdiction/>.

104 Area-based measures and marine spatial tools are commonly used for managing fisheries to protect target stocks and by-catch from excessive impacts. They are tools that have been improved over time as lessons are learned through their implementation. Area-based measures, including in the ABNJ, are tools within the framework of precautionary and ecosystem approaches. See Fisheries Management in the Areas Beyond National Jurisdiction (FAO, Rome) <www.fao.org/3/a-i5565e.pdf >.
105 An IUCN report finds that marine protected areas (MPA) plays a strong role in conserving marine biodiversity and thus can help combat climate change. See generally Simard, F., Laffoley, D. and J.M. Baxter (editors), Marine Protected Areas and Climate Change: Adaptation and Mitigation Synergies, Opportunities and Challenges (Gland, Switzerland: IUCN, 2016) 49–50; Marine Protected Areas and climate change report <www.iucn.org/news/marine-and-polar/201611/marine-protected-areas-and-climate-change-report>.
106 Peter Haugan, Chairman, IOC <https://en.unesco.org/ocean-decade>.
107 For this proposition see, generally, Santoro Francesca et al (eds), Ocean Literacy for All-A Toolkit (IOC Manuals and Guides, 80) (IOC/UNESCO & UNESCO Venice Office, Paris, 2017).
108 For this proposition see, generally, Steven Freeland, Addressing the Intentional Destruction of the Environment during Warfare under the Rome Statute of the International Criminal Court (Intersentia, Cambridge, United Kingdom, 2015) 1–293.
109 Oceans and the law of the sea, Agenda item 77 (a), UN Doc A/72/L.18, 5 December 2017 <https://en.unesco.org/sites/default/files/extract_decade_72omnibus_resolution.pdf>.
110 United Nations Decade of Ocean Science for Sustainable Development (2021–2030), UNESCO, <https://en.unesco.org/ocean-decade>.

References

Amador, F.G. (1959). *The Exploitation and Conservation of the Resources of the Sea: A Study of Contemporary International Law. Supplement.* AW Sythoff, Leyden.

Beatriz, de S. (2017). Imposing an international environmental jurisdiction: How developments on marine protected areas (MPAs) are fostering a new legal order for the conservation of ABNJ, paper presented in ABLOS Conference 10–11 October 2017, Monaco.

Franckx, E. (2006). *The Protection of Biodiversity and Fisheries Management Raised by the Relationship Between CITIES and UNCLOS, The Law of the Sea Progress and Prospects*, Oxford University Press, Oxford, pp. 210–232.

Greiber, T. (2011). Access and benefit sharing in relation to marine genetic resources from areas beyond national jurisdiction: A possible way forward. Bonn: IUCN. (BfN-Skripten, no. 301).

Haque, E. (2016). United Nations convention on the law of the sea (UNCLOS) and delimitation of maritime boundaries: A Bangladesh perspective, PhD Thesis, Western Sydney University, Sydney, Australia.

Hassan, D. (2009). Climate change and the current regimes of Arctic fisheries resources management: An evaluation. *Journal of Maritime Law and Commerce*, vol. 40.

Hassan, D., Kuokkanen, T., & Soininen, N. (Eds.) (2015). *Transboundary Marine Spatial Planning and International Law*, Routledge, London.

Herr, D, & Galland, G. (2009). *The Ocean and Climate Change. Tools and Guidelines for Action*, IUCN, Gland, Switzerland.

Hester, K., Peltzer, E., Kirkwood, W., & Brewer, P. (2008). Unanticipated consequences of ocean acidification: A noisier ocean at lower pH. *Geophysical Research Letters*, vol. 35, no. 19, doi: 10.1029/2008GL034913.

Jackson, J.B., Kirby, M.X., Berger, W.H., Bjorndal, K.A., Botsford, L.W., Bourque, B.J., . . . Hughes, T.P. (2001). Historical overfishing and the recent collapse of coastal ecosystems. *Science*, vol. 293, no. 5530, pp. 629–637.

Jianming Chen, Basics of Marine Genetic Resources < http://www.un.org/Depts/los/biodiversityworkinggroup/workshop1_chen.pdf>;

McGarry, B. (2017). Managing marine biodiversity in the Gulf of Guinea: What role for general principles of law?, paper presented in ABLOS Conference 10–11 October 2017, Monaco.

Mcleod, E., Salm, R.V., Anthony, K., Causey, B., Conklin, E., Cros, A., . . . Jokiel, P. (2008). The Honolulu declaration on ocean acidification and reef management, in *The Nature Conservancy*, USA, IUCN, Gland, Switzerland.

Myers, R.A., & Worm, B. (2003). Rapid worldwide depletion of predatory fish communities. *Nature*, vol. 423, no. 6937, pp. 280–283.

Pinto, D. (2012). *Fisheries Management in Areas Beyond National Jurisdiction: The Impact of Ecosystem Based Law-Making*, Vol. 13. Martinus Nijhoff Publishers, The Hague.

Planque, B., Fromentin, J.M., Cury, P., Drinkwater, K.F., Jennings, S., Perry, R.I., & Kifani, S. (2010). How does fishing alter marine populations and ecosystems sensitivity to climate? *Journal of Marine Systems*, vol. 79, no. 3, pp. 403–417.

Ryabinin, V., & Tang, Q. (2017). Foreword, in F. Santoro et al. (eds), *Ocean Literacy for All-A Toolkit (IOC Manuals and Guides, 80)*, IOC/UNESCO & UNESCO Venice Office, Paris.

Simard, F., Laffoley, D., & Baxter, J.M. (2016). *Marine Protected Areas and Climate Change: Adaptation and Mitigation Synergies, Opportunities and Challenges*, IUCN, Gland, Switzerland.

Tsamenyi, B. (1997). Mechanisms for integrated resource management. *Sustainable Development and Preservation of the Oceans: The Challenges of UNCLOS and Agenda*, vol. 21, p. 414.

Worm, B., Barbier, E., Beaumont, N., Duffy, J., Folke, C., Halpern, B., . . . Sala, E. (2006). Impacts of biodiversity loss on ocean ecosystem services. *Science*, vol. 314, no. 5800, pp. 787–790.

9
MARINE PROTECTED AREAS
Contemporary challenges and developments

Erika Techera

Introduction

More than 70% of the Earth's surface is covered in oceans and life on Earth began in the sea. Human influences on the natural environment date to the very earliest of times; whilst human populations were low and lifestyles traditional, our impacts were relatively minor. Over time unchecked resource exploitation began to have an effect on both land and in the sea. Today there is broad recognition that the marine environment and resources within it face anthropogenic threats from industries such as fishing, resource extraction and transportation, pollution from waste disposal, shipping and agricultural run-off and the introduction of invasive species. In coastal areas, even recreational use of our oceans is beginning to have an effect.

As we became aware of the decline in numbers, early efforts were made to conserve wildlife; some dating back to the 13th century (Meine, 2001). Although it was individual species that were often the first to be protected, the idea of setting aside specific zones is not new. Some areas were considered sacred and in other contexts had royal protection: deer preserves and royal game reserves, for example, in feudal Europe (Meine, 2001). The need to take measures to control activities in the oceans and protect critical marine habitats has also long been known. For instance, traditional marine governance regimes in the Pacific often included areas where fishing was not permitted, taboo areas and other restrictions including seasonal fishing bans in certain habitats (Johannes, 2002).

In industrialised contexts, the need to protect the marine environment also became clear as greater pressure was placed upon the oceans. Although impacts on individual species are perhaps easier to observe, it is uncontroversial that broader ecosystem health is also in decline. Living and non-living marine resources are impacted by human activities resulting in environmental degradation. In some cases, this is direct damage, such as the targeting of harvested species which disturbs the food web, or physical harm to the ocean floor through shipping or bottom trawling, pollution of the water column, or impacts from development including coastal and offshore infrastructure. In other cases, the damage is less direct including through tourism and recreational use. Climate change, for example, is having an impact on both the water column through temperature rise causing acidification as well as increased weather events which impact upon marine environments. In almost all cases the damage referred to here is anthropogenic and therefore the solution to the problem must lie in better governance of human activities combined with proactive conservation of species and their habitats (McCauley et al., 2015).

Initial management efforts focused upon protecting individual marine species, often for the specific aim of maintaining an industry: for example, the *International Convention for the Regulation of Whaling* (1946) originally focused on the conservation and development of stocks so that the whaling industry might continue. It is clear that the principle impact upon marine species is from fishing and this triggered rapid development in fisheries regulation. However, as marine species continued to decline in numbers, other approaches were explored. Some commentators directly link the call for more marine protected areas (MPAs) as a response to beliefs that fisheries management was failing worldwide (Kearney, Buxton, & Farebrother, 2012). But it is clear that protection of marine areas can have multiple benefits beyond harvested species, and therefore, over time and driven by developments in international environmental law, biology and the conservation movement itself, more holistic approaches were taken. This has led to the utilisation of mechanisms such as MPAs which have become 'one of the most widely used tools for marine conservation' (Spalding & Zeitlin Hale, 2016, p. 9).

Particular marine areas can be important because they are critical habitats for a rare species or are used by migratory species for breeding, birthing, nursery or feeding grounds, for example. MPA frameworks came about because of the need to take active measures to protect and conserve not just species but habitats such as these. The concept of protected area management arose early in relation to land and it is well known that Yellowstone was the first national park in the world. Australia declared the second area in the world – the Royal National Park designated in 1879 – but it is less well known that that Park included a marine area and is therefore perhaps the first marine protected area (Fitzsimons & Wescott, 2016).

Law plays an important part in the protection of the marine environment and can do so in a number of ways. It can regulate activities in and on our oceans, provide regimes for species-based protections and create frameworks for designation and management of protected areas. This chapter focuses on MPAs and commences with an exploration of the terminological issues. Thereafter the goals and purposes of MPAs are explored followed by a critical analysis of international law supporting their declaration. The chapter will conclude with an examination of gaps and challenges in current legal frameworks and how we can better protect and manage ocean areas.

Terminological issues

At its simplest an MPA is a marine zone declared for the primary purpose of conservation. In this sense it is an example of an area- or place-based measure which includes others such as aquatic reserves and marine monuments. Whilst the focus of MPAs is conservation, aquatic reserves are aimed at protecting harvested fish species, and marine monuments conserved for other specific purposes. Although in some cases fisheries or aquatic reserves provide for the protection of critical habitats, biodiversity and conservation, this does not usually extend to broader issues such as recreational uses and tourism.

It is clear though that the term 'marine protected area' is sometimes used interchangeably with 'marine reserve', 'marine park' and 'marine sanctuary'; and in other cases, it is used to distinguish between these phrases. Many of the terminological issues and differences can be distilled down to the utilisation of the areas in question. These can exist along a spectrum from a complete no-go zone, to others where commercial extractive activities are not allowed but recreation is permitted. In other cases areas are zoned with different uses in different zones: for example, controlled commercial activities, traditional use, diving and tourism and other recreation including boating and recreational fishing. Today MPAs can range from small, discrete no-go sites to multiple-use zoned areas with complex governance regimes for often large ocean areas.

A protected area has been defined by the *International Union for the Conservation for Nature and Natural Resources* (IUCN) as

> a clearly defined geographical space, recognised, dedicated and managed, through legal or other effective means, to achieve the long-term conservation of nature with associated ecosystem services and cultural values.
>
> *(Day et al., 2012)*

Such areas are classified into six categories and can include MPAs (Day et al., 2012, pp. 9–10). In the *Convention on Biological Diversity* (CBD) a protected area is similarly defined:

> [It] means a geographically defined area which is designated or regulated and managed to achieve specific conservation objectives.
>
> *(Article 2)*

In Decision VII/5 the CBD Conference of the Parties defined an MPA as

> any defined area within or adjacent to the marine environment, together with its overlying waters and associated flora, fauna and historical and cultural features, which has been reserved by legislation or other effective means, including custom, with the effect that its marine and/or coastal biodiversity enjoys a higher level of protection than its surroundings.

These definitions can include a wide array of area-based measures including complete no take and no access areas, areas with multiple use zones within them. The key issue is that the area has been designated with conservation as a primary focus. As noted previously, it is clear that other areas may have an incidental conservation benefit. Day et al. (2012) identify these as including

- Fishery management areas with no wider stated conservation aims,
- Community areas managed primarily for sustainable extraction of marine products,
- Marine and coastal management systems managed primarily for tourism, which also include areas of conservation interest,
- Wind farms and oil platforms that incidentally help to build up biodiversity,
- Marine and coastal areas set aside for other purposes but which also have conservation benefit: military training areas or their buffer areas . . . disaster . . . communications cable or pipeline protection areas; shipping lanes,
- Large areas . . . where certain species are protected by law across the entire region.

(Day et al., 2012, p. 10).

Some researchers have commented that the IUCN classification system focuses too heavily on the purposes for which the MPA was declared rather than protections provided (Costa et al., 2016). It appears to be agreed that the IUCN categories by themselves are insufficient to assess the quality of conservation within an MPA (Marinesque, Kaplan, & Rodwell, 2012). Costa et al. (2016) point to the recent declaration of large MPAs in remote areas, with no appropriate management plans and in which a range of extractive activities are permitted, and as an alternative it has been suggested that a regulation-based classification system is preferable where potential impacts of permitted activities are the focus. This draws attention to the issue of precisely what protections an MPA provides versus its articulated purpose.

MPAs as a tool for conservation

MPAs are not uncontroversial as a management tool. For example, one commentator has noted that they are an 'unjustified transposition of terrestrial paradigms into marine environments' given 'highly interconnected, volatile and mobile aquatic ecosystems' (Kearney et al., 2012, p. 1067). The arguments put forward are that fisheries regulation could serve an equal purpose. But this fails to recognise that MPAs not only seek to conserve and manage harvested fish and marine life, nor only living marine resources. Indeed MPAs have been 'linked to the most advanced concepts of environmental policy, such as sustainable development, precautionary approach, integrated coastal zone management, marine spatial planning, ecosystem approach and transboundary cooperation' (Scovazzi, 2011, pp. 14–15). The goal of MPAs is in part the conservation of species and biodiversity, but also of whole ecosystems including non-living structures. It has been recognised that 'MPAs often have a potentially larger positive non-use value than use (market) value' because they protect ecosystem resources which in turn provide goods and services that contribute to 'ecological and societal wellbeing' (Glenn et al., 2010, p. 422). Glenn et al. (2010) point to some of the difficulties faced by advocates of MPAs as a holistic marine management tool, because calculations of economic values have largely been limited to harvested species and the value of non-use benefits has been poorly quantified.

MPAs in essence conserve both habitats and biodiversity within them and therefore help maintain ecosystems including fisheries. Habitat protection directly protects the biodiversity that live in and around the area. This in turn provides ecosystem benefits because processes are assured contributing to water quality and overall ocean health. In addition, protecting these habitats can also support non-extractive industries such as tourism (Kelleher, 1999). In terms of fisheries, it is clear that species within the MPA are protected. They are of course mobile and may not be protected outside the area, but when used in conjunction with conventional fisheries regulation, MPAs provide a haven for recruitment with a spillover effect into fishing zones. Scientific evidence is well documented indicating that MPAs benefit ecosystems and marine species as well as human communities (Marine Parks Authority, 2008). The benefits include improved fish productivity, provision of recreational values as well as providing some security against future, as yet unknown, threats. The analyses include examinations of no take zones (Lester et al., 2009) as well as MPAs involving zoned activities (Marine Parks Authority, 2008).

Although national parks have tended to be well received by the public, the protection of marine areas has often been met with community opposition (National Research Council, 2001, p. 11). They remain controversial, in terms of their meaning, value and effectiveness, which demonstrates the necessity for further research in this particular field of social science work. They were also slow to be adopted as a tool and despite early examples, noted earlier, declarations of MPAs were not seen until the 1970s. Furthermore, as science has developed, so too has the knowledge that individual MPAs, unless extremely large (where they may become difficult to manage and monitor) may not achieve articulated goals. Most marine species are mobile, some highly migratory and, in response to this, networks of MPAs have been called for (see later).

All of these matters are ones where law has a role to play. Legal frameworks must incorporate the purposes for which the MPA is declared, how sites are selected and on what advice as well as the goals and objectives for different levels of protection. The process for declaration is critical, including participation of advisory bodies and the public. Post declaration there must be procedures for the adoption of a management plan, again involving expert advice and public participation. Other issues include advisory bodies and their composition and authority as well as initiatives for monitoring, compliance and enforcement.

The range of permitted uses and the process for approval is a key aspect of any MPA. As noted previously, at one end of the scale are completely protected areas where no activities, commercial or otherwise, are permitted and perhaps access is even prohibited. At the other extreme are areas in which activities are restricted but not prohibited and, in this way, impacts are managed and controlled but not outlawed. The issue of where an MPA might lie on the spectrum of protection is as old as protected areas themselves. For example, the Yellowstone Act (1872), establishing Yellowstone National Park, prohibited deliberate hunting and fishing for profit but allowed such activities for recreation (Glazer, 2001). Contemporary analyses of MPAs indicate that uses within zones can be grouped into five categories: 'commercial fisheries, recreational fisheries, aquaculture, bottom exploitation and non-extractive uses' (Costa et al., 2016, p. 193). How uses are determined, what permitting system is in place, what advice is sought in determining the zones and permit conditions, policing, enforcement, review and reporting are all issues the requisite legal framework must provide.

Legislation exists in one form or another in almost all countries in the world, but there is little uniformity both between and within countries. In Australia, for example, different legislation exists in each state which affects coherency and effectiveness (Techera, 2016). As will be explored later, there are steps that could be taken to provide not only greater coherency and clarity in this area, but also capacity building for States and jurisdictions where expertise and resources are limited. The focus of this chapter, however, is international law and the following analysis highlights key treaties and agreements which provide for MPAs. Similar to the national context, there is no 'model' or best practice MPA law and policy. What international law does is provide the mandate for the establishment of MPAs and sets quantitative and qualitative targets. As will be explored in the following section, there is an opportunity for international law to play a greater standard-setting role in this regard. Before examining this challenge, the international law frameworks must be analysed.

Legal responses

International law

There is no single international instrument focusing on MPAs. However, based upon the definition referred to previously, areas where conservation and protection are the focus, some treaties do create opportunities for MPA establishment, as explored below. Several early international agreements recognised the need not just to protect species but also relevant habitats including breeding, feeding, nursery and hunting grounds as well as hibernation areas. For example, the *Convention for the Conservation of Antarctic Seals* provides in Article 3 that

> Contracting Parties may . . . adopt other measures with respect to the conservation . . . of seal resources. . . (d) open and closed areas, including the designation of reserves, (e) the designation of special areas where there shall be no disturbance of seals.

Similarly, under Article V of the *International Convention on the Regulation of Whaling* (1946), whale sanctuaries may be established and 'provide a useful precedent of nations working together to agree upon conservation on the High Seas' (Hoyt, 2005, p. 33). Such sanctuaries have been established in the Indian and Southern Oceans. As thinking progressed beyond single species and sectors, broader provisions were adopted in new treaties. The *Convention on Migratory Species* (1979) is aimed at preventing migratory species from becoming endangered by taking action including protecting their habitats. Article III (4)(a) requires States to endeavour 'to conserve and ... restore those habitats of the species which are of importance in removing the species from danger of extinction'. Range States[1] for migratory species are encouraged to enter into agreements to restore the species utilising tools including conservation and restoration of habitats and networks of habitats (Article V 5).

The *Convention on Wetlands of International Importance especially as Waterfowl Habitat* (1973) (Ramsar Convention) was the first international instrument to focus specifically on habitats. Article 1 defines a wetland as 'including areas of marine water the depth of which at low tide does not exceed six metres'. Article 4 requires States to 'promote the conservation of wetlands ... by establishing nature reserves' and, if wetland boundaries are changed, requires the establishment of 'additional nature reserves for waterfowl and for the protection ... of an adequate portion of the original habitat'. Significantly each State party is required to nominate at least one wetland of international importance (Article 2) and many marine areas are listed Ramsar sites.[2]

The *Convention Concerning the Protection of World Cultural and Natural Heritage* (1972) (WHC) is also a treaty focusing on spaces and sites. It encourages the identification, protection and preservation of the natural and cultural heritage of outstanding value to all peoples. The Convention provides for the listing of sites including natural marine areas with 'outstanding universal value'. Importantly a State identifies (Article 3) and nominates site for inclusion on the World Heritage List but it is the World Heritage Committee that makes the listing decision (Article 11). Once listed a State has obligations to protect, conserve, present and transmit to future generations the cultural and natural heritage associated with that site (Article 4). Some well-known MPAs are World Heritage sites, including Australia's Great Barrier Reef, the US Northwest Hawaiian Islands (Papahānaumokuākea) and Ecuador's Galapagos Islands.[3]

These measures continue to operate, but perhaps the most significant development in terms of oceans governance was the *United Nations Convention on the Law of the Sea* (1982) (UNCLOS). UNCLOS establishes maritime zones, including the territorial sea,[4] Exclusive Economic Zones (EEZ)[5] and High Seas.[6] In relation to the territorial sea UNCLOS provides no specific obligations to establish MPAs or conserve that zone. In relation to the EEZ, UNCLOS grants coastal States sovereign rights for the purpose of conserving and managing its natural resources within that zone (Article 56(1)) and jurisdiction to protect and preserve the marine environment within its EEZ (Article 56(1)(b)(iii)). In relation to all zones, and importantly including the High Seas, UNCLOS creates general duties to protect and preserve the marine environment (Articles 192–196). Most of the general duties relate to pollution, however, there is also a distinct obligation to take measures 'necessary to protect and preserve rare or fragile ecosystems as well as the habitat of depleted, threatened or endangered species and other forms of marine life' (Article 194(5)). Although this would appear to create the power to protect marine areas, it has been said that these general obligations alone do not create the jurisdiction to create and enforce MPAs (Lagoni, 2003). Article 211 refers to pollution measures and provides for the protection of areas on the same basis as those applicable to MARPOL 'Special Areas' (see later), including additional laws for discharge measures or navigational practices in those areas (Article 211(6)(a) and (c)). Beyond the special provision in Article 211(6), UNCLOS provides rights to fish on the High Seas (Article 116) but also imposes obligations for the 'conservation of the living resources of the high seas' (Article 117) either alone or in cooperation with other States (Articles 118 and 119).

The only other relevant provisions under UNCLOS are those that provide for safety zones. Article 60 permits States to establish zones of up to 500 m around infrastructure such as artificial islands and installations to ensure the safety of those structures and navigation. Although these do not have the primary goal of the conservation of the marine environment and resources, they could have this effect.

Other relevant international law is found in the *International Convention for the Prevention of Pollution from Ships* (1973) (as modified by the Protocol of 1978) (MARPOL). MARPOL provides for the establishment of 'Special Areas' where particularly strict standards are applied to discharges from ships. Special Areas may include the high seas and, in some cases, encompass whole seas. A 'Special Area' is defined as

> a sea area where for recognized technical reasons in relation to its oceanographical and ecological conditions and the particular character of its traffic, the adoption of special mandatory methods for the prevention of sea pollution by oil, noxious liquid substances, or garbage, as applicable is required.
>
> *(Guidelines, Annex 1, (10))*

As such, to be designated three criteria must be met: oceanographic conditions, ecological conditions and vessel traffic characteristics. By comparison, in order for an area to be recognised as a Particularly Sensitive Sea Area (PSSA), it only needs to satisfy one of the ecological, scientific or socio-economic criteria. Special Areas are listed under the various headings of oil, sewage, noxious liquid substances, garbage or air pollution. Existing Special Areas include the Mediterranean (oil and garbage) and Baltics sea (oil, sewage and garbage) and Antarctica (oil, garbage and noxious liquid substances).

PSSAs protect against all impacts of shipping. In recognition that '[s]hipping activity can constitute an environmental hazard to the marine environment in general and consequently even more so to environmentally and/or ecologically sensitive areas' (Revised Guidelines, Annex, 2), a 'PSSA' is defined as

> an area that needs special protection . . . because of its significance for recognized ecological, socio-economic or scientific reasons and which may be vulnerable to damage by international shipping activities.
> *(Revised Guidelines, Annex, 1.2)*

PSSAs are identified and designated by the IMO upon a proposal by one or more coastal States (Revised Guidelines, Annex, 3). The criteria for the identification of a PSSA include ecological, social, cultural, scientific, educational and historic reasons. Ecological criteria include uniqueness, critical habitat, dependency, representativeness, diversity, productivity, spawning/breeding grounds, naturalness, integrity, fragility or bio-geographic importance (Revised Guidelines, Annex, 4.4.1–4.4.11). The PSSA guidelines are not confined to the territorial sea and EEZ and can extend beyond these limits (Lefebvre-Chalain, 2007, p. 47). The designation of a PSSA is accompanied by tailored 'associated protective measures' such as ships' routing measures, speed, discharge or anchoring restrictions or operational criteria and prohibited activities (Revised Guidelines, Annex, 7.5.2). However, as the PSSAs are not legally binding in their own right, these associated protective measures must have a legal basis in an international instrument (such as MARPOL itself or the *International Convention for the Safety of Life at Sea* [1974] for example) and be approved and adopted by the IMO. Existing PSSAs include the Great Barrier Reef (Australia), Galapagos Islands (Ecuador), Wadden Sea (Netherlands) and Papahānaumokuākea (USA); several of these areas are subject to other designations and legal protections.

In 1992 the *Convention on Biological Diversity* (CBD) was adopted and has had a profound effect on the declaration of MPAs. The CBD applies to processes and activities under the jurisdiction or control of each Contracting Party within or beyond national jurisdiction (Art 4(b) CBD). Article 8 provides for in situ conservation and requires Parties as far as possible and appropriate to

(a) Establish a system of protected areas or areas where special measures need to be taken to conserve biological diversity;
(b) Develop, where necessary, guidelines for the selection, establishment and management of protected areas or areas where special measures need to be taken to conserve biological diversity;
(c) Regulate or manage biological resources important for the conservation of biological diversity whether within or outside protected areas, with a view to ensuring their conservation and sustainable use;
 . . .
(e) Promote environmentally sound and sustainable development in areas adjacent to protected areas with a view to furthering protection of these areas.

Parties are required to 'implement this Convention with respect to the marine environment consistently with the rights and obligations of States under the law of the sea' (Article 22(2)).

Since the adoption of the CBD, developments have been directed at setting targets and goals for MPAs as well as networks and legal frameworks to support them. The *Jakarta Mandate on Marine and Coastal Biological Diversity* was adopted in 1995 and updated in 2004. It recommends legal and customary frameworks for MPAs as well as integrated networks of areas. At the World Summit on Sustainable Development in 2002 commitments were made to creating representative networks of MPAs by 2012 (WSSD, 2002, para 32). This was repeated at the 5th World Parks Congress in 2003 and at the 8th meeting of the parties to the CBD in 2006 where it was agreed to protect 20–30% of each marine habitat by 2012 and fully conserve 10% of marine eco-regions by 2010 (Marinesque et al., 2012). United Nations General Assembly Resolution 65/37 further reinforced the importance of conserving and managing vulnerable marine ecosystems and establishing MPAs. These goals were to be achieved through a global network of MPAs.

It is the CBD that has taken forward the issue of targets and quantitative goals. In 2004 a programme of work on protected areas was adopted and a *Working Group on Protected Areas* established. The mandate included options for MPAs including in areas beyond the limits of national jurisdiction. The CBD also adopted a *Programme of Work on Marine and Coastal Biodiversity*, which was agreed upon in 2004, noting that MPAs are essential for the conservation and sustainable use of marine biodiversity. In addition it was also agreed that a national framework of MPAs should include a range of levels of protection, encompassing both areas that allow sustainable uses and 'no-take' areas (CBD Decision VII/5). More recently in 2008, the CBD Conference of the Parties Decision IX/29 adopted criteria for 'ecologically or biologically significant areas' (EBSA) based upon uniqueness, special importance, status, vulnerability, productivity, diversity and naturalness.

The later adoption of the *Strategic Plan for Biodiversity 2011–2020* includes the Aichi Targets including Target 11:

> By 2020, at least 17 per cent of terrestrial and inland water, and 10 per cent of coastal and marine areas, especially areas of particular importance for biodiversity and ecosystem services, are conserved through effectively and equitably managed, ecologically representative and well connected systems of protected areas and other effective area-based conservation measures, and integrated into the wider landscapes and seascapes.

Significant attention and action has been catalysed through the CBD and Aichi Targets. As of May 2018, just over 7% of the world's oceans are under some form of marine protection.[7]

Regional treaties

In addition to the global instruments examined previously, a number of regional treaties provide for MPAs in offshore areas including the high seas.

The Antarctic Treaty was adopted in 1959 and provides for the use of the Antarctic only for peaceful purposes, scientific investigation and exchange of information between States. In 1964 an additional instrument was adopted, the *Agreed Measures for the Conservation of Antarctic Fauna and Flora*, which allowed for 'specially protected areas'. This category of protected area was replaced in 1991 by Annex V to the *Protocol on Environmental Protection to the Antarctic Treaty* (Environment Protocol) which provides for the designation of 'Antarctic Specially Protected Areas' (ASPA) and 'Antarctic Specially Managed Areas' (ASMA). ASPA can include any marine area designated to protect, *inter alia*, environmental and wilderness values (Article 3(1)). Such areas can require protection to ensure they are kept isolated from human activity, are representative of specific ecosystems, or of particular scientific interest, for example (Article 3(2)). A permit is then needed to enter an ASPA (Article 3(4)). An ASMA is an area to be managed because of particular activities being conducted within it and which may pose risks of 'mutual interference or cumulative environmental impacts' (Article 4(2)). Management plans are required for such areas (Article 5).

The *Convention on the Conservation of Antarctic Marine Living Resources* (CCAMLR) is another regional treaty which does allow for regulation of specific areas for conservation purposes. Article IX provides for the adoption of conservation measures which include, amongst other things, a 'designation of the opening and closing of areas, regions or sub-regions for purposes of scientific study or conservation, including special areas for protection and scientific study' (Article IX (2)(g)). In 2011 CCAMLR adopted a 'General framework for the establishment of CCAMLR Marine Protected Areas' with key criteria for the establishment of MPAs including objectives, utilisation of best scientific evidence and conservation measures. In 2009 CCAMLR established the South Orkney Islands southern shelf MPA, the world's first high seas MPA.[8]

CCAMLR is in essence a Regional Fishery Management Organisation (RFMO) and it is clear that other RFMOs implement area-based conservation measures. For example, the North-East Atlantic Fishery Commission (NEAFC) has closed some areas to bottom trawling and the South Eastern Atlantic Fishery Organisation has close 10 vulnerable marine areas to protect benthic environments (FAO). An analysis of the RFMOs demonstrates that overall management of the high seas by them is inadequate (Cullis-Suzuki & Pauly, 2010). However, these measures are often focused on conserving areas only to rebuild stocks so that fishing can be sustained. Therefore, they are not truly IUCN-defined MPAs.

In addition to the RFMOs are the Regional Seas Conventions (RSCs) adopted under the auspices of the United Nations Environment Program (UNEP). One such agreement is the *Convention for the Protection of the Marine Environment of the North-East Atlantic* (OSPAR) (1992). Annex V to the Convention extends the cooperation of the Parties to cover all human activities that might adversely affect the marine environment of the North-East Atlantic. In 2003 the OSPAR Commission adopted an agreement to create an 'ecologically coherent' network of well-managed MPAs by 2010 (O'Leary et al., 2012, p. 599).[9] By 2016, the OSPAR Network of MPAs comprised a total of 1,150 sites, including 1,140 MPAs situated within national waters of Contracting Parties and ten MPAs in Areas beyond

National Jurisdiction (ABNJ) (OSPAR Commission, 2016). Furthermore OSPAR has worked with other bodies such as NEAFC to achieve greater MPA outcomes (OSPAR Commission, 2015).

In the Pacific, the Coral Triangle Initiative (CTI) covers a large area of high marine biodiversity across the seas of Indonesia, Malaysia, the Philippines, Timor Leste, Papua New Guinea and the Solomon Islands (Fidelman & Ekstrom, 2012). A stated goal of the CTI is to scale up existing MPAs to place 20% of each major habitat under protected status by 2020 to 'form a connected, resilient and sustainably financed' MPA System.[10] Other examples of regional agreements involving special MPA arrangements are the Helsinki Commission's Baltic Sea Protected Areas (BSPAs),[11] and the 1995 Protocol to the 1976 Barcelona Convention: Specially Protected Areas of Mediterranean Importance (SPAMIs).[12]

In summary, international law provides for the protection of types of marine areas (such as wetlands), marine areas with specific values (outstanding universal value, particular sensitivity) and against certain types of impacts (shipping). More recently international law has set targets and quantitative goals for protection (Aichi Targets). In addition, it is clear that certain other areas or zones declared for various purposes may have the effect of conservation without that being their stated purpose (safety zones around offshore infrastructure). The combination of UNCLOS and the CBD, as well as other treaties where relevant, allows coastal States to establish MPAs in their territorial sea and EEZ as well as on the high seas in limited contexts. Nevertheless, a number of challenges remain, and these are explored in the next section.

Contemporary challenges

The previous analysis demonstrates that MPAs have been recognised as an important tool for the conservation and management of our oceans. Over the last few decades there has been a rapid expansion in MPAs driven in part by targets set at the global level. Despite this expansion, it is clear that global targets are unlikely to be achieved. To achieve more there is a need to look at optimum location and scale, networks and connectivity of those networks as well as advances that might be made with greater inter-disciplinary research. Whilst law cannot provide all the solutions there are also improvements that can be made within that field which also need to be explored.

Lack of legal coherency

The lack of any single international law instrument for MPAs has meant that each treaty regime has developed separately. International law could play a much greater role first by providing clarity and consistency across instruments and jurisdictions. The role of international governance should not be understated. Marinesque et al. (2012) found that the 'creation of large marine reserves . . . is apparently fostered by international events that promote marine conservation or integrated management of coastal areas' (p. 734). Therefore, there may well be a greater range of benefits to be achieved through a holistic approach to MPAs. This could be achieved by a global MPA instrument, but this is not necessarily desirable nor is it essential. Rather, one body could take the lead, perhaps the CBD for example, and establish best practice guidance which could then be adopted by other treaty regimes. In recent years there has been greater cooperation between international environmental law regimes such as the collaboration between the Rio Conventions.[13] Clarity could be achieved through the setting of standards for best practice MPA frameworks and creation of a forum for the exchange of information and discussion. Criticism has been levelled at the international agreements in terms of them providing little effective detail on protection measures (Marinesque et al., 2012, p. 736). A greater standard setting role could involve the development of model MPA legislation for example.

Location, time and scale

Associated with location of MPAs is an issue in several respects. There is the matter of who is empowered to propose an MPA and therefore whether optimum locations are chosen or sites which might be proposed for political reasons. On one level this is related to whether the views of all stakeholders (community and expert) are taken into account. A further location issue is whether legal frameworks facilitate integration, in particular at the land–water interface. It has been recognised that 'MPAs should be integrated with other policies for land use and use of the sea' (Kelleher, 1999, p.xi). For example, of the 10 largest MPAs in the world, only Australia's Great Barrier Reef was found along the coast of the State and many are in areas of very low impact where protection might not offer any considerable benefits over the status quo (Marinesque et al., 2012). One further location aspect relates to the disproportionate number and size of MPAs in industrialised versus developing countries. Marinesque et al. (2012), in analysing the global distribution of MPAs, found that 63% of the total number and 68% of the total areas protected were in advanced economies. This is despite the fact that the majority of marine biodiversity hotspots are in the waters of or adjacent to developing countries. Nevertheless, recent developments include a wave of new shark sanctuaries covering entire EEZs totalling 3% of the world's oceans to date (Ward-Paige, 2017).

Temporal issues are already incorporated into some area-based legal tools in terms of the opening and closing of waters depending on the health of fish stocks, for example, and seasonal harvesting bans. Mobility over time is an emerging issue as climate change is likely to alter species' ranges. Law and legal frameworks are ill-equipped to deal with mobility and, in particular, changing MPA boundaries. Finally, as noted previously, key international events such as the Jakarta Mandate (1995), World Summit on Sustainable Development (2002) and World Parks Congress (2003) all saw the establishment of new MPAs temporally connected to these events in an effort to achieve global targets (Marinesque et al., 2012). Therefore, temporal issues are relevant in many respects.

Scale is important too because it may determine whether an issue is dealt with at the global, regional, national or local level, each of which involves a different legal jurisdiction. Ecosystem-based approaches take no notice of jurisdictional boundaries. An eco-region might involve transboundary MPAs between two or more States, areas extending into the high seas, or crossing sub-national boundaries. These issues are also explored further in the next section. Another aspect of scale is the size of an MPA. We have seen some very large MPAs declared which can add to the complexity of governance. Indeed, along with the development of more sophisticated zoning within MPAs it may be possible and desirable to declare the whole of a State's EEZ to be an MPA with a range of zonings within it (Marinesque et al., 2012). This raises the issue of marine spatial planning discussed further later.

Areas beyond national jurisdiction

Although outside the 200 nm limits of the EEZ, no single State or authority has the power to designate MPAs or enforce compliance with regulations, UNCLOS provides general obligations to protect and preserve the marine environment and to conserve and manage high seas living resources. The effect of these provisions, as well as Article 194 of UNCLOS to protect 'rare and fragile ecosystems as well as the habitat of depleted, threatened and endangered species and other forms of marine life', is that States are in a strong position to take conservation measures on the High Seas, as long as they 'co-operate with other states, show that measures on the high seas they want to take would enhance the conservation of resources and that they are based on the best scientific evidence available' (Hoyt, 2005, p. 39). The position is strengthened by the other instruments analysed previously, including the CBD along with RFMOs and RSCs.

This has led to recent developments including the CCAMLR establishing the first high seas MPA, noted previously, and now the world's largest MPA covering Antarctica's Ross Sea.[14] In addition, OSPAR's creation of six MPAs in ABNJ establishes the world's first network of marine protected areas on the high seas, covering 286,200 km^2 of the North-East Atlantic. The UNGA has specifically addressed the issue of ABNJ. By UNGA Resolution 68/70 a Working Group was formed to explore the scope, parameters and feasibility of a new instrument under UNCLOS. In 2017 the Preparatory Committee submitted its report to the UNGA recommending that a legal instrument under UNCLOS be drafted focusing on ABNJ and suggesting potential elements it could contain to conserve and manage the use of biodiversity in these areas.[15] Although the content of such an instrument has not been agreed, it is likely that a new instrument will emerge, which will provide a stronger framework for MPAs on the High Seas.

Networks and transboundary MPAs

Just as we have seen the listing of iconic marine species, large marine parks have been established, such as the Papahānaumokuākea in the northwest Hawaiian

Islands and Chagos Islands. These areas are important, but attention has been drawn to the fact that often they are in remote areas where there are few people and therefore lesser impacts from humans. Large MPAs are often more complex in terms of institutional and legal arrangements, but so too are networks of MPAs. Marine science and conservation biology has drawn attention to the importance of a networked approach which provides connectivity conservation. Such an approach is necessary both because many marine species are highly mobile and/or migratory, but also as a way to provide biodiversity corridors to guard against impacts such as climate change. Beyond the establishment of networks, protective measures that straddle jurisdictional boundaries are needed to conserve biological diversity. This is particularly so if we are to achieve the protection of migratory species through mobile MPAs, a measure which is now deemed possible by scientists.[16]

A specific legal issue arises where networks of MPAs cross jurisdictional boundaries. There are several different scenarios where transboundary MPAs may be established to improve the protection offered, adjacent and non-adjacent existing MPAs, where an existing MPA borders an unprotected area and where new MPAs are to be created (Sandwith, Shine, Hamilton, & Sheppard, 2001). The potential benefits of transboundary MPAs include better management of transboundary sites, more cost-effective research and monitoring, facilitating holistic ecosystem-based management approaches as well as legal enforcement and cross-border policing (Unger, 2004).

In order to achieve these benefits 'issues such as different national legal and administrative systems, varying national commitments to marine conservation or residual economic interests, and differential ratification of international protocols or conventions will need to be overcome' (Unger, 2004, p. 35). There are some examples of transboundary MPAs and lessons need to be learned from these to assist other States seeking to establish such areas. Examples include the Pelagos Sanctuary for Mediterranean Marine Mammals designated between France, Italy and Monaco in 1999 and added to the Specially Protected Areas of Mediterranean Importance (SPAMI) list. It remains the first high seas MPA in the Mediterranean Sea. The Lubombo Transfrontier Conservation Area, the first transboundary area in Africa, was established in 2007 by Mozambique, South Africa and Swaziland, focusing on marine turtle conservation; it straddles the border between South Africa's KwaZulu-Natal province, Southern Mozambique and Swaziland (Zbicz, 1999). The bilateral Torres Strait Treaty of 1985 between Australia and Papua New Guinea establishes the Torres Strait Protected Zone is an innovative instrument for Transboundary marine protected area management (Sandwith et al., 2001). The treaty makes specific provision for the protection of the marine environment and the promotion of bilateral cooperation in conservation. More recently, Palau, the Marshall Islands and the Federated States of Micronesia have established the world's first regional shark sanctuary covering their respective adjoining EEZs.[17] Three transboundary sites are inscribed on the World Heritage List: the Kluane/Wrangell-St Elias/Glacier Bay/Tatshenshini-Alsek between Canada and the United States; the High Coast/

Kvarken Archipelago between Finland and Sweden and the Wadden Sea between Germany and the Netherlands, with Denmark also participating.

Marine spatial planning

Human uses of the ocean are expanding not only in terms of scale but also new areas of activity. Seabed mining, long discussed as an issue, may soon become a reality. Furthermore, energy from our oceans is also likely to have impacts in the coming decades, including the expansion of marine renewable energy projects involving wind, wave and tidal power to meet higher renewable energy targets (Kyriazi, Maes, & Degraer, 2016). A fragmented sectoral approach is unlikely to be adequate to deal with these issues. Therefore, it is likely that our ocean areas will need more sophisticated legal regimes to deal with the challenges of potential conflicts and impacts. One solution is marine spatial planning (MSP), which not only resolves conflicts between humans and marine conservation, but also between different human uses of the ocean (Soininen & Hassan, 2015). MSP frameworks have the advantage of being able to incorporate complex, three-dimensional planning which is more appropriate in ocean areas. Again, a zoned approach is taken and one in which exclusive use zones could be declared at different depths to take account of existing and future uses. Although the MoU between NEAFC and OSPAR has resulted in MSP in some areas, specific legislation to provide for MSP frameworks is emerging and likely to rapidly expand in coming years.

Interdisciplinary research

Historically, much research in the oceans has been undertaken by different disciplines in isolation. Law, however, cannot resolve ocean challenges without input from and engagement with other disciplines. Some efforts to embed science and technology in law and policy can be seen through the advisory committees under various treaties: for example, the *Subsidiary Body on Scientific, Technical and Technological Advice* under the CBD. However, scientific advice is often limited to species status and biological data. It is clear that broader engagement is needed: for example, engineering research has demonstrated that in situ decommissioning of oil rigs is possible and marine science has demonstrated the value of artificial reefs created from such structures (Techera & Chandler, 2015). Similarly, social science research has been embedded in protected area management, with the IUCN for example recognising Indigenous Community Conserved Areas (ICCAs) and the CBD focusing on traditional peoples. However, greater understanding is needed, particularly Indigenous and traditional peoples' conservation practices, and can be informed by disciplines such as anthropology and sociology. Many of the problems facing our oceans are influenced by politics (for example, tensions between fishing nations and those focused on conservation) and other fields such as economics and criminology. All of these disciplines must inform advances in MPA legal frameworks, as well as new and emerging sub-fields which international legal frameworks must make space for.

Monitoring and enforcement

The final contemporary issue is a perennial one for international environmental law: enforcement. Monitoring oceans is problematic given the vastness of the areas, remoteness from coastal States and the limited resources available to most States. Some cooperative measures have been adopted including bilateral arrangements such as ship rider agreements. However, as noted previously, there is much to be learned from other disciplines, including criminology and sociology, in terms of what drives certain behaviours and what would encourage compliance. One particular area which is likely to see rapid developments in the coming years is remote sensing technology in the form of drones and other autonomous vehicles, as well as satellite-based infrared cameras which can overcome some of the challenges of monitoring offshore ocean areas (Lindley & Techera, 2017).

Conclusion

Law has an important role to play in good oceans governance and legal frameworks for MPAs in particular. UNCLOS provides a firm foundation for marine conservation and management through setting standards for maritime zones and key concepts for fisheries management as well as general obligations to protect and preserve the marine environment. International environmental law treaties add to these measures in terms of conservation of species, habitats and ecosystems. Nonetheless, there is some tension between these agreements and regional approaches to fisheries management through RFMOs. Each regime cannot work in isolation and there are significant gaps and overlaps. Greater attention needs to be paid to creating a comprehensive and coherent framework for oceans governance and MPAs, which is perhaps best addressed through marine spatial planning. Finally, law alone cannot solve the problems and there is a need to engage better with other disciplines including conservation ecology, marine biology, oceanography, an engineering as well as business, economics, and social sciences such as anthropology, sociological and behavioural science.

If we are to achieve the goals set by key international instruments of networks of MPAs, and the positive outcomes necessary for connectivity conservation, comprehensive ranges of MPAs will be needed, crossing the territorial sea and EEZ of coastal States as well as on the high seas. Fragmentation across what are artificial maritime boundaries must be avoided if ecosystem-based approaches are to be truly achieved. Finally, as noted at the beginning of this chapter, the tools analysed here are necessary because of human behaviours which are having a negative impact on the oceans. In order for them to succeed we must find better ways to monitor and enforce law and policy including through innovative technologies. Only through identifying and adopting comprehensive and coherent frameworks and ensuring effective and efficient implementation and enforcement can we hope to achieve conservation and management goals across Earth's ocean areas.

Notes

1 Ranges States are those that exercise jurisdiction of any part of a migratory species range as well as States that have vessels registered to them that take migratory species on the high seas.
2 www.ramsar.org/sites/default/files/documents/library/sitelist.pdf.
3 http://whc.unesco.org/en/list/.
4 The first 12 nautical miles measured from coastal baselines, usually the low water mark (Articles 3–5).
5 A zone from the edge of the territorial sea to a maximum of 200 nautical miles over which the coastal State has sovereign rights to explore and exploit resources (Articles 55–57).
6 The water column beyond the EEZ (Article 86).
7 https://www.protectedplanet.net/marine.
8 www.ccamlr.org/en/science/marine-protected-areas-mpas.
9 OSPAR Recommendation 2003/3; Record of the Joint Ministerial Meeting of Helsinki & OSPAR Commissions 2003.
10 www.coraltriangleinitiative.org/collaboration-marine-protected-areas.
11 Guidelines for Designating Marine and Coastal Baltic Sea Protected Areas (BSPA) and Proposed Protection Categories, Helsinki-Commission, 16th Meeting, Helsinki 14–17 March 1995, Helcom 16/17.
12 Protocol Concerning Specially Protected Areas and Biological Diversity of a Mediterranean Sanctuary in the Mediterranean, Madrid 14 October 1994, Art 8.
13 www.cbd.int/rio/.
14 https://www.ccamlr.org/en/news/2016/ccamlr-create-worlds-largest-marine-protected-area.
15 http://www.un.org/depts/los/biodiversity/prepcom.htm.
16 www.independent.co.uk/environment/nature/mobile-marine-reserves-may-end-slaughter-of-endangered-sea-life-7079786.html.
17 http://www.pewtrusts.org/en/research-and-analysis/analysis/2016/04/21/pacific-islands-collaborate-to-enforce-worlds-first-regional-shark-sanctuary

References

Costa, B.H.E., Claud, J., Franco, G., Erzini, E., Caro, A. & Gonçalves, E.J. (2016). A regulation-based classification system for Marine Protected Areas (MPAs). *Marine Policy*, vol.72, pp. 192–198.

Cullis-Suzuki, S., & Pauly, D. (2010. Failing the high seas: A global evaluation of regional fisheries management organizations. *Marine Policy*, vol. 34, pp. 1036–1042.

Day, J., Dudley, N., Hockings, M., Holmes, G., Laffoley, D.D.A., Stolton, S., & Wells, S.M. (2012). *Guidelines for Applying the IUCN Protected Area Management Categories to Marine Protected Areas.* IUCN, Gland, Switzerland.

Fidelman, P., & Ekstrom, J.A. (2012) Mapping seascapes of international environmental arrangements in the Coral Triangle. *Marine Policy*, vol.36, pp. 993–1004.

Glazer, A.N. (2001). Natural reserves and preserves. *Encyclopaedia of Biodiversity*, vol. 4, pp. 317–327.

Glenn, H., Wattage, P., Mardle, S., Van Rensburg, T., Grehan, A., & Foley, N. (2010). Marine protected areas – substantiating their worth. *Marine Policy*, vol. 34, no. 3, pp. 421–430.

Hoyt, E. (2005). Sustainable ecotourism on Atlantic islands, with special reference to whale watching, marine protected areas and sanctuaries for cetaceans. *Biology and Environment: Proceedings of the Royal Irish Academy*, vol. 105B(3), pp. 141–154.

Fitzsimons, J., & Wescott, G. (Eds) (2016). Big, Bold and Blue: Lessons from Australia's Marine Protected Areas. CSIRO Publishing, Clayton South.

Johannes, R.E. (2002). The renaissance of community-based marine resource management in Oceania. *Annual Review of Ecology and Systematics*, vol. 33, no. 1, pp. 317–340.

Kearney, R., Buxton, C.D., & Farebrother, G. (2012). Australia's no-take marine protected areas: Appropriate conservation or inappropriate management of fishing? *Marine Policy*, vol. 36, no. 5, pp. 1064–1071.

Kelleher, G. (1999). *Guidelines for Marine Protected Areas*, IUCN, Gland, Switzerland and Cambridge, UK.

Kyriazi, Z., Maes, F., & Degraer, S. (2016). Coexistence dilemmas in European marine spatial planning practices. The case of marine renewables and marine protected areas. *Energy Policy*, vol. 97, pp. 391–399.

Lagoni, R. (2003). Marine protected areas in the exclusive economic zone, in Andree Kirchner (ed), *International Marine Environmental Law: Institutions, Implementation and Innovations*, Kluwer Law International, The Hague.

Lefebvre-Chalain H. (2007). Fifteen Years of Particularly Sensitive Sea Ares: A concept in Development. *Ocean and Coastal Law Journal*, vol. 13(1), pp. 47–69.

Lester, S.E., Halpern, B.S., Grorud-Colvert, K., Lubchenco, J., Ruttenberg, B.I., Gaines, S.D., & Warner, R.R. (2009). Biological effects within no-take marine reserves: A global synthesis. *Marine Ecology Progress Series*, vol. 384, pp. 33–46.

Lindley, J. & Techera, E. (2017). Overcoming complexity in illegal, unregulated and unreported fishing to achieve effective regulatory pluralism. *Marine Policy*, vol. 81, pp. 71–79.

Marine Parks Authority. (2008). *Natural Values of the Solitary Islands Marine Park*, NSW Marine Parks Authority, Hurstville.

Marinesque, S., Kaplan, D.M., & Rodwell, L.D. (2012). Global implementation of marine protected areas: Is the developing world being left behind? *Marine Policy*, vol. 36, no. 3, pp. 727–737.

McCauley, D.J., Pinsky, M.L., Palumbi, S.R., Estes, J.A., Joyce, F.H., & Warner, R.R. (2015). Marine defaunation: Animal loss in the global ocean. *Science*, vol. 347, no. 6219, p. 1255641.

Meine C. (2001). Conservation Movement, Historical. Encyclopaedia of Biodiversity vol. 1, pp. 883–896

National Research Council (2001). *Marine Protected Areas: Tools for Sustaining Ocean Ecosystems*, National Academy Press, Washington DC.

O'Leary, B.C., Brown, R.L., Johnson, D.E., Nordheim, H.V., Ardron, J., Packeiser T., & Roberts, C.M. (2012). The first network of marine protected areas (MPAs) in the high seas: The process, the challenges and where next. *Marine Policy*, vol. 36(3), pp. 598–605.

OSPAR Commission. (2015). Collective arrangement between competent international organisations on cooperation and coordination regarding selected areas in areas beyond national jurisdiction in the North-East Atlantic. OSPAR Agreement 2014-09. < https://www.ospar.org/documents?v=33030> accessed 22 May 2018.

OSPAR Commission. (2016). Key figures of the MPA OSPAR network. < http://mpa.ospar.org/home_ospar/keyfigures> accessed 22 May 2018.

Sandwith, T., Shine, C., Hamilton, L., & Sheppard, D. (2001). Protected areas for peace and co-operation (No. 7). Best Practice Protected Area Guidelines Series.

Scovazzi, T. (2011). The conservation and sustainable use of marine biodiversity, including genetic resources, in areas beyond national jurisdiction: A legal perspective. In Discussion Panel during the 12th meeting of the UN open-ended informal consultative process on Oceans and the Law of the Sea 20–24 June 2011. <http://www.un.org/Depts/los/consultative_process/ICP12_Presentations/Scovazzi_Abstract.pdf> accessed 22 May 2018.

Soininen, N., & Hassan, D. (2015). Marine spatial planning as an instrument of sustainable ocean governance, in D. Hassan, T. Kuokkanen & N. Soininen (eds), *Transboundary Marine Spatial Planning and International Law*, Routledge, London.

Spalding, M., & Zeitlin Hale, L. (2016). Marine protected areas: Past, present and future – A global perspective, in James Fitzsimons & Geoff Wescott (eds), *Big, Bold and Blue: Lessons from Australia's Marine Protected Areas*, CSIRO Publishing, Clayton South.

Techera, E.J. (2016). A review of Marine Protected Area legislation in Australia, in James Fitzsimons & Geoff Wescott (eds), *Big, Bold and Blue: Lessons from Australia's Marine Protected Areas*, CSIRO Publishing, Clayton South.

Techera, E.J., & Chandler, J. (2015). Offshore installations, decommissioning and artificial reefs: Do current legal frameworks best serve the marine environment? *Marine Policy*, vol. 59, pp. 53–60.

Unger, S. (2004). *Managing Across Boundaries: The Dogger Bank-a Future International Protected Area*, WWF Germany, Frankfurt.

Ward-Paige, C.A. (2017). A global overview of shark sanctuary regulations and their impact on shark fisheries' (2017) Marine *Policy*, vol. 82, pp. 87–97.

WSSD. (2002). Plan of implementation of the world summit on sustainable development. *Sustainable Development*, vol. 24, no. 46, p. 20.

Zbicz, D. (1999). Transboundary cooperation in conservation: A global survey of factors influencing cooperation between internationally adjoining protected areas, PhD Thesis, Duke University, Durham, NC.

10
RECOGNITION OF INDIGENOUS RIGHTS IN GOVERNANCE OF MARINE PROTECTED AREAS

Applying international law and Australian experiences

Donna Craig

Introduction

The expansion of protected areas (PAs) from the terrestrial to marine contexts has raised many complex governance issues. Most of the focus has been on the contested legal jurisdictions and management (responsibilities, resources and processes). Approximately 3% of the world's oceans are protected in implemented and actively managed marine protected areas. The World Conservation Union (IUCN) has representation from most governments and major environmental Non-Government Organisations (NGOs) from around the world. The IUCN PA categories and management guidelines (Dudley, 2008) are adopted, through law and policy, in most jurisdictions. Additional IUCN Guidelines have been developed for Marine Protected Areas (MPAs).

Significant issues remain about governance for integrated coastal zone management, ecosystem values and services. Indigenous Peoples' interests have belatedly been addressed through revisions of the IUCN categories, IUCN management guidelines and participatory approaches, collaborative management (co-management), joint management (Craig, 2002) and Indigenous Peoples' Territories and Areas Conserved by Indigenous Peoples and Local Communities (ICCAs) and the incorporation of traditional ecological knowledge into biodiversity and PA management. However, the international and domestic frameworks for MPA governance have failed to systematically address the rapid changes in normative and best practice approaches to recognising Indigenous rights. This has frequently led to a failure to recognise and implement key developments under the United Nations Declaration on the Rights of Indigenous Peoples (UNDRIP), The Convention on Biological Diversity 1992 (CBD) and the Convention Concerning Indigenous and Tribal Peoples in Independent Countries (ILO,169).

This chapter will briefly discuss the concepts of governance, focusing on common property resources, applicable to oceans and Indigenous Peoples. This will be followed by an overview of contemporary Indigenous rights and a critique of the IUCN PA governance approach adopted by most countries. The Australian PA category, known as Indigenous Protected Area (IPA) has been applied to Indigenous owned and controlled land (Smyth & Ward, 2008). This has been extended to Aboriginal and Torres Strait Islander 'sea country'. The Dhimmaru IPA will be used as an example of the strengths and weaknesses of the recognition of Indigenous rights in the Australian governance of MPAs.

Governance for sustainability

To a certain extent the need for integrated terrestrial and marine ecosystem governance requires new thinking about the nature and role of law. We are no longer trapped in the *Tragedy of the Common* (Hardin, 1968). Governance refers to the role and importance of institutions in *grouping different actors together and rules in steering their action* (Dovers & Connor, 2006; Evans, 2012). Evans (2012) expands modes of governance in the following way:

> Governance seeks to co-ordinate action between actors but there are a number of different ways in which this can be done. Modes comprise bundles of rules that guide interaction based on general principles about how actors are best motivated. Three different modes of co-ordination are generally recognised in the literature: hierarchy, network and market.

Ostrom (1990, 2009) and Laerhoven and Ostrom (2007) undertook research on traditional societies that depend on common property resources (such as fisheries or grazing land), arguing that they can develop internal rules and institutions to sustainably manage them (independent of markets or state regulation). There may be impediments relating to institutional and cultural fit in wider recognition and support of these approaches (Agrawal, 2002, 2003). Other impediments to sustainability governance relate to a mismatch between political and ecological scales and difficulties in designing integrated approaches at local, national and global scales (Dovers & Connor, 2006; Evans, 2012). Further insights can be gained through the literature on customary law (Australia Law Reform Commission, 1986; Craig & Gachenga, 2010; Techera, 2009, Kwa, 2006; New Zealand Law Commission, 2006; Orebech, 2005), legal pluralism (Griffiths, 1986; Merry, 1992; von Benda-Beckmann, 2002) and traditional ecological knowledge systems (Berkes, Colding & Folke, 2000; Berkes & Farvar, 1989).

Adaptive governance brings together actors with a stake in a social-ecological system (e.g., a fishery or an MPA) to enable the system to be monitored and to change their behaviour accordingly (Dovers & Connor, 2006; Evans, 2012):

> Governing takes place through a process of monitoring and experimentation that facilitates iterative learning and adaptation in the context of a changing environment.... The entire rationale of this mode of governance is to be highly flexible, allowing for change and adaptation.

Berkes, Colding and Folke (2003) influenced to a significant extent by common pool resource theory, highlight adaptive governance that increases the resilience of social-ecological systems by enhancing their capacity to adapt to cope with environmental changes and cope with extreme and uncertain events. A strength of their approach is the linking of institutions to ecosystem knowledge based on experimentation and learning (Dovers & Connor, 2006; Evans, 2012). On the down side, there are considerable impediments in developing methodologies and accessing resources for the vast number of contexts, difficulties in scaling up from local specificity (to a regional or larger scale) and a return to paradigms that promote expert-dominated processes and *threaten to depoliticise highly political aspects of social transformation* (Dovers & Connor, 2006; Evans, 2012). Adaptive governance can also privilege specific actors and cast them in different roles (Dovers & Connor, 2006; Evans, 2012).

Researchers at the Tyndall Centre for Climate Change (Hulme et al., 2007) conclude that there is a need for pluralist and inclusive decision-making to promote learning and inclusive decision-making. The qualitative and value dimensions of adaptive governance are inescapable. These insights about sustainability governance require a much deeper involvement by local communities and Indigenous Peoples (inclusive of their laws, knowledge systems and institutions). There is also a strong cultural basis and source of knowledge (TEK) for combining Indigenous rights and MPA governance:

> Traditional forms of marine spatial management, though varied in implementation and application to match local ecosystems and customs, are ubiquitous in Indigenous cultures that rely on marine resources. For example, marine customary tenures delimit areas of the ocean where rights of access and extraction are limited; 'periodically harvested closures', common in Melanesia and Polynesia, are off-limits to extractive activities except when opened for fishing for special occasions (e.g., village feasts, funerals, meeting cash needs).
>
> *(Ban & Frid, 2018, p. 180)*

More problematic is the reality that the objective of biodiversity conservation for MPAs often overlaps with Indigenous governance values and aspirations, but they cannot be assumed to be the same. The following discussion of Indigenous rights provides the foundation for recognition that Indigenous Peoples are more than stakeholders and have unique rights and relationships that should be recognised by the adaptive governance of MPAs. It argues that the older governance paradigms continue to privilege 'nature' over 'culture' and Indigenous rights.

Indigenous rights-based approaches

James Anaya (UN Special Rapporteur on the Rights of Indigenous Peoples) and Robert Coulter (Director of the Indian Law Resource Centre in the United States) argue that International Law can be effective in facilitating improved recognition of Indigenous rights at local, regional, national and international) Levels (Anaya, 2004, Coulter, 2006). The United Nations Declaration on the Rights of Indigenous Peoples (UNDRIP) is not a legally binding document in itself, but it re-states many existing human rights standards that are legally binding. Anaya advocates a realist approach to Indigenous rights and specifically rejects the resort to formalist and positivist jurisprudential positions (Anaya, 2005a; Griffiths, 2002; Nettheim, Meyers & Craig, 2006; Richardson, & Craig, 2006; von Benda-Beckmann, 2002). It is understood that international norms, and their application, change over time, as does Indigenous customary law. This approach is very important for environmental law and Indigenous rights, as many inappropriate laws, institutions and jurisprudence continue in post-colonial societies and the reality that sovereignty and self-determination have evolving and varied meanings (Allott, 2002; Barsh, 1994; Richardson, Mgbeoji, & Botchway, 2007).

It is important to highlight the research and activism of Anaya, the Indian Law Resource Centre and the case law under the Inter-American Human Rights Regime to demonstrate key aspects of the convergence and divergence of mainstream human rights–based approaches and Indigenous norms. The modern human rights system is based upon the Universal Declaration of Human Rights (UDHR) and in subsequent human rights treaties such as the International Covenant on Civil and Political Rights (ICCPR) and the International Covenant on Economic, Social and Cultural Rights (ICESCR). The Committee monitoring the UN Convention on the Elimination of All Forms of Racial Discrimination (CERD) noted that the situation of indigenous discrimination against indigenous peoples falls under

> the scope of the Convention. Under CERD, States should recognise and respect Indigenous peoples' distinct culture, history, language and way of life and ensure that indigenous communities can exercise their rights to practice and revitalise their cultural traditions and customs. This includes recognition and protection of the rights of Indigenous peoples to own, develop, control and use their communal lands, territories and resources, and where they have been deprived of their lands and territories traditionally owned or otherwise inhabited or used without their free and informed consent, to take steps to return those lands and territories.
> *(CERD, 1997)*

The major human rights treaties were developed before the ecological, social, cultural and economic dimensions of sustainable development were understood. Current legal instruments and trends in relation to environment law are insufficient to support the existence of a clear and specific right to an environment of a particular quality in international law, although a large number of national constitutions embody such a right (HREOC, 2008). Environmental human rights jurisprudence has mostly concerned itself with pollution claims. Shelton argues that *issues such as resource management and nature conservation or biodiversity are more difficult to bring under the human rights rubric, absent a right to a safe and ecologically-balanced environment.* Even without the articulation of a specific right to the environment, there are many broad rights recognised in the UDHR, ICCPR, ICESCR and the Convention Concerning Indigenous and Tribal Peoples in Independent Countries (known as ILO 169) which are relevant to the situation of Indigenous Peoples' marine territories.

The way in which these instruments should be implemented from an ecological standpoint has been well argued by the Australian Human Rights and Equal Opportunity Commission (HREOC), United Nations Office of the High Commissioner for Human Rights and by Grieber et al.

Falk (2001) considers that five conceptual structures have been used in Indigenous claims:

1   Human rights and non-discrimination claims
2   Minority claims
3   Self-determination claims
4   Historic sovereignty claims
5   Claims as indigenous peoples, including claims based on treaties or other agreements between Indigenous Peoples and states.

He argues that the first four categories are well established in legal practice (that has largely been unrelated to Indigenous Peoples rights and concerns) and questions how well they can be integrated with the specific Indigenous features in the fifth category (Falk, 2001). Falk elaborates how a variety of existing legal approaches to the first four categories may assist Indigenous claims to a limited extent, but concludes that:

> The construction and affirmation of a distinct programme of 'rights of Indigenous Peoples', going beyond universal human rights and existing regimes of minority rights, has been one of the objectives of the international Indigenous movement (Falk, 2001).

The task of formulating such substantive legal rules has largely fallen to the International Labour Organisation (explicit references to the environment and natural resources in the context of other rights can be found in Articles 2, 4, 7 and 15 of ILO 169). ILO 169 remains an important international treaty providing for a broad range of rights relevant to a comprehensive approach to climate adaptation. Most ratifications have been by developing nations and it falls short of the broader formulation of self-determination in UNDRIP Article 3. Indigenous Peoples should receive the full application of universally applicable civil, political, social, cultural and economic rights as well as national constitutional and domestic legal rights applying to all citizens (such as the right to self-determination expressed under the ICCPR and ICESCR). Indigenous Peoples have demonstrated leadership and taken advantage of changes in international law over the last three decades, particularly in the area of human rights, which is beneficial to humanity more broadly (Anaya, 2006). They should also be accorded recognition of rights that are specific and particular to Indigenous Peoples.

178 Donna Craig

The critical reference point for their integrated rights has become the UNDRIP. This a re-statement of much existing international treaty and international customary law but significantly expands the rights to self-determination, intellectual and cultural property and free prior informed consent. Davis (2008) argues that the 'cornerstone' of UNDRIP is the right to self-determination and that it is also a 'very clear exercise in translating the right to self-determination from international law into the domestic context' (p. 439). Therefore, it could be reasonably expected that Indigenous Peoples should be the beneficiaries of existing human rights, Indigenous rights and environmental regimes as they seek to address their urgent concerns in relation to ocean governance.

The UNDRIP formulation is critical to the approach taken by Anaya and Coulter, although they recognise that ILO 169 contains crucial normative standards with a significant level of international legal recognition. UNDRIP does not 'define' Indigenous Peoples (indeed, this would be inconsistent with many of the Articles). They are culturally distinct groups traditionally regarded, and self-defined, as descendants of the original inhabitants of areas to which they share a strong, often spiritual, attachment. The cultural distinctiveness of indigenous peoples includes the aspects of language, social organisation, religion and spiritual values, modes of production, laws and institutions. They generally share an experience of subjugation, dispossession, exclusion or discrimination, whether or not these conditions persist.

Anaya (2004) sees two major limits of sovereignty (for Indigenous Peoples). It upholds the status quo of political ordering protective of state territorial integrity and political unity and it limits the capacity of the international system to regulate the matters within the sphere of authority claimed by States (and recognised by the international system). There can be overlapping claims for sovereignty and self-determination, but most contemporary Indigenous claims use the language and norms of self-determination. Daes (1993) considers that this involves 'belated state building' through negotiation and other peaceful procedures involving meaningful participation by Indigenous Peoples:

> Through which indigenous peoples are able to join with all the other peoples that make up the state on mutually agreed terms, after many years of isolation and exclusion. This process does not require the assimilation of individuals, as citizens like all others, but the recognition and incorporation of distinct peoples in the fabric of the state, on agreed terms (Daes, 1993).

Anaya (2009a) maintains that internationally recognised human rights advances a multicultural model of political ordering and incorporation of indigenous peoples into the fabric of the State where indigenous peoples are to be able to join others in the States in which they live on the basis of equality in terms of cultural identity and not just individual citizenship. Anaya specifically advocates a human rights–based approach to Indigenous self-determination rather than a States rights–based framework (Anaya, 2006). He considers that international human rights norms, particularly those relating to non-discrimination and cultural integrity, supports this model and the concept of cultural integrity is at the very core of UNDRIP and ILO 169 (Anaya, 2009a).

The exercise of cultural self-determination may be limited by the human rights–based framework (for example to prevent harm and discrimination against women) and the UNESCO Declaration provides that *no one may invoke cultural diversity to impinge on other people's aspirations in all decisions affecting them.*

Anaya (2009a) identifies four key changes in international human rights law promoted by Indigenous Peoples:

- The move towards collective rights.
- The softening of state sovereignty.
- Evolution of the norm of self-determination.
- The role of non-state actors. (Anaya, 2006)

Indigenous Peoples are not just 'stakeholders' or 'participants'. The role of Indigenous participants in negotiating UNDRIP over 31 years, the UN Permanent Forum on Indigenous Issues(UNFIP) and their role in the Arctic Council and under the Arctic Environmental Protection Strategy (AEPS) are good examples of their distinct status:

> Indigenous peoples appear to be gaining recognition as having a unique or sui generis status among non-state actors within the international arena. Associated with this unique status is an enhanced level of participation. . . . Indigenous Peoples are by definition longstanding communities with historically rooted cultures and distinct political and social institutions.
>
> *(Anaya, 2006)*

The application of this approach in Indigenous governance to MPAs is complex. Some of the political and legal impetus may come from international regimes, but most legal responses will be domestic. This is evidenced by the increasing recognition of constitutional Indigenous rights and rights to environmental quality, common law rights (such as native title), treaty and statutory rights as well as gradual recognition of self-determination (often through negotiated self-governance and Comprehensive Land Claims Agreements as illustrated by Canadian experience) (Firestone, Lilley, & Torres de Noronha, 2004; Nettheim, Meyers, & Craig, 2002). Given the fluidity of international, regional and national legal systems, it is more important than ever to develop normative standards and approaches that will not be subject to constant erosion in litigation and negotiation with states and the private sector.

Indigenous rights and marine protected areas

A protected area (PA) is defined as a *geographical space recognised, dedicated and managed, through legal and other effective means, to achieve the long-term conservation of nature with associated ecosystem services and cultural values* (Dudley, 2008). This is intended to be applied to protected areas across biomes, ownership and governance types, motivations, management objectives and jurisdictional levels. The IUCN protected area guidelines provide a spectrum of governance and management arrangements that can apply to any PA category (Dudley, 2008). They can be managed solely by government agencies, or through co-management arrangements or solely by Indigenous groups, local communities or others. Throughout the IUCN guidelines there is a focus on achieving protected area outcomes rather than promoting particular governance and management models (Smyth, 2012).

Indigenous and Community Conserved Areas (ICCA) are defined by IUCN as:

> natural and/or modified ecosystems containing significant biodiversity values, ecological functions and benefits, and cultural values voluntarily conserved by indigenous peoples and local communities both sedentary and mobile – through customary laws or other effective means.

In Australia, terrestrial Indigenous Protected Areas (IPAs) are a form of ICCA that are formally recognised as part of the National Reserve System (NRS); the potential for IPAs to contribute to the National Reserve System for Marine Protected Areas (NRSMPA) is currently subject to debate (Smyth, 2009). The IUCN *Supplementary Guidelines for applying the IUCN Protected Area Management Categories to Marine Protected Areas* (2010) provide examples of how Indigenous interests in MPA should be addressed within each IUCN category (Smyth, 2012). Smyth illustrates this approach through the arrangements in the Great Barrier Reef Marine Park (GBRMP):

> where amendments to the Great Barrier Reef Marine Park 1975 (Cth) provide for the accreditation of Traditional Use of Marine Resource Agreements (TUMRAs), without the requirement for a native title determination. TUMRAs are agreements negotiated among and between Traditional Owners groups about how they intend to manage and sustainably use traditional marine resources (e.g. dugong, turtles, fish and shellfish) within their traditional sea country inside the GBRMP. TUMRAs may include a commitment to limit the harvesting of a particular species to an agreed number per year, or may include a moratorium on harvesting a species for a specified time. Once a TUMRA is accredited by the Great Barrier Marine Park Authority (GBRMPA), the TUMRA provisions are enforceable under the GBRMP Act – though native title rights are not affected. TUMRAs are being used effectively to ensure sustainability of traditional resource use by local Traditional Owner groups, and a way to manage use of these resources by other Indigenous groups who may wish to access resources in the specified TUMRA area. TUMRAs are also recognised under the Queensland Marine Parks Act 2004 (Qld).
>
> *(Smyth, 2012, p. 28)*

Such examples are ad hoc in the governance of MPAs. Butterfly argues that there is a fundamental problem in the definition and governance of PAs because of

> a nature–culture dualism insofar as the primary purpose of a protected area is nature conservation; cultural values are a secondary consideration where these are associated with nature. . . . The reductive and simplistic allure of classifying values as natural or cultural comes at the expense of articulating Indigenous worldviews and the richness of values that create the things worth conserving.

This suggests that inclusive Indigenous governance of MPAs requires a critical approach to embedded concepts such as 'nature', 'culture', 'heritage' and 'conservation' as well as the domestic implementation of Indigenous rights.

Australian indigenous protected areas for sea county: innovative indigenous governance?

The legal context for ocean governance, and the extent to which Commonwealth, state and territory governments recognise Indigenous rights to lands, waters, resources and seas (including their use and management), provides a necessary background to the development of marine and terrestrial IPAs.

The Commonwealth of Australia was formed when six partly self-governing British colonies united to become states of a nation (1901). The rules of government for this new nation were enshrined in the *Australian Constitution*. Under the federal system, powers are divided between a central government and individual states. In Australia, power was divided between the Commonwealth federal government and the six state governments. States retain the power to make their own laws. Territories are areas within Australia's borders that are not claimed by one of the six states. They can be administered by the Australian Government.

Australia has sovereignty over a band of waters called the 'territorial sea', which at present extends up to 12 nautical miles from the territorial sea baseline. This raises the question of how to divide management of resources and responsibilities in the territorial sea between the Commonwealth and the states. In 1975, the High Court determined that the Commonwealth has sovereignty over waters to the edge of the territorial sea, including the seabed beneath these waters. Subsequently, the Commonwealth and the states undertook negotiations resulting in the 'Offshore Constitutional Settlement' dealing with Commonwealth and state jurisdiction in the waters to the edge of the territorial sea. The settlement also includes arrangements on managing oil, gas and other seabed minerals, the Great Barrier Reef Marine Park, other marine parks, historic shipwrecks, shipping, marine pollution and fishing. In general, the states have responsibility for areas up to three nautical miles from the territorial sea baseline, which are termed 'coastal waters'. The settlement is not set out in one single document but is found in the legislation that implements it. The legislation generally extends the arrangements to the Northern Territory.

Australia's Oceans Policy (1998) was launched by the Australian (Commonwealth) government to promote ecologically sustainable development of marine resources, encourage internationally competitive marine industries, and ensures the protection of marine biological diversity. The government reinforced its commitment to the accelerated implementation of the National Representative System of Marine Protected Areas as a key component to the protection of marine biological diversity. Under the *Australia's Oceans Policy*, the government will seek to ensure the following:

- that traditional conservation and use practices are valued;
- that the reliance by many coastal Indigenous communities on marine resources is treated as an important ocean use; and
- that Indigenous communities are given every opportunity to take up commercial activities related to the oceans.

This provides the basis for involving Indigenous people in the management of Australia's marine environment, including the development of MPAs. Regional marine plans are developed as Marine Bioregional Plans, under s.176 of the *Environment Protection and Biodiversity Conservation Act 1999* (the EPBC Act). Marine bioregional plans give details about the various conservation and heritage-related statutory obligations under the EPBC Act that are operational in any region.

The link between Indigenous cultural values and biodiversity is well established in Australia in, for example, the EPBC Act and the *National Strategy for the Conservation of Australia's Biodiversity*. Marine bioregional plans prepared under s.176 of the EPBC Act are bound by the objects of the Act:

> f) to recognise the role of indigenous people in the conservation and ecologically sustainable use of Australia's biodiversity
> g) to promote the use of indigenous peoples' knowledge of biodiversity with the involvement of, and in cooperation with, owners of the knowledge.

In order to achieve its objects, the strategies include:

> (g) to promote a partnership approach to environmental protection and biodiversity conservation through
>
> > (ii) conservation agreements with land holders
> > (iii) recognising and promoting indigenous peoples' role in, and knowledge of, the conservation and ecologically sustainable use of biodiversity
> > (iv) the involvement of the community in management planning

The Australian Government also has responsibilities under the heritage provisions of the EPBC Act to assess and manage listed Indigenous heritage values, including in the marine environment. In making decisions under the EPBC Act, the Minister for the Environment and Heritage is bound by provisions of the Native Title Act 1993.

Indigenous use, occupation and enjoyment of the coastal zone was traditionally one of socio-cultural and economic integration with the ecology of the various bioregions that existed at the fringe of land and sea, and often into the ocean. Prior to contact, Indigenous land and seascapes were managed on a seasonal cycle so that both land and sea economies were sustained. Many coastal Indigenous communities regularly engaged in a mixed economy, enjoying both inland and sea country resources. The upholding of law and culture through recognition and maintenance of individual and clan rights and responsibilities geared to ecological rejuvenation was an integral part of Indigenous cultures.

The rights of Indigenous peoples to their lands and waters are recognised and made enforceable in Australian law through the native title and statutory land rights legislation (enacted by states and territories). The rights and interests recognised by native title are inherent to Indigenous peoples by virtue of their status as first peoples and it exists without requiring an application or determination. This legal position was clarified in the case *Mabo v. Queensland, 1992 (No.2)* (Mabo Case). However, the scope of native title to lands, waters and seas was limited by the conservative opinions of the High Court in Mabo and the limitations and procedures subsequently enacted by the Australian Government. The *Native Title Act 1993* (NT Act) declares that native title is recognised and protected according to the Act and cannot be extinguished except according to the procedures set out in the Act (ss.10–11). The Act provides for the Federal Court to make determinations as to whether native title exists (ss.13–15), and Indigenous peoples who make an application for determination must establish their claim according to the elements of proof captured by the definition set out in s.223(1). Recognition of rights over sea country was not directly considered in the *Mabo Case*.

In 2001, the High Court decision in *Yarmirr* clarified that native title extends to territorial waters (*Commonwealth v. Yarmirr*, 2001). Section 6 of the *Native Title Act 1993* also states that:

> This Act extends to each external Territory, to the coastal sea of Australia and of each external Territory, and to any waters over which Australia asserts sovereign rights under the Seas and Submerged Lands Act 1973.

The High Court in *Yarmirr* concluded that, except for the qualification of exclusivity, sovereignty in relation to the territorial seas showed no 'necessary inconsistency' with the continued recognition of native title. Each native title determination differs with respect to the rights and interests that are held by members of the native title group under their traditional laws and customs.

Indigenous Land Use Agreement (ILUAs), under the NT Act, may be entered into over any area and may concern the manner of exercise of native title rights and interests. An ILUA may be entered into with any or all registered native title claimant groups or prescribed body corporates (the holders of native title once determined) or with any person who claims to hold native title, and the Native Title Representative Body for the area. ILUAs can be entered into over marine areas. ILUAs may contain provisions relating to the validation of future acts or the manner and exercise of native title rights and interests. Registered ILUAs are binding to all native titleholders and interests. The subject matter over which an ILUA can be reached is broad and can cover most land, water and marine uses and management. Specifically, ILUAs are also being used for the co-management of national parks and the use of sea resources.

Aboriginal Peoples in the Northern Territory (NT) have gained significant recognition of their sea rights under the *Aboriginal Land Rights (Northern Territory) Act 1976* (Cth) (ALRA). The *Northern Territory v. Arnhem Land Aboriginal Land Trust*, 2008 (Blue Mud Bay case) held that pursuant to the ALRA land in the intertidal zone (the area between high and low water marks including river mouths and estuaries) in the NT could be claimed and recognised as Aboriginal land. Under the statutory land rights system in the NT (which is distinct from native title) Aboriginal land takes the form of inalienable fee simple, which the High Court has confirmed is the practical equivalent of full ownership.

Conservation agreements under the EPBC Act allow the relevant minister to enter into an agreement with a person, such as an Indigenous person, or incorporated or statutory Indigenous body, that has usage rights over the area. Native titleholders are covered by this provision as they hold a legal estate in the land. Conservation agreements can be entered into for the protection and conservation of biodiversity or heritage places or values and may include the protection, conservation or management of listed species, ecological communities or their habitats. Conservation agreements can be entered into in relation to marine areas. Agreements entered into voluntarily by native titleholders do not affect their underlying title. Agreements made outside the native title processes may be necessary because of the legal limits of native title law and the broad scope rights and activities involved in MPA governance.

National Indigenous cultural heritage and conservation operates at the national level under the *Aboriginal and Torres Strait Islander Heritage Protection Act 1984* (Cwlth). The *Aboriginal and Torres Strait Islander Heritage Protection Act 1984* (ATSIHPA) is intended to preserve and protect places, areas and objects in Australia and Australian waters that are places, areas or objects of particular significance to Aboriginals in accordance with Aboriginal tradition (s.4). The Act defines 'Australian waters' as:

a) the territorial sea of Australia and any sea on the landward side of that territorial sea
b) the territorial sea of an external Territory and any sea on the landward side of that territorial sea
c) the sea over the continental shelf of Australia.

A 'significant Aboriginal area' means:

a) an area of land in Australia or in or beneath Australian waters
b) an area of water in Australia
c) an area of Australian waters

being an area of particular significance to Aboriginals in accordance with Aboriginal tradition.

Under the Act, an area or object is deemed to be injured or desecrated:

if it is used or treated in a manner inconsistent with Aboriginal tradition; by reason of anything done in, on or near the area; if the use or significance of the area in accordance with Aboriginal tradition is adversely affected; or passage through or over, or entry upon the area by any person 'the body of traditions, observances, customs and beliefs of Aboriginals generally, or of a particular community or group of Aboriginals, and includes any such traditions, observances, customs or beliefs relating to particular persons, areas, objects or places'.

ATSIHPA applies within Australian territorial waters beyond the limit of three nautical miles. Within three nautical miles and on land, Aboriginal and Torres Strait Islander heritage is governed by state and territory legislations. ATSIHPA is 'not intended to exclude or limit the operation of a law of a state or territory that is capable of operating concurrently with the Act'. Aboriginal and Torres Strait Islander Peoples may also express views and values under the *Australian Heritage Council Act 2003* (Cwlth) processes and listing. However, there are significant limitations in national, state and territory heritage laws having regard to approach (separating culture from nature), limited coverage and inadequate recognition of Aboriginal and Torres Strait Islander rights and self-determination. Indigenous marine resource management may also be impacted by the EPBC Act, especially in matters of national environmental significance, and the *Fisheries Administration Act 1991* (Cwlth).

This overview has focused on Australian Commonwealth policy, legislation and case law. This indicates a growing recognition of Indigenous rights to 'country' that in many cases will involve integral relationships to land and sea. However, legislation and implementation are fragmented. There is an increasing amount of land and seas under Indigenous ownership (native title and statutory land rights). There is some recognition of sustainable use in PAs, limited protection of heritage and sacred sites and an extensive practice of Indigenous engagement in natural resource management in a wide variety of contexts. These developments, as well as the push for representative and connected ecosystems in PAs, led to the evolution of Indigenous Protected Areas (IPAs) as a new type of Australian PA.

IPAs are a voluntary agreement entered into by the Traditional Owners of the land and the Commonwealth government to promote biodiversity and cultural resource conservation on indigenous owned land. IPAs now form the second largest component of the National Reserve System.

The goals of the IPA program are as follows:

- To establish partnerships between government and indigenous land managers to support the development of a comprehensive, adequate and representative national system of protected areas which is consistent with the international protected areas classification by assisting indigenous people to establish and manage protected areas on estates for which they hold title and assisting indigenous groups and Commonwealth, State and Territory agencies to develop partnerships for cooperative management of existing protected areas.
- To promote indigenous involvement in protected area management by supporting the establishment of cooperatively managed protected areas in each jurisdiction and promotion of national best practice approaches to cooperative partnerships in protected area management.
- To promote and integrate indigenous ecological and cultural knowledge into contemporary protected area management practices, in accordance with internationally endorsed protected areas guidelines.

The first 12 years of the IPA Program focused almost entirely on Indigenous owned land:

> This is because the exercise of exclusive management authority over Indigenous owned land is more straightforward and less contested than on traditional Indigenous Country now held under a variety of non-Indigenous tenures. The inclusion of marine areas in IPAs has been viewed as problematic due to the lack of Indigenous tenure and exclusive authority in the sea.
>
> *(Smyth, 2009)*

> IPAs have now been dedicated – not only over Indigenous-owned land as has been the case until recently, but also over a range of other tenures within the traditional estate of an Indigenous group.
>
> *(Smyth 2009; Ross et al., 2009: pp. 245–247)*

The terms 'Sea Country' or 'Saltwater Country' refer to coastal, island and marine environments that together make up the traditional estates of maritime Indigenous groups in Australia:

> The ocean, or saltwater country, is not additional to a clan estate on land, it is inseparable from it. As on land, saltwater country contains evidence of the Dreamtime events by which all geographic features, animals, plants and people were created. It contains sacred sites, often related to these creation events, and it contains tracks, or Song lines along which mythological beings

travelled during the Dreamtime or creation period. The sea, like the land, is integral to the identity of each clan, and clan members have a kin relationship to the important marine animals, plants, tides and currents.

(Smyth, 1997)

Several Sea Country Plans, developed as part of the Australian Government's Marine Bioregional Planning Program for Australia's ocean environments, have documented Traditional Owners' aspirations to establish IPAs over their Sea Country, including both terrestrial and marine environments (Smyth, 2009):

> All of these proposals are pursuing a 'Country-based', rather than a 'tenure-based' approach to the IPA concept. They use the IPA concept as a management framework to achieve the goals of conservation and sustainable use of Sea Country, rather than limiting the IPA boundaries to those areas over which Indigenous peoples currently have exclusive control.

This is illustrated by the Dhimurru IPA in Northeastern Arnhem Land, which includes both coastal land and marine areas. The marine area contains many marine sacred sites registered under the *Northern Territory Aboriginal Sacred Sites Act 1989 (NT)*. This legal recognition of the cultural significance of the marine estate was sufficient for it to be included in the IPA, even though Traditional Owners' management authority over marine sacred sites is not as strong as over Aboriginal-owned land (Smyth, 2007).

Governance arrangements include Traditional-Owner organisations, Indigenous land and sea management agencies and community councils, regional Indigenous organisations and advised by relevant government and non-government organisations, some of whose representatives may sit on formal advisory committees for each IPA. The governance and management arrangements attempt to respect traditional owners' authority to make decisions about the country while also developing day-to-day management capacity. This usually involves a full-time IPA manager, Indigenous rangers and other specialist staff. Core funding has been provided by the Commonwealth Government along with variety of other grants. The adequacy of funding for the management of sea country IPAs, and insecurity of ongoing core government funding, is a significant impediment to good governance.

Conclusions

The international and domestic frameworks for MPA governance have failed to systematically address the rapid changes in normative and best practice approaches to recognising Indigenous rights. This has frequently led to a failure to recognise and implement key developments under UNDRIP, the CBD and ILO 169. Australian Commonwealth policy, legislation and case law reveals a growing recognition of Indigenous rights to 'country'. However, legislation and implementation is ad hoc, still focuses on the separation of land and seas, privileges nature over culture and does not provide for a clear or systematic recognition of Indigenous rights established under international law.

References

Agrawal, A. (2002). Common resources and institutional sustainability, in E. Ostrom et al. (eds), *The Drama of the Commons*, National Academies Press, Washington DC, pp. 41–85.

Agrawal, A. (2003). Sustainable governance of common-pool resources: Context, methods, and politics. *Annual Review of Anthropology*, vol. 32, no. 1, pp. 243–262.

Allott, P. (2002). *The Health of Nations: Society and Law Beyond the State*, Cambridge, Cambridge University Press.

Anaya, J. (2004). *Indigenous Peoples in International Law*, Oxford University Press, Oxford.

Anaya, J. (2005a). Divergent discourse about international law, indigenous peoples and rights over lands and natural resources: Towards a realist trend. 16 *Colorado Journal of International Environmental Law*, 237–258

Anaya, J. (2005b). Divergent discourses about international law, indigenous peoples, and rights over lands and natural resources: Toward a realist trend. *Colorado Journal of International Environmental Law and Policy*, vol. 16, p. 237.

Anaya, J. (2006). Indian givers: What indigenous peoples have contributed to international human rights law. *Washington University Journal of Law & Policy*, vol. 22, p. 107.

Anaya, J. (2009a). International human rights and indigenous peoples; The move toward the multicultural state, Arizona Legal Studies Discussion Paper 09–34, p. 15.

Anaya, J. (2009b). *International Human Rights and Indigenous Peoples*. Aspen Publishers, New York, NY.

Anaya, J., & Williams Jr, R. (2001). The protection of indigenous peoples' rights over lands and natural resources under the Inter-American human rights system. *Harvard Human Rights Journal*, vol. 14, p. 33.

Australia Law Reform Commission. (1986). *The Recognition of Aboriginal Customary Laws*, Government Printer, South Africa.

Ban, C., & Frid, A. (2018). Indigenous peoples' rights and marine protected areas. *Marine Policy*, vol. 87, pp. 180–185.

Barsh, R. (1994). Indigenous peoples in the 1990s: From object to subject of international law. *Harvard Human Rights Journal*, vol. 7, p. 33.

Berkes, F., & Farvar, M. (1989). Introduction and overview, in Fikret Berkes (ed.), *Common Property Resources: Ecology and Community-Based Sustainable Development*, Belhaven Press, London p. 1.

Berkes, F., Colding, J., & Folke, C. (2000). Rediscovery of traditional ecological knowledge as adaptive management. *Ecological Applications*, vol. 10, no. 5, pp. 1251–1262.

Berkes, F., Colding, J., & Folke, C. (Eds.) (2003). *Navigating Social-Ecological Systems*, Cambridge University Press, Cambridge, pp. 433–434.

Convention on the Elimination of All Forms of Racial Discrimination 1966 (CERD), 97. *General Recommendation 23: Indigenous Peoples*, A/52/18, paragraphs 3.2, 4a, d and e and 5

Coulter, R. (2006). Using international human rights mechanisms to promote and protect rights of Indian nations and tribes in the United States: An overview. *American Indian Law Review*, vol. 31, no. 2, pp. 573–591.

Coulter, R. (2008). UN declaration on the rights of indigenous peoples: A historic change in international law. *The Idaho Law Review*, vol. 45, p. 539.

Craig, D. (2002). Recognising indigenous rights through co-management regimes: Canadian and Australian experiences. *New Zealand Journal of Environmental Law*, vol. 6, p. 199.

Craig, D., & Gachenga, E. (2010). The recognition of Indigenous customary law in water resource management. *Water Law*, vol. 20, pp. 1–7.

Daes, E. (1993). Some Considerations on the Right of Indigenous Peoples to Self-Determination. *Transnational Law & Contemporary Problems*, vol. 3, p. 1.

Daes, E. (1995). Standard-setting activities: Evolution of standards concerning the rights of Indigenous People. United Nations. Sub-Commission on Prevention of Discrimination and Protection of Minorities. Working Group on Indigenous Populations.
Davis, M. (2008). Indigenous struggles in standard-setting: The United Nations Declaration on the rights of indigenous peoples. *Melbourne Journal of International Law*, vol. 9.
Dovers, S., & Connor, R. (2006). Institutional and policy change for sustainability in *Environmental Law for Sustainability: A Reader*. Hart Publishing, Oregon.
Dudley, N. (Ed.) (2008). *Guidelines for Applying Protected Area Management Categories*. IUCN, Gland, Switzerland.
Evans, J. (2012). *Environmental Governance*, Routledge, London.
Falk, R (2001) "Reconciling Five Competing Structures of Indigenous Peoples' Claims in International and Comparative Law"), extracted in Anton, D and Shelton, D (2011) *Environmental Protection and Human Rights*. Cambridge University Press, p. 546.
Firestone, J., Lilley, J., & Torres de Noronha, I. (2004). Cultural diversity, human rights, and the emergence of Indigenous peoples in international and comparative environmental law. *American University International Law Review*, vol. 20, p. 219.
Griffiths, A. (1986). Legal pluralism, in R. Banakar & M. Travers (eds), *An Introduction to Law and Social Theory*, Hart Publishing, Oregon.
Griffiths, A. (2002). Legal pluralism, in R. Banakar & M. Travers (eds), *An Introduction to Law and Social Theory*, Hart Publishing, Oregon.
Hardin, G. (1698). Extensions of 'the tragedy of the commons'. *Science*, vol. 280, no. 5364, pp. 682–683.
HREOC, *Human Rights and Climate Change*, Background Paper, 2008
Hulme, M., Adger, W.N., Dessai, S., Goulden, M., Lorenzoni, I., Nelson, D., . . . Wreford, A. (2007). *Limits and Barriers to Adaptation: Four Propositions*. Tyndall Center for Climate Change Research. University of East Anglia, Norwich.
Kwa, E. (2006). Traditionalizing sustainable development: The law, policy and practice in Papua New Guinea, Doctoral dissertation, Research Space@ Auckland.
Laerhoven, F., & Ostrom, E. (2007). Traditions and trends in the study of the commons. *International Journal of the Commons*, vol. 1, no. 1, pp. 3–28.
Merry, S. (1992). Anthropology, law, and transnational processes. *Annual Review of Anthropology*, vol. 21, no. 1, pp. 357–377.
Nettheim, G., Meyers, G., & Craig, D. (2002). *Indigenous Peoples and Governance Structures: A Comparative Analysis of Land and Resource Management Rights*, Australian Institute of Aboriginal and Torres Strait Islander Studies. Canberra, p. viii.
Nettheim, G., Meyers, G., & Craig, D (2006). *Indigenous Peoples and Governance Structures: A Comparative Analysis of Land and Resource Management Rights*, Aboriginal Studies Press, Canberra.
New Zealand Law Commission. (2006). *Converging Currents: Custom and Human Rights in the Pacific*, New Zealand Law Commission. Wellington.
Orebech, P. (2005). *The Role of Customary Law in Sustainable Development*, Cambridge University Press, Cambridge.
Ostrom, E. (1990). *Governing the Commons: The Evolution of Institutions for Collective Action*, Cambridge University Press, Cambridge.
Ostrom, E. (2009). A general framework for analyzing sustainability of social–ecological systems. *Science*, vol. 325, no. 5939, pp. 419–422.
Richardson, B., & Craig, D. (2006). Indigenous peoples, law and the environment, in *Environmental Law for Sustainability*, Hart Publishing, Oxford, Chapter 7.
Richardson, B, Mgbeoji, I., & Botchway, F. (2007). *Environmental Law in Post-Colonial Societies: Aspirations, Achievements and Limitations, Environmental Law for Sustainability*, Hart Publishing, Oxford.

Ross, H, Grant, C, Robinson, C, Izurieta, A, Smyth, D & Rist P 2009, 'Co-management and Indigenous protected areas in Australia: achievements and ways forward', *Australian Journal of Environmental Management*, vol. 16, no. 4, pp. 242–252

Smyth, D. (1997). *Saltwater Country Aboriginal and Torres Strait Islander Interest in Ocean Policy Development and Implementation*. Department of the Environment, Canberra

Smyth, D. (2007). Dhimurru indigenous protected area: Sole management with partners, in T. Bauman and D. Smyth (eds), *Indigenous Partnerships in Protected Area Management in Australia: Three Case Studies*. Australian Institute of Aboriginal and Torres Strait Islander Studies, Canberra pp. 100–125.

Smyth, D. (2009). Just add water? Taking indigenous protected areas into sea country, in D. Smyth & G. Ward (eds), *Indigenous Governance and Management of Protected Areas in Australia,*. Australian Institute of Aboriginal and Torres Strait Islander Studies, Canberra, pp. 95–110.

Smyth, D. (2012). Best practice recognition and engagement of aboriginal traditional owners and other indigenous people in the use and management of Victoria's marine protected areas. A Discussion Paper for the Victorian Environment Assessment Council. P.28

Smyth, D., & Ward, G.K. (2008). *Protecting Country: Indigenous Governance and Management of Protected Country*, AIATSIS, Canberra.

Techera, E. (2009). Law, custom and conservation: The role of customary law in community-based marine management in the South Pacific, Doctoral dissertation, Macquarie University.

Von Benda-Beckmann, F. (2002). Who's afraid of legal pluralism? *The Journal of Legal Pluralism and Unofficial Law*, vol. 34, no. 47, pp. 37–82.

Cases

Commonwealth of Australia v Yarmirr (2001). 208 CLR 1.
Mabo v Queensland (No 2) (Mabo case) [1992] HCA 23.
Northern Territory of Australia v Arnhem Land Aboriginal Land Trust (2008). 236 CLR 24.

PART IV
Polar regions

11
PROTECTION OF THE ANTARCTIC MARINE ENVIRONMENT
Dimensions, relationships and fields

Tuomas Kuokkanen

Introduction

Antarctica is a continental landmass that covers about 14 million square kilometres and has 17,968 kilometres of coastline. It is surrounded by ocean, called the Southern Ocean or sometimes as the Southern Seas or the South Polar Sea (McIvor, 2009). The Southern Ocean constitutes about one-tenth of the world's ocean space and covers approximately 36 million square kilometres (Joyner, 1992).

The Antarctic Treaty was concluded in 1959 (Antarctic Treaty). According to the treaty, Antarctica shall be used for peaceful purposes only. The treaty gives special attention to the freedom of science and sets aside territorial claims to Antarctica. In addition, the Antarctic Treaty system[1] includes the following treaties: the 1972 Convention for the Conservation of Antarctic Seals (Antarctic Seals Convention), the 1980 Convention on the Conservation of Antarctic Marine Living Resources (CCAMLR)[2], the 1988 Convention on the Conservation on the Regulation of Antarctic Mineral Resource Activities (CRAMRA) and the 1991 Protocol on Environmental Protection to the Antarctic Treaty (Antarctic Environmental Protocol)[3].

Environmental principles concerning the planning and conduct of activities are set forth in Article 3 of the Environmental Protocol. One of the Protocol's key provisions is Article 7, which prohibits any activity relating to mineral resources, other than scientific research. The Protocol has six annexes, which include specific provisions on environmental impact assessment (Annex I), fauna and flora (Annex II), waste disposal (Annex III), marine pollution (Annex IV), protected areas (Annex V) and Liability (Annex VI). The liability annex was adopted in 2005 and has not yet entered into force.

Also, other international instruments outside the Antarctic regime can be relevant in relation to Antarctic issues.[4] This is the case also with regards to the protection of the Antarctic marine environment. As Joyner (1992) notes, '[i]nternational ocean law for the Antarctic is not arranged in a single new legal document, nor available in a concise set of regulations. Rather, law for circumpolar Antarctic waters has evolved piecemeal into a complex regime that reflects political realities' (p. 274).

The present chapter explores the protection of the Antarctic marine environment from a legal point of view. In order to better understand how the system works, the chapter examines the field of Antarctic issues by distinguishing four dimensions: subjective, spatial, temporal and substantive.[5] To begin with, the subjective dimension includes various actors in the field, as the consultative parties of the Antarctic treaty. The spatial dimension refers to areas and territories, particularly to marine areas. While the temporal dimension means issues referring to time, the substantive dimension refers to material instruments. The dimensions have many components, which have relationships with each other. While exploring different dimensions, the chapter seeks to identify both issues from inside and outside the Antarctic Treaty system.

The chapter does not aim to be an exhaustive inquiry of all the issues relating to the protection of the Antarctic marine environment. Rather, the purpose is to understand the dimensions and relationships in this field.

Actors in the protection of the Antarctic environment: subjective dimension

Seven states, namely Australia, Argentina, Chile, France, New Zealand, Norway and the United Kingdom of Great Britain and Northern Ireland, made territorial claims to parts of Antarctica. The claims of Chile, Argentina and the United Kingdom overlap. For this reason, the United Kingdom submitted to the International Court of Justice an application against Argentina and Chile relating to the sovereignty over certain islands and lands in Antarctica. As the court did not have jurisdiction to deal with the applications both cases were removed from the court (Antarctica case, *United Kingdom v. Argentina*; Antarctica, *United Kingdom v. Chile*). The United States and the Soviet Union did not recognise territorial claims made by other States and have reserved a right to make claims (Guyer, 1973).

In the late 1940s and the 1950s, tension increased in the South Atlantic and neighbouring parts of Antarctica (Watts, 1992). Therefore, it was necessary to endeavour to reach a compromise, as Triggs (1987) put it, 'to avoid rivalry between Argentina, Chile and the United Kingdom and the brooding dangers of Cold War between the United States and the Soviet Union' (p. 54). As the legal paradigm began to change after World War II, countries had to adjust their argument also over Antarctic issues (Guyer, 1973). Likewise, scientists were active in pursuing solutions to the Antarctic question. As Hambro (1974, p. 218) notes, the Antarctic Treaty 'is probably the best example in history of politicians being drawn into action by scientists'.

The Antarctic Treaty was signed by 12 countries that were active in Antarctica during the International Geophysical Year of 1958–1959 and participated in the treaty negotiations in the diplomatic conference in Washington 1959. These signatory States gained the status of 'Consultative Parties' which are allowed to make decisions. After the entry into force of the Antarctic Treaty, further parties have been allowed to accede to the treaty and gain the Consultative Party status pursuant to Article XII and IX provided that a State is a member of the United Nations.

The Antarctic Treaty established the Antarctic Consultative Meeting (ATCM) as a decision-making body. The meeting consists of representatives of the Consultative Parties, non-Consultative Parties, observers and invited experts. Currently, the Scientific Committee on Antarctic Research (SCAR), the Commission for the Conservation of Antarctic Marine Living Resources (CCAMLR) and the Council of Managers of National Antarctic Programs (COMNAP) are observers. As experts, the ATCM has invited for example the Antarctic and Southern Ocean Coalition (ASOC) and the International Association of Antarctica Tour Operators (IAATO). The Antarctic Treaty secretariat was established in 2003 and is located in Buenos Aires, Argentina.

The ATCM can adopt measures, decisions and resolutions. However, only the Consultative Parties may take part in decision-making while observers and invited experts may participate in the discussions. Thus, the Antarctic Treaty system and the ATCM can be characterised as an international regime which Stephen D. Krasner has defined as 'a set of implicit or explicit principles, norms, rules and decision-making procedures around which actors' expectations converge' (Krasner, 1983, p. 2). Over the years, the role of non-governmental organisations (NGOs) and epistemic communities has increased.

The Antarctic marine area: spatial dimension

Antarctica is in many respects an extraordinary place. It is the coldest, windiest, iciest and driest continent. It was part of the ancient Gondwana continent. Once Antarctica was separated from Gondwana, water began to circulate around it in the Antarctic Circumpolar Current.

Before the end of the World War II, the claimant States had made unilateral claims to parts of Antarctica, which cover also ocean areas. Only 15% of the Antarctic continent remained unclaimed (Rotkirch, 1987). The Antarctic treaty froze these territorial claims.

According to the preamble of the Antarctic Treaty, Antarctica 'shall not become the scene or object of international discord'. Furthermore, in Article 2 of the Environmental Protocol, the parties commit themselves to the comprehensive protection of the Antarctic environment and dependent and associated ecosystems and designate Antarctica as a natural reserve, devoted to peace and science.

According to Article VI, the treaty applies to the area south of 60 degrees South Latitude, including all ice shelves. The article further specifies that 'nothing in the present Treaty shall prejudice or in any way affect the rights, or the exercise of the rights, of any State under international law with regard to the high seas within that area'. One consequence of this distinction has been that parties have concluded separated conventions when regulating issues that 'affect their rights of the exercise of their rights with regard to the seas within the area of application of the Treaty' (Harlan K, 2002, p. 2).

The 60 degrees boundary was selected for historical reasons and it is, as Joyner (1992) notes, 'arbitrary and without biogeographical basis' (p. 19). However, in negotiating the CCAMLR it was recognised that the effective conservation of marine living resources required a broader definition of the scope of the convention. Therefore, the northern limit of the Antarctic marine ecosystem was extended to the Antarctic Convergence, which means the point where the cold northerly-moving Antarctic waters meet warmer southerly-moving waters (Harlan K, 2002, p. 2; Joyner, 1992).

Annex V of the environmental protocol concerns protected areas. It provides for the designation of Antarctic Specially Protected Areas (ASPA) and Antarctic Specially Managed Areas (ASMA). Such areas may also include marine areas. So far, the ATCM has established a number of ASPAs and ASMAs with marine components as well as coastal ASMAs and ASPAs to protect marine values on land (The role of Antarctic Treaty Consultative Meeting, 2014, p. 21).

Issues related to time: temporal dimension

The claimant States made their claims to Antarctica between 1908 and 1943. In discussing the history of the Antarctic Treaty, Guyer points out the change of political and legal factors during this time period. He notes that prior to 1914, public opinion and doctrine admitted territorial claims 'as colonial expansions and inherent superiority of certain nations'. He notes that after World War II the situation changed as countries that 'originally started their Antarctic involvement due to imperial considerations gradually evolved to one of predominant scientific presence' (Guyer, 1973, p. 364).

With regards to the territorial claims, the Antarctic Treaty made a twofold modification to its Article IV. First, it safeguards the positions of those parties that had 'previously asserted rights of or claims to territorial sovereignty in Antarctica', that consider themselves as having a 'basis of claim to territorial sovereignty in Antarctica', and that do not recognise 'any other State's right of or claim or basis of claim to territorial sovereignty in Antarctica'. Second, the article turns to the future by stating that

> no acts or activities taking place while the present Treaty is in force shall constitute a basis for asserting, supporting or denying a claim to territorial sovereignty in Antarctica or create any rights of sovereignty in Antarctica. No new claims, or enlargement of an existing claim, to territorial sovereignty in Antarctica shall be asserted while the present Treaty is in force.

According to the preamble of the Antarctic Treaty Antarctica 'shall continue forever to be used exclusively for peaceful purposes'.

Substantive issues related on the protection of the marine environment: material dimension

The regulatory process on the protection of the Antarctic marine environment developed gradually. The conclusion of the Antarctic Treaty provided a basis for protection. Thereafter, the process started to evolve from the protection of marine living resources to the prevention of marine pollution and finally to the protection of the Antarctic ecosystems.

Even though the Antarctic treaty does not directly refer to the protection of the environment, it includes several provisions that are also relevant from the environmental point of view. For example, according to Article I, any measures of a military nature are prohibited. Furthermore, any nuclear explosions in Antarctica and the disposal of radioactive waste material in the continent are prohibited (Article V). In addition, the treaty authorised the ACTM in its Article IX to give measures in furtherance of the principles and objectives of the treaty. Pursuant to that mandate, the ATCM had already adopted in 1964 the Agreed Measures for the Conservation of Antarctic Fauna and Flora (Recommendation III-8), which provided a basis for the further work developed in relation to nature conservation and environmental protection.

The first separate treaty was the Convention for the Conservation of Antarctic Seals, which was concluded in London on 1 June 1972 as a response to the concern about the vulnerability of Antarctic seals to commercial exploitation (Convention of Antarctic Seals). The parties to the agreement recognised in the preamble of the convention that 'the stocks of Antarctic seals are an important living resource in the marine environment which requires an international agreement for its effective conservation'. The convention applies to the Antarctic treaty area and covers all species of seal in Antarctic waters: southern elephant seal, leopard seal, Wedddell seal, Crabeater seal, Ross seal and southern fur seals.

As a next step, the Convention on the Conservation of Antarctic Marine Living Resources (CCAMLR) was concluded in Canberra on 20 May 1980. The main concern behind the convention was the potential over-exploitation of krill, which is a small crustacean and which plays an important role within the Antarctic marine ecosystem (McIvor, 2009). In order to provide for the effective conservation of krill and other Antarctic marine living resources, the Convention introduced a number of innovative approaches.

Annex II of the Environmental Protocol includes specific provisions to protect the Antarctic fauna and flora from human disturbance. It applies also to marine species. For instance, the Ross seal is a specially protected species according to the Appendix A of the Annex.

The prevention of marine pollution is regulated through Annex IV of the Environmental Protocol; it concerns the prevention of marine pollution. According to Article 2 of the annex, it applies, 'with respect to each Party, to ships entitled to fly its flag and to any other ship engaged in or supporting its Antarctic operations, while operating in the Antarctic Treaty area'. The annex regulates the discharge of oil, noxious liquids and sewage generally, as well as the specific discharge of sewage. Furthermore, the annex includes provisions, *inter alia*, on cases of emergency, ship retention capacity and reception facilities, design, construction, manning and equipment of ships, sovereign immunity, preventive measures and emergency preparedness and response. The provisions of the annex are drafted to be consistent with the International Convention and Protocol for the Prevention of Pollution from Ships (MARPOL 73/78).

Also, other provisions of the Madrid Protocol are relevant for the protection of marine environment. For instance, Article 8 and Annex I provide detailed rules on environmental impact assessments. In addition, Annex III includes provisions on waste disposal and waste management. According to Article 5 of that Annex, sewage and domestic liquid waste may be discharged into the sea in certain situations. The Protocol does not only cover a range of preventive actions but also lays down in its Article 15 regulations for emergency response action. Furthermore, in 2005 the ATCM meeting held in Stockholm adopted Annex VI to the protocol. The new Annex, which has not yet entered into force, provides rules for liability arising from environmental emergencies.

Outside the Antarctic treaty system

Several international conventions outside the ATS may relate to the protection of the Antarctic marine environment. While the UNCLOS deals with the protection and preservation of the marine environment in a general manner, several conventions dealing with specific issues are relevant in the Antarctic context. This is the case, for example, in relation to the MARPOL 73/78, the Whaling Convention, the Basel Convention and the CITES convention. Moreover, under the International Convention for the Regulation of Whaling, the Antarctic Ocean South of the convergence has been designated as a whale sanctuary where commercial whaling is banned and under the MARPOL 73/78 Convention: the whole Antarctic Treaty area has been designated as a special area (The role of the Antarctic Treaty Consultative Meeting, 2014).

Furthermore, the work of many international organisations and bodies are also concerned with the protection of the Antarctic marine environment. One recent example is the adoption of a Polar Shipping Code by the International Maritime Organization, which is designed for shipping in both the Arctic and the Antarctic waters (Polar Code). The code was adopted during the 94th session of IMO's Safety Committee in November 2014 and the environmental provisions and MARPOL amendments during the 18th session of IMO's Marine Environmental Protection Committee in May 2015.

In the 1980s, the Antarctic mineral resource negotiations led to the debate on the relationship between the Antarctic Treaty system and the United Nations. Malaysia was primus motor in initiating the discussion in the UN. Already at the signing ceremony of the Law of the Sea Convention at Montego Bay, the Foreign Minister of Malaysia stated that the international community should turn its attention to Antarctica, which he described as another area of common interest 'where immense potentialities exist for the benefit of all mankind' (cited in Hayashi, 1986, p. 276). Subsequently, Malaysia, together with many like-minded third world countries, submitted the question of Antarctica to the agenda of the General Assembly in 1983. They criticised the Antarctic Treaty parties and argued that it is unjust that a small group of powerful countries should agree on the exploitation of Antarctic mineral resources, and argued that the Antarctic resources are the common heritage of mankind like the minerals on the deep seabed (Hayashi, 1986; Rotkirch, 1987). Conversely, the Antarctic Treaty parties denied that Antarctic mineral resources can be compared to the mineral resources on the deep seabed which have not been subject to a regulatory system as opposed to the Antarctic treaty system which already exists (Rotkirch, 1987). The debate gradually cooled down once it appeared that the CRAMRA would not enter into force and the Environmental Protocol was concluded in 1991, which banned the mineral activities in the Antarctic treaty area.

Currently, there are two ongoing processes which also relate to the relationship between the Antarctic treaty system and the Law of the Sea.[6] First, the relationship between the Law of the Sea and the claims made by some of the Antarctic countries to the continental shelf is a pending issue (Comba, 2009; Vicuña, 1988). The objective of the Commission on the Limits of the Continental Shelf is to facilitate the implementation of the United Nations Convention on the Law of the Sea in respect of the establishment of the outer limits of the continental shelf beyond 200 nautical miles from the baselines from which the breadth of the territorial sea is measured. Under the Convention, the coastal State shall establish the outer limits of its continental shelf where it extends beyond 200 nautical miles on the basis of the recommendation of the Commission. The following consultative parties have made submissions to the Commission: Australia, Norway, New Zealand, Australia, France and Argentina (Commission on the Limits of the Continental Shelf). In addition, Chile has submitted preliminary data. Pursuant to Article 76(8) of the Law of the Sea Convention, the Commission shall make recommendations to coastal States on matters related to the establishment of the outer limits of their continental shelf. So far, the commission has not issued any recommendations relating to Antarctica.

The second pending issue relates to areas beyond national jurisdiction. For example, in 2004, the United Nations General Assembly established an Ad Hoc Open-ended Informal Working Group to study issues relating to the conservation and sustainable use of marine biological beyond areas of national jurisdiction (BBJN). After the working group had concluded its work, on 19 June 2015 the General Assembly adopted a resolution on the 'Development of an international legally-binding instrument under the United Nations Convention on the Law of the Sea jurisdiction' (Resolution 69/292). In the resolution, the General Assembly established a preparatory committee (PrepCom) to make substantive recommendations on the elements of a draft text of an international, legally binding instrument under the United Nations Convention on the Law of the Sea and to report to the General Assembly by the end of 2017.

Processes outside the ATS may raise concern among the ATS parties as the question can be asked; which forum has legitimacy to make decisions relating to particular Antarctic issues. Such a question may arise, for instance, in relation to the BBJN process and the biological prospecting in Antarctica (Rayfuse, 2008; Leary, 2008; Lohan & Johnston, 2005). The matter was discussed at the 38th Consultative Meeting held in Sofia in 2015. In the meeting several parties highlighted that the collection and use of biological material from the Antarctic should be discussed with the Antarctic Treat System (Antarctic Treaty Consultative Meeting, 2015). In the discussion, it was noted that parties 'should be mindful of the regulatory system of the Antarctic Treaty System and be careful of engaging in discussions on the possible application of other, possibly conflicting, regimes' (Rayfuse, 2008; Leary, 2008; Lohan & Johnston, 2005). Thereafter, the meeting reaffirmed that 'the Antarctic Treaty system was the appropriate framework for managing the collection of biological materials in the Antarctic Treaty and for considering its use (Rayfuse, 2008; Leary, 2008; Lohan & Johnston, 2005).

Yet, it is clear that Antarctic issues cannot be dealt with in a vacuum. One challenge is activities of third parties in Antarctica like, for instance, tourism (Guyer, 1973). Moreover, many global environmental problems, such as climate change, ozone depletion and transboundary air pollution may also affect Antarctica. Sometimes even certain individual matters outside the Antarctic regime have had an impact on Antarctic matters. For example, the *Exxon Valdez* disaster had an impact to abandonment of the mineral resource convention and the conclusion of the environmental protection protocol (Howkins, 2016).

Against this background, the ATCM and the ATS parties have recognised that international cooperation is required to deal effectively with Antarctic issues. For example, in the context of the Fiftieth Anniversary of the Antarctic Treaty, parties were encouraged to work through other appropriate international organisations that have expertise in respect of activities that may also take place in the Antarctic treaty area, such as maritime activities (Washington Ministerial Declaration, 2009: para 8). In particular, the effects of climate change are a deep concern for the ATCM. In the Santiago Declaration, adopted on the occasion of the 25th Anniversary of the signing of the Madrid Protocol, parties reaffirmed their intention to work together to better understand changes and to address the effects of climate change on the Antarctic environment and dependent associated ecosystems (Santiago Declaration, 2016, para 6).

Relationships and fields

Reuter (1995) notes in his book on the law of treaties that a treaty 'does not produce its effects in a legal vacuum', and that surrounding each treaty 'there is an intricate web made up of all the treaties in force, of customary rules, and acts of international organizations' (p. 129). He points out that 'a number of treaties may be linked among themselves, as well as with other acts and sources of international law, with differing degrees of closeness and varying effects' (Reuter, 1995, pp. 130–131).

The Antarctic treaty and instruments relating to it are a good example of the web that Reuter referred to.

The Antarctic Treaty System 'is the whole complex of arrangements made for the purpose of coordinating relations among states with respect to Antarctica' (Handbook: 1). Over the years, the Antarctic Treaty system has managed to balance various interests. For instance, the way how the treaty deals with territorial claims is a good illustration of successful management. Even though Article IV does not solve territorial or sovereignty issues, the non-solution provided by the article has, paradoxically enough, allowed Antarctic regime building. Thus, the treaty 'maintains equilibrium of the web of competing national political interests, and thus served as the treaty's *modus vivendi* for facilitating negotiations on various Antarctic-related issues to go forward' (Joyner, 1992, p. 64). Watts (1992, p. 140) points out that the 'carefully crafted network of provisions comprising Article IV and the provisions based on it are a central part of a series closely interrelated and interdependent elements which have established for Antarctica a distinctive and carefully balanced regime'.

Also, the protection of the marine environment involves the management of various relationships and interests. For instance, the concept of Antarctic marine ecosystems according to Article 1 of the CCAMLR means, 'the complexity of relationships of Antarctic marine living resources with each other and with their physical environment'. In the preamble of that convention, parties recognise 'the importance of safeguarding the environment and protecting the integrity of the ecosystem of the seas surrounding Antarctica'. The parties to the seals convention emphasise the balancing of different interests by aiming 'to promote and achieve the objectives of protection, scientific study and rational use of Antarctic seals, and to maintain a satisfactory balance within the ecological system' (Seals Convention, preamble).

The Madrid Protocol seeks to protect the Antarctic environment and dependent and associated ecosystems in a comprehensive manner. As the protocol applies both to the Antarctic continent and to the surrounding Southern Ocean, there is no a rigid distinction between terrestrial and marine protection. Indeed, as Boyle (1997) notes, the Antarctic marine environment is 'simply part of a much larger "macro-region" of land *and sea* to which the Antarctic Treaty System applies throughout' (p. 29). In the preamble of the protocol, the parties also emphasise the value of the protection outside of Antarctica by noting that the protection is 'in the interest of mankind as a whole'.

The Antarctic treaty system can be seen as a general field of Antarctic issues and rules. Thus, when speaking on Antarctic questions, one often refers to this general field.[7] Yet, there are also specific fields. The protection of the Antarctic marine environment can be regarded as such a field. While it includes rules and principles from the general field, that is the Antarctic system, it has also applicable rules outside the Antarctic system. For example, as discussed previously, there are global marine conventions which are applicable in the Antarctic waters. Therefore, it is important to take into account all those rules, and not only the ATS rules, when dealing with the Antarctic marine protection.

The Antarctic treaty system has proven to be effective in responding to both internal and external challenges. On the one hand, this has required that the work of the ATS has been effective so that it has gained legitimacy in the outside world. Thereby, the ATS has been able to strenuously resist 'outside interference in Antarctic matters and demands for the Antarctic to be internationalised and managed by the United Nations' (Scott, 2010, p. 5).

Conclusions

The present chapter first divided issues relating to Antarctic marine protection to subjective, spatial, temporal and material dimensions focusing on the Antarctic Treaty system. Thereafter, the chapter briefly dealt with issues outside the Antarctic Treaty system. The chapter then discussed the relationships both inside and outside the Antarctic Treaty system. Finally, the chapter pointed out that while the Antarctica treaty system represents a general field of Antarctic issues there are also specific fields such as the protection of the marine environment. Both the general field and specific field have a number of components that are partly interrelated and have specific relationships.

The success of the treaty regime is that it has separate instruments that are, as Watts (1992) put it, 'carefully interrelated so that various parts of the system respect and complement each other' and have 'given rise to a single coherent system' (p. 291–292). As opposed to a static arrangement, the Antarctic Treaty System has been a dynamic, flexible and adaptive one (Joyner, 1992). Also, in the future, the ATs must deal with both internal and external challenges and their various relationships.

The protection of the Antarctic marine environment is not based on a single instrument but rather it is made up of a complex relationship between different instruments and interests. Depending on context, these various relationships might have different impacts. Sometimes the field might be in a delicate balance and sometimes a certain powerful instrument or interest might produce a force on other instruments or interests. Sometimes forces might or might not work in synergy. The effective protection of the Antarctic marine environment requires, first, the identification of those various dimensions and relationships and, second, their proper management.

Notes

1 See Cohen (Ed.) (2002); Jackson (1995); Rothwell (1996)
2 See Rose & Milligan (2009)
3 See Bestmeijer (2003), Francioni (1993), Redgwell (1993).
4 See Vigni (2000).
5 See discussion by Fitzmaurice (1986) and Heiskanen (2013) on jurisdictional dimensions.
6 See United Nations Commission on the Limits of the Continental Shelf (2016).
7 See discussion on the term general field, Fitzmaurice (1986) and Heiskanen (2013).

References

Bastmeijer, Kees. (2003). *The Antarctic Environmental Protocol and Its Domestic Legal Implementation*, Kluwer Law International, The Hague.

Boyle, A. (1997). Globalism and regionalism in the protection of the marine environment, in Davor Vidas (ed.), *Protecting the Polar Marine Environment. Law and Policy for Pollution Prevention*, Cambridge University Press, Cambridge, pp. 19–33.

Cohen, H. (Ed.) (2002). *Handbook of the Antarctic Treaty System*. US Department of State. https://www.state.gov/documents/organization/15271.pdf

Comba, D. (2009). The polar continental shelf challenge: Claims and exploitation of mineral resources – An Antarctic and Arctic comparative analysis. *Yearbook of International Environmental Law*, vol. 20, pp. 158–187.

Francioni, Francesco (1993). The Madrid protocol on the protection of the Antarctic environment. *Texas International Law Journal*, vol. 28, pp. 47–72.

Fitzmaurice, Gerald. (1986). *The Law and Procedure of the International Court of Justice*. Cambridge, Grotius Publications.

Guyer, R. (n.d). The Antarctic system (1973). *Academy of International Law*. Leyden, p. 211.

Hambro, E. (1974). Some notes on the future of the Antarctic treaty collaboration. *American Journal of International Law*, vol. 68, no. 2, pp. 217–226.

Harlan, K. Cohen (Ed.) (2002). *Handbook of the Antarctic Treaty System*, 9th edn, U.S. Departement of State, www.state.gov/e/oes/rls/rpts/ant/.

Hayashi, M. (1986). The Antarctica question in the United Nations. *Cornell International Law Journal*, vol. 19, pp. 275–290.

Heiskanen, V. (2013). Ménage à trois? Jurisdiction, admissibility and competence in investment treaty arbitration. *ICSID Review*, vol. 29, no. 1, pp. 231–246.

Howkins, A. (2016). *The Polar Regions. An Environmental History*, Polity Press, Cambridge, MA.

Joyner, C. (1992). *Antarctica and the Law of the Sea*, Martinius Nijhoff Publishers, Dordrecht, Boston, London.

Jackson, Andrew. (1995). *On the Antarctic Horizon; Proceedings of the International Symposium on the Future of the Antarctic Treaty System*, Ushuaia, Argentina.

Leary, D. (2008). Bi-polar disorder? Is bioprospecting an emerging issue for the Arctic as well as for Antarctica? *Review of European, Comparative & International Environmental Law*, vol. 17, no. 1, pp. 41–55.

Lohan, D., & Johnston, S. (2005). Bioprospecting in Antarctica. United Nations University-Institute of Advanced Studies, Yokohama, Japan. 31.

McIvor, E. (2009). Looking South: Antarctic environmental governance, in Ed Couzens & Tuula Honkonen (eds), International Environmental Law-making and Diplomacy Review 2008, University of Eastern Finland, UNEP Course Series 8, pp. 139–152.

Rayfuse, R. (2008). Protecting marine biodiversity in polar areas beyond national jurisdiction. *Review of European, Comparative & International Environmental Law*, vol. 17, no. 1, pp. 3–13.

Reuter, P. (1995). *Introduction to the Law of Treaties*. Routledge, London.

Redgwell, Catherine (1994). Environmental protection in Antarctica: The 1991 protocol, *International and Comparative Law Quarterly*, vol. 43, pp. 599–634.

Rose, Gregory & Milligan, Ben (2009). Law for the management of Antarctic marine living resources: From normative conflicts towards integrated governance? *Yearbook of International Environmental Law*, vol. 20, pp. 41–87.

Rothwell, Donald R. (1996). *The Polar Regions and the Development of International Law*, Cambridge University Press, Cambridge.

Rotkirch, H. (1987). The growing significance of Antarctica: The efforts to establish an international Antarctic mineral resources regime, in Matti Tupamäki (ed.), *Finnish Branch of International Law Association 1946–1986. Essays on International Law*, Helsinki, pp. 169–189.

Roura, R.M., Steenhuisen, F., & Bastmeijer, C.J. (2014). The role of the Antarctic Treaty Consultative Meeting in protecting the marine environment through marine spatial protection, Information paper submitted by Netherland, www.ats.aq/documents/ATCM37/ip/ATCM37_ip049_e.doc.

Scott, K. (2010). Managing sovereignty and jurisdictional disputes in the Antarctic: The next fifty years. *Yearbook of International Environmental Law*, vol. 20, no. 1, pp. 3–40.

Secretariat of the Antarctic Treaty. (2015). *Final Report of the Thirty-Eight Antarctic Treaty Consultative Meeting*, Volume I and II, Buenos Aires, Bulgaria.

Triggs, G. (1987). *The Antarctic Treaty Regime: Law, Environment and Resources*, Cambridge University Press, Cambridge.

United Nations Commission on the Limits of the Continental Shelf. (2016). Preliminary information* indicative of the outer limits of the continental shelf beyond 200 nautical miles, Viewed 7 August 2016, www.un.org/Depts/los/clcs_new/clcs_home.htm.

Vicuña, F. (1988). The law of the sea and the Antarctic treaty system: New approaches to offshore jurisdiction, in Joyner Christopher C. & Chopra Sudhir K. (eds), *The Antarctic Legal Regime*, Martinus Nijhoff Publishers, The Hague, pp. 97–127.

Vigni, Patrizia. (2000). *The Interaction Between the Antarctic Treaty System and the Other Relevant Conventions Applicable to the Antarctic Are: A Practical Approach versus Theoretical Doctrines*. The Max Planck Yearbook of United Nations Law, The Hague, pp. 481–542.

Watts, A. (1992). *International Law and the Antarctic Treaty System*, Vol. 11. Cambridge University Press, Cambridge.

Conventions and declarations

Convention for the Conservation of Antarctic Seals, London, 1 June 1972, 11 ILM (1972) 251.

Convention on the Conservation of Antarctic Marine Living Resources, Canberra, 20 May 1980, 19 ILM (1980) 869.

Convention on the Regulation of Antarctic Mineral Resource Activities, Wellington, 2 June 1988, 27 ILM (1988) 868.

International Convention for the Prevention of Pollution by Ships, London, 2 November 1973, 12 ILM (1973) 1319 and Protocol Relating to the Convention for the Prevention of Pollution from Ships, London, 17 February 1978, 17 ILM (1978) 246 (MARPOL 73/78).

International Convention for the Regulation on Whaling, Washington, 2 December 1946, 161 UNTS 72.

International Code for Ships Operating in Polar Waters (Polar Code), MEPC 68/21/Add.1 Annex 10, www.imo.org/en/MediaCentre/HotTopics/polar/Documents/POLAR%20CODE%20TEXT%20AS%20ADOPTED.pdf (visited 7 August 2016).

Protocol on Environmental Protection to the Antarctic Treaty, Madrid, 4 October 1991, 30 ILM (1991) 1461.

Santiago Declaration on the Twenty Fifth Anniversary of the Signing of the Protocol on Environmental Protection to the Antarctic Treaty, XXXIX Antarctic Treaty Consultative Meeting, Santiago, Chile 2016, www.ats.aq.

United Nations Convention on the Law of the Sea, Montegor Bay, 10 December 1982, 21 International Legal Materials (1982) 1261.

Washington Ministerial Declaration on the Fiftieth Anniversary of the Antarctic Treaty, Antarctic Treaty Consultative Meeting XXXII, Washington, 6–7 April 2009, www.ats.aq.

Cases

Antarctica (United Kingdom v. Argentina), Order of 16 March 1956, ICJ Reports 1956, p. 12.
Antarctica (United Kingdom v. Chile), Order of 16 1956, ICJ Reports 1956, p. 15.
Antarctic Treaty, Washington, D.C., 1 December 1959, 402 UNTS 71.

12
PROTECTION OF THE ARCTIC MARINE ENVIRONMENT

Timo Koivurova and Nengye Liu

Introduction

The Arctic Ocean is the smallest and shallowest of Earth's oceans, covering an area of some 14 million square kilometres, of which 2.8 million square kilometres is beyond areas of national jurisdiction – as part of the high seas.[1] There was no need to develop legal regulations to protect the Arctic Ocean and the associated marginal seas, as these waters used to be ice-covered. There was only limited navigation near the coastal regions. The environmental impacts therefore could be handled by national regulations.

However, as climate change has progressed more intensely in the Arctic, this has had concrete and dramatic impacts on the sea ice. The extent of summer sea ice has been declining over the past 50 years at an average of 8% per decade (Stroeve, Holland, Meier, Scambos, & Serreze, 2007) and on 15 September 2007, the ice cap was 22% smaller than it was in 2005, the last record year (Renfrow, 2007). The 2007 record exceeded the computer model predictions used to prepare for the Fourth Assessment Report of the Intergovernmental Panel on Climate Change in 2007.[2] According to a 2016 report from NASA, the Arctic has lost almost 95% of its older ice cover since 1984.[3]

As a result of, among other factors, reduced sea ice, the Arctic waters are being used more and more for various activities. Obviously, increasing the amount of human activities leads to emerging needs for governance pertaining to the Arctic Ocean. More importantly, it is projected that the Arctic Ocean ecosystem is on the verge of a full-scale system change.

There are various serious threats to the marine environment of the Arctic Ocean. With the receding sea ice, Arctic marine areas open increasingly to shipping and resource extraction, which affects Arctic ecosystems and traditional ways of life for indigenous peoples. The increasing commercial access will also have impacts on marine biodiversity. Even if there are no commercial fisheries in ice-covered parts of the Arctic Ocean, this may gradually change. As the Arctic Council's 2013 Arctic Biodiversity Assessment (ABA) states: 'There is increasing concern that the global demand for seafood outside the Arctic combined with increasing accessibility of Arctic seas as a result of sea ice loss creates the potential for increased risks to poorly known fish and crustacean stocks'.[4] In general, 'habitat loss and degradation pose the main threats to biodiversity. The relative well-being of many Arctic ecosystems today is largely the fortuitous result of a lack of intensive human encroachment',[5] which are now being affected by increasing human activities. As the ABA also states

> climate change is the most serious threat to biodiversity in the Arctic, in particular, the marine Arctic. Climate-induced effects on species and ecosystems, associated with a decrease in sea ice extent and duration, are already being observed. Of key concern is the rapid loss of multi-year ice in the central Arctic basins and changes in sea ice dynamics on the extensive Arctic shelves, which affect the biodiversity and productivity of marine ecosystems.[6]

The Arctic Council's Arctic Monitoring and Assessment Programme (AMAP) Working Group adopted the Arctic Ocean Acidification Overview Report in 2013. It found that the Arctic Ocean is rapidly accumulating carbon dioxide (CO_2) leading to increased ocean acidification – a long-term decline in seawater pH.[7] This ongoing change impacts Arctic marine ecosystems that are already affected by rising temperatures and melting sea ice. In addition, the threats of invasive species and pollutants arriving at the Arctic from mid-latitudes threaten the Arctic marine ecosystems.

This chapter will hence try to do two main things. First, examine what is the current framework and governance system for the Arctic marine environment to counter the various threats outlined previously. Second, and perhaps even more importantly, given that the Arctic Ocean will likely be opened for the first time during the summer months in 2030–2040,[8] it will be important to examine how this governance 'landscape' and the various levels of governance are already preparing themselves for the emergence of a new Ocean. One crucial development in the coming years is whether the governance of the Arctic Ocean is done by its coastal States or in the predominant forum of current intergovernmental cooperation in the region – the Arctic Council. It will be shown that the tension between these forums already exists.

Before all this, it is important to be clear on a few fundamental issues from the viewpoint of Arctic marine governance. What can be considered the extent of the marine Arctic, and how is it being considered in this chapter? It is also of importance to identify which entity has what governance powers in different regions of the Arctic, and what type of intergovernmental forum the Arctic Council is.

What is the Arctic and Arctic marine governance?

It is in general difficult to define what areas constitute the Arctic. This is a complex question since several different criteria can be presented when thinking where the southernmost boundary of the Arctic would lie. Possible natural boundaries are, for instance, the tree line, i.e., the northernmost boundary where trees grow, or the 10 C isotherm, i.e., the southernmost location where the mean temperature of the warmest month of the year is below 10 C. In the Arctic-wide cooperation, now operating as the Arctic Council, the Arctic Circle has been used as a criterion for membership. Only those states that possess areas of territorial sovereignty above the Circle (five Nordic states, the Russian Federation, the United States and Canada) would be invited to participate in cooperation.

The same complexity applies to the Arctic marine area. There is no accepted definition of the Arctic Ocean. A widely used definition is adopted by the Arctic Monitoring and Assessment Programme (AMAP) of the Arctic Council, which uses the working definition of marine areas north of the Arctic Circle (66°32'N), and north of 62°N in Asia and 60°N in North America (as modified to include the marine areas north of the Aleutian chain, Hudson Bay and parts of the North Atlantic Ocean, including the Labrador Sea).[9] It does seem generally accepted, however, that there are only five coastal states, namely, Canada, Denmark (through Greenland), Norway, the Russian Federation and the United States. This has caused some political friction since the Arctic Ocean coastal states have not invited Iceland to be part of this constellation of political action, Iceland arguing that it should be treated as an outlying portion of the Arctic Ocean (Parliament, 2011).

The Arctic region falls predominately under the national jurisdiction of the eight Arctic States, which results in some complex jurisdictional questions concerning the region. As mentioned previously, the Arctic Ocean is currently melting. This means that the high seas areas in the central Arctic Ocean, amounting to 2.8 million square kilometres, may, in the future, be at least partly suitable for the capture fisheries. After the Arctic States have delineated the outermost limits of their continental shelves, which will still take quite some time, there will likely be small deep-sea pockets that belong to the Area and be considered the common heritage of humankind and administered by the International Seabed Authority (ISA). From the viewpoint of navigation, the melting of the sea ice means that ever greater areas will become open for navigation, given that the United Nations Convention on the Law of the Sea (UNCLOS),[10] which codifies customary international law, guarantees navigational freedoms in the high seas, and innocent passage in territorial sea.

Furthermore, the Arctic is also a complex area from the viewpoint of how power is exercised and divided within the nation-States that have sovereignty in the region. The three federal states – the Russian Federation, the United States and Canada – exercise some powers in the Arctic region through both the federal level and at sub-national levels, e.g., Alaska in the United States or Nunavut in Canada (Poelzer & Wilson, 2014). Three other Arctic states, Denmark, Finland and Sweden, are members of the European Union (EU).[11] In addition, Norway and Iceland are part of the European Economic Area (EEA).[12] As regards environmental protection, the EU environmental law applies in respect of its Member States, and also to a large extent the EEA countries. Yet, it is important to note that the Faroe

Islands and Greenland are not part of the EU. Greenland was recently elevated to the status of self-government (in contrast to its old Home-Rule status), with large, corresponding, autonomous powers, and a possibility to secede from Denmark and establish its own State.[13] The Svalbard Islands, even though they are under the sovereignty of Norway, are excluded from the EEA agreement, and are governed by an international treaty concluded in 1920 (Treaty Concerning the Archipelago of Spitsbergen).[14] Nevertheless, Norway is competent to enact legislation in most policy areas for the Svalbard Islands. In some parts of the Arctic, Indigenous peoples still – at least to a limited extent – govern themselves via their customary laws.

It is also of interest to examine briefly what type of body is the Arctic Council, the predominant governance institution in the Arctic. The Finnish initiative for Arctic-wide cooperation, the Arctic Environmental Protection Strategy (AEPS) that ran from 1991–1997, was merged with the Canadian initiative on the Arctic Council during the transition period 1996–1998. The Council is a soft law forum, as it was established via a declaration (Koivurova & VanderZwaag, 2007). Canada, Denmark, Finland, Iceland, Norway, Sweden, the Russian Federation and the United States are members of the Council, and can make the decisions. Uniquely, six Indigenous peoples' organisations are so-called permanent participants, who must be consulted before any decision-making occurs in the Arctic Council. There is also an increasing number of observers to the Council. Six new observers (China, India, Japan, Italy, South Korea and Singapore) have been approved at the ministerial meeting in Kiruna, Sweden in 2013.[15] Senior Arctic Officials and the recently established permanent secretariat in Tromsø, Norway, manage the everyday coordination of the Council, while biannual ministerial meetings make major policy decisions (Graczyk, 2011.; Graczyk, & Koivurova, 2014).

It is important to acknowledge that the core work of environmental protection has progressed unimpeded from the beginning of the AEPS in 1991. Over time, the Arctic Council's products have included assessments, overview reports, brochures, guidelines, capacity-building projects and numerous technical and progress reports.[16] The four core working groups – Arctic Monitoring and Assessment Programme (AMAP), Conservation of Arctic Flora and Fauna (CAFF), Protection of the Arctic Marine Environment (PAME) and Emergency Prevention Preparedness and Response (EPPR) – have been able to work continuously for almost 25 years, allowing for a long-term learning process.[17] The role that has gradually evolved as a core task of the Arctic Council is to increase knowledge about the circumpolar Arctic in order to influence both national and international policy-making. The work of the Arctic Council has focused on producing major scientific assessments, such as the 2004 Arctic Climate Impact Assessment (ACIA, 2004; Symon, Arris & Heal, 2005), the 2009 Arctic Marine Shipping Assessment[18] and the 2013 Arctic Biodiversity Assessment (Meltofte, 2013). The production of science-based information in various formats has proved to be the niche activity for the Arctic Council. It has enabled the Arctic Council to influence international treaty-making processes via producing scientific assessments that have identified threats to the Arctic ecosystems coming from outside the region. As an example, the Arctic Council has been able to influence global negotiation processes in very innovative ways. For example, several Arctic Council reports have contributed to the global understanding of mercury and its effects in the Arctic in particular.[19] This becomes a driver of the negotiations towards the adoption of the 2013 Minamata Convention on Mercury.[20]

Until recently, Arctic cooperation has functioned in a fairly consistent mode of operation, having environmental protection and sustainable development as its mandate. In response to alarming climate change, the Arctic Council has recently strengthened its institutional capacity. At the Nuuk Ministerial Meeting in May 2011, Arctic Ministers decided to establish the Standing Arctic Council Secretariat at the Fram Centre in Tromsø. The Standing Secretariat became operational 1 June 2013.[21] Two international, legally binding agreements have been adopted under the auspices of the Council, namely the Agreement on Cooperation on Aeronautical and Maritime Search and Rescue in the Arctic,[22] the Agreement on Cooperation on Marine Oil Pollution Preparedness and Response in the Arctic[23] and the Agreement on Enhancing Arctic Scientific Cooperation will likely be signed in the next ministerial meeting in May 2017.[24]

Marine governance framework for the Arctic Ocean

The most important segments of the current international governance of the marine environment of the Arctic Ocean are the UNCLOS and multilateral environmental agreements (MEAs) that apply also in the Arctic (Johnsen, Alfthan, Hislop, & Skaalvik, 2010). This is so because the eight Arctic states have over the years assumed MEA legal commitments, which apply in their jurisdiction. All Arctic states are parties to the UNCLOS except for the United States, which accepts most of UNCLOS as customary international law. We will first examine the impact of UNCLOS and a few of the most important MEAs for protecting the Arctic marine environment. Thereafter, it is useful to identify what the Arctic Council has done in terms of protecting the Arctic marine environment.

The UNCLOS has many times been referred to as the constitution of the oceans. It comprehensively regulates human activities in the world's oceans. It also provides general legal guidance for protecting the marine environment, including the Arctic Ocean. In its Part XII, the UNCLOS provides a general legal framework for the protection of the marine environment, which sheds light on the rights and obligations of states. For example, Article 192 obliges States to 'protect and preserve the marine environment'. The UNCLOS identifies various sources of marine pollution, such as ships, land-based discharges, seabed activities and dumping and lays out duties for States in a general manner to tackle these types of pollution. It provides that States shall take measures 'necessary to protect and preserve rare or fragile ecosystems as well as the habitat of depleted, threatened or endangered species and other forms of marine life'.[25] States must also act to prevent, reduce, and control pollution from any source using the 'best practicable means at their disposal'.[26]

Another crucial international framework is the Convention on Biological Diversity (CBD),[27] a convention with almost universal global membership and all the Arctic States, with the exception of the United States, are parties to it. The CBD is a comprehensive convention, covering the diversity of ecosystems, species and genetics. The key objectives of the CBD are the conservation and sustainable use of biodiversity as well as the fair and equitable sharing of benefits from the use of genetic resources. From an Arctic perspective, it is also important that the CBD includes provisions to protect the traditional knowledge, innovations and practices of Indigenous and local communities in relation to biodiversity management. The CBD is a vast regime itself. It also acts as an umbrella regime for other biodiversity-related conventions,[28] such as the Convention on Wetlands (Ramsar Convention),[29] the Convention on International Trade in Endangered Species of Wild Fauna and Flora (CITES),[30] the Convention on the Conservation of Migratory Species of Wild Animals[31] and the World Heritage Convention.[32]

Apart from the UNCLOS and the CBD, which apply to the marine Arctic as framework conventions, there are also global and regional instruments that specifically regulate human activities in the Arctic. Due to retreating sea ice in the Arctic, shipping, fisheries and offshore oil and gas operations are probably the most pressing activities that might threaten the Arctic marine environment. Global and regional regimes regarding these sectors are introduced respectively in the next paragraph (for in-depth analysis, see Liu, 2014, 2015, 2017).

Under the auspices of the International Maritime Organization (IMO), a series of international conventions and instruments have been adopted to regulate shipping, i.e. International Convention on the Prevention of Pollution from Vessels (MARPOL),[33] International Convention on the Safety of Life at Sea (SOLAS),[34] International Convention on the Control of Harmful Anti-Fouling Systems on Ships (Anti-fouling Convention),[35] International Convention for the Control and Management of Ships' Ballast Water and Sediments (BWM Convention)[36] and International Convention on Oil Pollution Preparedness, Response and Co-operation (OPRC).[37] The global regulatory regime is also applicable to the Arctic Ocean, though Article 234 of the UNCLOS (ice-covered area)[38] includes a significant exception extending coastal state jurisdiction in ice-covered areas. Moreover, the International Code for Ships Operating in Polar Waters (Polar Code)[39] were adopted by the IMO in 2015 and entered into force from 1 January 2017. The Code is designed to supplement rather than replace existing IMO instruments. The Polar Code constitutes technical amendments to Annexes I, II, IV and V of MARPOL and a new Chapter XIV of SOLAS with a specific focus on the Polar Regions. The introduction to the Polar Code contains mandatory provisions applicable to both Part I (maritime safety measures) and Part II (pollution prevention measures). Parts I and II are each subdivided into subparts A (mandatory provisions) and B (recommendations). The Polar Code has left several issues of vessel-source pollution, such as a ban on heavy-fuel grade oil and the prevention of invasive species from ballast waters, in its recommendatory part. Albeit an initial step to deal with vessel-source pollution in the polar waters by the international community, the Polar Code is no doubt the most important regulation for shipping in the Arctic (Liu, 2016).

There are a multitude of existing international, regional and bilateral fora and instruments that regulate fisheries in the Arctic Ocean. In order to sustainably manage straddling[40] and highly migratory fish stocks,[41] the United Nations Agreement for the Implementation of the Provisions of the United Nations Convention on the Law of the Sea of 10 December 1982 relating to the Conservation and Management of Straddling Fish Stocks and Highly Migratory Fish Stocks (UN Fish Stocks Agreement)[42] was adopted in 1995. The Food and Agriculture Organization of the United Nations (FAO) has been actively managing global fisheries by adopting a series of legally binding and non-binding instruments. For example, the Agreement to Promote Compliance with International Conservation and Management Measures by Fishing Vessels on the High Seas (FAO Compliance Agreement)[43] was adopted to cope with the problem of reflagging.[44] It became part of the Code of Conduct for Responsible Fisheries[45] in 1995. Furthermore, for combating illegal, unreported and unregulated (IUU) fishing, the FAO has produced instruments such as the 2001 International Plan of Action to Prevent, Deter and Eliminate Illegal, Unreported and Unregulated Fishing (IPOA-IUU)[46] and the 2009 Agreement on Port State Measures to Prevent IUU Fishing.[47]

At the regional level, several regional fisheries management organisations (RFMOs), such as the North-East Atlantic Fisheries Commission (NEAFC), cover some parts of the Arctic Ocean.[48] Although no commercial fishing occurs in the central Arctic Ocean yet, due to the rapid loss of sea ice, fisheries may begin in the foreseeable future. As will be discussed later, the coastal states of the Arctic Ocean, the so-called Arctic Five – United States, Russia, Canada, Norway and Denmark – believe they have a stewardship role in the conservation and management of Arctic marine living resources.[49] But to achieve the sustainable management of fisheries, non-Arctic states, especially high seas fishing states and policy entities, such as China and the European Union, must also be involved in any regulatory efforts. On 16 July 2015, the Arctic Five adopted the Declaration Concerning the Prevention of Unregulated High Sea Fishing in the Central Arctic Ocean, or the Oslo Declaration. It acknowledges the interest of other coastal states in preventing unregulated high seas fisheries in the central Arctic Ocean and starts a so-called 'broader process' of developing fisheries management measures for the central Arctic Ocean with non-Arctic states and policy entities.[50] As a result, China, the EU, Iceland, Japan and the Republic of Korea – the five leading non-Arctic fishing states – were invited to help develop a regional fisheries organisation or arrangement for the central Arctic Ocean. Known as the Arctic 5+5, the group held its first meeting on fisheries in Washington in December 2015. A series of follow-up meetings has been held since in Washington (again), Iqualuit in Canada and Torshavn, in the Faroe Islands. At the time of writing this chapter, all delegations reaffirmed their commitment to prevent unregulated commercial high seas fishing in the central Arctic Ocean during the Torshavn meeting.[51] But a formal agreement has not yet been reached. Another meeting is to be held in Iceland in 2017.

Perhaps because most offshore oil and gas operations are operating in areas within national jurisdiction, there is no general multilateral convention dealing specifically with environmental control of petroleum operations. Annex III of the Convention for the Protection of the Marine Environment of the North-East Atlantic (OSPAR)[52] deals with the prevention and elimination of pollution from offshore sources. The OSPAR covers part of the Arctic Ocean.[53] Moreover, there are two regional instruments that have been adopted under the auspices of the Arctic Council that address this issue. First, the Arctic Offshore Oil and Gas Guidelines (AOOGC)[54] proposes a non-binding set of suggested best practices for oil and gas extraction designed to advise industry officials and government regulators. Second, as mentioned previously, the Agreement on Cooperation on Marine Oil Pollution, Preparedness and Response in the Arctic was adopted in 2013, but it has yet to enter into force.

The Arctic Council is engaged in various kinds of activities related to the Arctic marine environment, in particular through the AMAP and PAME working groups, but to some extent through CAFF's projects as well. The main driver in the Council's marine policy is PAME's Arctic Marine Strategic Plan (AMSP), which urges actions on many fronts. The AMSP identifies the largest drivers of change in the Arctic as climate change and increasing economic activity.[55]

The AMSP encourages the Arctic states to do the following: 1) develop guidelines and procedures for port reception facilities for ship-generated wastes and residues; 2) examine the adequacy of the AOOGC, which led to the third revision of these Guidelines, endorsed by the April 2009 ministerial;[56] 3) identify potential areas where new guidelines and codes of practice for the marine environment are needed; 4) promote application of the ecosystem approach; 5) support the establishment of marine protected areas, including a representative network, work which is still to be commenced (Koivurova, 2009); 6) call for periodic reviews of both international and regional agreements and standards and 7) encourage the implementation of contaminant-related conventions or programmes and possible additional global and regional actions. The PAME has also regularly reviewed the IMO's Polar Code. One of the important outcomes of the April 2009 Ministerial Meeting of the Arctic Council was the Best Practices in Ecosystem Based Oceans Management in the Arctic (BePOMAR) project (Hoel, 2009), which highlighted some of the best practices in Arctic marine area management and encouraged the use of certain principles in future marine governance work in the region. The more recent marine work of the Arctic Council will be reviewed in the following section.

Prospects for stronger environmental governance for the Arctic marine environment

As was reviewed previously, the Arctic-wide cooperation started in 1991 and operates currently as the Arctic Council among eight Arctic States. It is not self-evident that this constellation of States is best equipped to counter the challenges posed to the Arctic marine environment, given that two of the Council's members do not have a coastline on the Arctic Ocean (Finland and Sweden) and Iceland is not seen as a littoral State of the Arctic Ocean. In fact, the five Arctic States met in 2008 in Ilulissat, Greenland and issued the so-called Ilulissat Declaration.

Coastal State cooperation

The coastal States argue that they are the ones who are well-positioned to respond to the fast-changing Arctic:

> The Arctic Ocean stands at the threshold of significant changes. Climate change and the melting of ice have a potential impact on vulnerable ecosystems, the livelihoods of local inhabitants and indigenous communities, and the potential exploitation of natural resources. By virtue of their sovereignty, sovereign rights and jurisdiction in large areas of the Arctic Ocean, the five coastal states are in a unique position to address these possibilities and challenges.[57]

After rejecting the Arctic treaty as a governance solution for the Arctic, stating that the law of the sea provides an 'extensive international legal framework' applicable to the Arctic Ocean, the Arctic Ocean coastal States provide the following:

> The Arctic Ocean is a unique ecosystem, which the five coastal states have a stewardship role in protecting. Experience has shown how shipping disasters and subsequent pollution of the marine environment may cause irreversible disturbance of the ecological balance and major harm to the livelihoods of local inhabitants and indigenous communities. We will take steps in accordance with international law both nationally and in cooperation among the five states and other interested parties to ensure the protection and preservation of the fragile marine environment of the Arctic Ocean.[58]

This was at the time interpreted as an outright challenge to the Arctic Council, given that the Arctic Council conducts such work, and that permanent participants and three of the Member States of the Arctic Council were not invited to this meeting. The second such meeting took place in Canada in 2010. The UNCLOS can also be interpreted as favouring this solution proposed by the Arctic Five. According to Article 197 of the UNCLOS, it encourages its contracting parties to

> cooperate on a global basis and, as appropriate, on a regional basis, directly or through competent international organizations, in formulating and elaborating international rules, standards and recommended practices and procedures consistent with this Convention, for the protection and preservation of the marine environment, taking into account characteristic regional features.

It has been suggested that Articles 122 and 123 on semi-enclosed seas would also imply legal obligations on Arctic Ocean coastal States. It is important to examine this issue since it is not excluded that coastal States at some point need to think under which forum and with whom they would like to conduct Arctic marine cooperation.

As argued by some scholars, the Arctic Ocean constitutes a semi-enclosed sea as defined in Article 122 and hence the littoral States would be under the legal obligations of 123 (Scovazzi, 2009). According to Article 122:

> For the purposes of this Convention, 'enclosed or semi-enclosed sea' means a gulf, basin or sea surrounded by two or more States and connected to another sea or the ocean by a narrow outlet or consisting entirely or primarily of the territorial seas and exclusive economic zones of two or more coastal States.

This provision identifies two types of sea areas to be within its scope: either those that are covered primarily by territorial seas and exclusive economic zones (EEZs) of coastal States or those that are connected to other sea areas only by a narrow strait. Since the terms used in Article 122 are fairly vague, it is difficult to provide a clear-cut answer as to whether the Arctic Ocean is an enclosed or semi-enclosed sea in the meaning of Article 122. As regards the first type of sea area, it should be noted that a large part of the Arctic Ocean consists of high seas and thereby would not convincingly satisfy the requirement of 'primarily'. As regards the second type of sea area, in comparison to the seas which clearly are enclosed or semi-enclosed – such as the Baltic or Mediterranean Seas – the Arctic Ocean opens relatively broadly to the North-East Atlantic.

But even if the argument could be made that the Arctic Ocean is an enclosed or semi-enclosed sea in the meaning of Article 122, Article 123 does not provide a clear-cut legal obligation for regional cooperation. It reads:

> States bordering an enclosed or semi-enclosed sea should cooperate with each other in the exercise of their rights and in the performance of their duties under this Convention. To this end they shall endeavour, directly or through an appropriate regional organization: (a) to coordinate the management, conservation, exploration and exploitation of the living resources of the sea; (b) to coordinate the implementation of their rights and duties with respect to the protection and preservation of the marine environment; (c) to coordinate their scientific research policies and undertake where appropriate joint programmes of scientific research in the area; (d) to invite, as appropriate, other interested States or international organizations to cooperate with them in furtherance of the provisions of this article.

According to the phrasing of this provision, it seems more adequate to interpret Article 123 as encouraging regional sea cooperation over marine environmental protection, management of living resources and marine scientific research rather than imposing on coastal States a legally binding obligation to do so. In international treaty practice, 'should' is normally used to denote non-legally binding encouragement rather than a legal obligation (for which 'shall' or 'must' are used). Moreover, the use of 'shall' in the second sentence is significantly qualified by the term 'endeavour'. It seems, hence, a better argument that Article 123 merely contains a weak obligation to cooperate, but it does urge the coastal States – perhaps together with other States and international organisations – to engage in regional cooperation over the policy areas enumerated in the provision.

If the coastal States were to regard the Arctic Ocean as an enclosed or semi-enclosed sea in the meaning of Article 122, and if they were to be prepared to commence negotiations over how to implement cooperation in the fields mentioned in Article 123, they would also need to figure out the relationship between this initiative and the Arctic Council, given that the Council's work so far also extends to marine environmental protection and scientific research in the Arctic Ocean.

Yet, the Arctic Ocean coastal States have not continued the general cooperation meetings, and even the two organised in Ilulissat, Greenland, and Chelsea, Canada, were not based on any reliance on Articles 122 and 123. The coastal State setting has thus far been used to negotiate central Arctic Ocean fisheries regulation, even if such fisheries do not yet exist, and this is done on the basis of the Fish Stocks Agreement, to which all the Arctic states are parties.

Arctic Council's most recent efforts

Arctic Council's work on the marine environment has become increasingly ambitious. The 2004 Arctic Marine Strategy Plan (AMSP) was replaced by a new 2015–2025 AMSP,[59] which addresses both short-term and long-term challenges and opportunities, through 40 Strategic Actions comprised under four Strategic Goals. It is clearly visible that the Arctic marine environment should be managed via an adaptive ecosystem-based management approach:

> (a) Improve knowledge of the Arctic marine environment, and continue to monitor and assess current and future impacts on Arctic marine ecosystems. (b) Conserve and protect ecosystem function and marine biodiversity to enhance resilience and the provision of ecosystem services. (c) Promote safe and sustainable use of the marine environment, taking into account cumulative environmental impacts. (d) Enhance the economic, social and cultural well-being of Arctic inhabitants, including Arctic indigenous peoples and strengthen their capacity to adapt to changes in the Arctic marine environment.

The Arctic Council working groups will coordinate and cooperate closely in its implementation, and the Arctic Council will need to look to governments and agencies for support and participation.

The overarching *approach* for the protection of the Arctic marine environment has become the adaptive ecosystem marine governance, which has been advanced by a special Ecosystem-Based Management (EBM) Expert Group, which started its work in 2011 and delivered its final report to the ministers in the 2013 ministerial meeting. The committee provided in its final report a policy commitment, a definition of EBM in the Arctic, a set of principles for EBM in the Arctic and a number of high-priority activities for coordinating and improving the EBM work of the Arctic Council. Moreover, the Ministerial Meeting in Kiruna adopted the revised map of 18 large marine ecosystems (LMEs), and encouraged the Arctic States to ensure the coordination of their approaches and the implementation of recommendations from the expert group both within and across boundaries. For the EBM expert group, EBM is the comprehensive, integrated management of human activities based on the best-available scientific and traditional knowledge about the ecosystem and its dynamics, in order to identify and take action on influences that are critical to the health of ecosystems, thereby achieving the sustainable use of ecosystem goods and services and the maintenance of ecosystem integrity.[60]

At the Arctic Council Ministerial Meeting in Iqaluit 24 April 2015, a Task Force on Arctic Marine Cooperation was founded. The mandate is to consider future needs for strengthened cooperation on Arctic marine areas (for instance drawing inspiration from other regional seas frameworks), devise mechanisms to meet these needs and make recommendations on the nature and scope of any such mechanisms. The Task Force is expected to complete its analysis of the issues no later than the 2017 ministerial meeting, which ends the US chairmanship.

A broader process

There is no doubt that the Arctic States (Arctic Five or Arctic Eight) are the key players in Arctic marine governance. Nevertheless, non-Arctic States ought to play a part in Arctic governance in order to better protect the vulnerable and unique Arctic environment. This is evident because, for example, the most severe threat to the Arctic – climate change – is mainly caused by greenhouse gases emitted from outside the Arctic, such as Germany and China. Moreover, both China and the EU are potential users of Arctic shipping routes, especially the North-East Passage (NEP).[61] It is estimated that by using the NEP, Chinese cargo ships can save nearly 5,200 kilometres and nine days compared with the traditional voyage to Europe through the Strait of Malacca and the Suez Canal (Pettersen, 2014). Since 2008, the European Commission has published three Arctic policy documents: the European Commission Communication of 20 November 2008 on the European Union and the Arctic Region, COM (2008) 763;[62] the Joint Communication of the European Commission and High Representative of the European Union for Foreign Affairs and Security Policy of 26 June 2012 on Developing a European Union Policy towards the Arctic Region: Progress since 2008 and Next Steps, JOIN (2012) 19[63] and the Joint Communication of the European Commission and High Representative of the European Union for Foreign Affairs and Security Policy of 27 April 2016 on An Integrated European Union Policy for the Arctic, JOIN (2016) 21.[64] This clearly shows the EU's strong interests to be involved in Arctic governance. The EU is not alone. China is also quite motivated to get into the 'Arctic club'. For example, in the 4th Arctic Circle Assembly in Reykjavik, Iceland 2016, the Chinese Chief Negotiator on Climate Change, Feng Gao, stated that Arctic cooperation must be inclusive, comprehensive and diversified.[65] From the Arctic side, to accept China and other Asian economies as observers of the Arctic Council is an initial step for broader Arctic governance. The Arctic 5+5 negotiation on fisheries in the central Arctic Ocean is another positive sign. The key issue that remains is how Arctic and non-Arctic States could effectively work together to achieve sustainable development in the Arctic.

Concluding remarks

It is clear that the Arctic marine environment is facing severe challenges in the near and long-term future. Climate change and other stressors will put the Arctic marine regions under heavy stress, as reviewed previously.

Currently, it seems that the marine environment of the Arctic Ocean will be managed under the Arctic Council. There are ambitious policies in place, such as the 2015–2025 AMSP, which, however, is a non-legally binding document.

It will be interesting to see whether the marine work that tries to respond to the vast challenges of the Arctic Ocean will be done by the Arctic Council or whether the coastal States will take over at some point in time, with perhaps a stronger regional hard-law approach. Currently, this does not look likely, but we have to remember that the Arctic Ocean will change dramatically over the course of the next decades. In particular, the United States is pushing for very proactive fisheries regulation and also proposing new institutional measures to bolster the Arctic Council in terms of its marine work. It is not difficult to predict that there will be pressures for the Arctic Ocean coastal States to take a stronger approach, if they cannot do this within the Arctic Council.

Whichever constellation will be countering these challenges to the Arctic marine environment, there is a fair amount of consensus that this will be done on the basis of an ecosystem-based management approach.

Notes

1 There are four high seas pockets in the marine Arctic, namely the 'Banana Hole' in the Norwegian Sea, the 'Loophole' in the Barents Sea, the 'Donut Hole' in the central Bering Sea and the 'Central Arctic Ocean' around the North Pole.
2 University Corporation for Atmospheric Research, 2007. Arctic Ice Retreating More Quickly Than Computer Models Project, viewed 12 December 2016, www.ucar.edu/news/releases/2007/seaice.shtml.
3 NASA, 2016, See How Arctic Sea Ice is Losing its Bulwark Agaist Warming Summers, viewed 15 December 2016, www.nasa.gov/feature/goddard/2016/arctic-sea-ice-is-losing-its-bulwark-against-warming-summers.
4 Arctic Council, 2013. Arctic Biodiversity Assessment. Akureyri: Conservation of Arctic Flora and Fauna Working Group (CAFF).
5 Ibid.
6 Ibid.

7   Arctic Council, 2014. Arctic Ocean Acidification 2013: An Overview. Oslo: Arctic Monitoring and Assessment Programme (AMAP).
8   See, e.g., viewed 12 December 2016 www.pewtrusts.org/en/projects/arctic-ocean-international/solutions/faqs.
9   Geographical coverage, Arctic Monitoring and Assessment Programme, viewed 13 December 2016, www.amap.no/AboutAMAP/GeoCov.htm.
10 United Nations Convention on the Law of the Sea (Montego Bay, 10 December 1982, in force 6 November 1994) (1982) 21(6) ILM, pp. 1261–1354.
11 The EU is a unique economic and political partnership between 28 European countries that together cover much of the continent of Europe. Viewed 13 December 2016, europa.eu/about-eu/index_en.htm.
12 The Agreement on the European Economic Area, which entered into force on 1 January 1994, brings together the EU Member States and the three EEA EFTA States – Iceland, Liechtenstein and Norway – in a single market, referred to as the 'Internal Market'. Viewed 13 December 2016, www.efta.int/media/documents/legal-texts/eea/the-eea-agreement/Main%20Text%20 of%20the%20Agreement/EEAagreement.pdf.
13 Act on Greenland Self-Government (no. 473 of 12 June 2009), viewed 13 December 2016, naalakkersuisut.gl/~/media/Nanoq/Files/Attached%20Files/Engelske-tekster/Act%20on%20Greenland.pdf.
14 Agreement on the European Economic Area (Brussels, 17 March 1994). A special Protocol was adopted as part of the EEA Agreement to the effect that Norway may decide whether to apply the EEA Agreement to Svalbard or not. Norway decided to exclude the Islands. EFTA, EEA Agreement, Protocol 40 on Svalbard (1994).
15 Eighth Ministerial Meeting of the Arctic Council 2013, Kiruna Declaration, Kiruna, Sweden, viewed 14 December 2016, https://oaarchive.arctic-council.org/bitstream/handle/11374/93/MM08_Final_Kiruna_ declaration_w_signature.pdf?sequence=1&isAllowed=y.
16 For a general overview of these projects, see Koivurova and VanderZwaag 2007, supra note 18.
17 There are also two other working groups that have been established later, the Sustainable Development Working Group and the Arctic Contaminants Action Programme.
18 PAME (Protection of the Arctic Marine Environment) & AMSA (Arctic Marine Shipping Assessment) 2009, viewed 14 December 2016, www.pame.is/index.php/projects/arctic-marine-shipping/amsa.
19 Arctic Council 2013, Statement to the Diplomatic Conference on the Minamata Convention on Mercury, Kumamoto, Japan, viewed 14 December 2016, www.arctic-council.org/images/PDF_attachments/ AC_statements/2013_10_11_final_minamata_statement.pdf.
20 Minamata Convention on Mercury (adopted 10 October 2013 at Kumamoto), viewed 14 December 2016, www.mercuryconvention.org.
21 Arctic Council 2015, The Arctic Council Secretariat, viewed 14 December 2016, www.arctic-council.org/index.php/en/about-us/arctic-council/the-arctic-council-secretariat.
22 Agreement on Cooperation on Aeronautical and Maritime Search and Rescue in the Arctic 2011, viewed 14 December 2016, https://oaarchive.arctic-council.org/handle/11374/531.
23 Agreement on Cooperation on Marine Oil Pollution Preparedness and Response in the Arctic 2013, viewed 14 December 2016, https://oaarchive.arctic-council.org/handle/11374/529.
24 Arctic Council 2016, Task Force on Scientific Cooperatino meets in Ottawa, viewed 14 December 2016, www.arctic-council.org/index.php/en/our-work2/8-news-and-events/408-sctf-ottawa-july-2016.
25 Article 194 (5), UNCLOS.
26 Article 194 (1), UNCLOS.

27 Convention on Biological Diversity (Nairobi, 22 May 1992, in force 29 December 1993) (1992) 31 ILM pp. 842–847.
28 Convention on Biological Diversity, Biodiversity-related Conventions, viewed 14 December 2016, www.cbd.int/brc/.
29 Convention on Wetlands of International Importance especially as Waterfowl Habitat, Ramsar, 2 Feburary 1971, as amended by the Protocol of 3 December 1982 and the Amendments of 28 May 1987, viewed 14 December 2016, www.ramsar.org/sites/default/files/documents/library/scan_certified_e.pdf.
30 Convention on International Trade in Endangered Species of Wild Fauna and Flora, viewed 14 December 2016, www.cites.org/eng/disc/text.php.
31 Convention on the Conservation of Migratory Species of Wild Animals, viewed 14 December 2016, www.cms.int/en/convention-text.
32 Convention Concerning the Protectiong of the World Cultural and Natural Heritage, viewed 14 December 2016, http://whc.unesco.org/en/conventiontext/.
33 International Conference on Marine Pollution: International Convention for the Prevention of Pollution from Ships, ILM, 12 (1973), pp. 1319–1444.
34 Inter-Governmental Maritime Consultative Organization: International Convention for the Safety of Life at Sea, 1974, ILM, 14 (1975), pp. 959–978.
35 International Conference on the Control of Harmful Anti-Fouling Systems for Ships, AFS/CONF/26, 18 Oct 2001, Agenda item 8.
36 International Convention on Ballast Water Management for Ships, BWM/CONF/36, 16 Feb 2004, Agenda item 8.
37 International Maritime Organization: International Convention on Oil Pollution Preparedness, Response and Co-Operation, 1990, and Final Act of the Conference, ILM, 30 (1991), pp. 733–761.
38 It reads: 'Coastal States have the right to adopt and enforce non-discriminatory laws and regulations for the prevention, reduction and control of marine pollution from vessels in ice-covered areas within the limits of the exclusive economic zone, where particularly severe climatic conditions and the presence of ice covering such areas for most of the year create obstructions or exceptional hazards to navigation, and pollution of the marine environment could cause major harm to or irreversible disturbance of the ecological balance. Such laws and regulations shall have due regard to navigation and the protection and preservation of the marine environment based on the best available scientific evidence'.
39 International Code For Ships Operating In Polar Waters (adopted May 15, 2015), viewed 14 December 2016, www.imo.org/en/MediaCentre/HotTopics/polar/Documents/POLAR%20CODE%20TEXT%20 AS%20ADOPTED.pdf.
40 Stocks occurring both without and in an area beyond and adjacent to the Exclusive Economic Zone.
41 Highly migratory species (HMS) are defined as those species listed in Annex 1 of the 1982 Convention. This list includes tuna, tuna-like species (billfish, dolphins and sharks), and certain cetaceans. These species were categorised and so labelled because they move considerable distances over vast expanses of ocean areas.
42 United Nations Agreement for the Implementation of the Provisions of the United Nations Convention on the Law of the Sea of 10 December 1982 relating to the Conservation and Management of Straddling Fish Stocks and Highly Migratory Fish Stocks (adopted 4 August 1995, entered into force 11 December 2001) (1995) 34 (6) ILM, pp. 1542–1580.
43 The Agreement to Promote Compliance with International Conservation and Management Measures by Fishing Vessels on the High Seas (adopted 24 November 1993) (1993) 33 ILM, p. 968.
44 The practice of vessel operators reflagging their vessels with flags of convenience, those from other countries or countries not party to fisheries agreements or arrangements to avoid obligation to comply with conservation and management measures. See

Weidemann, L 2013, International Governance of the Arctic Marine Environment, with Particular Emphasis on High Sea Fisheries, Springer, Berlin, p. 148.
45 Code of Conduct for Responsible Fisheries, viewed 14 December 2016, www.fao.org/docrep/005/ v9878e/v9878e00.HTM.
46 International Plan of Action to Prevent, Deter and Eliminate Illegal, Unreported and Unregulated Fishing, viewed 14 December 2016, www.fao.org/docrep/003/y1224e/y1224e00.htm.
47 Agreement on Port State Measures to Prevent, Deter, and Eliminate Illegal, Unreported and Unregulated Fishing (adopted 22 November 2009, not yet in force), viewed 14 December 2016, www.fao.org/fileadmin/user_upload/legal/docs/2_037t-e.pdf.
48 The NEAFC Convention Area covers the Atlantic and Arctic Oceans east of a line South of Cape Farewell – the southern tip of Greenland (42°W) – north of a line to the West of Cape Hatteras – the Southern tip of Spain (36° N) – and West of a line touching the western tip of Novya Semlya (51°E). See Where is the NEAFC Regulatory Area?, viewed 14 December 2016, www.neafc.org/what-neafc/117; See also Map of the NEAFC Regulatory Area, viewed 14 December 2016, www.neafc.org/page/27.
49 The Ilulissat Declaration, viewed 14 December 2016, www.oceanlaw.org/downloads/arctic/Iluliss at_Declaration.pdf.
50 Declaration Concerning the Prevention of Unregulated High Sea Fishing in the Central Arctic Ocean (Oslo Declaration), www.regjeringen.no/globalassets/departementene/ud/vedlegg/folkerett/declarati on-on-arctic-fisheries-16-july-2015.pdf.
51 Meeting on High Seas Fisheries in the Central Arctic Ocean (Tórshavn, The Faroe Islands, 29 November – 1 December 2016), Chairman's Statement, viewed 14 December 2016, http://arcticjournal.com/press-releases/2733/meeting-high-seas-fisheries-central-arctic-ocean.
52 Convention for the Protection of the Marine Environment of the North-East Atlantic (1993) 32 ILM, p. 1069 (OSPAR Convention).
53 See OSPAR Convention Article 1, definition of 'maritime area'. For graphic representation see Region I – Arctic Waters, viewed 15 December 2016, www.ospar.org/content/content.asp?menu=00420211000000_ 000000_000000.
54 Arctic Offshore Oil and Gas Guidelines (AOOGG), viewed 15 December 2016, https://oaarchive.arctic-council.org/handle/11374/62.
55 Arctic Marine Strategic Plan (2004), p. 8, viewed 15 December 2016, http://web.arcticportal.org/uploads /bi/D8/biD8EROnocY8aTetM8KZOQ/PAME-Bklingur-A4.pdf.
56 See supra note 65.
57 The Ilulissat Declaration, *supra* note 49.
58 Ibid.
59 The new AMSP was developed by the Working Group for the Protection of the Arctic Marine Environment (PAME) in cooperation with the Arctic Council members, its subsidiary bodies and observers. Viewed 15 December 2016, https://oaarchive.arctic-council.org/handle/11374/413.
60 Arctic Council, Ecosystem-Based Management in the Arctic: Rep. Submitted to Senior Arctic Officials By The Expert Group On Ecosystem-Based Management, 2013.
61 The NEP is defined as the set of sea routes from Northwest Europe around North Cape (Norway) and along the North coast of Eurasia and Siberia through the Bering Strait to the Pacific. Arctic Marine Shipping Assessment Report, PAME of the Arctic Council, p. 34, viewed 15 December 2016, https://oaarchive.arctic-council.org/handle/11374/54.
62 COM (2008) 763, viewed 15 December 2016, eur-lex.europa.eu/LexUriServ/LexUriServ.do?uri=COM:2008:0763:FIN:EN:PDF.
63 JOIN (2012) 19, viewed 15 December 2016, eeas.europa.eu/arctic_region/docs/join_2012_19.pdf.
64 JOIN (2016) 21, viewed 15 December 2016, http://eur-lex.europa.eu/legal-content/EN/TXT/PDF/?uri= CELEX:52016JC0021&from=EN.

65 4th Arctic Circle, viewed 15 December 2016, www.arcticcircle.org/assemblies/2016/videos.

References

Arctic Climate Impact Assessment (ACIA). (2004). *Impacts of a Warming Arctic-Arctic Climate Impact Assessment. Impacts of a Warming Arctic-Arctic Climate Impact Assessment, by Arctic Climate Impact Assessment.* ISBN 0521617782, Cambridge University Press, Cambridge, December 2004, p. 144.

Graczyk, P. (2011). Observers in the Arctic council – evolution and prospects. *The Yearbook of Polar Law Online*, vol. 3, no. 1, pp. 575–633.

Graczyk, P., & Koivurova, T. (2014). A new era in the Arctic Council's external relations? Broader consequences of the Nuuk observer rules for Arctic governance. *Polar Record*, vol. 50, no. 3, pp. 225–236.

Hoel, A.H. (2009). *Best Practices in Ecosystem-Based Ocean Management in the Arctic.* Norsk Polarinstitutt.

Johnsen, K, Alfthan, B. Hislop, L., & Skaalvik, J. (Eds.) (2010). Protecting Arctic biodiversity. United Nations Environment Programme, GRID-Arendal, Norway. www.grida.no.

Koivurova, T. (2009). Governance of protected areas in the Arctic. *Utrecht Law Review*, vol. 5, no. 1, pp. 44–60.

Koivurova, T., & VanderZwaag, D. (2007). The Arctic Council at 10 years: Retrospect and prospects. *University of British Columbia Law Review*, vol. 40.

Liu, N. (2014). China's role in the changing governance of Arctic shipping. *The Yearbook of Polar Law Online*, vol. 6, no. 1, pp. 545–558.

Liu, N. (2015). Protection of the marine environment from offshore oil and gas activities, in R. Rayfuse (ed.), *Research Handbook on International Marine Environmental Law*, Edward Elgar, Cheltenham.

Liu, N. (2016). Can the polar code save the Arctic? *American Society of International Law Insights*, vol. 20, no. 7.

Liu, N. (2017). The European Union and regulation of fisheries in the central Arctic ocean, in N. Liu, E. Kirk & T. Henriksen (eds), *The European Union and the Arctic*, Brill Nijhoff, Chapter 10, forthcoming.

Meltofte, H. (2013). Arctic biodiversity assessment: Status and trends in Arctic biodiversity. Conservation of Arctic Flora and Fauna (CAFF), https://www.caff.is/assessment-series/233-arctic-biodiversity-assessment-2013.

Parliament, I. (2011). A parliamentary resolution on Iceland's Arctic Policy, www. mfa.is/media/nordurlandaskrifstofa/A-Parliamentary-Resolution-on-ICE-Arctic-Policy-approved-by-Althingi. Pdf.

Pettersen, T. (2014). China to release guidebook on Arctic shipping. *Barents Observer*, www.barentsobserver.com/en/arctic/2014/06/china-release-guidebook-arctic-shipping-20.

Poelzer, G., & Wilson, G.N. (2014). Governance in the Arctic: Political systems and geopolitics. Arctic human development report. Regional processes and global linkages, pp. 183–220. Nordic Council of Ministers.

Renfrow, S. (2007). Arctic sea ice shatters all previous record lows. National Snow and Ice Data Center (NSIDC).

Scovazzi, T. (2009). Legal issues relating to navigation through Arctic waters. *The Yearbook of Polar Law Online*, vol. 1, no. 1, pp. 371–382.

Stroeve, J., Holland, M.M., Meier, W., Scambos, T., & Serreze, M. (2007). Arctic sea ice decline: Faster than forecast. Geophysical Research Letters, vol. 34, no. 9.

Symon, C., Arris, L., & Heal, B. (Eds.) (2005). *Arctic Climate Impact Assessment Final Scientific Report*, Cambridge University Press, Cambridge.

PART V
Settlement of disputes and conclusions

13
CONTEMPORARY MARINE ENVIRONMENTAL DISPUTES

Daud Hassan and Beatriz Garcia

The judicial settlement of marine environmental disputes

Scope of marine environmental disputes

Environmental disputes are difficult to define. One of the reasons for this is that the term *environment* also lacks a precise definition (Romano, 2000). The meaning of the word *environment* has not been defined in key environmental instruments, such as the 1972 Stockholm Declaration and the 1992 Rio Declaration. Multilateral environmental treaties only provide definitions in a specific context. For example, the 1988 Convention on the Regulation of Antarctic Mineral Resources Activities defines 'damage to the Antarctic environment'. The 1985 Vienna Convention on the Protection of the Ozone Layer defines the scope of 'adverse effects on the environment'.

There have been attempts to define the term *environment*. For example, the Working Group of Experts on Liability and Compensation of Environmental Damage arising from Military Activities, established by the United Nations Environmental Program in 1996, in the context of the occupation of Kuwait, proposed the following definition: 'it is safe to say that the term environment includes a-biotic and biotic components, including air, water, soil, flora, fauna and the ecosystems formed by their interaction' (UNEP, 1998, p.119). According to the Working Group, the term should also include: 'cultural heritage, features of landscape and environmental amenity'.

In the advisory opinion rendered in 1996 on the *Legality of the Threat or Use of Nuclear Weapons*,[1] the International Court of Justice (ICJ) proposes a broad and rather vague definition:

> The Court . . . recognizes that the environment is not an abstraction but represents the living space, the quality of life and the very health of human beings, including generations unborn.

When it comes to international environmental disputes, another aspect to be considered is the overlapping of disciplines in a given dispute. These disputes often involve many areas such as international law, water law, human rights law, international fisheries law and international trade law, among others. For instance, in the Order for Provisional Measures in the *Southern Bluefin Tuna* cases,[2] which involved the sustainability of fishing activities for Southern Bluefin Tuna in the Pacific Ocean, Japan contested that the dispute did not involve the United Nations Convention on the Law of the Sea (UNCLOS) but strictly the 1993 Convention for the Conservation of Southern Bluefin Tuna. In fact, one could question whether this case could be defined in terms of environmental law, notably marine environmental law, or in terms of the conservation of marine biological diversity (Low & Hodgkinson, 1995). As international disputes often involve various issues and areas of international law, it may be difficult to identify the nature of the dispute.

Environmental issues typically involve complex scientific, technical and political aspects. The legal issues under environmental disputes rarely arise in isolation of other concerns, such as political or trade considerations (Romano, 2000, p. 101). In principle, there are *lato sensu* no differences between environmental and other international disputes. In the *Mavrommatis Palestine Concessions* case,[3] the ICJ defined a dispute as:

> a disagreement on a point of law or fact, a conflict of legal views or of interest between the parties.

Those are the basic elements of any dispute. An environmental dispute, like other international disputes, is a 'disagreement on a point of law or fact'.

Yet environmental disputes differ *ratione materiae* from other international disputes. They result *stricto sensu* of a disagreement on a point of law or fact related to an *environmental* issue.

Bilder (1975) proposes four features of environmental disputes, which distinguish them from other types of international disputes. First, environmental problems tend to involve situations in which the knowledge of the facts is limited and the assessment of risks uncertain. For instance, the causes of pollution, the extent of the problem it causes, and its effects are often unclear. Second, environmental problems usually require collaborative action for their solutions. For example, all countries contribute to air or oceanic pollution and these problems therefore require joint actions. This is particularly true in the case of shared natural resources, such as air, waterways, migratory species, etc. Third, environmental issues involve balancing the benefits of activities that may affect the environment and the costs of controlling them. Lastly, environmental problems pose threats of a unique kind in terms of the number of people affected and the importance of their interests. Most environmental problems are inherently international ones. In Bilder's view, a dispute is *environmental* when it relates to 'the alteration through human intervention of natural environmental systems' (Bilder, 1975, p. 153).

As noted by Alan Boyle, most of what we regard as *environmental* relates to issues such as 'pollution of air, freshwater and oceans; climate change; unsustainable use of natural resources; loss of biodiversity, ecosystems and habitat; and conservation of endangered species and natural heritage' (Boyle & Harrison, 2013, p.131). However, as he points out, even these concepts are not without difficulty, because environmental disputes involve not only these but also various other issues and areas of law. For example, the *Gabcikovo-Nagymaros* case is about environmental law, but it is also about the law of treaties, water resources law, state succession and state responsibility (Boyle & Harrison, 1997).

Boyle identifies two approaches in the literature that discuss the nature of environmental disputes: the first one tries to categorise the applicable rules, while the second looks at the real-world problem the rules address (Boyle & Harrison, 2013). This latter approach, which involves looking at the 'heart of the issue' or real-world problem, might give better guidance as to whether a dispute is an *environmental* dispute. This is the approach used here.

Principles and obligations

States have a duty to protect and preserve the marine environment under Article 192 of UNCLOS. The degree of acceptance of various treaties relating to marine pollution and the consensus expressed by States negotiating Part XII of UNCLOS suggest that its provisions, notably Article 192, are supported by a strong *opinio juris* and represent a codification of general principles that have achieved customary international law status (Birnie & Boyle, 2002, p. 351). The obligation to protect the environment is addressed to the State Parties and also extended to international organisations that become parties to the Convention.[4] Underlying the duty to protect and preserve the marine environment is the no-harm principle in international law. All States have a basic duty to act in a way so as not to harm the interests of other States.[5] Generalising this principle, one arrives at an international obligation upon States to control and reduce environmental pollution, including marine pollution or harm.[6]

In practice, there is little positive guidance in determining a globally accepted environmental pollution threshold, as there is no constant view of a pollution threshold. There is no sufficient basis as to an international concept of pollution, and most categories of marine pollution focus on major damage and substantial impairment of the use of the environment.[7] Therefore, some environmental disturbances or harm caused to the marine environment, which do not neatly fit into the definitions of pollution and the different sources of pollution under UNCLOS, may not be given proper consideration. There are forms of environmental harm, such as damage caused to marine mammals by noise, or physical damage caused to marine habitats by anchors or by ships, which may not fall under the definition of 'pollution'. Pollution is defined in Article 1(4) of UNCLOS as the 'introduction by man, directly or indirectly, of substances or energy into the marine environment', which may result 'in such deleterious effects as harm to living resources and marine life, hazards to human health, hindrance to marine activities, including fishing and other legitimate uses of the sea'. For example, as noted by the Global Environment Facility, the introduction of harmful alien species into new environments through ships' ballast water is one of the great threats to the marine environment.[8] However, it is questionable whether this form of harm is considered 'pollution' under UNCLOS. In addition, Article 193 of UNCLOS balances the sovereign right of States to exploit their natural resources with their duty to protect the marine environment. This provision does not give environmental protection priority over State sovereignty, and to that extent does not prohibit all risk of harm at all (Boyle, 2007).

Prevention is a way of exercising the duty to protect and preserve the marine environment, and it is a key feature of UNCLOS's dispute settlement mechanism. Article 194 of UNCLOS obliges States to take all necessary measures to prevent marine pollution from any source. This provision contains a presumption of marine environmental protection. However, it also allows states wide discretion in performing their duties by including reference to the use of 'the best practicable means' and 'in accordance with their capabilities in this respect'.

Article 194 introduces an uncertain standard for marine environmental protection. A less-developed State, with limited capabilities, may not be required to take the same costly or sophisticated steps as a highly developed State. The insertion of those words gives a 'licence of reluctance' to States in relation to their responsibility to take adequate measures for marine environmental protection, since the assessment of pollution control depends entirely on their capability to do so. The ambiguous standard for marine environmental protection may lead to disputes between developed and developing countries regarding their obligation to prevent, reduce and control the pollution of the marine environment.

In order to prevent marine pollution and other forms of environmental harm, States are requested to conduct environmental impact assessments (EIA). As per Article 206, State Parties are expected to conduct EIA when there is 'reasonable grounds for believing that substantial pollution or significant harm' may result from activities under their jurisdiction or control. State Parties are given considerable discretion to define what 'reasonable grounds' or 'substantial or significant' harm mean. This also creates an uncertain standard as to which activities require EIA.

Generally, States have a duty to cooperate vis-à-vis the protection of the marine environment and all other obligations under UNCLOS. For example, they shall cooperate in relation to the establishment of navigational and safety aids,[9] in enquiries concerning marine casualty or incidents,[10] in the repression of piracy,[11] in the suppression of illicit traffic in narcotic drugs or other substances,[12] in the conservation and management of the living resources,[13] in the construction and improvement of means of transport[14] and in promoting the transfer of technology and scientific knowledge,[15] among others. This duty is stated in Article 197, particularly in relation to the protection and preservation of the marine environment:

> States shall cooperate on a global basis and, as appropriate, on a regional basis . . . for the protection and preservation of the marine environment, taking into account characteristic regional features.

In line with the duty to cooperate is the obligation to settle disputes concerning the interpretation or application of UNCLOS by peaceful means, as defined under Article 279. States must cooperate in order to reach a peaceful settlement of disputes. A breach to the obligations under Part XII of UNCLOS and potential disputes in relation to its application or interpretation are likely to be 'marine environmental disputes' in nature and they must be settled by peaceful means, according to both Articles 197 and 279 of UNCLOS.

International courts and tribunals/international judicial organs

International Law imposes a general prohibition on the threat or use of force by one State against another.[16] States shall settle their disputes by peaceful means.[17] This duty is reflected in Article 2(3) of the United Nations Charter:

> All members shall settle their disputes by peaceful means in such a manner that international peace and security, and justice are not endangered.

The UN Charter sets a corresponding obligation to resolve disputes through any of the peaceful means listed in Article 33:

> The parties to a dispute shall, first of all, seek a solution by negotiating, inquiry, mediation, conciliation, arbitration, judicial settlement, resort to a regional agencies or arrangements, or other peaceful means of their choice.

These various means of dispute settlement have been included in numerous multilateral environmental agreements. Article 279 of UNCLOS refers to the settlement of disputes by peaceful means as an *obligation*.

There are two basic ways to settle international disputes: by diplomatic or legal methods. By diplomatic means, the parties retain control over the dispute insofar that they may accept or reject a proposed settlement (Sands,1994). They include negotiation, consultation, good offices, mediation, inquiry and conciliation. The legal methods involve international arbitration and adjudication, and the use of national courts. They require the application of the law by a third party and result in a binding decision (Cooper, 1986).

Generally, international courts and tribunals both at the regional and global levels are competent to hear environmental disputes, including marine environmental disputes. The International Tribunal for the Law of the Sea (ITLOS) is the judicial body established by UNCLOS to adjudicate disputes arising out of the interpretation and application of this Convention.[18] Other judicial bodies at the global level include, for example, the International Court of Justice, the World Trade Organization's Dispute Settlement Body and arbitral tribunals.

As a general rule, States are never compelled to refer disputes to adjudication without their consent. This is one of the reasons why international adjudication is not often used or not used enough. States are wary to refer their disputes to a third party and tend to protect their sovereign rights and national interests.

The international tribunal for the law of the sea

The ITLOS became operational in October 1996.[19] It consists of 21 members, elected for nine years by the assembly of the State Parties.[20] The Statute of the Tribunal is provided for in Annex VI of UNCLOS.

The Tribunal has jurisdiction to settle disputes concerning the interpretation or application of UNCLOS, and also disputes under another treaty or convention concerning the subject matter covered by UNCLOS, if the parties to the dispute so agree.[21] The jurisdiction of the ITLOS with regards to marine environmental disputes is not subject to any of the limitations listed in Article 297 or the optional exceptions provided for in Article 298. Therefore, wherever the parties to an environmental dispute have accepted the jurisdiction of the ITLOS under Article 287, the Tribunal will have unchallenged competence to deal with it (Mensah, 1998).

The ITLOS may set up chambers to deal with certain types of disputes and *ad hoc* chambers for specific disputes.[22] The ITLOS established a Chamber for Marine Environmental Disputes consisting of seven judges of the Tribunal.[23] The aim was to deal more quickly with queries concerning the marine environment and prevent any serious damages.

So far, the ITLOS has heard just a handful of cases dealing with the protection of the marine environment. These include notably the *Southern Blue-Fin Tuna*[24] *Cases (New Zealand v. Japan; Australia v. Japan)*, the *Land Reclamation* Case[25] (*Malaysia v. Singapore*), and the *MOX Plant Case*.[26]

The potential of the ITLOS, and the judges' skills and expertise, has not been fully utilised.[27] As of February 2017, of the current 168 States and non-State entities that ratified the convention,[28] only 51 expressed their choice of procedure upon ratification.[29] Even fewer countries, 38 States, accepted the compulsory jurisdiction of the ITLOS.[30] The other parties reserve their right to do so at any other time as per Article 287 (Choon-ho Park, 200). In its 21 years of existence, the Tribunal has decided 25 cases. With regards to the choice of procedures, arbitration has proven to be the rule, while opting for the ITLOS or the International Court of Justice remains the exception.[31] In this context, one may enquire whether there is any need for a broader framework with strong compulsory settlement procedures for dealing with marine environmental disputes.

The International Court of Justice

The International Court of Justice (ICJ) has jurisdiction over contentious cases referred to it and all matters specially provided for in the United Nations Charter or in other treaties and conventions.[32] The ICJ may also give advisory opinions at the request of States or other authorised bodies.[33]

International adjudication, including arbitration, is an exceptional means of dispute settlement. The contentious jurisdiction of the ICJ depends on the consent of all parties to a dispute. According to Article 36, paragraph 2, of the ICJ Statute:

> The States parties to the present Statute may at any time declare that they recognize as compulsory ipso facto and without special agreement, in relation to any other state accepting the same obligation, the jurisdiction of the court in all legal disputes.

Acceptance of the jurisdiction of the Court under Article 36, Paragraph 2, may be made unconditionally, or on the condition of reciprocity, or for a limited period of time. The consent of the States can be given in advance of any dispute, for instance when a State ratifies a treaty. Recent practice in multilateral environmental treaties allows parties, at the time of signature, ratification, or accession, or at a later stage, to accept compulsory dispute settlement (CDS) by recourse to arbitration or to the ICJ. For example, compulsory jurisdiction is provided for in the 1992 *Climate Change Convention*,[34] the 1992 *Biodiversity Convention*,[35] and the 1997 *Watercourses Convention*.[36] Consent to refer cases to the ICJ may be also given by special agreement.[37] Unlike the ITLOS, the ICJ hears contentious cases between States only.[38]

In 1993, the ICJ established a Chamber for Environmental Matters that has been periodically reconstituted. The Chamber was created 'in view of the developments in the field of environmental law and protection which have taken place in the last few years'.[39] In 13 years of existence, no State has ever referred a case to the Chamber, and it was finally closed in 2006.[40]

Although the ICJ has never dealt with a major international environmental dispute,[41] the Court has had the opportunity to consider matters related to environmental protection and establish key principles of international environmental law. The ICJ record of environmental jurisprudence includes cases such as the *Icelandic Fisheries* and *Nuclear Tests*, the *Nuclear Weapons Advisory Opinion*, *Gabcikovo-Nagymaros* and *Pulp Mills Provisional Measures*.[42]

The ICJ has also heard cases related to maritime international law, particularly fisheries, for example in the case *Fisheries Jurisdiction (United Kingdom of Great Britain and Northern Ireland v. Iceland)*.[43] This dispute involved Iceland and several North Atlantic fishing States, especially Great Britain, between 1952 and 1976. The dispute was caused because Iceland established fisheries jurisdiction zones in the waters surrounding the island and tried to enforce them against foreign vessels. In 1972, the United Kingdom referred the dispute to the ICJ challenging Iceland's extension of its zone to 50 miles.

On the merits,[44] the ICJ first found that the Icelandic Regulations of 14 July 1972 were not opposable to the United Kingdom (and Germany). The objective of such regulations was to establish an exclusive fishery zone in which all fishing by vessels registered in other States would be prohibited. The Court argued that the concept of the coastal State's preferential rights was not compatible with the exclusion of all fishing activities of other States. The ICJ concluded that those Regulations represented an infringement of the right of fishing conferred to the other disputing parties. However, this did not mean that they should disregard Iceland's fishing rights. On the contrary, all States should observe each other's rights and comply with fishery conservation measures. According to the ICJ,[45]

> It is one of the advances in maritime international law, resulting from the intensification of fishing, that the former laissez-faire treatment of the living resources of the sea in the high seas has been replaced by a recognition of a duty to have due regard to the rights of other States and the needs of conservation for the benefit of all.

Alarming scientific data concerning the rapid depletion of marine living resources in the waters of Iceland triggered a reaction by the Icelandic Government. In 1975, it issued regulations extending its fisheries jurisdiction to 200 nautical miles. An increasing number of States claimed a 200-mile exclusive zone. Finally, Iceland and the United Kingdom signed an agreement and a limitation was imposed on the number of British trawlers that could fish within the 200-mile limit.

Arbitral tribunals

Most environmental treaties provide for arbitration. For instance, the 1969 *Oil Pollution Intervention Convention* contains detailed provisions on the composition of an arbitration tribunal.[46] Other treaties provide for the submission of disputes to arbitration, such as the 1973 International Convention for the Prevention of Pollution from Ships,[47] or the 1974 Baltic Convention.[48]

The success enjoyed by arbitration can be attributed to its great flexibility. It combines the fundamental features of judicial settlement, such as binding settlement, and previously agreed-upon procedures, with a large degree of influence by the States. They can decide on issues such as the composition of the court and the rules of procedure among others (Romano, 2000).

Generally, each party has the right to designate one of the arbitrators. The third arbitrator, who is normally the chairman of the arbitral tribunal, is usually chosen jointly by the parties, by the two other arbitrators, or by a neutral party. The arbitral award, like adjudication, results in a binding decision, unless the relevant convention or the parties have provided otherwise. International arbitration has produced a few noteworthy decisions such as the *Trail Smelter*,[49] *Lac Lanoux*[50] and *Gut Dam*[51] arbitrations.

World Trade Organization (WTO)

The WTO Dispute Settlement Body is composed of all WTO members. It operates under the principles of being 'equitable, fast, effective, and mutually acceptable'.[52] The first stage in the dispute settlement procedure is consultation. This is the stage

Contemporary marine environmental disputes   233

in which the parties attempt to solve the dispute on their own and may ask the Director-General of the WTO to mediate or assist.[53]

If the parties cannot come to a solution during consultation, then a panel is created. Before the first hearing, each party presents its case in writing to the panel. Then, during the first hearing, each party makes its case. Written rebuttals are later submitted and, at the second panel meeting, oral arguments are heard. At this point, the panel may consult experts.

The panel then submits a draft of the descriptive sections of its report, which includes the facts of the case but not the expected ruling. Each party comments on the draft, after which an interim report with findings is given to the parties for review. Additional panel meetings may be held during this time. A final report is then submitted to the parties and all WTO members. Unless a consensus rejects this report, it becomes the ruling. The panel's ruling can only be overturned by a consensus of the Dispute Settlement Body.

Both parties can appeal the panel's ruling. Appeals cannot bring in new information, but must be based on points of law such as legal interpretation.[54] Each appeal is heard by three out of seven members of a permanent Appellate Body. The Dispute Settlement Body must accept or reject (rejection must be made by a consensus vote) an appeal report. The 'losing' party has a 'reasonable period of time' to correct its wrongdoings and may ask the Dispute Settlement Body for more time if required.

The environmental jurisprudence of WTO includes cases such as *Shrimp-Turtle*,[55] *EC-Asbestos*[56] and *EC-Hormones*.[57] These cases address issues concerning environmental protection and human health, such as the protection of species (sea turtles) from harm; the ban of environmental toxins (asbestos) to protect animal, human, plant life or health; and human health (*hormones used in beef products*).

Other WTO cases that relate to the law of the sea include the *EC – Seal Products*[58] and the *US – Tuna II (Mexico)*.[59] In that first case, Canada and Norway are concerned about products deriving or obtained from seals, including meat, oil, blubber, organs, raw fur skins and tanned fur skins, among others. Canada asks the EU to bring its measures back to conformity with the 1995 Agreement on Technical Barriers to Trade (TBT) or the 1994 General Agreement on Tariffs and Trade (GATT). There is a particular focus on the inhumane nature of some seal hunting (including clubbing). The decision of this case states that hunting should be conducted with respect to environmental sustainability, using scientific population models of marine resources and applying the ecosystem-based approach, and not exceed catch quotas. The second case, *US – Tuna II (Mexico)*, relates to the labelling of 'dolphin-safe' tuna. Mexico claims that the US 'dolphin-safe' labelling is inconsistent with the GATT 1994 and TBT Agreement and is discriminatory against them and unnecessary. The Panel found that the US's labelling provisions do not discriminate against Mexican tuna (and are therefore not in violation of TBT Article 2.1), but also that the labelling provisions are more trade-restrictive than necessary under Article 2.2 of TBT. The Panel also found that setting on dolphins (using them to catch tuna) is harmful to them and could cause both observed and unobserved adverse effects.

Courts and tribunals at the regional level

Some courts and tribunals at the regional level have also developed a significant environmental jurisprudence. Albeit not their primary role, these organs can hear environmental disputes and, potentially, marine environmental disputes.

Court of justice of the European Union

There is both an oral and written part of this court's proceedings.[60] The written part of the procedure contains the lodging of procedural documents, including a written report. After the written report, a preliminary report containing proposals as to the organisation of procedure is created. During the oral portion, there is a hearing. Witnesses may be asked to be brought in during the oral part of the Court proceedings. This Court has dealt with a few environmental disputes, including cases related to fisheries,[61] maritime zones,[62] waste disposal[63] and oil pollution.[64]

Other courts and tribunals

The two regional Human Rights Courts – the European Court of Human Rights and the Inter-American Court of Human Rights – as well as the African Commission on Human and Peoples' Rights have made an outstanding contribution to environmental rights jurisprudence (Boyle, 2007, p. 372). They have jurisdiction to hear cases concerning human rights, but they could theoretically hear marine environmental disputes that involve breaches to basic human rights, such as the right to life[65] and to a 'satisfactory environment'.[66]

For example, the European Court of Human Rights has heard cases related to the contamination of water supplies and the right to private and family life,[67] the management of water reservoirs and the right to life[68] and the conservation of coastal dunes and the right to freedom of expression.[69] The Inter-American Court of Human Rights has developed an extensive jurisdiction on Indigenous peoples' rights.[70] The Court has clarified the scope and application of Indigenous peoples' rights in the Americas, and the relationship between these communities and their land and natural resources.[71] The African Commission on Human and Peoples' Rights has made a remarkable contribution to the environmental jurisprudence with the *Ogani* case.[72]

In the Americas, a sub-regional Court, the Andean Court of Justice,[73] is the judicial body under the Andean Community (CAN),[74] which involves Bolivia, Colombia, Ecuador and Peru. The Court is competent to determine the legality of decisions, resolutions and agreements adopted by the member States, and provide authoritative interpretations of the Andean Community law. The decisions of the Court are binding on the Member States. When CAN Member States fail to comply with obligations under CAN law, the General Secretariat can activate a *non-compliance procedure*.[75] In cases where the defaulting State continues with the behaviour that motivated the non-compliance procedure, the General Secretariat can require a decision by the Andean Court of Justice.[76] This Court has developed extensive jurisdiction in non-compliance actions.[77]

Over the years, the Andean Community has developed a significant body of law dealing with different aspects of the sub-region's environment and has also created specialised institutions dealing with environmental matters. By adopting decisions on areas such as access to genetic resources, industrial property or agriculture and food security, this organisation has created a sub-regional regime that includes common norms and procedures applicable to its member States.[78]

Settlement procedure under the ITLOS

Choice of procedure

States parties are free to settle their disputes by any peaceful means of their own choice, according to Article 280 of UNCLOS. In fact, flexibility in the choice of procedures was key to ensure the widest possible consensus on dispute settlement provisions, as evidenced during UNCLOS's negotiations (Boyle, 1999).

If a dispute arises concerning the interpretation or application of UNCLOS, State Parties are under an obligation to exchange views[79] or submit the dispute to conciliation by mutual consent.[80] If no settlement is reached, the compulsory dispute settlement procedure under Section 2, Part XV of UNCLOS applies, except for certain types of disputes listed in Article 197.

States may choose, upon ratification of UNCLOS or at a later time, one or more dispute settlement mechanisms from a menu of four procedures listed in Article 287, the 'choice of procedure' clause. The four options are the ICJ, the ITLOS, arbitration or special arbitration. If the parties to a dispute have selected the same procedure, this will apply in disputes between them.[81] In the absence of agreement concerning the adjudication forum, the disputes will be referred to arbitration in accordance with Annex VII of UNCLOS.[82] Disputes that cannot be resolved through procedures agreed between the parties will always be subject to the mandatory procedure of arbitration.

Part XV of UNCLOS does not apply if the parties to the dispute agree to submit it to another procedure. States can choose another procedure that entails a binding decision under a general, regional or bilateral agreement agreed upon between the parties *in lieu* of the procedures provided for in Part XV.[83] The CDS procedures under Section 2 of Part XV are 'residual' procedures in that they are applicable only in the absence of other procedures acceptable to the parties (Vidas & Østreng, 1999). In addition, they only apply after local remedies have been exhausted, where this is required by international law.[84]

Compulsory dispute settlement regime

The inclusion of a comprehensive system of disputes consisting of both voluntary and compulsory procedures was a fundamental innovation of UNCLOS.[85] This system applies to the vast majority of the provisions of the Convention.[86] As noted previously, parties that fail to settle a dispute through voluntary procedures are obliged to resort to CDS procedures entailing binding decisions provided for in Section 2 of Part XV. In the absence of a declaration, parties are deemed to have accepted arbitration. This has proven to be the general rule, while selecting the ITLOS or the ICJ remains the exception.[87]

The jurisdiction of an adjudicating body becomes compulsory when the parties to a dispute have accepted it by virtue of a declaration.[88] A fundamental principle of international adjudication is the consent of the parties. In practice, disputes relating to the marine environment have usually not been subject to interstate claims, even in cases as serious as the *Amoco Cadiz*,[89] but instead have been dealt with under national law, civil liability and compensation schemes (Mazzeschi, 1991).

A party to a dispute can initiate the CDS procedures under Section 2 of Part XV by the submission of an application to the competent court or tribunal listed under Article 287. Upon receipt of the application, the court or tribunal immediately notifies the other party or parties of the application.[90] The decisions rendered by a court having jurisdiction under Section 2 are final and binding on the parties to the dispute.[91]

The ITLOS also has an advisory function. This is based on Article 21 of its Statute, which states that the Tribunal's jurisdiction comprises 'all disputes and all applications submitted to it' and 'all matters specifically provided for in any other agreement which confers jurisdiction on the Tribunal'. Even disputes under another treaty or convention concerning a subject matter covered by UNCLOS can be submitted to the ITLOS, if the parties to the dispute so agree.[92] The advisory function of the Tribunal may offer an alternative to contentious proceedings, particularly in view of its non-binding nature.[93] The State Parties or other entities seeking an advisory opinion may obtain legal guidance on a specific question and an indication of how a particular dispute may be solved.[94] By doing so, they may avoid the contentious proceedings under UNCLOS. The advisory procedure has already been used,[95] and can assist conflicting parties to reach an agreement and prevent them from engaging in a dispute.

Settlement regime for sea-bed disputes

Part XI of UNCLOS establishes a special system for settling disputes related to the International Seabed Area. Disputes concerning activities in the Area will trigger this special dispute settlement procedure rather than the mechanisms under Part XV of UNCLOS. The Seabed Dispute Chamber has jurisdiction to settle disputes concerning the prevention of pollution or other forms of degradation of the marine environment of the Area. The Chamber also has jurisdiction to give an advisory opinion on matters pertaining to Part XI of the Convention.[96] The Chamber has received its first request to render an Advisory Opinion in 2010 from the Council of the International Seabed Authority.[97]

Exceptions to compulsory jurisdiction

There are certain types of disputes that States would not readily agree to submit to compulsory procedures, particularly those relating to matters considered to be of vital national interest. As a result, it was decided to subject UNLCOS's CDS procedures to certain limitations and exceptions. This was to reassure States that the acceptance of the Convention would not compromise their sovereign rights and their ability to settle certain disputes outside the compulsory adjudicatory process ((Vidas & Østreng, 1999, p. 84). These limitations and exceptions are listed in Section 3, Part XV of UNCLOS.

A State, when signing, ratifying or acceding to the Convention or at a later time, may declare in writing that it does not accept one or more of the procedures provided for in Section 2 with respect to certain types of disputes. As per Article 298, the disputes that may be excluded from UNCLOS's CDS procedures include the following: the delimitation of the territorial sea (Article 15), the exclusive economic zone (Article 74) and the continental shelf (Article 83), and those involving historic bays or titles.

The fact that a State Party may exclude disputes from CDS procedures by virtue of Article 298, Paragraph 1(a), does not mean that the dispute is entirely exempted from settlement. As a general rule, States must seek to resolve the dispute peacefully.[98] Therefore, they may use any of the mechanisms under Article 33 of the UN Charter to settle a dispute, or any other arrangement agreed upon between the parties.

There has been criticism regarding UNCLOS's dispute settlement mechanism. Alan Boyle describes the problems associated with Part XV as the 'cafeteria' and 'salami-slicing' approaches (Boyle, 2007). The 'cafeteria' approach relates to the various possible forums for compulsory settlement that State Parties can choose from. The four procedures on the menu are ITLOS, ICJ, arbitration and special arbitration. This is due to the fact that, during UNCLOS's negotiations, disagreement on the most appropriate process was such that no single forum could be given general compulsory jurisdiction (Boyle, 2007, p. 40). A problem related to the cafeteria approach is fragmentation: there is no single forum for disputes arising under UNCLOS and there is no mechanism to ensure uniformity in the outcome of similar cases before different tribunals (Boyle, 2007, p. 41). The *Swordfish case* is an example of this, as it was briefly pursued simultaneously under the WTO and UNCLOS (Boyle & Harrison, 2013).

The 'salami-slicing' approach relates to the possibility of categorising and separating different types of disputes – some of which will lead to a binding, compulsory settlement while others will not (Boyle, 2007, p. 42). In practice, it is hard to categorise a dispute and fit it squarely under the CDS procedures. As noted by Boyle, everything turns in practice not on what each case involves but on how the issues are formulated (Boyle & Harrison, 2013, p. 45).[99] Boyle concludes that the 'exceptions from the general principle of compulsory jurisdiction are such that procedural fragmentation is inevitable and will lead in practice to greater emphasis on consensus rather than compulsory settlement' (Boyle & Harrison, 2013, p. 45).

Settlement of marine environmental disputes

When it comes to control and prevention of marine pollution, the concession by maritime States of enforcement powers to coastal States was actually conditioned on compulsory third-party or adjudication to prevent the abuse of those powers and to secure the prompt release of vessels (Dupuy & Vignes, 1991, p. 210). The compulsory settlement of marine environmental disputes was considered an essential element of compromise and a means to discourage both the insufficient zeal by flag States and the excessive zeal by coastal States likely to hamper the freedoms at sea (Dupuy & Vignes, 1991, p. 210).

States are under an obligation to protect and preserve the marine environment and shall be held liable for causing environmental harm, as per Article 235. This clause can be traced to Principle 22 of the 1972 Stockholm Declaration on Human Environment, according to which:

> States shall co-operate to develop further the international law regarding liability and compensation for the victims of pollution and other environmental damage caused by activities within the jurisdiction or control of such States to areas beyond their jurisdiction.

Liability under the law is the obligation and responsibility borne by the person concerned for any breach of law. It implies the notion of answerability as it indicates accountability for an act and the obligation to answer for it (Brodeur, 1999, p. 137). This liability may add incentive to take due care to avoid damage (Mensah, 1999, p. 322) and ensure the effective protection of the marine environment from pollution. It is to be noted that in relation to marine environmental issues, liability for damage occurs without any subjective fault. This non-fault liability is useful for complicated marine pollution issues where pollution results from disposal of pollutants and proof is difficult.

Article 235 of UNCLOS addresses the liability issue for the protection of the marine environment. It provides

- States are responsible for the fulfilment of their international obligations concerning the protection of the marine environment. They shall be liable in accordance with international law.
- States shall ensure that recourse is available in accordance with their legal systems for prompt and adequate compensation, or other relief, in respect of damage caused by pollution of the marine environment by natural or juridical persons under their jurisdiction.
- With the objective of assuring prompt and adequate compensation in respect of all damage caused by pollution to the marine environment, States shall

cooperate in the implementation of existing international law and the further development of international law relating to responsibility and liability for the assessment of, and compensation for, damage and the settlement of related disputes, as well as, where appropriate, development of criteria and procedures for the payment of adequate compensation, such as compulsory insurance or compensation funds.

This indicates that States will be liable for the non-fulfilment of obligations concerning pollution damage. Although legal redress is to be available to States, uncertainties exist. Section 2 of Article 235 obliges States to provide recourse in their national law with respect to damage caused by pollution to the marine environment by persons under their jurisdiction, i.e., civil liability. However, it does not include cases in which a State rather than individuals causes damage. The Convention deftly avoided the issue of State liability for sub-standard performance by providing only that States 'shall be liable in accordance with international law' (Article 235).

An effective system for the resolution of marine environmental disputes between coastal States within a given region is important to encourage development of appropriate marine and coastal environmental standards. Part XV of UNCLOS (Articles 279–299) creates scope to resolve the disputes between States in various matters including disputes involving protection and preservation of the marine environment.[100] In establishing the compulsory dispute settlement (CDS) system, these provisions constitute a major advance. As noted earlier, the principal provision of compulsory dispute settlement in UNCLOS is Article 286. It establishes that, subject to specific limitations, if parties are unable to reach an alternative settlement proceeding on their own then 'any dispute concerning the interpretation or application of this convention shall . . . be submitted at the request of any party to the dispute to the court or tribunal having jurisdiction under this section'.[101]

Disputes in relation to marine environmental protection are clearly subject to the CDS procedures since no exemption exists to allow UNCLOS to redirect this type of dispute to a non-compulsory procedure.[102] Under CDS, the decision of the court or tribunal is final.[103]

The ITLOS has an important role to play in the protection and preservation of the environment, particularly through the competence conferred to it concerning provisional measures.[104] The Tribunal may prescribe provisional measures to prevent serious harm to the environment.[105] Importantly, the ITLOS has a 'residual' competence to prescribe provisional measures even in cases where the dispute has been submitted to an arbitral tribunal under UNCLOS (Mensah, 1998). There are conditions governing the exercise of this competence. The ITLOS may prescribe provisional measures only when pending the constitution of an arbitral tribunal, or when the parties to the disputes have failed to agree on a court or tribunal to deal with the request for provisional measures.[106] The jurisdiction of the ITLOS under Article 290(5) is compulsory. Provisional measures have been requested for example in the *Southern Blue-Fin Tuna*[107] *Cases*, *Land Reclamation* Case,[108] and the *MOX Plant Case*.[109]

Article 290 of UNCLOS allows for preliminary or provisional measures to prevent serious harm to the marine environment at the request of one of the Parties where a dispute has been submitted to a court or tribunal.[110] Prescribing binding provisional measures substantially advances opportunities for the protection of the marine environment from pollution by enabling its prevention, instead of a post hoc declaration of liability. *The MOX Plant Case* is an example in this respect.

The MOX Plant Case concerned the protection of the Irish Sea from the risk of radioactive pollution through a proposed plant being constructed on the English coast. Ireland initiated arbitration proceedings against the United Kingdom in view of the fact that the United Kingdom declined to indicate any willingness to suspend authorisation or prevent operation of the proposed MOX (Mixed Oxide) Plant.[111] Ireland considered that the discharges were incompatible with the United Kingdom's obligations to:

> protect the marine environment (Article 192 of LOSC); cooperate to protect and preserve the marine environment (Article 123 and 197 of LOSC);[112] take all ... measures ... that are necessary to prevent reduce and control pollution from all sources,[113] minimise to the fullest possible extent ... the release of toxic, harmful and noxious substances, especially those which are persistent, from land-based sources.
>
> *(194(3)(a))*[114]

Ireland also considered that the proposed operation was in violation of obligations under Article 207 of UNCLOS on pollution from land-based sources (in particular Article 207(2) and (5) of UNCLOS) and Article 213 of UNCLOS, on the enforcement of laws with respect to pollution from land-based sources.[115] On the basis of these considerations, and because of the urgency of the situation, Ireland requested the Tribunal to prescribe provisional measures suspending construction of the proposed plant, relying upon Article 290(5) of UNCLOS.[116] The United Kingdom requested the Tribunal to reject Ireland's request for provisional measures, as the proposed plant was yet to be operational.[117] In its order, the Tribunal rejected Ireland's request as it did not consider that the situation was urgent, but, nevertheless, it considered that the UK had a duty to cooperate as a fundamental principle for marine pollution control under part XII of UNCLOS and general international law[118] and prescribed unanimously, Ireland and the United Kingdom shall cooperate and shall, for this purpose, enter into consultations forthwith in order to:

> Exchange further information with regard to possible consequences for the Irish Sea arising out of the commissioning of the MOX Plant;
>
> Monitor risks, or the effects, of the operation of the MOX plant for the Irish Sea; and
>
> Devise, as appropriate, measures to prevent pollution of the marine environment, which might result from the operation of the MOX Plant.[119]

Relying upon CDS procedures, this case made a significant development for the protection of the marine environment from land-based sources of marine pollution (LBSMP). It was considered that the rights of coastal States are important, but they need to be accountable for compliance with their obligations when activities affect other States and communities. This provisional prescription also generated the application of environmental impact assessment as one of the noteworthy features of international law of marine pollution. Although this case brought a success in terms of the application of UNCLOS's CDS procedures, some uncertainties have also been observed that could affect the efficacy and credibility of this system to control LBSMP.[120]

UNCLOS provides a comprehensive basis for the resolution of disputes in relation to a case on marine pollution. Relying upon these procedures, the *MOX Plant Case*[121] took a bold step forward for the prevention of potential marine environmental harm from pollution. In this case, ITLOS considered that coastal States need to be accountable for compliance with their obligations when their activities affect other States and communities. The Tribunal described the 'duty to cooperate' as a fundamental principle for international control of marine pollution and for the resolution of marine environmental disputes.[122]

This case made a significant contribution to international law relating to LBSMP control by helping to define the scope of Part XV of UNCLOS concerning compulsory provisional measures to resolve an international dispute also covered by another international agreement. Article 282 of UNCLOS provides that if the Parties have entered into another agreement covering the same subject matter and entailing a binding decision-making process, then a dispute can be resolved through the procedures under that other agreement.[123] However, in the *MOX Plant Case*, Article 282 was considered to apply only to a dispute concerning the interpretation or application of UNCLOS specifically, and no other agreement.[124] In this respect the Tribunal considered

> that even if the OSPAR Convention, the EC Treaty and the Euratom Treaty contain rights or obligations similar to or identical with the rights and obligations set out in the Convention, the rights and obligations under those agreements have a separate existence from those under the Convention on the Law of the Sea.[125]

Thus, Article 282 is about disputes over interpretation or application of UNCLOS alone. The agreement – general, regional, bilateral or otherwise – to resolve disputes must concern exclusively disputes under UNCLOS.

This case successfully cleared another hurdle to ITLOS's exercise of its jurisdiction, as set out in Article 281(1) of UNCLOS. Article 281(1) states:

> If the state Parties which are Parties to a dispute concerning the interpretation or application of this Convention have agreed to seek settlement of the

dispute by a peaceful means of their own choice, the procedures provided for in this Part apply only where no settlement has been reached by recourse to such means and the agreement between the Parties does not exclude any further procedure.[126]

Since Article 32(1) of the OSPAR Convention related to settlement of disputes in the OSPAR maritime area but did not enable provisional measures, it did not preclude the ITLOS from prescribing provisional measures under Article 290(5) (Lagoni, 2002, p. 11).

However, Article 282 may not always be so limited. The separate opinion of Vice President Dolliver Nelson in the *MOX Plant Case* itself could indicate that Article 282 has a potentially broader reach covering disputes over final rather than provisional measures. He commented that:

> I am in the agreement with the Tribunal that 'for the purpose of determining whether the Annex VII arbitral tribunal would have prima facie jurisdiction, Article 282 of the convention is not applicable to the dispute submitted to the Annex VII arbitral tribunal'.[127] However, I have doubts concerning the reach of paragraph 51 which may well render article 282 and 281 ineffective.[128]

Paragraph 51 of the Order of the *MOX Plant Case* considered

> that the application of international law rules on interpretation of treaties to identical or similar provisions of different treaties may not yield the same results, having regard to, *inter alia*, differences in the respective contexts, objects and purposes, subsequent practice of Parties, and *travaux preparatoires*.[129]

This opinion could constrain the utilisation of the compulsory binding dispute resolution system of UNCLOS.

Some other provisions of UNCLOS could undermine its compulsory adjudication system. For example, Parties may choose any other peaceful means to settle a dispute without submitting to the compulsory adjudication of ITLOS or any of UNCLOS' arbitral chambers[130] and two or more Parties may conclude agreements modifying or superseding the operation of the dispute resolution provisions of UNCLOS.[131]

Therefore, UNCLOS's interaction with other treaties may create problems where such treaties overlap in subject matters and exclude adjudication or arbitration without the express consent of individual states. Any treaties providing for an alternative form of dispute resolution can supersede UNCLOS's compulsory adjudication (Sturtz, 2001, p. 467). The *Southern Bluefin Tuna Case* is an example in this respect, where compulsory adjudication under UNCLOS was undermined by a small trilateral regional agreement, the *Convention for the Conservation of Southern Bluefin Tuna* (CCSBT). In this case Australia and New Zealand sued Japan for overfishing of the Southern Bluefin Tuna. Australia and New Zealand argued that Japan violated obligations under both the Convention for the Conservation of Southern Bluefin Tuna (CCSBT) and the LOSC. Although the ITLOS issued protective provisional measures against Japan, the Arbitral Tribunal found that it was an issue under the CCSBT, and therefore undermining UNCLOS Part XV.[132] The Arbitral Tribunal concluded that UNCLOS 'falls significantly short of establishing a truly comprehensive regime of compulsory jurisdiction entailing binding decisions'.[133] This award supported the adoption of consent-based agreements and challenges the viability of the continuing compulsory nature of UNCLOS's dispute resolution regime.[134]

Above all, it is necessary to bear in mind that the application of provisional measures, as in the *MOX Plant Case*, is temporary. The final determination of this case will depend on the decision of another Arbitral Tribunal, which is yet to be established for this case. Therefore, whether that final Tribunal will undermine the ITLOS's provisional prescription, as in the *Southern Bluefin Tuna Case*, is yet to be seen.

However, whatever the outcome may be, it is clear that the status of UNCLOS's compulsory adjudicative system is uncertain and needs clarification. Therefore, a broader framework with strong compulsory procedure is needed. This strong procedure would promote effective cooperation in LBSMP control.

Other treaties, such as the 1982 Fish Stock Agreement,[135] contain stronger dispute settlement provisions than UNCLOS (Hassan, 2009, p. 528). According to Article 30 of this Agreement, the provisions relating to the settlement of disputes under Part XV of UNCLOS apply *mutatis mutandis* to *any* dispute between the parties. These disputes may involve the interpretation or application of a sub-regional, regional or global fisheries agreement relating to straddling fish stocks or highly migratory fish stocks to which the disputing States are Parties, *whether or not* they are also Parties to UNCLOS.

Lastly, some environmental disturbances or harm caused to the marine environment that do not necessarily fit into the definitions of *pollution* under UNCLOS may be left out of its CDS procedures. Some forms of environmental harm, for instance damage caused to some marine mammals by noise or physical damage caused to marine habitats by anchors or by ships, do not neatly fit into the definition of 'pollution' (i.e. *introduction by man, directly or indirectly, of substances or energy into the marine environment*). In such cases, the provisions of Part XII might need to be interpreted extensively.

Conclusions

The dispute settlement of international disputes is inherently limited. A fundamental principle of international adjudication is the consent of the parties. States are free to submit a dispute to the appreciation of a third party, and they are usually free to choose the available procedures for resolving their disputes. Even compulsory dispute settlement procedures, such as that established by UNCLOS, require States to accept to be bound by them. In practice, States rely on their sovereign rights and prerogatives to protect national interests and avoid referring disputes for consideration by a third party. Therefore, international adjudication is the exception rather than the rule.

In fact, in many situations, such as the case with UNCLOS, States are conferred significant freedom regarding dispute settlement options in order to ensure that a treaty can be adopted in the first place. Therefore, some of the deficiencies of UNCLOS may be attributed to the compromises made by the State Parties during its negotiations. In the ideal world, all matters covered by UNCLOS and maritime disputes should be subject to CDS procedures and submitted to the ITLOS, but this is not always the case. The various limitations and exceptions under UNCLOS's CDS procedures raise some problems. As framed by Boyle, the 'cafeteria' and 'salami-slicing' approaches used by the Convention may lead to fragmentation (i.e., different Courts or Tribunals dealing with the same or similar cases) and uncertainty as to which disputes may actually fit under the CDS procedures.

Some provisions of UNCLOS could also undermine its compulsory adjudication system. For example, State Parties may choose any other peaceful means to settle a dispute without submitting to the compulsory adjudication of ITLOS or any of its arbitral chambers, and two or more Parties may conclude agreements modifying or superseding the operation of the dispute resolution provisions of UNCLOS.

Therefore, UNCLOS's interaction with other treaties may create problems where such treaties overlap in subject matters and exclude adjudication or arbitration without the express consent of individual states. In such situations, other treaties providing for an alternative form of dispute resolution can potentially supersede UNCLOS's compulsory adjudication. The *Southern Bluefin Tuna Case* is an example in this respect, where compulsory adjudication under UNCLOS was undermined by a small trilateral regional agreement, the 1993 *Convention for the Conservation of Southern Bluefin Tuna*. Therefore, some maritime disputes, including marine environmental disputes that in principle fall under UNCLOS's CDS procedures, may be excluded from it by virtue of its interaction with other treaties. In view of the current deficiencies related to UNCLOS's CDS procedures, a broader framework with strong and clear compulsory procedures should be envisaged. This would ensure that marine environmental disputes are settled through international adjudication without much hesitation or uncertainty.

Notes

1 Legality of the Threat or Use of Nuclear Weapons in Armed Conflicts Advisory Opinion, ICJ Reports, Vol. 35, 1996, pp. 809–938.
2 Order for Provisional Measures in the Southern Bluefin Tuna Cases, International Tribunal of the Law of the Sea (ITLOS), on 27 August 1999.
3 Mavrommatis Palestine Concession, (Jurisdiction), Permanent Court of International Justice, Ser. A, No 2 (1924), p. 11.
4 Article 305 (1) (f), United Nations Convention on the Law of the Sea (UNCLOS).
5 This rule can be found in several treaties; for example, Article 7 of the 1997 Convention on Law of Non-navigational Uses of International Watercourses includes it as the 'obligation not to cause significant harm'.

6 About this principle and other environmental law principles, see D. Hassan, "Territorial Sovereignty and State Responsibility, An Environmental Perspective," *Environmental Policy and Law*, Vol. 45, No. 3–4, 2015, pp. 139–145, p. 139.
7 Ibid., p. 144.
8 General Assembly, Report of the Secretary-General, Oceans and the Law of the Sea, (A/57/57) Fifty-seventh Session, 7 March 2002.
9 Article 43.
10 Article 94 (7).
11 Article 100.
12 Article 108.
13 Articles 65, 117, 118.
14 Article 129.
15 Article 144 (2).
16 According to Article 2(4) of the United Nations Charter (UN Charter), 'All members shall refrain in their international relations from the threat or use of force against the territorial integrity or political independence of any state, on in any manner inconsistent with the Purposes of the United Nations'.
17 The General Assembly Declaration on the Principles of International Law Concerning Friendly Relations and Cooperation among States in accordance with the Charter of the United Nations, G.A. Res. 2625 (XXV), 24 October 1970, modelled on Article 33(1) of the UN Charter provides: 'States shall seek early and just settlement of their international disputes by negotiation, inquiry, mediation, conciliation, arbitration, judicial settlement, resort to regional agencies or arrangements or other peaceful means of their choice'.
18 Article 21, ITLOS Statute.
19 See the ITLOS website, www.itlos.org/the-tribunal/history/.
20 Articles 2 and 4, ITLOS Statute.
21 Article 22, ITLOS Statute.
22 Article 15, ITLOS Statute.
23 See ITLOS website, www.itlos.org/the-tribunal/chambers/.
24 Southern Bluefin Tuna Cases (New Zealand v. Japan; Australia v. Japan), Provisional Measures.
25 Case concerning Land Reclamation by Singapore in and around the Straits of Johor (Malaysia v. Singapore), Provisional Measures.
26 The MOX Plant Case (Ireland v. United Kingdom), Provisional Measures.
27 Statement by Mr. Rudiger Wolfrum, President of the ITLOS, at the Plenary of the Sixty-First Session of the United Nations General Assembly, on 8 December 2006.
28 www.un.org/Depts/los/reference_files/chronological_lists_of_ratifications.htm.
29 www.itlos.org/jurisdiction/declarations-of-states-parties/declarations-made-by-states-parties-under-article-287/.
30 States that ratified the Optional Protocol of Signature concerning the Compulsory Settlement of Disputes: https://treaties.un.org/Pages/ViewDetails.aspx?src=TREATY&mtdsg_no=XXI-5&chapter=21&clang=_en.
31 Wolfrum, 2008, p. 7.
32 Article 36, paragraph 1, International Court of Justice (ICJ) Statute.
33 Article 65, ICJ Statute.
34 Article 14(2).
35 Article 27(3).
36 Article 33 (10).
37 Article 36 (2), ICJ Statute.
38 Article 36, ICJ Statute.
39 ICJ, Press Communiqué 93/20 "Constitution of a Chamber of the Court for Environmental Matters", 19 July 1993.
40 www.icj-cij.org/court/index.php?p1=1&p2=4.
41 Boyle (note 19). This author notes that in its first 10 years the ICJ decided only one case with tangential relevance to international matters, the Corfu Channel case, p. 371.

42 The following cases influenced the development of international environmental law: Corfu Channel (United Kingdom v. Albania) Merits, Judgement, ICJ Reports 1949, pp. 4–127; Fisheries Jurisdiction (United Kingdom v. Iceland) Merits, Judgement ICJ Reports 1974, pp. 3–173, (Germany v. Iceland), Merits, Judgement, ICJ Reports 1974, pp. 175–251; Nuclear Test Cases (Australia v. France) Judgement, ICJ Reports 1974, pp. 253–455, (New Zealand v. France), Judgement, ICJ Reports 1974, pp. 457–528; Certain Phosphate Lands in Nauru (Nauru v. Australia), Order of September 13, 1993, ICJ Reports 1993, pp. 322–323; Gabcikovo-Nagymaros Project (Hungary v. Slovakia), Judgement, ICJ Reports 1977, pp. 1–72, Pulp Mills on the River Uruguay (Argentina v. Uruguay), Provisional Measures, Order of 13 July 2006, I.C.J. Reports 2006, p. 133.
43 There are two cases against Iceland which were brought before the ICJ, one by the United Kingdom, and the other by the Federal Republic of Germany.
44 Fisheries Jurisdiction (United Kingdom v. Iceland) Merits, Judgement, ICJ Reports 1974, pp. 3–173.
45 Fisheries Jurisdiction (United Kingdom v. Iceland) Merits, Judgement, ICJ Reports 1974, pp. 3–173, para. 72, p. 31.
46 Chapter 2 of the 1969 International Convention relating to Intervention on the High Seas of Oil Pollution Casualties.
47 Article 10.
48 Article 18.
49 Trail Smelter arbitration (United States v. Canada), United Nations, Reports of International Arbitral Awards, Vol. 3, 1949, pp. 1903–1982.
50 Lac Lanoux Arbitration, International Law Reports, Vol. 24, 1957, pp. 101–142.
51 Canada-USA Settlement of Gut Dam Claims, September 22, 1968, Report of the Agent of the United States before the Lake Ontario Claims Tribunal, International Legal Materials, Vol. 8, 1969, pp. 118–143.
52 See Understanding the WTO: Settling Disputes, www.wto.org/english/thewto_e/whatis_e/tif_e/disp1_e.htm.
53 Article 5 (6). Annex 2 of the World Trade Organization (WTO) Agreement.
54 Article 17 (6), Annex 2 of WTO Agreement.
55 United States – Import Prohibition of Certain Shrimp and Shrimp Products, WTO case Nos. 58 (and 61), Ruling on adopted on 6 November 1998. This is a case brought by India, Malaysia, Pakistan and Thailand against the United States.
56 European Communities – Measures Affecting Asbestos and Products Containing Asbestos, Appellate Body Report adopted on 5 April 2001. This case was initiated by Canada against the European Community on 28 May 1998 (Request for Consultations). WTO Reports adopted on 5 April 2001.
57 European Communities – Measures Concerning Meat and Meat Products (Hormones). This case was initiated by the United States on 26 January 1996 (Request for Consultations) against the European Community, with a mutually acceptable solution on implementation notified on 25 September 2009.
58 European Communities – Measures Prohibiting the Importation and Marketing of Seal Products. This case was initiated by Canada against the European Community, on 2 November 2009 (Request for Consultations). The WTO Reports were adopted, with recommendation to bring measure(s) into conformity on 18 June 2014.
59 United States – Measures Concerning the Importation, Marketing Tuna Products. This case was initiated by Mexico against the United States on 24 October 2008 (Request for Consultations). Compliance proceedings ongoing on 9 May 2016.
60 Court of Justice of the European Union's website, http://curia.europa.eu/jcms/jcms/T5_5119/en/.
61 Commission of the European Communities v United Kingdom of Great Britain and Northern Ireland, Case 32/79, Judgment of the Court of 10 July 1980: fisheries are limited to Member States' coastal waters, extending maximum up to 12 nautical miles; Kingdom of Spain v Council of the European Union Conservation and exploitation

of fisheries resources – Regulation (EC) No 2371/2002, Case 91/03, Judgment of the Court of 17 March 200: authorisation for Member States to restrict fishing in their coastal waters to fishing vessels that traditionally fish in these waters; Commission of the European Communities v French Republic, Case 304/02, Judgment of the Court of 12 July 2005: failure of a Member State to fulfill obligations – Fisheries – Control obligations placed on the Member States.
62 Commission of the European Communities v Ireland. Sea fisheries, Case 61/77, Judgment of the Court of 16 February 1978: extending maritime zones.
63 Procureur de la République v Association de défense des brûleurs d'huiles usagées, Case 240/83, Judgment of the Court of 7 February 1985: disposal of waste oils; Chemische Afvalstoffen Dusseldorp BV and Others v Minister van Volkshuisvesting, Ruimtelijke Ordening en Milieubeheer, Case 203/96, Judgment of the Court of 25 June 1998: shipments of waste for recovery.
64 The Queen, on the application of International Association of Independent Tanker Owners (Intertanko) and Others v Secretary of State for Transport, Case C-308/06, Judgment of the Court of 3 June 2008: oil pollution caused by the sinking of a tanker; Commission of the European Communities v Council of the European Union, Case C-176/03, Judgment of the Court of 13 September 2005: environmental protection.
65 Article 2, European Convention for the Protection of Human Rights and Fundamental Freedoms; Article 4, American Convention on Human Rights.
66 Article 24, African Charter on Human and Peoples' Rights.
67 Case of Dzemyuk v. Ukraine, Judgment 4 September 2014: the applicant alleged that the construction of a cemetery near his house had led to the contamination of his water supply, both for drinking and gardening purposes, leaving his home virtually uninhabitable and his land unusable.
68 Case of Kolyadenko and Others v. Russia, Judgment of 28 February 2012: the applicants lived in Vladivostok near the Pionerskaya river and water reservoir. They were all affected by a heavy flash flood in Vladivostok in August 2001. The applicants submitted in particular that the authorities had put their lives at risk by releasing the water without any prior warning and by having failed to maintain the river channel, and that there had been no adequate judicial response in that respect. They also complained that their homes and property had been severely damaged, and that they had had no effective remedies in respect of their complaints.
69 Vides Aizsardzības Klubs v. Latvia, Judgment of 27 May 2004: the applicant was a non-governmental organisation for the protection of the environment. In 1997 it had adopted a resolution addressed to the competent authorities expressing its concerns about the conservation of coastal dunes on a stretch of coast in the Gulf of Riga. The resolution, which was published in a regional newspaper, contained, *inter alia*, allegations that the local mayor had facilitated illegal construction work in the coastal area. The mayor brought an action for damages against the applicant, claiming that the statements in the resolution were defamatory.
70 About this jurisprudence see B. Garcia, The Amazon from an International Law Perspective, Cambridge University Press, 2011.
71 See for example, Case Mayagna (Sumo) Awas Tingni Community vs. Nicaragua, Preliminary Objections, Judgment of February 1, 2000, I/A Court H.R. Series C, no. 66, Case Yakye Axa Indigenous Community vs. Paraguay, Merits, Reparations and Costs, Judgment of 17 June 2005, I/A Court H.R. Series C, no. 125, Case Saramaka People vs. Suriname, Preliminary Objections, Merits, Reparations, and Costs, Judgment of 28 November 2007, I/A Court H.R. Series C, no. 172.
72 155/96 Social and Economic Rights Action Center (SERAC) and Center for Economic and Social Rights (CESR) / Nigeria, decided on merits on 27 October 2001. The case deals with irresponsible oil development on the part of the government in Nigeria, and a human rights violation of the Ogoni people residing there. The Social and Economic Rights Action Centre (SERAC) and the Centre for Economic and Social

Rights (CESR), both NGOs, brought up the case. The complaint was brought up in March 1996, and was settled by the African Commission in October 2001. The Complainants allege that the government is 'directly participating in the contamination of air, water and soil and thereby harming the health of the Ogoni population'. Article 24 of the African Charter says 'All peoples shall have the right to a general satisfactory environment favourable to their development'. 'The pollution and environmental degradation to a level humanly unacceptable has made living in the Ogoni land a nightmare'.

Available at the African Commission on Human and Peoples' Rights: www.achpr.org/communications/decision/155.96/.
73 Established by the 1979 Treaty Creating the Court of Justice of the Andean Community.
74 Based on the 1969 Subregional Integration Agreement (the Andean Pact or Cartagena Agreement).
75 Chapter 1 ('Nullification or Non-compliance') of 1979 Treaty Creating the Court of Justice of the Andean Community.
76 Article 23, 1979 Treaty Creating the Court of Justice of the Andean Community.
77 About the Andean Community and the Andean Court of Justice, see Garcia (note 84), pp. 132–137.
78 For example, Decision 391 on the Common Regime for Access to Genetic Resources of 2 July 1996, which adopted standardised registration and control systems for chemical pesticides for agricultural use; Decision 436 of 11 June 1998 (Norma Andina para el Registro y Control de Plaguicidas Químicos de Uso Agrícola); or Decision 486 of 14 September 2000 (Régimen Común sobre Propiedad Industrial). The Andean countries have also established common guidelines, for example with regard to their rich biodiversity, through Decision 523 of 7 July 2002 on a Regional Biodiversity Strategy for Tropical Andean Countries. These decisions are available at www.comunidadandina.org/INGLES/biodiversity.htm.
79 Article 284, UNCLOS.
80 Article 284, UNCLOS.
81 Article 287 (4), UNCLOS.
82 Article 287 (5), UNCLOS.
83 Article 283, UNCLOS.
84 Article 295, UNCLOS.
85 Wolfrum, 2008, p. 2.
86 Ibid.
87 Ibid.
88 Ibid.
89 In 1978, another major oil spill, the *Amoco Cadiz* incident, sparked new debates on marine pollution. The *Amoco Cadiz*, a Liberian-registered tanker operated by a US oil company, ran aground off the coast of Brittany. Several tonnes of crude oil were spilled into the sea, causing the pollution of intensively used fishing grounds and of several hundred kilometres of beaches. This incident was a turning point in the history of marine pollution because of its gravity and the various questions it has raised specifically concerning liability. Encyclopedia of Public International Law, Vol. 1, Amsterdam, Elsevier, 1992, p. 153.
90 Article 294.
91 Article 295.
92 Article 22, ITLOS Statute.
93 Wolfrum, 2008, p. 7.
94 Ibid.
95 Request for an Advisory Opinion submitted by the Sub-Regional Fisheries Commission (SRFC) (Request for Advisory Opinion submitted to the Tribunal).
96 Article 191, UNCLOS.
97 Responsibilities and obligations of States sponsoring persons and entities with respect to activities in the Area (Request for Advisory Opinion submitted to the Seabed Disputes Chamber).
98 Article 279, UNCLOS.

99 'For example, take a dispute involving EEZ claims around a disputed island or rock and the exercise of fisheries jurisdiction by one State within this EEZ. How do we categorise this dispute? Does it relate to the exercise of sovereign rights and law enforcement within the EEZ, excluded under Articles 297 and 298 from compulsory jurisdiction? Is it a maritime boundary dispute concerning the interpretation or application of Article 74 and excluded from binding compulsory jurisdiction under Article 298 if one of the parties opted out under that Article? Or is it a dispute about entitlement to an EEZ under Part V and Article 121 (3) of the Convention? If it is the last, it is not excluded from compulsory jurisdiction under either Article 297 or 298'.

100 For a detailed history of the dispute settlement regime of UNCLOS, see A. Adede, The System for Settlement of Disputes Under the United Nations Convention on the Law of the Sea, Dordrecht, Martinus Nijhoff, 1987; and S. Rosenne and L. Sohn (eds), United Nations Convention on the Law of the Sea, 1982: A Commentary, Dordrecht, Martinus Nijhoff, 1989.

101 Article 286, UNCLOS.

102 Article 297(3), see A. Adede, "The Basic Structure of the Disputes Settlement Part of the Law of the Sea Convention," Ocean Development and International Law, 1982, Vol. 11, p. 137.

103 Article 288, UNCLOS.

104 Article 290 (5), UNCLOS.

105 Article 25, ITLOS Statute.

106 Article 25, ITLOS Statute.

107 Southern Bluefin Tuna Cases (New Zealand v. Japan; Australia v. Japan), Provisional Measures. In this case, New Zealand requested that the ITLOS evaluates its dispute with Japan over Southern Bluefish Tuna, pending the constitution of an Arbitral Tribunal under Annex VII of UNCLOS.

108 Case concerning Land Reclamation by Singapore in and around the Straits of Johor (Malaysia v. Singapore), Provisional Measures. This case concerns land reclamation activities by Singapore impinging upon Malaysia's rights in and around the Straights of Johor inclusive of the areas around 'Point 20'. In this case, Malaysia requests provisional measures, pending the constitution of the Arbitral Tribunal under Annex VII of UNCLOS.

109 The MOX Plant Case (Ireland v. United Kingdom), Provisional Measures.

110 Article 290(5), UNCLOS.

111 MOX Plant Case (Ireland v United Kingdom), 9 November 2001, paras 51 and 52.

112 Ibid para 56.

113 Ibid, para 113.

114 Ibid, para 114.

115 Ibid, para 114.

116 Ibid, para 150.

117 International Tribunal for the Law of the Sea, Press Release (ITLOS /Press 61) 29 November 2001.

118 MOX Plant Case, Order 3 December 2001, para 82.

119 Ibid, para 89.

120 Ibid, para 85.

121 Ibid, para 83.

122 Ibid, para 81.

123 Article 282 of the LOSC states, 'If States Parties which are parties to a dispute concerning the interpretation or application of this Convention have agreed, through a general, regional, bilateral agreement or otherwise, that such dispute shall, at the request of any party to the dispute, be submitted to a procedure that entails a binding decision, that procedure shall apply in lieu of the procedures provided for in this Part, unless the parties to the dispute otherwise agree'.

124 The International Tribunal for the Law of the Sea, Order of 3 December 2001, The MOX Plant Case (Ireland v United Kingdom), para 52.

125 Order of 3 December 2001, The MOX Plant Case, ibid, para 50.

126 Article 281(1) of LOSC.
127 The MOX Plant Case, para 53.
128 In the *MOX Plant Case*, Separate Opinion of Vice President Nelson, para 7. Paragraph 51 of the Order of the *MOX Plant Case* considered 'that the application of international law rules on interpretation of treaties to identical or similar provisions of different treaties may not yield the same results, having regard to, inter alia, differences in the respective contexts, objects and purposes, subsequent practice of Parties and travaux preparatoires'.
129 Ibid.
130 Article 280 of the LOSC.
131 Article 311 of the LOSC.
132 Southern Bluefin Tuna Case, Award on Jurisdiction and Admissibility, August 4, 2000, 39 ILM 1359 (2000) para 66.
133 See Southern Bluefin Tuna Case Judgment (Australia and New Zealand v Japan), para 62.
134 See Article 16 of the CCSBT; 'Southern Bluefin Tuna Case: Australia and New Zealand v Japan', p. 479. However, in the *Southern Bluefin Tuna Case*, Justice Sir Kenneth Keith came to very different conclusion, i.e., that ITLOS had jurisdiction because Article 16 of the CCSBT did not exclude such jurisdiction (Southern Bluefin Tuna Case, Award on Jurisdiction, 1401:30).
135 Agreement for the Implementation of the Provisions of the United Nations Convention on the Law of the Sea of 10 December 1982 Relating to the Conservation and Management of Straddling Fish Stocks and Highly Migratory Fish Stocks (Fish Stock Agreement).

References

Bilder, R. (1975). The settlement of disputes in the field of the international law of the environment. *Hague Academy of International Law, Collected Courses*, vol. 144, pp. 139–240.

Birnie, P., & Boyle, A. (2002). *International Law and the Environment*, Oxford University Press, New York.

Brodeur, J. (1999). Accountability: The search for a theoretical framework, in E. Mendes et al. (eds), *Democratic Policing and Accountability*, Ashgate, Aldershot, p. 137.

Boyle, A. (1997). Dispute settlement and the law of the sea convention: Problems of fragmentation and jurisdiction. *International and Comparative Law Quarterly*, vol. 46, pp. 37–54.

Boyle, A. (1999). Problems of compulsory jurisdiction and the settlement of disputes relating to straddling fish stocks. *The International Journal of Marine and Coastal Law*, vol. 14, no. 1, pp. 1–25.

Boyle, A. (2007). The environmental jurisprudence of the international tribunal for the law of the sea. *The International Journal of Marine and Coastal Law*, vol. 22, no. 3, pp. 368–381.

Boyle, A., & Harrison, J. (2013). Judicial settlement of international environmental disputes: Current problems. *Journal of International Dispute Settlement*, vol. 4, no. 2, pp. 245–276.

Choon-ho Park, Hon. (2002). Judicial settlement of international marine disputes – An overview of the current system. *Stetson Law Review*, vol. 28, pp. 1035–1046.

Cooper, C. (1986). The management of international environmental disputes in the context of Canada-United states relations: A survey and evaluation of techniques and mechanisms. *Canadian Yearbook of International Law*, vol. 24, pp. 247–313.

Dupuy, R., & Vignes, D. (Eds.) (1991). *A Handbook of the New Law of the Sea*, Nijhoff, Dordrecht.

Hassan, D. (2009). Climate change and the current regimes of Arctic fisheries resources management: An evaluation. *Journal of Maritime Law and Commerce*, vol. 40, no. 4, pp. 511–536.

Lagoni, R. (2002). Regional protection of the marine environment in the North East Atlantic under the OSPAR convention of 1992, paper presented in the Conference on Stockholm Declaration and Law of the Marine Environment, Stockholm University, Sweden, 22–25 May 2002.

Low, L., & Hodgkinson, D. (1995). Compensation for wartime environmental damage: Challenges to international law after the Gulf war. *Virginia Journal of International Law*, pp. 405–483.

Mazzeschi, R. (1991). Forms of responsibility for environmental harm, in F. Francioni & T. Scovazzi (eds), *International Responsibility for Environmental Harm*, Nijhoff, London, pp. 15–35.

Mensah, R. (1999). The international legal regime for the protection and preservation of the marine environment from land-based sources of pollution, in A. Boyle & D. Freestone (eds), *International Law and Sustainable Development*, Oxford University Press, Oxford, p. 322.

Mensah, T. (1998). The international tribunal and the protection of the marine environment. *Environmental Policy and Law*, vol. 28, pp. 216–129.

Romano, C. (2000). *The Peaceful Settlement of Environmental Disputes*, Kluwer, The Hague.

Sands, P. (1994). *Principles of Environmental Law*, Vol. 1, Manchester University Press, UK

Smith, B. (1988). *State Responsibility and the Marine Environment*, Clarendon Press, Oxford, pp. 117–118.

Sturtz, L. (2001). Southern Bluefin tuna case: Australia and New Zealand v Japan. *Ecology Law Quarterly*, vol. 28.

UNEP (1998). Group of experts on liability and compensation for environmental damage arising from military activities. Compilation of Documents, *Environmental law* /3/Inf.1, Nairobi.

Vidas, A., & Østreng, W. (Eds.) (1999). *Order for the Oceans at the Turn of the Century*, Kluwer, The Hague.

Wolfrum, Rüdiger.(2008). Statement of the International Tribunal for the Law of the Sea. International Law Commission, Geneva.

14
FUTURE OF INTERNATIONAL MARINE ENVIRONMENTAL LAW AND POLICY

Concluding remarks

Daud Hassan and Asraful Alam

The oceans provide the fluidity of the Earth and maintain its ecosystem. Any detrimental impact on the oceans brings significant threat to the productivity of the oceans and marine environment. Protection of marine environment is the key issue to maintain the productivity of the oceans. However, the global marine environment is facing numerous threats, including unsustainable use of marine living resources, impacts of climate change, land-based marine pollution, pollution from ships, offshore hydrocarbon exploration and mining and other human activities in the oceans. Over-exploitation, for example, overfishing, is causing unsustainability in the oceans, and long-term losses in the biological productivity and the functioning of the oceans (Chapters 1 and 2). Moreover, the marine environment is being severely polluted by habitat loss due to conflicting human activities in the oceans, which is considered to be a high risk for the marine environment all over the world (Chapters 3 and 4). In addition, climate change is bringing overwhelming challenges to the marine ecosystems by an unprecedented increase of ocean warming, ocean acidification, coral bleaching, changes in species distribution and other biological changes (Chapters 1 and 6).

Marine environmental problem is a global phenomenon which needs international and regional initiatives towards sound preservation and protection. It requires strong legal protection at the national, regional and international level. Although a variety of theories, principles and legal instruments have emerged and are working, those are either not directly applicable for the marine environment or do not contain specific provisions relating to the marine environment (Chapters 2 and 5).

The framework of international marine environmental law and policy has emerged based on the principles of international environmental law. The scope of the principles of environmental law have extended to the marine environment through a reasonable analogical deduction. The principle of a State's sovereignty over natural resources, the duty not to cause transboundary harm, the intergenerational and intragenerational equity, the precautionary principle, the principle of prevention, the principle of cooperation, the polluter-pays principle, the common but differentiate responsibilities principle and the principle of sustainable development have been crystalised to develop international marine environment regime. These principles of the international environmental law have played an important role in evaluating and developing international marine environmental law and policy (Chapter 2).

The United Nations Convention on the Law of the Sea (UNCLOS), 1982, established a legal order of the seas to facilitate international communication and promote the peaceful use of the oceans, the equitable utilisation of the resources, the conservation of the living resources and the protection of marine environment (Chapters 2 and 5). UNCLOS 1982 provides not only the general framework for protection and preservation of the marine environment but also an introduction to the actual institutional arrangements for the protection of the marine environment. The Convention accelerates the subsequent institutional arrangement of the International Maritime Organization (IMO) along with some regional organisations in Europe, Asia, America and Africa to develop and implement international marine environmental law (Chapters 2 and 4).

The framework of international marine environmental law has been embodied from different aspects due to the different sources of marine pollution. Land-based sources of marine pollution, pollution from ship and pollution from offshore hydrocarbon and mineral exploration are the common dimensions of marine pollution, which lead to the respective aspect of international marine environmental law.

Land Based Sources of Marine Pollution (LBSMP) is a major problem affecting the world's marine and coastal environment as it is responsible for 80% of marine pollution. But there is no global treaty which exclusively deals with LBSMP control. Several legal and policy arrangements have been undertaken at the international level in the prevention and control of LBSMP such as UNCLOS, 1982, the Montreal Guidelines on the Protection of the Marine Environment from Land Based Sources, 1985, Agenda 21 of the United Nations Conference on Environment and Development, 1992 and the Global Program of Action for the Protection of the Marine Environment from Land Based Sources, 1995. Many Regional Sea Programmes and the UNEP coordination office have taken initiatives at the regional level to control, reduce and prevent LBSMP. However, the question remains as to how far the present legal frameworks have gone for the effective protection of the marine environment from LBSMP (Chapter 3).

Apart from LBSMP, international shipping has many other unintended impacts on the marine environment. Marine environment is being remarkably polluted by oil leakage, ballast water, sediments and ship recycling, which lead to the development of an international legal framework to prevent and reduce marine pollution by ships. The International Convention on Oil Pollution Preparedness, Response and Co-Operation, 1990 under the International Maritime Organisation (IMO) is a response to marine pollution by oil. The Conventions relating to ballast water and sediments, bio-fuelling and harmful anti-fouling, recycling of ship and the protection of the Sensitive sea area provide a comprehensive regime of international marine environmental law concerning marine pollution from ships (Chapter 4). The International Convention for the Prevention of Pollution from Ships (MARPOL 73/78) is the most important international convention for the prevention of vessel-source marine pollution (Chapters 4 and 5).

Marine pollution from offshore hydrocarbon development and production carries another risk for the marine environment because of its involvement of harmful substances for the exploration and exploitation of resources, and discharge of emissions. Further, accidental pollution, blowout and oil spills are significant environmental risks accompanying offshore hydrocarbon and mineral operations. The issue of prevention and control of marine pollution from offshore petroleum and mineral resources operations has been the subject of international law at global, regional and national policy levels (Chapter 5). UNCLOS, 1982, provides certain specifics in relation to pollution from offshore oil and gas activities. Article 194 requires State parties to take measures to prevent, reduce and control pollution of the marine environment, including with installations and devices used in the exploration or exploitation of the natural resources of the seabed and subsoil. The regional and bilateral framework for protection of the marine environment, including accidental pollution prevention arrangements under UNEP Regional Seas Framework Conventions and Action Plans are a strong protest against such types of marine pollution (Chapter 5 and 2).

Despite the inter-operational marine pollution, climate change is an existential threat to the health of ocean ecosystems and marine biodiversity. Ocean acidification is a phenomenon resulting from increased concentration of carbon dioxide (CO_2) in the atmosphere. It has a drastic consequence for marine species and ecosystems (Chapters 6 and 8). Ocean acidification is not directly covered by any international treaty. However, the UN Framework Convention on Climate Change and the Paris Agreement addressed the issue of CO_2 as a general concept. Moreover, the Convention on Biological Diversity, 1992, refers to the protection of biodiversity, although the convention declines to cover specific aspect of marine biodiversity (Chapters 6 and 8).

A legal regime should have not only preventive aspects but also protective aspects to preserve the subject matter of that regime. Therefore, an effective international marine environmental law requires a regulatory framework for the protection of the marine environment by a balanced approach in economic and environmental interests. The rapid growth of human activities in the Ocean for shipping, fishing, energy, defence and tourism are increasing day by day. This ever-increasing human activity is creating intra- and inter-conflicts, which ultimately causes marine pollution. Various global and regional assessments of the marine and coastal environment indicate that the biodiversity in marine and coastal areas are declining continuously due to conflicting uses of ocean spaces. In order to protect and preserve the marine and coastal environment from various adverse effects including climate change, an improved planning and implementation system is urgently needed. (Chapter 7 and 1).

Future of international law and policy 255

In this respect, marine spatial planning (MSP) is a proven tool to establish a more rational use of marine space and the interactions between its uses. MSP allows both a high level of environmental protection and a wide range of human activities. It emphasises coordinated networks of national, regional and global institutions. MSP has been considered as a way forward for the effective ocean governance as it includes integrated, adaptive, strategic, area-based and participatory measures. However, the international marine environmental law lacks substantially to provide a solid basis for MSP (Chapter 7).

Both living and non-living resources of ocean are critically important to sustaining life on Earth. In this case, fisheries, one of the most important living resource, attracts more concentration than others. But oceanic climatological change due to marine pollution has a profound effect on fishing resources (Chapters 8 and 6). But the legal and policy regime of international marine environment has a significant shortcoming for fisheries resources management in a sustainable manner. UNCLOS, 1982, the Fish Sticks Agreement, 1995, and other international law and policies relating to fisheries management are not adequate to ensure sustainable fisheries resources management. Various obstacles and challenges that the current fisheries resources management is facing requires an effective conservation and management framework. The framework should include both fisheries resource management in areas within National Jurisdiction and areas beyond National Jurisdiction. In this case, the final recommendation of the UN committee for fisheries resource management can be a clear guideline to proceed forward (Chapter 8).

Marine Protected Areas (MPA) may be another approach to ensure sustainable fisheries resources management. Over the last 50 years, marine protected areas have emerged as a critical tool for the protection of marine species, habitats and ecosystems. More recently marine protected areas have featured in both international and domestic environmental law context as an important mechanism to protect the ocean environment. Nonetheless, continuing declines in marine biodiversity have led to further measures including targets being set for the designation of greater ocean areas. However, merely declaring more protected areas will not ensure ocean health. Arguably, marine protected areas must be 'reconceived' to achieve more positive environmental outcomes (Chapters 9 and 8). MPA, under the conservation of Biological diversity, 1992, may be rationally be applied in marine biodiversity for the protection of fishing resources as well as other living resources (Chapters 9 and 6).

The expansion of MPA to a marine context has raised many complexities in ocean governance. Indigenous rights, ownership and community engagement is one of those issues (Chapters 10 and 9). The existing international marine environmental law does not contain any explicit provision as to the legal rights of Indigenous peoples in ocean resources (Chapters 10 and 12). In this concern, the current Indigenous involvement in the management of the Great Barrier Reef may be a lesson for necessary changes and policy framing for sustainable and equitable ocean governance (Chapter 10).

International marine environmental law should be adoptive to the context of unique necessity and situation. The Antarctic and the Arctic are two unique marine regions which are quite different from others because of complex formation and nature. The current legal framework in Antarctic (the Antarctic Treaty 1959, The Antarctic Seal Convention, 1972, Convention on the conservation of Antarctic Marine living resources, 1980) deserves appreciation. But in order to ensure better protection of the marine environment, the legal regime should be according to the nature and the causes for marine pollution in that area (Chapter 11).

The Arctic region is more concerned for climate change issues which cause oceanic acidification. It has triggered States to formulate a legal framework for the Artic marine environment. Currently, the marine environment of the Arctic Ocean is managed under the Arctic Council. It has adopted 2015–2025 AMSP which addresses both short-term and long-term challenges and opportunities, through 40 Strategic Actions comprised under four Strategic Goals. But though the Policy is ambitious, it is a non-binding document (Chapter 12).

The extension of sea area and the rights of the coastal States have been producing an increasing number of marine environmental dispute. But the legal regime to resolve these marine environmental disputes is not adequate. The current disputes settlement procedures through the International judicial forum – including the International Court of Justice, the International Tribunal for the Law of the Sea, the International Arbitral Tribunal and the Dispute settlement forum of the World Trade Organization – have a remarkable loophole of compulsory and binding effect of procedure and judgement. States are free to submit a dispute to the appreciation of a third party, and are usually free to choose the available procedures for resolving their disputes. Even compulsory dispute settlement procedures, such as that established by UNCLOS, require States to accept to be bound by them. Moreover, the regional arrangements have less focus on marine environmental aspect (Chapter 13).

The goal of the protection and preservation of the marine environment in a sustainable manner is to achieve a sound marine environmental condition around the globe for the sake of current and future generations. An effective regime supported with contemporary and newly developed concepts and principles are the first step to deliver this goal. Effective implementation of the marine environmental regimes at national, regional and global levels are crucial in this respect. It appears that the current arrangements and their implementation systems at national, regional and global levels fall far short to achieve the goals and objectives of the sustainable development of the marine environment. There is a compelling need for an effective cooperative approach which will facilitate to improve the current regimes and their implementation by reducing marine environmental disputes, developing economic collaboration without contravening international obligations and further encouraging in the participatory process in marine environmental development and control. Sufficient political will and adequate partnership building are essential to pave the way for an effective result in this respect.

INDEX

ABNJ. *See* areas beyond national jurisdiction
Aboriginal and Torres Strait Islander Heritage Protection Act 1984 (ATSHIPA) 184–185
Aboriginal Land Rights (Northern Territory) Act 1976 184
access and benefit sharing (ABS) 135
adaptive governance 174–175
AEPS. *See* Arctic Environmental Protection Strategy
AFS Convention 75–76
Agenda 21 51
Aichi Biodiversity targets 94–95, 98, 164
air pollution 64–65
AMSP. *See* Arctic Marine Strategic Plan
Andean Court of Justice 234–235
Antarctica 193
Antarctic Consultative Meeting (ATCM) 195
Antarctic Environmental Protocol 193
Antarctic marine environment: introduction to 193–194; mineral resources 198–199; outside of treaty system 198–200; protection of 193–202, 256; spatial dimension of 195–196; subjective dimension of 194–195; temporal dimension of 196
Antarctic Specially Managed Areas (ASMA) 163, 196
Antarctic Specially Protected Areas (ASPA) 163, 196
Antarctic Treaty 163, 193–198, 200–202

Antigua Convention (2002) 28
aquatic invasive species 65, 153, 207
arbitral tribunals 232
Arctic Biodiversity Assessment (ABA) 207, 209
Arctic Climate Impact Assessment (ACIA) 209
Arctic Council 209–210, 213–218
Arctic Environmental Protection Strategy (AEPS) 179, 209
Arctic marine environment: coastal states cooperation on 214–216; defined 207–209; governance of 207–218; impact of climate change on 206; introduction to 206–207; nation-states in 208–209; offshore oil and gas operations in 212–213; protection of 206–222, 256; shipping routes 217; threats to 206–207
Arctic Marine Shipping Assessment (AMSA) 209
Arctic Marine Strategic Plan (AMSP) 213, 216
Arctic Monitoring and Assessment Programme (AMAP) 207, 208, 209
Arctic Ocean 10, 206, 208, 215
Arctic sea ice sheets 88
Arctic States 208–214, 217–218
areas beyond national jurisdiction (ABNJ) 4, 127, 129–131, 135, 137–139, 166, 199
areas under national jurisdiction (AWNJ) 127–128, 135

258 Index

ASMA. *See* Antarctic Specially Managed Areas
ASPA. *See* Antarctic Specially Protected Areas
ATCM. *See* Antarctic Consultative Meeting
ATSHIPA. *See* Aboriginal and Torres Strait Islander Heritage Protection Act 1984
Australia: indigenous protected areas in 180–187; legislation on offshore oil and gas production 79–80; Oceans Policy 182
Australian Heritage Council Act 2003 185
AWNJ. *See* areas under national jurisdiction

Balance project 115n25
ballast water 60, 65, 253–254
Barcelona Convention (1995) 77, 164
Basel Convention (1989) 29, 65–66
biodiversity. *See* marine biodiversity
biofouling 60, 65
Black Sea Convention (2009) 26
black water 9
Blue Economy 104, 114n21
blue growth 101, 107
Bonn Convention on the Prevention of Pollution of the North Sea (1969) 54
bottom trawling 5–6
British Petroleum 81
Brundtland Report 30
BWM Convention (2004) 65
by-catch 5–6

CAFF. *See* Conservation of Arctic Flora and Fauna
capacity building 141–142
carbon dioxide 6, 7, 45, 87, 88; emissions reduction 96–97; and ocean acidification 88–89, 90, 92–93, 124, 207. *See also* climate change; greenhouse gases
Caspian Sea 78–79
CDB. *See* Convention on Biological Diversity
CERD. *See* Convention on the Elimination of All Forms of Racial Discrimination
chemical discharge 63–64
Chevron Nigeria Ltd oil rig 81
China 217–218
cleaner production principle 51
climate change 45; and Arctic 206; impacts of 6–7, 101, 124–125, 254; introduction to 87–88; and marine living resources 124–125; and ocean acidification 87–98, 154; UN Framework Convention on Climate Change 93, 96–98
coastal zones: defined 53; development 45; importance of 123; indigenous use of 183; integrated management of 55, 173
Code of Conduct for Responsible Fisheries 31
Comite Maritime International (CMI) 76
common but differentiated responsibilities principle 29–30
Common Heritage of Mankind 135
common pool resource theory 175
Commonwealth v. Yarmirr 183
Conservation of Arctic Flora and Fauna (CAFF) 209
continental shelf 134–135, 199
Convention Concerning the Protection of the World Cultural and Natural Heritage (World Heritage Convention) 18
Convention for the Conservation of Antarctic Marine Living Resources (CAMLR Convention) 26
Convention for the Conservation of Antarctic Seals 158, 193
Convention for the Prevention of Marine Pollution by Dumping of Wasters and Other Matter 49
Convention for the Protection of the Marine Environment of the Baltic Sea Area 77
Convention for the Protection of the Marine Environment of the North-East Atlantic (OSPAR) 24–25, 26, 77, 163–164, 213
Convention on Biological Diversity (CBD) 17–18, 93–95, 135, 155, 161–162, 173, 210–211
Convention on Fishing and the Conservation of the Living Resources of the High Seas 126–127
Convention on Migratory Species 159
Convention on the Conservation of Antarctic Marine Living Resources (CCAMLR) 163, 193, 197
Convention on the Conservation on the Regulation of Antarctic Mineral Resource Activities (CRAMRA) 193
Convention on the Elimination of All Forms of Racial Discrimination (CERD) 176
Convention on the International Trade in Endangered Species of Wild Flora and Fauna (CITES) 18

Index **259**

Convention on the Prevention of Marine Pollution by Dumping of Wastes and Other Matter 17
Convention on Wetlands of International Importance 18, 159
cooperation principle 26–28
coral bleaching 7, 90
coral reefs 7, 90
Coral Triangle Initiative (CTI) 164
Corfu Channel case 21
Court of Justice of the European Union 234
cultural diversity 179
customary international law: on control of LBSMP 46–47; on offshore oil and gas operations 80. *See also* international law

dangerous goods 63–64
Decade of Ocean Science for Sustainable Development 143
Declaration of the United Nations Conference on the Human Environment (Stockholm Declaration) 19–20, 23, 26–27, 47, 127
Deepwater Horizon oil spill 69, 81
developing countries: and climate change 60; equity toward 29–30; and intragenerational equity 22; and marine environmental protection 228; MPAs in 165; needs of 22, 31
due diligence 25
duty to protect 227–228

ecosystem-based fisheries management (EBFM) 138–139
ecosystem based management (EBM) 55, 103–104, 216–217
ecosystem services 112n3
Emergency Prevention Preparedness and Response (EPPR) 209
endangered species 160, 211
energy efficiency, of ships 64–65
Energy Efficiency Design Index (EEDI) 64
environment, defined 225
environmental disputes. *See* marine environmental disputes
environmental impact assessment (EIA) 50, 228
Environmental Protection Conservation Act (EPBC Act) 182–183, 184
equity 29–30
European Court of Human Rights 234
European Economic Area (EEA) 208–209

European Union 35, 101; and Arctic area 208, 217–218; MSP framework 107–110
Exclusive Economic Zones (EEZ) 81, 105, 110, 127, 159–160, 169
exclusive-use zones 105
Exxon Valdez oil spill 9

FAO Code of Conduct for Responsible Fisheries 131
FAO Deep Sea Fisheries Guidelines 131
Faroe Islands 208–209
Fisheries Jurisdiction case 47, 231–232
fisheries management 123–151, 255; Arctic 212; current regimes for 125–139; ecosystem-based approach to 138–139; effective 133–139; introduction to 123; proposal for sustainable 139–143; traditional 138
fishing: bottom trawling 5–6; by-catch 5–6; and climate change 125; depletion of fish stocks 5; illegal 5, 10n1; unsustainable 4–6
Fish Stock Agreement (1995) 24, 34–35, 123, 129–130, 135–136, 212
Food and Agricultural Organization (FAO) 31–32; Code of Conduct for Responsible Fisheries 25
food chain 90
food security 123

garbage, from ships 9, 63–64
general use zones 105
geographic range boundaries 7
Global Ocean Acidification Observing Network 91
global organisations. *See* international institutions
Global Programme of Action (GPA) to Prevent, Reduce and Control LBSMP 52–53, 54
good neighborliness principle 20–21, 46–47
governance. *See* marine governance
Great Barrier Reef Marine Park 7, 90; and indigenous rights 180; marine spatial planning in 111–112
greenhouse gases 9, 60, 64–65, 88, 96–97. *See also* carbon dioxide; climate change
Greenland 209
green shipbuilding 66
Gulf of Mexico 79

habitat loss 5–6, 207
habitat protection 157, 160

Helsinki Convention (1992) 25, 28, 35
highly migratory species (HMS) 24, 31, 124, 146n35, 157, 212, 220n41, 243
High Seas 159–160, 212
Hong Kong Convention 66
horizontal fragmentation, of marine governance 103
human activities: and climate change 87, 124; impact on marine ecosystems 3, 45, 101, 153, 254; and ocean acidification 88–89
human rights 176–179, 234
Human Rights Courts 234

ICES. *See* International Council for the Exploration of the Sea
illegal fishing 5, 10n1
ILUAs. *See* Indigenous Land Use Agreements
Indigenous Community Conserved Areas (ICCAs) 168, 180
Indigenous Land Use Agreements (ILUAs) 183–184
Indigenous Protected Areas (IPAs) 180–187
indigenous rights: Australia 180–187; and governance 175–179; and human rights 178–179; limits of 178; and MPAs 173–187
indirect pollutants 92–93
Integrated Coastal Zone Management (ICZM) 55
Integrated Maritime Policy (IMP) 107, 108
Inter-American Court of Human Rights 234
intergenerational equity 22–23, 30
International Convention for the Control and Management of Ship's Ballast Water and Sediments (2004) 65
International Convention for the Prevention of Pollution from Ships (MARPOL) 8, 17, 60, 61, 63–64, 75, 160, 198
International Convention for the Prevention of Pollution of the Sea by Oil (OILPOL) 8, 17
International Convention for the Regulation of Whaling 18, 154, 159
International Convention for the Safety of Life at Sea (SOLAS Convention) 8, 33
International Convention on Oil Pollution Preparedness, Response and Co-operation (1990) 28, 63, 74–75

International Convention on the Control of Harmful Anti-Fouling Systems on Ships (AFS Convention) 75–76
International Council for the Exploration of the Sea (ICES) 126
International Court of Justice (ICJ) 21, 46, 47, 225, 230–232
International Covenant on Civil and Political Rights (ICCPR) 176
International Covenant on Economic, Social, and Cultural Rights (ICESCR) 176
International Criminal Court (ICC) 142
international dispute resolution 229–235
International Energy Agency 9
international environmental law: principles of 18–31, 36. *See also* international law
International Labour Organisation (ILO) 177
international law 4, 8, 17–18; on control of LBSMP 46–47; on fisheries resources management 125–139; and indigenous rights 175–179; on marine environmental disputes 229–235; on marine protected areas 158–162; on ocean acidification 90–92; on offshore oil and gas operations 71–76, 80; principles of environmental 252–253; to protect against ship-based pollution 60–62
International Law Commission (ILC) 126
International Maritime Organization (IMO) 4, 16, 31–33, 60–65; on dumping activities 74; Polar Shipping Code 198, 211; shipping regulations 211
international organisations 16, 31–33
International Panel on Climate Change (IPCC) 87
International Plant Protection Convention 21
International Seabed Authority 142, 208
international shipping industry 8–9, 60. *See also* ships
International Technical Conference on the Conservation of the Living Resources 126
International Tribunal for the Law of the Sea (ITLOS) 27, 229, 230, 235–243
International Union for the Conservation for Nature and Natural Resources (IUCN) 155, 173, 180

Index 261

intragenerational equity 22–23, 30
invasive species 65, 153, 207
Iron Rhine arbitration 80

Jakarta Mandate on Marine and Coastal Biological Diversity 130, 162
Jeddah Convention 23
Johannesburg Declaration (2002) 4

Kuwait Convention (1975) 23, 78
Kyoto Declaration 131

land-based sources of marine pollution (LBSMP) 7–8, 45–46, 253; customary international law on 46–47; instruments specifically dealing with 52–53; problems and future challenges 55–56; regional regulation of 53–55; role of treaty instruments in controlling 47–49; sustainability instruments for control of 50–51
Land Reclamation case 27
Law of the Sea Convention. *See* United Nations Convention on the Law of the Sea
Legal Committee 32
London Convention (1972) 49, 73–74
London Protocol (1996) 24, 30, 49, 73–74
Lubombo Transfrontier Conservation Area 167

Mabo v. Queensland 183
Madrid Protocol 77–78, 198, 200, 201
mangroves 125
marine animals: impacts of climate change on 7; and oil spills 9. *See also* marine living resources
marine biodiversity: and climate change 7; conventions on 93–95, 135, 155, 161–162, 173, 210–211; degradation of 3; impact of overfishing on 4–6; and indigenous cultural values 182; loss of 101, 125
Marine Climate Change Impacts Partnership (MCCIP) 125
marine environment: Antarctic 193–202; Arctic 206–222; human impacts on 3, 45, 101, 153–154, 254; impact of ocean acidification of 89–90; impacts of climate change on 6–7, 101, 124–125, 254; protection of 17–18, 131–133, 153–154, 157, 193–202, 206–222, 228, 252–256; threats to 3–10, 123, 153, 252

marine environmental disputes 225–250, 256; choice of procedure in 235; compulsory dispute settlement regime 235–236; exceptions to compulsory jurisdiction 237–238; international courts and tribunals for 229–235; judicial settlement of 225–229; principles and obligations 227–229; scope of 225–227; sea-bed disputes 236; settlement procedures under ITLOS 235–243
marine environment conservation: challenges in 3–10; international laws for 17–18; introduction to 3
Marine Environment Pollution Committee (MEPC) 32
marine genetic resources (MGRs) 124, 135, 143, 144n3, 149n76
marine governance 4, 35–36; Arctic area 207–218; conceptual framework for 17–18; fragmentation of 103–104; indigenous rights-based approach to 175–179; international organisations for 31–33; introduction to 173–174; of marine protected areas 173–187; and marine spatial planning 101–118; and principles of international environmental law 18–31, 36; regional organisations for 33–35; for sustainability 174–175
marine living resources: and climate change 124–125; conservation of 123–151, 153, 255; impact of ocean acidification of 89–90; and marine pollution 125; unsustainable use of 4–6
marine parks 166–167
marine pollution: in Arctic area 197–198; defined 70; international laws against 33; introduction to 45–46; land-based 7–8, 45–56, 253; and marine organisms 125; from offshore hydrocarbon and mineral resources development 69–85, 254; prevention of 26, 228; from ships 8–9, 17, 33, 60–67, 253–254; sources of 45
marine protected areas (MPAs) 95, 137, 153–170, 255; contemporary challenges for 164–169; controversy over 157; defined 155; governance of 173–187; and indigenous rights 173–187; interdisciplinary research on 168; international law 158–162; introduction to 153–154; legislation on 157–158, 164–165; location of 165; monitoring and enforcement of 169; networks and transboundary 166–168; regional treaties

on 162–164; scale of 166; temporal issues with 165; terminology 155–156; as tool for conservation 156–158
marine resources 112n2, 123–124. *See also* marine living resources
marine spatial planning (MSP) 101–118, 168, 255; adaptivity of 106–110; basic elements of 102–105; certainty in 106–107; characteristics of 105–106; concept of 137; European Union framework for 107–110; in Great Barrier Reef Marine Park 111–112; history of 113n8; introduction to 101–102; zones 105, 114n20, 115n24
marine technology 141–142
maritime zones 101
MARPOL Convention 8, 17, 26, 33, 60–64, 75, 160, 198
Mavrommatis Palestine Concessions case 226
MCCIP. *See* Marine Climate Change Impacts Partnership
Mediterranean Sea 77–78, 79
MEPC. *See* Marine Environment Pollution Committee
Montara Platform Blowout 69, 81
Montreal Guidelines 51, 52
MOX Plant case 27, 240–242
MPAs. *See* marine protected areas
MSP. *See* marine spatial planning
multilateral environmental agreements (MEAs) 34, 210

Nagoya Protocol 135, 149n74
national jurisdictions 4
nationally determined contributions (NDCs) 97
national parks 154, 157, 158
Native Title Act 1993 183
natural gas 9–10
natural resources: exploitation of 141; and no-harm principle 20–21; of oceans 123–124; state sovereign rights over 19–20. *See also* marine resources
Niger Delta oil spill 9
nitrogen 9
no-harm principle 20–21
non-governmental organisations (NGOs) 19, 53, 173, 187, 195
Nordic Council of Ministers (NCM) 35
North-East Atlantic Fishery Commission (NEAFC) 163
North West Atlantic Fisheries Convention 126
Norway 208–209
Nuclear Test Ban Treaty 21

obsolete ships, disposal of 65–66
ocean acidification 6–7, 45, 87–98; about 88–89; in Arctic area 207; and Convention on Biological Diversity 93–95; impacts of 89–90; increase in 124–125, 154, 254; international response to 90–92; and Law of the Sea 92–93; and Paris Agreement 96–98
Ocean Acidification International Coordination Centre (OA-ICC) 91
ocean ecosystems. *See* marine environment
ocean governance. *See* marine governance
oceans: area covered by 87, 153; natural resources of 123–124; role of 16, 45, 87, 123–124, 252; threats to 16, 252
ocean temperatures 87–88
offshore hydrocarbon exploration and mining 9–10; accidents 69, 71, 81; in Arctic area 212–213; background on 70–71; global legal regime 71–76; international customary law on 80; introduction to 69–70; marine pollution from 69–85, 254; national responses 79–80; regional arrangements on 76–80
offshore oil rigs 76
oil and gas exploration and mining 9–10; accidents 69, 71, 81; in Arctic area 212–213; background on 70–71; global legal regime 71–76; international customary law on 80; marine pollution from 69–85, 254; regional arrangements on 76–80
oil demand 9
oil discharge 63–64
oil spills 9, 10, 69, 71, 81, 253–254
OPRC. *See* International Convention on Oil Pollution Preparedness, Response and Co-operation
Organization for Economic Cooperation and Development (OECD) 55
OSPAR Convention (1992) 24–25, 26, 77, 163–164, 213
overfishing 4–6, 45, 101

Pacific Fur Seal case 23
Paris Agreement 6, 96–98, 254
Paris Convention (1960) 28
Paris Convention for the Prevention of Marine Pollution from Land Based Sources (1974) 77
Particularly Sensitive Sea Areas (PSSAs) 64, 160–161
Persian Gulf 78, 79

Index 263

petroleum resources, marine pollution from 69–85
pH of seawater 89, 97, 124. *See also* ocean acidification
Polar Regions 10. *See also* Antarctic marine environment; Arctic marine environment
Polar Shipping Code 198, 211
pollutant discharge 63–64
polluter-pays principle 28, 51, 103, 113n15, 253
pollution 3; air 64–65; defined 227–228; land-based 7–8; prevention of 26; transboundary 20–21. *See also* marine pollution
precautionary approach 23–25
precautionary principle 23–25, 50, 103, 113n14, 253
Prestige oil spill 9
prevention principle 25–26
protected areas. *See* marine protected areas
Protection of the Arctic Marine Environment (PAME) 209, 213
pteropods 90

Ramsar Convention on Wetlands of International Importance 18, 159
recreation uses 153, 154
Regional Activity Centre (RAC) 35
Regional Coordinating Units (RCUs) 35
regional courts and tribunals 234–235
regional fisheries management organisations (RFMOs) 135–136, 163, 169, 212
regionalism, importance of 53–54
regional organisations 16, 31–35
Regional Organization for the Protection of Marine Environment (ROPME) 35, 78
regional regulations: on LBSMP 53–55; on offshore oil and gas operations 76–80
Regional Seas Conventions (RSCs) 163
Regional Seas Programme (RSP) 7–8, 33–35, 54
regional treaties, on MPAs 162–164
renewable energy projects 168
resource extraction 45
restrictive-access zones 105
Rio Declaration (1992) 4, 20, 23, 27, 28, 29, 50–51, 147n38
Royal National Park 154

safety zones 160
Santiago Declaration 200
sea-bed disputes 236
seabed mining 168
seabirds, and oil spills 9

seafood production, impact of ocean acidification of 90
sea level rise 88, 114n22, 125
sewage discharge 9, 63–64
shared fish stocks 146n35
shark sanctuary 167
shipbreaking 65–66
shipping regulations 211
ship recycling industry 60, 66, 253
ships: disposal of obsolete 65–66; energy efficiency of 64–65; pollution from 8–9, 17, 33, 60–67, 253–254
sic utere tuo principle 80
soft laws 131
SOLAS Convention 33
Southern Bluefin Tuna case 226, 242–243, 244
sovereign rights 141
Special Areas 160–161
state sovereignty, over natural resources 19–20
Stockholm Conference 47
Stockholm Declaration (1972) 19–20, 23, 26–27, 47, 127
sulphur 8–9
sustainability: of fisheries 139–143; governance for 174–175; instruments 50–51
sustainable development 4, 30–31, 50, 55
Sustainable Development Goals (SDGs) 18, 55, 91–92, 94–95, 98, 139–140, 150n99
sustainable use 30
Svalbard Islands 209

targeted management zones 105
technology transfer 141–142
Tehran Convention (2003) 78–79
Torres Strait Protected Zone 167
tourism 154, 157
Tragedy of the Commons 174
Trail Smelter case 21, 80
transboundary harm, duty not to cause 20–21
transboundary MPAs 166–168
transboundary stocks 146n35
treaty instruments, to control LBSMP 47–49

UNCLOS. *See* United Nations Convention on the Law of the Sea
UNEP. *See* United Nations Environment Programme
UNEP Coordination Office 54–55
UN Fish Agreement 135–136

UN Framework Convention on Climate Change (UNFCCC) 90, 93, 96–98, 254
UN General Assembly 91, 98, 140, 199
United Nations Charter 8, 47, 229
United Nations Conference on Environment and Development (UNCED) 50
United Nations Conference on the Human Environment (UNCHE) 47
United Nations Convention on the Law of the Sea (UNCLOS) 4, 16–20, 47–49, 71–73, 208, 253; and Antarctica 199; and Arctic area 210–211; and common but differentiated responsibilities principle 29–30; and cooperation 27–28, 32, 33; and environmental disputes 235–243; and fisheries resource management 123, 127–133; framework of 35; and intragenerational equity 22, 23; and marine protection 131–133; maritime zones 101; and MSPs 159–160; and no-harm principle 21; and ocean acidification 92–93; and precautionary principle 24; and prevention principle 25–26; on regional initiatives 34; and ship-based pollution 61–62; and sustainable development 30–31
United Nations Declaration on the Rights of Indigenous Peoples (UNDRIP) 173, 178, 179

United Nations Environment Programme (UNEP) 16, 163
United Nations Fish Stock Agreement (1995) 17–18, 24, 31, 34–35, 123, 129–130, 135–136, 212
United Nations General Assembly 31
Universal Declaration of Human Rights (UDHR) 176

vertical fragmentation, of marine governance 103
vessel-source pollution 60–67, 253–254

Washington Conference 52–53
whales 18, 159
wildlife protection 153
wind farms 115n26
World Conservation Union 173
World Heritage Convention 21
World Heritage List 159, 167–168
World Summit on Sustainable Development (WSSD) 55, 162
World Trade Organization (WTO) 232–233

Yellowstone Act 158
Yellowstone National Park 154, 158